Total Speech

Post-Contemporary Interventions

Series Editors: Stanley Fish and

Fredric Jameson

otal Speech

An Integrational Linguistic Approach to Language

Michael Toolan

Duke University Press   Durham and London

1996

© 1996 Duke University Press   All rights reserved
Printed in the United States of America on acid-free paper ∞
Typeset in Times Roman with Monotype Joanna display
by Keystone Typesetting, Inc.
Library of Congress Cataloging-in-Publication Data
appear on the last printed page of this book.

Contents

Acknowledgments   vii

Introduction   1

1 On Inscribed or Literal Meaning   24

2 Metaphor   56

3 Intentionality and Coming into Language   98

4 Further Principles of Integrational Linguistics, or, On Not Losing Sight of the Language User   140

5 Relevance in Theory and Practice   181

6 Repetition   226

7 Rules   271

References   323

Index   335

Acknowledgments

I should particularly like to thank the following, for reading and reacting to parts of this work in draft form, or for their conversations with me on the issues involved: Rukmini Bhaya Nair, Ron Carter, George Dillon, P. M. S. Hacker, M. A. K. Halliday, Roy Harris, J. L. Mackenzie, Talbot Taylor, George Wolf, and students at the University of Washington.

A special kind of thanks goes to Julianne Statham and to our children, Roisin, Patrick, and Miriam; they best understand my "whole bodily behavior" if anyone does; they are the stream of life in which these words have meaning.

Earlier versions of sections of this book have previously appeared in print. Most of chapter 1, on literal meaning, is reprinted from "Perspectives on Literal Meaning," *Language and Communication* 11, no. 4 (1991): 333–51, copyright 1991, with the kind permission of Elsevier Science Ltd., The Boulevard, Langford Lane, Kidlington OX5 1GB, United Kingdom. Section 4 of chapter 3 appeared as "Largely for against Theory," *Journal of Literary Semantics* 19, no. 3 (1990): 150–66. Some material in chapter 5 originated as "On Relevance Theory," in *New Departures in Linguistics*, ed. G. Wolf (New York: Garland, 1992), 146–62, reprinted with the kind permission of Garland Publishing Inc.; and as "On Recyclings and Irony," in *Literature and the New Interdisciplinarity: Poetics, Linguistics, History*, ed. R. Sell and P. Verdonk (Amsterdam and Atlanta: Rodopi, 1994), 79–92, reprinted with the kind permission of Editions Rodopi B.V. I am also grateful to the estate of Sylvia Plath, for permission to reproduce her poem "Cut."

Introduction

> And as I walked I became possessed of a strange and trembling intimation: the whole corporeal world . . . had shed [its] physical reality and had become mere imaginings. . . . And that intimation in turn gave way to a stronger sense: that even we had ceased to be physical and existed only in spirit, only in the need we had for each other. — The character Frank, at the close of the play *Faith Healer*, by Brian Friel

> Words have meaning only in the stream of life. — Wittgenstein, *Last Writings on Philosophy and Psychology*

Another book about language? Another book about language.
Because language is both endlessly fascinating and profoundly natural. Metaphor has been called the dream work of language; but it is language itself that is our life-supporting atmosphere, effortlessly filling our waking days and dreaming nights, and making so many human activities possible. In particular, that of belief. Language manages to be both a constant source of conflict and controversy and, otherwise, utterly unreflected on. It is one of the most essential and significant of human attributes, alongside and interwoven with memory, imagination, bodily experience, and mortality. It is of the utmost importance, as much because of as despite the fact that human beings can live out their lives without consciously reflecting on the part that language plays therein. In particular, it is quite imaginable that speakers within a settled and isolated community might conduct themselves without ever thinking of their own speech as a language (among the world's languages), as a complex system harnessed to the activities of exchanging goods, services, and information.

But if the thought experiment is extended, so as to set down this community alongside some other community with noticeably different speech ways ("a different language"), it seems reasonable to suppose that, in both communities, a new awareness of languages (here, of two languages), and of *a* language as a complex codified accompaniment to the diverse activities of life, a *separable* "accompaniment," might naturally and logically develop. But this supposition, about just that "naturally developed" awareness of languages and the separability of a language from the rest of life, is the intellectual and imaginative crux of this book. Is it the case that, where two communities display the use of noticeably different signifying patterns, an awareness of the separability of languages is fostered? And is it further the case that just such an increased awareness points to the logical soundness and explanatory power of that inference — namely that our (autonomous, separable) languages embed us in our worlds? The majority view, within linguistics and far beyond (throughout both Western science and the world of everyday common sense), is that an awareness of the kind indicated is a major step up in the "cognitive ascent" that leads to an understanding of languages as coherent and complete systems, essentially autonomous of direct influence from other mental, social, or cultural influences, enabled by the arbitrariness of the sign (the sound-meaning nexus), and structured by complex patterns or rules (but emphatically not rules of the easily learned schoolroom kind, such as "*i* before *e* except after *c*").

Thus attention to languages, rather than language, and then to the natural soundness of treating each language as a separable code-like system is usually viewed as an essential and logical first step if any sort of headway is to be made with such questions as how children acquire a language, how translation works, what kinds of language pathology there are and how their effects may be mitigated, and innumerable other questions of a similar nature, geared to a reasoned, analytic, and explanatory understanding of language rather than a prescientific stance of credulous trust. It is the difference between the understanding of a car's engine displayed and used by a competent auto mechanic and the near nonexistent understanding that may be displayed by the car's owner-driver. These arguments and analogies have the powerful familiarity of everyday common sense; they are, therefore, immensely difficult to unsettle. Nevertheless my hope in this book is to cause an unsettling of the received view and its separatist, mechanist, codificatory logic — not on the grounds that it is entirely wrong but on the grounds that it is so to a significant degree. So I wish to emphasize from the outset that this book is not "against" segregationalist linguistic analysis and the treatment of languages as mechanistic codes; rather, it attempts to show the inadequacies of any thoroughgoing adoption and application of those principles. A decidedly skewed conceptualization of language develops when certain ideas that are useful as simplifying aids to such pragmatic tasks as translation and language teaching — that is, generally useful rules of thumb — are recast as unquestionable foundational axioms, on which and without which the scientific study of languages would be impossible. Among these ideas is the claim that a language is an autonomous, decontextualizable biplanar code.

At the same time, the book is not intended as a series of negative strictures. On the positive side, I seek to show that a different way of looking at language, one that consistently pays attention to its inevitable contextual embeddedness, can be of explanatory value for a number of purposes that have tended to remain neglected or devalued in academic linguistic studies. What I have in mind by attention to the "inevitable contextual embeddedness" of language is foundational for all that follows, so a part of this introduction is devoted to clarifying this notion. I intend the phrase to be equivalent to what Roy Harris has called (foregrounding the contrast with post-Saussurean segregationalist and autonomous linguistics) an "integrational" perspective on linguistic interaction. This book as a whole is "integrational" in spirit, a kind of dialogue incorporating uses and mentions of work by Harris and those sympathetic, to one degree or another, to this perspective (among recent work propounding this approach, see Harris 1981a; Love 1990b; Davis and Taylor 1990; and Wolf 1992; and, for a robust critique, see the papers in Love and Wolf, in press). With any luck, the influence of Harris's thinking will be apparent at numerous points in the chapters that follow, and if this book does no more than provoke readers to turn or return to Harris's remarkable final chapter of *The Language Myth* (1981a), "Linguistics Demythologized," then something worthwhile will have been achieved. The present book hopes to be a drawing out of the arguments that Harris presents there, particularly putting them to work on some foundational contemporary linguistic notions (such as literal meaning and rule governedness) as well as on some of the important context-sensitive proposals in current linguistics (such as relevance theory). The following paragraphs briefly introduce the key tenet of an integrational perspective, the contextual embeddedness of language.

An important element in the integrational conception of situated language is a guarded skepticism concerning such old and sacred partners as text and context. The integrationist argues that we are much too confident in thinking that we know just what is text and just what is context. We treat these as foundational categories (we think that — in advance — we can judge that the lecturer's words will be part of the text, the size of the room in which the lecture is delivered and the fact that the lecturer is blind parts of the context) when they are (and not so much "merely" as "importantly") contingent ones. Integrational thinking declines to accept that text and context are distinct and stable categories, prior to consideration of particular cases. Striving to understand the language user's own perspective on his or her world, it recognizes that, in our everyday world and our everyday uses of language, we make no clear separation of experience into "texts" and "contexts." An integrational perspective sees also that in many oral cultures, where oral verbal performance constitutes the closest analogy to textuality in a literate culture, a sharp text-context division is difficult to make, or simply inappropriate. It notes too that even in the case of the most canonized of literary texts — such as *Hamlet*, *David Copperfield*, or *The Prelude* — some indeterminacies as to what is in or part of the text, what is outside, often persist. Which ending of *David Copperfield* belongs to the "true" text — surely not both endings? Is *Hamlet* on the page or *Hamlet* in the theater the actual text? Which *Prelude* — 1805 or 1850 — is *The Prelude*? What is true of texts is far more apparent of contexts, namely, that they are multiple and impossible of predetermined delimitation. Context is both indispensable to our making sense of language and shockingly, liberatingly variable; it is only locally determinate, as occasions of communication arise. As a result, there really is no such thing as *the* context, even to the extent that we can continue to think of certain things as texts: there is only a recurrent activity of contextualizing.

Perhaps nothing has done as much to promote the text-context binarism in linguistics — in linguistics, the science of language famously committed to the idea of the primacy of speech as the most natural human linguistic medium — as the development and spread of writing. Indeed, the association of the word *text* with writing has become so strong that for many hearers the phrase "spoken text" sounds anomalous. At the same time, no linguist doubts that the text-context distinction applies as directly to speech as it does to writing. Nothing demonstrates this as strongly as the continued faith, among linguists, in the efficacy of transcription as a means of capturing all — unquestionably all — the textual essentials of a spoken interaction. Transcription methods and inclusiveness have changed in recent years, but the idea that transcription remains a coherent means by which to reduce to writing all of a *text* (with or without varying details of context) remains secure. And when transcriptions are supplemented or displaced by audiovisual recordings in contemporary discourse studies, the assumption is not that the former failed to represent all the text, only that they failed to represent enough context. But for integrational linguists, transcription converts an interactional event (or series of events) into a textual product (separable from "the" contextual setting), a property. Transcription is a kind of absconding with that part of an interaction most easily reduced to writing, leaving the remainder as disposable residue.

The text-context binarism derives its staying power most directly from the power and ubiquity, in many cultures, of writing. But other cultural developments have helped sustain the distinction: multiple-copy printing, dictionaries, written grammars, discipline formation, scientism, and computers. That a foundational way to study language is first to separate text from context, that is, raise up the "linguistic" and set aside the "nonlinguistic," is part of the powerful and environing picture that now holds us captive. But ultimately there is no absolute separability of text from context; text (language) is never autonomous, and context is never permanent or stably linked to but distinct from text. Both *text* and *context* are ontological derivatives, an after-the-fact sense making, and just what is deemed to be the text and what the (relevant) context is decided locally, from within the interactional situation at hand. In other words, text and context finally do not exist at all, except situationally. And, since future situations cannot be fully known in advance, what will be text, what context, cannot be reliably or scientifically predicted either. This wrenching away from the standard conceptions of text and context is one of the necessary preconditions if a coherent narrative explanation of why languages change at all is to be formulated. Relatedly, the extant views of text and context are irremediably retrospective and recuperative, a post hoc sorting of "what has gone before": they are not established entities known at the outset of an interaction, such that interactants can automatically recognize certain material as text, certain other material as context, in their use of the interaction to further their respective communicational goals. Rather than enacting a mechanical recognition, interactants perform an active and revisable assigning of material to *text* and *context* categories, if they are so minded. Nor is a type-token relation involved, as if there were an established type, *text*, of which the present instance was a token. The integrationist resists here, as in other areas of linguistics, the overly determined picture of linguistic interaction that "type-token" theorizing presents.

But more needs to be said concerning context, not least since, for all its unsatisfactoriness as a term, falsely suggestive of a static entity with definite extension, nevertheless the term is virtually indispensable. The word is used in many pages that follow, but used with the qualification that an emphasis on local provisional determination (of what, on any particular occasion, may count as context) applies. Several recent studies have undertaken to enlarge our understanding of context (Duranti and Goodwin 1992; Auer and di Luzio 1992; Gumperz 1989), but the fact remains that, while in particular circumstances interactants evidently take particular factors as significant attributes of context (and, concomitantly, use these as "contextual cues," etc.), beyond particular cases it is contentious to specify, in any absolute way, just what is or constitutes context and what does not. It is hard to find any necessary or sufficient elements constitutive of context in a generalizable way.

Consider, for example, Lyons's often-cited description of the canonical speech situation (Lyons 1968: 275ff., 413ff.). There, the situational context of a spoken utterance includes "a particular spatiotemporal situation which includes the speaker and hearer, the actions they are performing at the time and various external objects and events." But Lyons adds that the context of an utterance cannot be identified simply with the spatiotemporal situation and relevant objects and actions. It must also include interactants' shared knowledge of what has been said earlier "in so far as this is pertinent to the understanding of the utterance"; that is, the context of an utterance must include accumulated cotextually derived information. More complexly yet, it must include interactants' tacit knowledge of various conventions and beliefs subscribed to by "the speech-community to which the speaker and hearer belong" (p. 413). Lyons suggests that, despite their undoubted importance, a full account of these contextual features is impossible in practice, "and perhaps also in principle," and notes that such considerations cast doubt on the possibility of ever being able to construct a complete theory of the meaning of utterances.

The present book is entirely in agreement with these observations of Lyons's, but it differs from Lyons concerning their consequences for linguistic studies. For Lyons, the consequence — presentationally, a step already taken, four chapters earlier in his conspectus — is that linguistics must concern itself not with actual "raw" utterances, but with abstract theoretical items, confusingly known by a term familiar to nonlinguists, *sentences*. In arguing for a sharp distinction between utterances and sentences Lyons echoes the binarist linguistic strategy of Saussure, who postulated a domain of *parole*, the more efficiently to set it aside, as Chomsky in turn did with *performance*. Lyons proceeds to articulate what is perhaps still today the linguistic orthodoxy, built on such theoretical notions as the sentence: a linguistics turned resolutely away from situated utterance. The use of the term *sentence* is predictably confusing and even misleading, in that it suggests to the nonlinguist that the categories and interests of standard linguistics are closely related to an everyday understanding of language. However, a contrasting remoteness is often more apparent in that linguistics: "When we use language to communicate with one another, we do not produce sentences, but utterances. . . . Since sentences are never produced by speakers . . . there can be no direct relationship between sentences and particular contexts" (Lyons 1968: 419–20). Yet on other occasions it would seem that utterance and sentence are not profoundly distinct entities. In his very introduction of the sentence as a theoretical linguistic unit, Lyons quotes without comment from Zellig Harris, who declares that "The utterance is, in general, not identical with the 'sentence' " (which implies that, on occasion, it is); he also cites Bloomfield's discussion of *How are you? It's a fine day. Are you going to play tennis this afternoon?* in which Bloomfield declares "the utterance consists of three sentences" (Lyons 1968: 172). As is recurrently the case with foundational demarcations in linguistics (e.g., in relation to *langue* vs. *parole*), the robustness of the theoretical distinction between sentences and utterances is thus problematic from the outset.

However, if — as from an integrational position — no sharp division between sentences and utterances is endorsed and the relevance of locally determined contextualizing of utterances is revealed, then all the factors that Lyons noted — cotextually displayed information, background knowledge, assumed shared conventions and beliefs — together with numerous further potentially relevant variables, are again matters for attention. Those further contextual variables may include, but cannot be limited to, the gender, ethnicity, nationality, class, expertise, etc. of interactants and their use of paralinguistic factors such as tone of voice, gaze, posture, and facial expression. Since just which of these factors will influence the uptake of an utterance on a particular occasion can emerge only from that particular interaction event, it is impossible to provide a general predictive account of "the nature of context."

If, for integrationists, the local determinations of text and context are routinely and mistakenly assumed to be reflexes of a general predictable demarcation of text and context, the same neglected variability also underlies relations between context and meaning. In normal circumstances, what counts as communicationally relevant or criterial context is revisable and indeterminate in nature. The revisionary adjustment of provisional meanings of utterances or acts is evident not merely in the fluid dynamics of everyday conversation but also in just that domain that seems, to the layperson, to attempt to expel with most vigor the ambiguities and indeterminacies of natural language: the law. We may imagine that we have a pretty clear idea of the literal or conventional meaning of such words and phrases as *chicken, fire, souvenir, race,* and *sausage.* But various commentaries have charted in some detail how minor and major judicial cases are in practice determined in highly contextualized ways (Benn Michaels 1980; Harris 1981a; Love 1984; Williams 1991). In all these cases, the criteria for what counts as a souvenir or a sausage emerge from the particular circumstances of each controversy (and what the adjudicatory parties take to be the salient circumstances in those controversies); there is little direct submission to literal or dictionary (i.e., decontextualized) definition.

An instance of this tension between an imagined decontextualized literalism and the situated determination of meaning recently emerged on the Linguist internet discussion list, concerning the suitability of the term *informant* to designate native-language speakers whose judgments about language and use are sought out by linguists. For many people in North America, linguists and nonlinguists alike, the term *informant* has some unsavory or pejorative connotations and is felt to be demeaning to those to whom it might be applied. In rebuttal, some commentators made reference to dictionary definitions, especially of *informer*; they claimed that an erroneous transfer of connotations from that quite different word triggered an unwarranted sensitivity toward and a mistaken avoidance of an entirely blameless word. But the general view of contributors to the discussion was that invoking dictionary definitions of *informer* and *informant* was either prescriptivist or irrelevant, or both. Contemporary usages and asssociations could not be set aside so simply. Here one of the more powerful pieces of evidence was the citing of recent occasions on which agencies such as the FBI have referred to people in refugee camps, whom they had hired to supply them with inside information, as *informants.* In this situation, as in those cases that involved judicial arbitration, it is clear that consulting dictionaries cannot be relied on to resolve issues. This is partly because dictionaries rarely provide a "single" answer to any interpretive or definitional question posed of them but more generally because present circumstances can always override received lexicographical wisdom. Making appeals to dictionaries is recurrently found to be more a rhetorical strategy than a procedure assumed to be definitive, and appearing to defer to dictionaries takes place only if no pressing argument not to do so emerges.

Integrational linguistic emphases in the study of language invariably include the following:

a) *Cotemporality* (a term of art proposed in Harris 1981a: 157ff.): cotemporality refers to and emphasizes the profoundly synchronized nature of verbal and nonverbal events; it relatedly acknowledges the "now-ness" of language in use. The foundational assumption here is that utterances are interpretable, in the first or default instance, by reference to the speaker's here and now, even in all its extralinguistic complexity. All our linguistic acts — like all our nonlinguistic ones — are invariably assumed to be immediately relevant to the current situation, unless indications to the contrary are provided. It is in part because immediate relevance is the norm that linguistic and nonlinguistic acts are so often intersubstitutable.

b) The privileging of local relevance, rather than the precedent of remote behavior, in the situational determination of the meaning of an utterance or exchange.

c) Sequentiality of linguistic production.

d) The uniqueness of experience (language can never, strictly, be rerun and played over again: our sense of repetition is always a sense of the close relatedness — and not of identical reproduction — between pairs or groups of utterances, things, or events).

In practice, the potentially infinite diversity of language practices that these four tenets project is held in check, for individuals are born into highly socialized normative communities, within which they are taught to find their own socialized normative place. Thus, while language is never a code, it is apparent that most individuals become habituated to a code-like predictability of usage, forms, and meanings. Nor need the habituation be thought of as necessarily undesirable or demeaning; it will often be a constructive acceptance of the limits to communicative innovation and the desirability of recognizably shared public forms. Also among the forces constraining and delimiting our individualistic excesses with language (as within other domains) must be counted time, aging, and mortality. Taking the long view, life strikes us as short, aging comes sooner than we might wish, and finiteness constrains all our processes. It also gives them shape and helps give language shape. Part of the human response to finiteness and normativity is the tireless schematizing that we evidently undertake, the sorting of past experiences into remembered scripts, activities, and stereotyped situations. It is through this shifting multidimensional mental network of scripts, situations, and styles that we undertake the making of contextualized sense of particular episodes of linguistic interaction. The crucial intermediate role played by our interpretive schematizations of situations, between "the" language and "the" world, is discussed more fully in chapter 4.

Some of the recurrent themes adduced by an integrational approach include the following: that language learning is a process of growing familiarity and proficiency with a grammar of possibilities (possible expressions, possible gestures, possible intonations, possible kinesics, etc.); that the reinforcement of those possibilities is achieved in part by what Whorf called "habituation"; that grammar is therefore quite as appropriately conceptualized as constantly developing or emergent (Hopper and Traugott 1993) rather than as fixed; and that the interrelations between such a provisionalized grammar and speakers' interpretive schematizations of situations (the latter equivalent to what Wittgenstein termed "forms of life") entail a dialogism that truly merits the adjective Bakhtinian.

This book probes a network of questionable assumptions about language that enjoy wide currency within and beyond linguistics. The book is also concerned to characterize language anew, with those assumptions held at bay, where not vanquished. The notions to be reconsidered principally concern literal meaning, metaphor, intention-free signification, use of words versus mention of them, repetition, ostensive behavior, directness versus indirectness of speech, and language as the following of mental rules. From those principal concerns a number of secondary suppositions follow. In exploring these topics, I introduce a variety of textual examples (inter alia, poems, lawsuits, and the language of children). The goal has not been wholesale rejection of the network of notions (literal meaning etc.) found to be suspect: each notion has played and continues to play an important role in various cultures' thinking about language and society. What is argued for is the need for radical change in the way these notions operate as the foundations of contemporary theorizing about language and communication. If the revised account presented here of literal meaning, metaphor, intention, repetition, etc. and their interrelation in language has any merit, it inescapably entails major changes in the way linguistics and language are conceptualized.

The conclusion to which the present studies point is that the foundational requirements and characteristics of language using are quite general ones and that human language does not crucially rest on specific and language-exclusive mental faculties and mechanisms (below I will term this *the cognitivist-mechanist approach*). That is to say, whatever language-dedicated cognitive predispositions the normal human may be endowed with — and there is plentiful evidence that humans are predisposed toward the grasp and use of certain kinds of structuring — those predispositions are not, as many have claimed, crucial for language. It is one thing for humans to have such a genetic endowment, facilitating language acquisition and use; and that humans do, in some form, is not here disputed. It is quite another thing to claim that, for language to be possible, such an endowment — a biologically given predisposition to comprehend and reproduce linguistic structure rapidly — is needed. It is argued here that it is not so needed, that the human genetic disposition to handle a particular kind of linguistic structure with facility is strictly neither necessary nor sufficient for language.

The codificatory and systematizing impulses of modern linguistics have been so powerful as to render the idea of a language as a system and a code — in essence, a species-wide and species-specific complex mental program to be progressively deciphered by linguists via slow but steady advances in technical modeling — utterly standard and barely questionable common sense. The present book tries to show some of the ways in which this common sense often glosses over incoherence. Additionally, that cognitive-mechanist approach to language has created some regrettable gaps and distortions in the academic study of language: either a general reluctance, in disciplines that neighbor linguistics (child development and education, anthropology, sociology), to undertake a thoroughgoing critique of the cognitive-mechanist model, a model sometimes taken to be as prestigious and irrefutable as a branch of mathematics; or a general respectful acceptance and tentative application of the paradigm (the tentativeness sometimes brought on by a sense of an insecure grasp of what have often been immensely complex arguments and proposals). As a result, such matters as the study of language use and language development in everyday situations, the analysis of patternings and exploitations of language in literary texts and elsewhere, the shifting development of societal attitudes toward particular forms of language whether at the level of the individual or of government policy, have been treated as far more marginal to linguistics, hence far less widely examined within linguistics, than seems justified.

But this book intends to do more than lament linguistic wrong turnings. The purpose of delineating what arguments cannot hold is to highlight the aspects of language, and the assumptions about its cognitive bases in humans, that are foundational. As noted above, and offered in place of explanations in terms of language-specific principles and rules espoused by those of a cognitive-mechanist persuasion, it is argued here that language draws primarily on quite general characteristics of humans (and, to a degree, of some other animals also). These can be summarized as the following partially overlapping attributes: faith; trust; orientedness to others; faculties of memory and imagination; goal orientedness; and the ability to perceive the relatedness and nonrelatedness of phenomena (understood as the perception of similarity and difference rather than of identity and difference). Among these attributes, I take orientedness to others to be preeminent — the predisposition that Frank, in the epigraph of this introduction, refers to as "the need we have for each other." Endowed with these very general and natural attributes, humans equally naturally develop language; all the more arcane and technical principles introduced into the picture by cognitive mechanists are by contrast epiphenomenal, no matter how locally illuminating they may be. (The words *natural* and *naturally* in the preceding sentence are probably open to criticism. I do not wish to suggest that orientedness to other has always been a major human characteristic or deny that its emergence may have been environmentally conditioned in ways too complex to fathom here; I accept that it may more accurately be represented as something fostered culturally for so long that it has come to be called simply *natural*.)

Language is essentially rooted in trust, goal orientedness, memory, and acuity of perception since — like those very attributes — it is an integral part of human life (and not an autonomous faculty or organ, like a board or card added to a primitive computer, which miraculously developed along its own lines in our prehistory). If language is an integral part of life, much of one's grasp of the former will depend on how one views the latter, that is, what one understands life to be or what one understands life to entail. Whatever else it entails, all the evidence suggests that human life is a continual and creative puzzle solving (or attempting), in which we are repeatedly called on to make sense anew of things (as distinct from merely retrieving old solutions to things). This is not to deny that past experience is a resource in the puzzling out of present experience but rather to stress that such past experience cannot be applied with a certainty of its relevance in anything like the way that, with a scientific law, one is confident of the certain, relevant, and consequential occurrence of the specified outcome when the specified initial conditions for the application of that law have arisen. And the reason for our experiential uncertainty is that taken as a whole, as distinct from the separated subparts of it that particular scientific laws characterize, life is not a matter of doing the same things over and over again in anything like the way that a scientific law asserts that, given such and such conditions, the same thing will follow over and over again. Life is, then, among other things, a working of puzzles rather than an "observing" of laws. I hope to sustain this claim in the course of discussing a variety of texts or language events in the following chapters. Each case in its own way supports these claims: that language is essentially a flexible practice, shaped by profound interacting principles of self-awareness, normativity, other orientedness, and rational risk taking, integral to the larger phenomenon of risk-entailing puzzle working entailed in life itself.

The essential tenet of an integrational linguistic analysis is that language is always contextually embedded and that this contextualization is always open to change. For integrationists, "contextualizedness" amounts to a design feature of language. The implications of an integrational perspective need to be reflected in our theorizing about literal meaning, metaphor, irony, repetition, "bad" language, uses and mentions, and rule following. From this viewpoint, the crucial mistake of established linguistics, a linguistics that champions the decontextualizedness or autonomy of the linguistic structure, is that it effectively regards a language as a theory before it is a practice. In the following chapters, fundamental topics in the theorizing of language as a branch of human activity are broached. I begin with literal meaning, long a cornerstone of linguistic semantics and many forms of pragmatics. Numerous models of linguistic meaning uncritically accept the idea that literal meaning comes first and is foundational and proceed from there; I present arguments in support of the view that, on the contrary, literal meaning is a rather late-emerging construct, a derivative. Evidence from psycholinguistics and elsewhere suggests that literal meaning is no first foundation, sometimes a descriptive convenience, and often irrelevant to interpretation. Literal meaning is a precipitation, from countless occasions of use, of a purportedly stable or core meaning, under the catalyzing influence of pressures from a culture that has taken a "scriptivist" turn; by "a scriptivist turn" I mean a pronounced orientation in favor of written language (concerning which more is said in chapter 6). The conclusion is that the idea of literal meaning must be reconceptualized: proper weight must be given to the indeterminacies of meaning in context, which in turn compel us to discard altogether the notion of a stable, permanent phenomenon or level called *meaning*. In the longer run, in the phrase *literal meaning* it is not the term *literal* that is the more unsatisfactory but the term *meaning*.

The critique of the idea of decontextualizable linguistic meaning is pursued in the following chapter, on metaphor. On the one hand, the diversity of uptake of a fresh metaphor (i.e., the diversity of meanings derived from particular metaphors) would seem to be overwhelming confirmation for the "no fixed meaning" view. On the other hand, numerous linguists and philosophers have denied that all those illuminations we get from metaphors are meanings. For some, at most, metaphors trigger derivative "meanings" that may attach to the speaker or utterance but not to the language itself or its sentences. On the contrary, the diverse illuminations that we derive from a sentence used metaphorically can "go through" only if that sentence's first or standard meaning — and no other meaning besides — stands ready to be used as a springboard for interpretation. In all these deeply influential views, a counterpart to the binarism discernible in the first chapter (literal meaning vs. nonliteral meaning) is apparent. Thus, metaphor is contrasted with everyday language, or literal language, or even simile: at any event, metaphor must be characterized and conceptualized as radically different from the typical case. Linguists and philosophers can then damn it with extravagant praise as exuberant language, exotic and abnormal, and as not so much a challenge to but a powerful confirmation of the received constricted view of ordinary nonmetaphoric language.

In recent years, however, abundant evidence has been advanced in support of the idea that metaphoricality is no exoticism in the garden of language but a widespread indigenous part of the flora. Everyday language itself is riddled with metaphors, albeit often rather faded or worn ones. At the same time, a reconsideration of the "damning praise" that theorists have heaped on metaphor is in order, for what is striking in such treatments is how very much less than satisfactory they are when applied to genuinely fresh metaphors. Most such accounts fail to supply even so much as a sketch of how a producer or an interpreter derives the rich but not unconstrained array of suggestive associations that a creative metaphor triggers. The conclusion that I work toward, using evidence from linguistic philosophy, psycholinguistic studies, cognitive linguistics, and the interpretation of poems, is that metaphor should be conceptualized as different not in kind but only in degree from language in general; indeed, an inspection of fresh metaphors at work (in a poem by Sylvia Plath) gives us some insight into the nature and workings of language as a means of communication. Metaphors are high-risk redescriptions or reinterpretations with the goal of securing enhanced intimacy or insight.

Chapter 3 turns to intentionality — insisted on as intrinsic to any coherent notion of linguistic communication — and speculations concerning the development of language in the species and in the typical child. By *intentionality* is meant the Gricean idea that language is used in the furtherance of specific interactional goals, where speaker and hearer can be taken to have the expectation that part of the communication of intents and purposes will be undertaken by the suitable use and uptake of whatever language is employed. It is not assumed here, however, that a speaker's intentions somehow "govern" the utterance's meaning or that those intentions are recoverable or determinate. More important, I argue, is the contingent but crucial process of attributing intentions, by the hearer to the speaker particularly but vice versa also, guided by foundational faculties of pattern construction and perception, other-orientedness, memory, normativity, and abstraction. Those faculties seem the necessary elements for "coming into language," a phrase that, although a clumsy formulation, often seems a preferable description to established but problematic ones such as "language development" or "language acquisition." "Coming into language" is examined in relation to two imagined contexts of use: the accomplishment of a work task and the maintenance of mother-infant connection. In both cases, what is crucial is that instinctive processes become increasingly reflected on: what was first and necessarily a single integrated activity becomes dis-integrated or open to analysis (e.g., into the verbal and the nonverbal), for certain purposes. In part, the individual emerging into a languaged world is performing creative interpretation of (perceived) near repetitions, so that this chapter needs to be read in conjunction with the broader examination of repetition and codification in chapter 6. The issues of "coming into language" also relate directly to chapter 7 in two important ways: there the alleged "rule governedness" of natural languages and the child's tacit recourse to such rules in the course of developing a more and more adult-like phonological system are considered; and the child's creative interpretation mentioned above is set beside "radical interpretation" of the kind Davidson has claimed underlies language use.

The chapter closes with a guarded grappling with the Derridean notion of iterability and the "antitheory" theory espoused by the neopragmatists Knapp and Benn Michaels (others of a mind with this position — even if Knapp and Benn Michaels take them to task on specific points — would include Fish and Rorty). While neopragmatism is broadly endorsed, it is suggested that, in the antitheorists' rejection of any divergence between authorial intention and textual meaning, insufficient attention is paid to the independent role of the addressee. And, despite Derrida's trenchant critique of linguistic claims from Saussure to Searle, the uptake of his notion of iterability seems to reinstate the power of the sign, or the language as a system of signs, as a "thing" inherently unchanging or stable, which can then be put to uncannily changed uses, with radically different intentions or none at all, in every new context. A signifier may float free from its signified, but there is still the assumption — indeed, it is claimed, just as Saussurean linguists might, that it is a necessity — that it is the same signifier, constant in form, that occurs again, untrammeled by speaker intentions, in each new context with a new force. This, I contend, is halfhearted contextualism. Taking language in context seriously entails deconstructing the very idea of language as a stable thing, to be shifted from one context to another. To view language thus is already to be viewing it at an abstract level, for the actuality is that in ever-changing circumstances speakers are constantly coping with shifts and indeterminacies of form and meaning — even if usually that coping takes the form of interpretive appeal to prior abstract types of form and meaning.

One of the themes that is important particularly to discussions in chapters 3, 4, and 5 concerns assumptions about the role in communication of mutual knowledge and a shared and presupposed background. Background or mutual knowledge has often been postulated as a prerequisite for the swift computation or processing of abbreviated or culturally embedded utterances; at the same time, a plausible characterization of such knowledge that steers clear of infinite regression has been hard to achieve. A critique of linguists' appeals to mutual (background) knowledge, of various kinds, is pursued in chapter 5; the general thesis is that orientedness to other (mutuality but not mutual or shared knowledge) is the pertinent prerequisite for coming into language, which is also to say coming into understanding. For potentially effective linguistic communication, it is enough that each of us assumes that we are jointly oriented to others and seek to converge on understanding, although we share no more than the orientedness and an awareness of that orientedness: we share no knowledge held in common. As far as mother-child interaction is concerned, the essential question is, If we accept that mutual knowledge is not present at the outset, prior to interaction and the beginnings of communication, at what point shall we say that it does become implanted (and, crucially, mutually implanted)?

In chapter 4, an attempt is made to identify some of the ways in which taking language in context seriously entails a revised account of the relations between language and society. In the process, I explore some of the key tenets of an integrational linguistic view of the nature of language. A crucial intermediary between language and society would seem to be linguistic meaning: what a particular society, or speech community, is said to take particular utterances to mean. Here, the very characterization of linguistic meaning in such collectivist terms (a collectivism that is, however, skewed in favor of the powerful within society, whose linguistic authority, like their money, talks) is treated as an accommodation with hegemony. There needs to be renewed recognition that collectivism is an enforced stabilization of the much more fluid intrinsic conditions of language use, in which the key intermediary between language and society is not an autonomous and determinate plane of linguistic meaning but a multidimensioned, user-varying network of activity-type schemata. The interpretation of linguistic signs in any interaction is not undertaken by direct and independent consultation of a mental store of such signs without concurrent and coordinated reference to a mental record of multiply variable situations; and, while these coordinated referrals can guide current interpretation, they can never predetermine it — as linguistic and situational innovations everywhere confirm.

As a result, the socially embedded nature of language should not be emphasized at the expense of the role of the creatively interpretive individual, whose engagement with language is characterized rather differently from that of the fluent automaton sometimes presupposed by linguistic theories. Here the language user's memory limitations and shifts of interests are treated as potentially significant determinants of the nature and use of language — and not as theoretical irrelevances. We know rather less about what goes on in the brain to support and enable linguistic production than psycholinguistics sometimes implies. Nevertheless, some cognitive speculations are in order, if only to set an integrational sketch of the individual's processing faculties beside the integrational picture of language in social practice. Accordingly, some proposals are outlined concerning how language interactions are in the first instance remembered with their contexts attached (i.e., primary memory is memory of occasions, and not selectively or exclusively of the verbal part of those occasions or of any structural pattern in those occasions). For specific purposes, and under the pressure of specific needs and perceptions of cost effectiveness, the individual sifts, sorts, backgrounds, and foregrounds aspects of that rich continuum of remembered contextualized interactions; the upshot of such constrained sorting may be the postulation of rather abstract patternings, which are the basis for metadescriptions such as mental models, schemas, prototypicality, grammatical rules, and word meanings. These patternings, and the appropriate ways to use language so as to accord with those patternings, are what seem to lie in the forefront of our everyday awareness of language; hence — by way of example — the word *chair* has innumerable meanings in innumerable contexts, but, when asked its meaning, we are likely to say first "a piece of furniture to sit on," or words to that effect. While memory is foundational to language use, it operates neither mechanically nor alone: attention must also be given to the role of imagination in language development and the establishment of meanings. It is in the scope of the abstract patternings that individuals assign to their unique and diverse linguistic experiences that convergence on a complex shared linguistic practice becomes possible. And convergence is nurtured by our other-oriented drive to connect, to trust and be trusted. Individuals are born into highly socialized normative communities, within which they are taught to find their own socialized normative place. As a result, although language is never a code, nevertheless it is quite apparent that individuals and groups — especially subordinated and disempowered ones, although here the issue of what constitutes subordination must not be prejudged — may be habituated to a code-like predictability of usage, forms, and meanings.

Aspects of the work of several theorists who variously contextualize language within society are discussed here. Among these is Bakhtin, who had some of the most sociologically interesting things to say about what might otherwise be regarded as a minor flourish of literary technique: the style known as "free indirect discourse." In addition to being a favored narrative strategy, free indirect discourse is an instructive instance of a larger tension in language — one that emerges also wherever quotation is apprehended as more than a reporting, as an actual saying (e.g., in newspaper reports, oral recountings, references, or testimonials). The ramifications of incorporating this tension into an account of language — as I argue an integrational perspective can while an orthodox linguistic one cannot — lead to the conclusion that categorical separation of uses of expressions from mentions is an impossibility. What fails in the case of literal meaning fails also in the inherently hierarchical binary notion of uses and mentions (and its close grammatical counterpart, types and tokens). That any theoretical segregation into uses and mentions is always open to reinterpretation in which these are newly conflated is utterly characteristic of language. Particular efforts to assert that here are uses, there are mentions, are always inconclusive. This is true both generally and in particular instances such as the plight of Salman Rushdie, who continues to suffer on account of a deeply hostile and distrustful reception, as uses, of material in *The Satanic Verses* that he has protested are mentions. It is so also in the very different situation of anyone reading Henry James: the reader struggles to identify those judgments that, despite seeming narratorial use, appear on closer inspection to be an ironized mentioning of a particular character's partisan views. There is no foundationalist, freestanding basis on which to arbitrate or transcend the picture of flux and emergence within which any use may be seen as a mention, or vice versa, and where indeed neither extreme of assessment — all uses are really mentions, all mentions are really uses —

can be noncontingently ruled out. Also pertinent here is Bakhtin's proposal that in dialogic discourse a present utterance is always cast or slanted so as to deflect the answering utterance it foresees. This is other-oriented constrained guesswork if anything is, and it is thoroughly congruent with an integrational view of intentionality: intentionality, I argue, must in essence be the intentions that a hearer attributes to a speaker, without hope, possibility, or need of confirmation (by the speaker) of their accuracy. The hearer makes those attributions prior to his or her involvement in an interactional response, informed by those attributions.

The emphasis on the role of the hearer in communication, as the attributor of speaker intentions, is maintained in chapter 5, not least because such an emphasis prompts the question whether this is any different from a Gricean account of communication or its influential offspring, Sperber and Wilson's theory of relevance. Chapter 5 argues that in important respects both Grice's account and relevance theory appeal to an excessively determinate base, where language is code. There is an overreliance also on ostensive-inferential processing and the relevance of the inferences that such processing yields — a guaranteed relevance, its proponents have claimed. Once again, normatively constrained inferencing and an assumption of probabilism, within an assumed environment of other-oriented communicational convergence, are preferred as prerequisites for the understanding of how linguistic communication works. Besides offering a general theory of communication, Sperber and Wilson's model is important for the light that it attempts to throw on specific ways of language use, such as irony, metaphor, and indirect speech acts. Their most developed treatment is of irony, the essence of which they have characterized as "echoic interpretively resemblant use." Their arguments, and the application of these arguments to particular examples, are examined in detail. In view of the discussion of use-mention in chapter 4 and elsewhere, it is interesting to note that, while Sperber and Wilson now call irony "use," an earlier important paper of theirs labeled it "echoic mention." What is constant in their treatment, however, is the idea of irony as echoic. In qualification of this, I argue that echoism is neither necessary nor sufficient for irony and that the understanding of irony (verbal or situational) begins rather with the perception of mismatch, between words and world. In the case of intentional verbal irony, the hearer assumes the mismatch to be intentional and intended to be perceived (this distinguishes it from simple lying). So much is necessary for intentional verbal irony; it is not, however, sufficient since these conditions hold in the case of metaphor also. I try to specify the further necessary features of irony and also to clarify its differences from metaphor. Although irony and metaphor appear to be comparable figures of speech, of equivalent status, I argue that they operate discoursally in rather different ways and at different levels.

Chapter 6 looks at relevance in a more global context, as the basis for the perception of repetition on which rest, in turn, our standard notions of what a language is. In examining repetition in detail, issues raised in chapters 4 and 5 are also carried further. Earlier, the Derridean account of citation and iteration, as permanent possibilities of the sign, was discussed. That was by way of a preliminary to making a case for fuller acknowledgment that the same possibilities of variation and difference accorded to context must be extended also to the linguistic mark or sign, no matter the degree to which, in modern habitualized and normative practice, that variation in the phonic, graphic, or kinesic nature of signs is set aside by language users. At the phenomenal level, in the first-order experience of language as an integrated part of "the whole bodily behaviour" of individuals (Firth 1964: 19), there is no such thing as repetition. The picture of a language as a system of reliable repetitions and the extensions of that picture in such notions as an inventory of reliably repeatable performative verbs or a grammar of the conditions for the effective performance of particular and determinate speech acts (proposed by Austin and Searle, respectively) are metalinguistic abstractions. As Love has succinctly summarized the matter: "A language is a second-order construct arising from an idea about first-order utterances: namely, that they are repeatable" (Love 1990c: 101). And, as Love adds, a language is permanently such an idea-based construct: by its nature it cannot ever become, by any miraculous metamorphosis, a first-order reality for individuals.

Part of what is interesting in these issues is the clarification of why it is that our culture has come so widely to assume something different, namely, that a language (English, Spanish, Cantonese) is indeed a first-order reality, containing agreed-on and relatively fixed forms and meanings. Here, as indicated earlier, the impact of writing has been significant to a degree still not fully appreciated. With the coming of writing, language ceases to be equated simply with speech; language can begin to be contemplated as thoroughly detached from speakers and events, as freestanding in an "autoglottic space," for in writing we find a "*general* model of unsponsored language" (Harris 1989: 104). The emergence of writing brings an immense shift in conceptualizations of the nature of language and verbal communication, and writing dominates and appears to govern written communication in a way that, in an oral-language community, speech cannot govern communication involving speech. The contrast has much to do with what seems natural or plausible in the effort to attribute intentions: it is possible and even routine to attribute quite particular meanings and intentions to an addresser or coparticipant, in the course of interactions involving speech, even when the "speech channel" is severely restricted (even to the point of, e.g., the total lack of access to acoustic signals). In such circumstances, it is not bizarre to look for intentions and meanings (and expect to find them) in the coparticipant's behavior taken as a whole, that is, without exhaustive attention to the specificities of the stream of speech. But to attempt anything parallel in the case of written language, namely, to attempt to deduce authorial meaning and intentions with only a secondary attention to the specificities of the stream of written signs, seems ill judged when not simply ludicrous. Examples of such improbable undertakings would be attempting to read a text that was held up behind one's back or was displayed at such a distance that the characters could be seen only as a blurred mass. Even speech in a totally foreign language, in use in an ordinarily observable situation, remains interpretable by an outsider to a degree that is normally quite impossible in the face of situated writing in a foreign language, and this contrast in interpretability has profound consequences. Readable writing itself has an indispensable role in written communicative acts, and this gives rise to such corollary conceptualizations as that writing is ordinarily meaningful, that what is meant is "in" the writing, and that the reliably meaningful character of written language is ensured by the foundations provided by literal meanings.

Finally, in chapter 7, modern linguistics' attractive characterization of language use as "rule-governed creativity" is considered. The chapter reviews in detail how rule-governed creativity is claimed to apply in the intriguing cases of a child's development of a fuller and more adult-language-like phonological system from a simpler one and in hearers' frequent success at "unscrambling" malapropisms and slips of the tongue. Among the changes of emphasis that I urge, in discussions of child language, is greater circumspection in characterizing the child's "immature" language system as deficient or primitive and the infant years of language acquisition as ones in which, gradually and systematically, lacks and errors are remedied. While it is acknowledged that generative phonological studies of child language have identified systematic patterns of (diverging) comprehension and production of particular sound clusters by the same child, I argue that more of those patterns may be explicable in terms of salience (especially interactional salience) than is recognized by a generativist account of stored underlying forms on which various derivational rules operate. A salience-oriented analysis of language development in children amounts to an account that places greater weight on the criterion of relevance. The integrational revision proposes that language is, in many respects and circumstances, less rule governed and more creative and, in other circumstances, rule governed but less creative than the orthodox view allows. To support this revised perspective, the chapter attempts to comment from a linguistic point of view on some of the host of overlapping or contrasted terms invoked in discussions of the systematicity of languages: among these are rules, laws, acting in accordance with a rule rather than following a rule, constraints, innate predispositions or principles, working hypotheses, rules of thumb, and passing theories. The book concludes by emphasizing the importance of individuals to languages.

While at many points appeal is made to integrational principles in reasserting the contextual determinedness of language, no uniquely integrational-linguistic methodology is presented in these chapters. It is not clear that a radically new methodology is either possible or necessary: it is open to question whether a perspective so definitively sensitive to the varying requirements of each new communicational situation could yield anything so determinate as a methodology. At the same time, it is arguable that what is chiefly required is not a new methodology but rather a revised application of extant methods. In this book, insofar as analytic methods and procedures are discussed, the latter view is advanced. Numerous established methods are potentially congruent with integrational assumptions, ranging from conversation and discourse analysis, distributionalism, attitude surveys, and matched-guise tests to corpus linguistics and questionnaires probing speakers' attitudes toward their own and others' speech. The fundamental questions that the integrationist seeks always to introduce, whatever the analytic method harnassed, are to what extent the inquiry has adopted an ordinary language user's own stance toward the material under scrutiny (Saussure's neglected principle [Saussure 1983 [1916] 128ff.]) and to what extent "the total speech act in the total speech situation" (Austin's underlying concern [Austin 1962: 147]) has remained in view. As these desiderata indicate, the integrationist seeks above all an "inward" account of language, as opposed to a detached, abstracted, and idealized one. In a discipline pervaded by models and representations, the integrational approach would have us distrust models and representations — at least to the extent of addressing the question whether what is modeled is truly the lay language user's own understanding of the given phenomena.

At the same time, it is very probable that the demand that integrational criticism of current linguistic assumptions and theory should come with a developed alternative methodology for language analysis reflects a way of thinking deeply committed to the prevailing post-Saussurean cognitivist-mechanist paradigm. *Integrational linguistics* names a principle rather than a method, the principle that understanding language must entail considering how it is actually used and understood by language users, who in turn are acknowledged to be more genuinely creative in their linguistic communication (hence unpredictable changers of "the" language) than is usually conceded. It would run the risk of theoretical self-contradiction for a book concerned with the inherent limitations of linguistic models and methods to attempt to set out an alternative methodology of its own. My preference is to retain, shorn of their more extravagant theoretical underpinnings, as much of a number of extant models as is possible.

1

On Inscribed or Literal Meaning

> It might seem that the thesis that there is no such thing as literal meaning is a limited one, of interest largely to linguists and philosophers of language; but in fact it is a thesis whose implications are almost boundless, for they extend to the very underpinnings of the universe as it is understood by persons of a certain cast of mind. — Stanley Fish, *Doing What Comes Naturally*

> It is crucial to distinguish between what a sentence means, that is, its literal sentence meaning, and what the speaker means in the utterance of the sentence. We know the meaning of a sentence as soon as we know the meanings of the elements and the rules for combining them. — J. Searle, "Literary Theory and Its Discontents"

Preliminaries

This chapter, together with the one following, discusses literalness, metaphoricality, and figurative language: what they are and how they emerge, are understood, and are related. Although the first chapter is "on" literal meaning while the second is on metaphor, they are not on these subjects respectively; that is to say, chapter headings notwithstanding, literalness and metaphoricality are treated not as essential kinds or strictly separable phenomena but as names that are artifacts of convenience. The categorization separating literal meaning from metaphor, and the substantial delimitation of one in relation to the other, is a deeply embedded convenience of literate Western culture, a culture within which contemporary theorizing about language has its place. Nor is the term *convenience* intended to be denigratory: its close kinship to more authoritative terms such as *purpose*, *relevance*, and *intention* needs acknowledging. All are touchstones in the larger argument that is to emerge. The larger argument is that language should be viewed essentially as other-

25 Inscribed or Literal Meaning

oriented situated behavior: but other oriented not at the expense of self-interest but by way of calculated pursuit of reasonable self-orientedness.

The focus on literal meaning here, and on metaphor in the next chapter, reflects a prevalent classification of utterance interpretation in such fields as pragmatics and psycholinguistics. But my treatment is intended to be unitary, classing the literal and the metaphoric as aspects of a single phenomenon of sense making in language: the two chapters should be read as one, with the subsuming title and topic of "Figuration," for it will be argued that conceptualizations in terms of literalness versus metaphoricality are themselves essentially a form of figuration: the ascribing of "literal meaning" is a kind of troping, and metalinguistic exercises of separating out literal sheep from metaphoric goats (or wolves) is a parallel "figuring things out."

In this chapter, I argue that, although a conceptualization of literal meaning as the basic, determinate, and context-free meaning of words and sentences is necessary for standard linguistic treatments of the semantics and pragmatics of a language, in practice no such domain of context-free meaning exists. The standard linguistic procedure is to concede that some kind of "background" is a necessary frame for literal meaning but also to represent that background as neutral and inconsequential. I review and critique some recent discussions that attempt to maintain an account of literal meaning as "context-transcending" meaning. I argue, on the contrary, that literal meaning is itself a highly contextualized notion, that it is a cultural and ideological construct very much designed to characterize some language practices as orderly, authorized, and authoritative (and others as not so); it is therefore well suited to and reflective of societal interests in literacy, order, and authority.

In the introduction to an influential collection of articles in pragmatics (Searle, Kiefer, and Bierwisch 1980), the editors compare and contrast different treatments of the term *pragmatics*, and notions (of denotation, sense, and use of linguistic expressions) surrounding it, in three analytic traditions: formal philosophy, linguistic semantics, and ordinary language philosophy. Despite major differences, they feel able to conclude: "In all three traditions something like a notion of literal meaning is essential, and some contrast between literal meaning and speaker's utterance meaning seems essential to any account of language. Speaker's utterance meaning may differ from literal meaning in a variety of ways. Speaker's meaning may include literal meaning but go beyond it, as in the case of indirect speech acts, or it may depart from it, as in the case of metaphor, or it may be the opposite of it, as in the case of irony" (p. xi).

Literal meaning is essential and foundational, then, in this account. At the same time, it is not a plane of meanings that is context free or interpretable without reference to a background. The literal meaning of an expression is never meaning in a "zero context," Searle argues in the same volume, but rather always is meaning relative to background assumptions that cannot themselves be part of the expression's meaning. Searle proceeds to discuss a series of sentences in which the "same" verb, *cut*, is used literally and yet determines different sets of truth conditions in each case (*cutting the grass, the cake, the cloth,* etc.):

> The reason that the same semantic content, "cut," determines different sets of truth conditions in these different sentences . . . derives not from any ambiguity of a semantic kind, but rather from the fact that as members of our culture we bring to bear on the literal utterance and understanding of a sentence a whole background of information about how nature works and how our culture works. A background of practices, institutions, facts of nature, regularities, and ways of doing things are assumed by speakers and hearers when one of these sentences is uttered or understood. . . . My knowledge that cutting grass is a different sort of business from cutting cakes is part of this larger system of knowledge. (Searle 1980: 227)

By this postulation of a required "background" in the interpretation of a literal sentence, Searle appears able to protect the notion of the invariance of literal meaning. The literal meaning of *cut* is said not to change: only the truth conditions (and, shaping these, the background assumptions) do.

However, if we adopt Searle's arguments for the necessity of background assumptions, certain issues remain unclear. The first of these concerns the literal meaning of *cut*: nowhere does Searle offer a formulation as to what this is, although he insists on its identity across the five sentences he discusses. His own characterization of *cut* as "a physical separation by means of the pressure of some more or less sharp instrument" he dismisses as "very misleading." The same example, of cutting the grass (vs. cutting the cake) is used in Searle (1994a: 640), where again it is claimed that the literal meaning of *cut* is univocal and determinate — "We do not have different definitions of the word 'cut,' corresponding to these two occurrences" — and that we secure correct understanding of such utterances by interpreting them against "a whole cultural and biological Background," which is of a very different order than literal meaning and linguistic factors. Evidently Searle would not accept the idea that there are certain established commonest senses of the verb *cut* (such as "to crop or shorten," "to divide into parts," etc.), along the lines that a detailed dictionary reflects. Rather, there is one, literal, all-purpose meaning of *cut* — still not spelled out in Searle (1994a) — and then a depth of "background" contextualizing that jointly enables us to understand or reject particular utterances in which the word is used. But if the literal meaning of *cut* is such a feeble guide to the interpretation of the word in contexts of use, one is prompted to ask why — and whether — it is "crucial" to separate out literal or sentence meaning at all. It is not clear that the exercise is crucial for actual users of a language. In what way would communication be impaired if users began with the assumption that every word was associated and associatable with a range of senses, from common to rare, and that some selection from among these was to be expected in every case of situated utterance? "Sentences have to have standing, conventional sentence meanings in order that we can use them to talk with," writes Searle (1994a: 646), but what is the justification, other than the pressure for an elegant simplicity of modeling, for assuming that such standing meanings are single — that any utterance will have just one "standing sentence meaning" associatable with it? If we question that unificationism, we are questioning also the inflated status of the notion *literal meaning*. It is no accident that Searle's (1994a) "reiteration" defends the literal or sentence meaning versus speaker meaning distinction alongside a series of other ones (principally, type vs. token; sentence vs. utterance; use vs. mention). Each of these binary distinctions entails the others; they are a mutually justifying network of assumptions. The very first rejoinder from an advocate like Searle to a critic of any one of these notions (e.g., literal meaning) is that the critic has neglected or misunderstood one of the related orthodox distinctions, such as that between types and tokens. But for radical critics such as integrationists the point is rather that a quite different view of types and tokens, too, is necessary.

The second point not fully resolved concerns the means of identification of the intended background assumptions determining an utterance's meaning: What might these means be, and how are they used by a hearer? But an outline of standard linguistic views of literal meaning and utterance meaning is desirable before these issues are pursued more fully.

Literal, Conventional, and Utterance Meaning

An informal characterization of literal meaning might be the following:

The conventional meanings of words of a language and the meanings of sentences in that language, where any sentence meaning is derived from a complex synthesis of the meanings of its composite words.

Such a characterization seeks to distinguish literal meaning from conventional sentence meaning. The distinction is clear in the contrast between two interpretations of the sentence

    John got the sack.

The conventional interpretation, sensitive to the usual idiomatic use of *get the sack*, might offer the paraphrase "John was fired." But the literal meaning purports to express more "basic" or foundational meanings, those residing first in a sentence's component words, and so would produce the paraphrase "John fetched/received the (nonrigid) container." One assumption is that idiomatic meanings are some kind of overlay of the literal meaning, such that a conventional sense, attached to a fixed sequence of words taken as an unanalyzed unit, supplants the literal interpretation of the component words. Idiomatic conventional meanings thus occupy an in-between area, being neither literal nor fully metaphoric.

The definition of literal word and sentence meanings above amounts to an appeal, in determining meanings, to the information enshrined in a reliable grammar and dictionary of a language. But such an appeal may often yield several possible literal meanings for a sentence. Consider the following:

    Can you pass the salt?

The literal meaning of the sentence may vary considerably, given the multiple conventional meanings of *can* and *pass*, as should be evident if we imagine the sentence used in a chemistry laboratory or in a medical interview with a patient, besides the dinner-table setting. Thus, polysemy too (in addition to idiomaticity) overlays literal meaning. It is important to note, however, that even in the last-mentioned context of use, at the dinner table, the literal paraphrase will be "Are you able (is it possible for you) to convey the salt?" that is, something rather different from its probable conveyed or speaker meaning, which would not be an inquiry about ability or possibility at all but rather a polite request. Thus literal meanings and conveyed (or speaker or utterance) meanings are in principle quite different from each other. Indeed, much contemporary linguistic pragmatics purports to explain how language users seemingly proceed inferentially from decontextualized literal meanings of sentences to their conveyed meanings in particular contexts of utterance.

Even thus situated, however, the characterization of literal meaning given above retains many problems. The definition refers to *meaning synthesis*, a variant term for the projection, combination, or predication analysis that semanticists have postulated as the necessary means for capturing the semantic representation of sentences. But just how such a synthesis might take place in a language user's mind — and even the assumption that it does at all — remains highly controversial. Before pursuing the issues involved, a more formal definition of *literal meaning* may now be in order, to set beside the earlier informal one:

> Literal meaning is always language-specific. The meaning of an utterance of a sentence s of language L is said to be literal if it is only composed of the meanings of the words and phrases in s in accordance with the syntactic conventions in L. It is, however, not always clear what the meaning of the words and phrases in s actually is, because the words may have different meanings, and because their meaning often depends on the context c of the utterance. For example, the meaning of indexical expressions such as *I*, *here*, *now* in an utterance, or the meaning of anaphoric expressions such as *he*, *then*, *that* in an utterance depends on c. Even words such as *enough*, *but*, *otherwise*, *big*, *can*, and many others, have a context-dependent meaning, i.e., their meaning includes a context variable x. (Wunderlich 1980: 298)

This formulation introduces the crucial issue of context dependency. The determination of an utterer's meaning in using a particular sentence can be seen to rest, typically and heavily, on principles or phenomena that are in a sense both semantic and pragmatic. The expressions are grammaticized, distinctions built into the language (hence semantic); but their specific sense and reference can be determined only in relation to some concrete context. Within the latter area fall (at least) deixis and anaphora and, probably, presupposition. But there are in addition other relatively systematic principles at work, which it is arguable we use in the determination of utterance meaning: within this area lie proposals concerning conversational implicature and cooperativeness and speech act theory (or, as a recent counterproposal, relevance theory) and the designs of talk identified by conversational analysts.

Searle on Literal Meaning Relative to a Background

In fact Wunderlich's description of literal meaning would seem to leave very few sentences sufficiently context free to have a purely literal meaning. While that might suit antiliteralists, it is clearly not what Searle and other speech act theorists have in mind when they speak of literal meaning. They might complain that, in writing of "the meaning of indexicals" and similarly, Wunderlich has not distinguished sentence from utterance: there is a specifiable literal meaning of words such as *I*, *here*, and *enough*, and without this the derivations and determinations of particular context-bound referents and values for these words, in actual utterances, would be impossible. Or, as Searle has put it, literal meaning as such is not affected by the particular reference of an indexical or the truth or otherwise of a particular statement in context: the truth conditions may vary, but the literal meaning cannot.

As indicated above, for Searle literal meaning is not entirely context free. He has emphasized a certain "contextualizedness" of literal meaning: "The notion of the literal meaning of a sentence only has application relative to a set of background assumptions, and furthermore these background assumptions are not all and could not all be realized in the semantic structure of the sentence in the way that presuppositions and indexically dependent elements of the sentence's truth conditions are realized in the semantic structure of the sentence" (Searle 1979: 120). But this necessary background is hardly of the kind stipulated as required by thoroughgoing contextualists. For example, Searle has subjected the sentence *The cat is on the mat* to detailed scrutiny. He imagines the cat and mat floating freely in outer space; or, on earth, suspended separately but contiguously from wires; or with the mat poking stiffly out of the floor and a drugged cat perched on the elevated end of it. It transpires that whether it is literally true to say that the cat is on the mat in any such case depends on context-specific assumptions as to what might constitute being on the mat. Searle offers such outlandish contexts in order to advance his thesis that the literal meaning of a sentence and its associated determinate truth conditions have application only relative to potentially variable background assumptions that are quite different from the familiar semantic/pragmatic parameters such as indexicality, change of meaning, and presupposition. Furthermore, these background assumptions are too numerous to have a place in the semantic structure of the sentence, and, besides, the very statement of those assumptions, in literal terms, relies on yet other background assumptions in order to be intelligible.

This account may cause confusion. On the one hand, by conceding that literal meaning varies and is context bound only in relation to the sort of differences of background that most of us would regard as remote from typical utterance comprehension (cats perched on vertical mats, the supply of a mile-wide hamburger on ordering "a hamburger" in a restaurant), Searle seems to be tenaciously protective of literal meaning as a firm foundation for utterance interpretation, in all "normal circumstances." On the other hand, in proceeding to add that such crucial background assumptions are too numerous and endless to permit semantic characterization, he seems more radical than ordinary contextualist pragmaticists who attend to the indexicals, presuppositions, etc. that are believed to admit principled specification.

Searle's position amounts to saying that the truthfulness of asserting "The cat is on the mat" will always involve a kind of provisionality. He represents this provisionality as a provisionality "relative to background assumptions" without much clarification. But some clarification can be attempted. A first crucial background assumption is an awareness, on the part of both speaker and addressee, that even the conventional meanings of *cat, on, mat, hamburger*, etc. are multiple. While relatively institutionalized meanings of *on, hamburger*, etc. are all potentially available for adducement, there is typically an implicit ranking of those possible meanings in any particular context, and interactants usually operate on the "in good faith" assumption that there is considerable orientation to, and awareness of, this context or (as Searle calls it) background. In the restaurant, when the customer asked for a hambruger, did she mean a mile-wide hamburger? Certainly not. As socialized members of the hamburger-eating world, we know what to expect when we order a hamburger in a restaurant, just as surely as the waitperson and cook know what is expected. Furthermore, if we contrast the idea of a hamburger in a fast-food establishment and in an independent restaurant, all the relevant parties know that, in the latter context, *hamburger* has a somewhat different sense.

On the other hand, is it not the case that a mile-wide hamburger is still a hamburger? In a sense, yes it is, we have to concede. But it is not a hamburger in the sense (or in any of the senses) that a customer could in good faith assume as one to which the customer and waitperson would be mutually oriented when the order was made. There is, then, for each speaker of the language familiar with hamburgers, a preferential or probabilistic ranking of the meanings of *hamburger*, those rankings (each speaker has their own; nor can we assume identity of rankings by any two speakers) having grown up entirely on the basis of previous experience (the linguocultural experiences of eating out, of categorizing foods, of glossing the language of menus, etc.). As we proceed through the interactions that punctuate our lives (and even the business of identifying some point as the close of one interaction and some other point as the commencement of another interaction is provisional), we are constantly making provisional assessments of the current gestalt — of where we are at now and of what will likely be understood (what probable sense will be made or taken) if our talking or actions now orient to hamburgers or cats on mats.

An integrationally minded starting point will be that each speaker carries in memory a fluid field of probable and possible meanings of every word of which they have had some experience (confining the discussion to previously encountered words, at this stage, and also postponing the question of how one processes the stream of ongoing experience so as to identify particular words). It would be a mistake to stress that this is cultural experience or social experience, as if to imply that these were contrastive with something to be termed linguistic experience. Experience is experience, whatever its provenance: even having encountered a word only in a dictionary may leave experiential traces in the memory, which may be drawn on in subsequent encounters. Lakoff's "experientialist semantics" (Lakoff 1987: 205ff.) might be cited here: "In experientialist semantics, meaning is understood via real experiences in a very real world with very real bodies." However, that perspective subscribes to a familiar but questionable distinction between firsthand experience and communicated knowledge, experienced at secondhand: "My understanding [of molybdenum] is based on what has been indirectly communicated to me of their [molybdenum experts'] experience" (Lakoff 1987: 207).

In the course of any situation in which a particular word (e.g., *hamburger*) is used, a complex network of interconnecting assumptions and preferences provides the provisional and revisable justification for the senses of *hamburger*, and of, for example,

> Give me a hamburger, medium rare, with ketchup and mustard, but easy on the relish,

that the speaker, in interactional good faith in mutual orientedness, intends.

We go through any new interaction armed with the provisional knowledge and construction of the world derived from previous encounters. That knowledge amounts to a running commentary to ourselves that, in the case of ordering a hamburger, might give rise to interpretive processing dramatizable along the following lines:

This *is* a fast-food establishment (again), isn't it? It *is* open (again), isn't it? I have come here to eat (again), haven't I? This individual in front of me across the counter (it is a counter, isn't it?) (again) *is* (and knows that he is, doesn't he?) taking orders, isn't he? Etc., etc.

With the copious use of the word *again* here, the issue of repetition or iterability looms large. But no great theoretical weight should be placed on the everyday term *again*. When we assume ourselves to be going through routines or normative activities "again," we are not in fact misled into imagining that the present activity and communication could possibly be truly identical with

33   Inscribed or Literal Meaning

previous experiences, or that here and now we are once more going through that experience first undergone there and then, or that a present encounter could be merely a mechanical replication of an earlier one—even in the emphatically routine-laden patterns of communication in fast-food restaurant chains. At the very least, we know ourselves to be different and removed from the person we assume ourselves to have been in the past; our very memories of that previous encounter (or those previous encounters), on the basis of which remembrances our sense of repetition is postulated, are equally the guarantors that the present encounter, however many ways analogous with previous ones, is not pure replication. In short, we remember the gap: the fact of the orientational shift and the fact that we remember it are crucial. If to remember the gap is as important as is here claimed, what might be the consequences of failing to do so? In such a dysfunctional condition, where an individual fails to register experiential difference and the corollaries of temporality and linearity, a psychosis of lived repetition may be apparent, of the kind reported in the case histories of Oliver Sacks.

The *again*'s that we attribute to the elements in our ongoing interactive lives by no means imply identity of current features with prior ones, but rather an assumed and trusted similarity with previous, remembered features. The rational assumptions that interactants make as to the similarities between a current experience and earlier ones are fundamental to this account of meaning in interaction. This making sense and pattern of past experience, in memory, may be the basis for the important role in language use and language learning that Tannen and others have attributed to repetition (see Tannen [1987a] and a special issue of the journal *Text* [Johnstone 1987] on the same topic). From an integrational perspective, the term *repetition* remains in need of qualification, being a potentially misleading abbreviated way of referring to perceived relatedness. These issues are explored in detail in chapter 6.

A similar interactional good faith in mutual orientedness, within a network of assumptions and preferences, is the provisional grounding for the waitperson's interpretation of the "Give me a hamburger . . ." request. But, to repeat, the speaker's intended meaning and the addressee's interpreted meaning are, by definition, distinct (i.e., separate); they are also potentially rather different from each other. In short, interactants are guided in utterance construction and utterance interpretation by their current sense of the likely uses of such words as — in the example under discussion — *hamburger* and *give* in such situations as fast-food restaurants and so on.

It may be worth reviewing just what Searle might object to in this account. In Searle (1979), it is insisted that, just because "Give me a hamburger, medium rare . . ." is defectively fulfilled when a mile-wide hamburger is delivered, this does not show that the speaker "failed to say exactly and literally what [he] meant" or that he should have said: " 'Give me a hamburger, medium rare, with ketchup and mustard, but easy on the relish; and don't encase it in plastic and no mile wide hamburgers, please.' If we say that, then it will become impossible ever to say what we mean because there will always be further possible breakdowns in our background assumptions which would lead us to say that the obedience conditions of the sentence were not satisfied in a given context" (Searle 1979: 128). Here, Searle attempts to force acceptance of the inviolate status of literal meaning by contrasting a seemingly reasonable and "transparent" utterance ("Give me a hamburger, medium rare, with ketchup and mustard, but easy on the relish") with an evidently ludicrous one ("no plastic, no mile-wide hamburgers"). No one would reasonably want all such contextual assumptions spelled out before we would agree that the conditions for a felicitous order had been met. Such background assumptions should ordinarily stay in the background. The more interesting issue is whether Searle's alternative solution needs to be followed instead: "What we should say in such cases is that I did say exactly and literally what I meant but that the literal meaning of my sentence, and hence of my literal utterance, only has application relative to a set of background assumptions which are not and for the most part could not be realized in the semantic structure of the sentence" (Searle 1979: 128). A similar logic prevails here as will be found at numerous points in this book, where an overarching conception of what linguistics should be like is confronted with problematic aspects of one of the categories or notions deemed to be a foundational component of that linguistics. The logic in the present case runs as follows:

1. A linguistic account of language behavior must in some sense take the form of an abstract, finite, systematized model or representation, like a code with instructions.

2. If the background assumptions attached to literal meanings were addressed fully within the linguistic account, then no systematic abstract account of literal meaning — or, by extension, of linguistic behavior — will be practically possible.

3. Therefore, it is essential to make a sharp demarcation between literal meanings and their background assumptions. We will say that the latter are outside linguistics (because, if the given conception of linguistics is to survive, they will have to be kept outside linguistics).

In the contest between "how to do linguistics" and "how to account for literal meaning," the powerful former interest holds sway. The integrational alternative is to see the difficulties with modeling so-called literal meaning as, precisely, an indication of the need to revise premise 1 and to explore the ways in which linguistic accounts may have to be nonabstract, nonfinite, and so on.

In Searle's account of meaning, background assumptions are there, and they are not there: they are there insofar as even literal meaning is relative to them; they are not there insofar as they cannot be realized in the semantic structure of the sentence. Additionally, the position now invokes a separate notion, in need of clarification, namely, "the semantic structure of the sentence." But, postponing consideration of this further notion, it is clear that, by tolerating a considerable vagueness as to the status of "background assumptions," Searle seeks to protect the notions of literal meaning and the semantic structure of a sentence as stable, calculable groundings for subsequent utterance interpretation. First we have literal meanings, sentential semantic structures, conditions on felicitous speech acts, and intentions; then we build on those literal meanings, mindful of speech-act conditions, in expressing our intentions. What Searle seems reluctant to pursue is the logical conclusion of the argument concerning meanings and background assumptions, namely, that every aspect of what we metalinguistically recast as "the meaning of a word, the meaning of a sentence," is relative to the interpreter's background assumptions and that what we have come to speak and write about as the literal and conventional meanings of words are simply indirect expressions of the normative and privileged background assumptions about particular words (and ways of using them) declared by influential commentators on the language—grammarians, lexicographers, philosophers, etymologists, literary critics, and writers. All these would seem to have a stake in persuading others of their special expertise in the language, their more-than-everyday—indeed, authoritative—grasp of the language. A standard stratagem used to display expertise and authority is to show chaos and uncertainty (e.g., the multiplicity of uses of a word) reduced to order and seeming certainty (e.g., a description of the literal, conventional, and figurative meanings of a word). Human beings crave such order and certainty in their languages and particularly so in written language, as is reflected in the innumerable everyday references to correct English, bad English, poor English, standard English, the proper meaning of a word, and sloppy grammar. Here, as in some other areas of metalinguistic practice, such preoccupations point to a communal—or intercommunal—lack of trust and confidence, of a quite significant kind. Trust and confidence are as important in linguistic activity as they are in economic activity.

But everyday prejudices and cravings may not be the healthiest ground on which to build a theory of language. Relatedly, we should resist the illusion of advantage that seems to accrue from asserting that literal meaning is independent of the provisional experience-based meanings of individual speakers. Those remembered uses are the only legitimate source for what otherwise amounts to invention or reification. If the plural and provisional remembered senses or uses (and not literal meaning) are our basis for utterance interpretation, then what status does "the semantic structure of the sentence" have, and what sort of role does it play in interpretation? The short answer to this is that the very notion of "*the* semantic structure of the sentence" — and perhaps even that of "a semantic *structure* of a sentence" — is put in question. Searle takes the infinity of background assumptions, and the infinity of statements that would be needed to make them intelligible, as grounds for excluding them from the literal-meaning-backed semantic structure of the sentence: on the contrary, that same evidence of infinity of background needs to be incorporated into a revised picture of sense making and semantic structure — one that emphasizes that such attributions of structure and sense come from language users and should not be thought of as in the sentence, in any a prioristic way. Mutatis mutandis, conventional meanings, and principles of utterance interpretation, begin and end in users of a language and are never elements of the language, conceived of as a freestanding body of knowledge (e.g., as a set of units and rules).

In another paper, Searle asks the reader to compare and contrast the following two utterances: "The fly is on the ceiling" and "The cat is on the ceiling." But first consider the following account of how our understanding of these two utterances differs:

We can without hesitation imagine saying, "The fly is on the ceiling," but not, "The cat is on the ceiling." The latter we can imagine saying only after pausing to devise a suitable context. With the former utterance, we can instantly picture a world in which the remark might fit, or be relevant or true; in the latter case, the picturing is less instantaneous. Either way, the hesitation or lack of it is in us, and not the sentences: for us, an utterance like "The fly is on the ceiling" is habitual and routine, while "The cat is on the ceiling" is not so. The former is such an established use that we find it unexceptional even in the *sui generis* contextualization that is citation in the course of a linguistic discussion.

Now compare the foregoing (the position espoused here) with what follows, which is Searle's view of our differential responses to these utterances:

37 Inscribed or Literal Meaning

We know without hesitation what are the truth-conditions of, "The fly is on the ceiling," but not of, "The cat is on the ceiling," and this difference is not a matter of meaning, but a matter of how our factual background information enables us to apply the meanings of sentences. (Searle 1979: 80)

While the earlier formulation makes no mention of word or sentence meaning, in Searle's account it is both instrumental and invariant: it is the constant sense of the words (and their combination) that undergoes "application," enabled by background knowledge. The account rests on an analytic separation of verbal meaning from extralinguistic background and the use of the latter in "applying" the meanings of sentences. In effect, "application" is a machine or device by means of which sentence meanings are processed so as to become, in contexts, speaker or utterance meanings. But what is most crucially unclear is just what the nature and limits of this activity of "applying" are. Searle states explicitly, above, that the act of applying is distinct from both word and sentence meanings and background information; it is some kind of function or matrix or algorithmic procedure by which the former two interact in the construal of utterance meaning. Occasionally, Searle's position and that of integrational linguistics seem closely aligned: for example, when he remarks that his argument against context-free literal meaning "has the consequence that there is no sharp distinction between a speaker's linguistic competence and his knowledge of the world" (1979: 134). Yet significant differences in the account of interactional meaning are at issue. Searle insists, as a speech-act theorist perhaps must, that literal meanings and semantic content are secure and reliable and that it is the background knowledge (and hence the conditions for fulfillment of the various speech acts that use those literal meanings) that varies.

Componentialism

Componential analysis is only one of many accounts of how the semantic interpretation of sentences proceeds. Nevertheless, it probably remains the most influential, the one most widely accepted within mainstream linguistics as at least promising explanatory adequacy. (For trenchant criticism of one of the other most influential theories, truth-conditional semantics, see Harris [1981b].)

The following characterization of semanticist analysis (from Rumelhart 1979: 81) is a fair representation of the theory:

The traditional program of semantic analysis (cf. Katz & Fodor, 1963) provides a set of *meanings* for the individual lexemes of the language and then provides a set of *rules of composition* whereby the individual meanings of the lexemes are *combined* to form the *meaning of the sentence*. Likewise, for any discourse, the meanings of the individual sentences of the discourse can be combined to form the meaning of the discourse. Arguably, this program of semantic analysis can provide a reasonable account of the *conveyed meanings* (that is, what the listener understands upon hearing the sentence uttered in context) of many sentences in English.

Where conveyed meanings evidently depart rather far from literal meaning, as in metaphors, semanticists want to resist both a solution involving postulating multiple senses and any adducement of extracontextual criteria and insist on the continued validity of their methods of analyzing words into core components of meaning and the systematic combinations of such components. In the case of metaphor, semanticists (Cohen 1979; Levin 1977) hold to the need for an ordered process of cancellation of incompatible features from the metaphoric vehicle as it is applied to the literal tenor. Other important domains where conveyed utterance meaning is said to depart from the literal meaning of sentences are indirect speech acts and irony.

Although the focus of much attention in the 1960s (see esp. Katz and Fodor 1963; Bierwisch 1967, 1970), componential semantic theories have failed to live up to expectations. Aitchison's verdict on the attempt in Schank (1972) to specify the semantic primitives underlying common verbs is representative of the general conclusion:

It seems unlikely that Schank has specified "primitives" in any psychological sense. He has simply found a convenient way of describing "family resemblances" between the groups of words he was dealing with. . . . It is important to distinguish between useful ways of describing things and structures which are likely to exist in speakers' minds. Judging from the work of Schank, there is no reason to believe that verbs are assembled out of pieces in the human mind—even though we might well adopt his system if we were trying to write a computer program which explained relationships between words in a helpful, though non-realistic way. And the problems found with Schank's primitives—difficulty of deciding what they are, their decomposability, and their incompleteness for specifying meaning—occur in most other attempts to identify primitives (e.g., Jackendoff, 1983). (Aitchison 1987b: 79)

At its core, a componential semanticist perspective claims that sentence meaning is objective, invariant, and relatively context free, that to share a language is to share — or be potential sharers of — an inventory of determinate words and their meanings, the contents of that inventory remaining constant regardless of changes of interactional setting, mood, or purpose. Word meanings, capturable by a relatively delimited set of componential features variously applying to each item in a language's lexicon, and the predictable meanings of grammatical combinations of those word meanings are uniformly shared by all the members of a speech community, who employ this fixed biplanar code (tying determinate forms to determinate meanings) to communicate. Such an assumption of form-meaning determinacy is at the core of most versions of semantics, even though semanticists are ready to acknowledge the innumerable departures from that determinacy in contextualized speech practice, for in all such practice (or performances), it is argued, the foundational system is built on, so that particular, context-bound additional meanings are conveyed by utterances. Semanticists thus postulate a crucial distinction between sentences and utterances, sentence meaning and utterance meaning, and so on. But they argue that the second of each of these pairs depends entirely on the first, that the first is the necessary precondition of the second and should be the focus of linguistic study, being part of the language proper or competence, the second being merely part of language use or performance. Relatedly, semantics or semantic representation (or logical form) is a distinct enterprise, fully a part of (rule-governed) grammar. The "rough and ready distinction" restated in Leech (1983: 6) remains widely adhered to — "Meaning in pragmatics is defined [in relation to speech situations], whereas meaning in semantics is defined purely as a property of expressions in a given language, in abstraction from particular situations, speakers, or hearers" — particularly in its indication that semantics unequivocally attempts less than pragmatics does (or, in semanticists' own terms, seeks a properly constrained theory of sentence meaning, about which falsifiable claims may be made). The chief reason to mention componential semantics in the present chapter is to indicate that here, as in Searlean pragmatics, there is a clear swerving away from "the total speech act in the total situation" (Austin 1962), so as to make meaning, literal or otherwise, a manageable concept within an autonomous and decontextualized linguistics.

The Pragmaticist Tradition

At least partly in competition with the semanticist tradition, pragmaticists hold that meaning can be fully determined only by adducing certain delimited aspects of context: for adequate and coherent determination, must word and sentence meaning themselves be determined in relation to aspects of interaction that will emerge only from within the relevant speech encounter, rather than being given essentially by the lexicon or grammar. Such contextual aspects include information specifying who speaks (the deictic orientation point) and who or what the referents intended by particular expressions are. Other relevant factors include judgments as to whether interlocutors are being cooperative (seemingly truthful, adequately informative, relevant, suitably brief, and orderly): apparently intentional departures from those norms are then assumed to be creative exploitations conveying extra inferences or calculable implicatures. For those who espouse a speech-act-theory version of pragmatics, other factors such as the orderly application of principles and procedures for associating utterance meaning with sentence meaning will be germane: for example, application of the theory of indirect speech acts and the lexical force hypothesis so that sentence meaning, locution, or sense (what is said) may be mapped onto utterance meaning, illocution, or force (what is intended and conveyed by what is said).

But again, as in semantics, some notion of literal meaning seems crucial for these versions of pragmatics. Insofar as their project is more ambitious than that of semanticists, being the goal of identifying the principles and conventional forms by means of which intentional meanings are conveyed in performance, their work diverts attention from the problematic notion of literal meaning in the process of attempting to specify, in predictable ways, actual meanings. That is to say, declared interest in interlocutors' actual meanings brings in train such an enlarged attention to the multiple linguistic and extra-linguistic dimensions of utterances (as these arise in response to the particular perceived needs, interests, and goals of the equally heterogeneous set of individuals within a speech community) that doubts grow concerning the role of literal meaning in such complex negotiations. Nevertheless, as in the work of Searle, and as is evident in various remarks in Austin (1962: 94ff.) and Grice (1975: 44, 50), some notion of literal or conventional meaning remains a model-shaping element in pragmatic accounts.

Whatever idealization called literal or conventional meaning is retained by the theorist, the crucial need is that such constructs be depicted much more explicitly as a matter of cultural habituation and contingency than has hitherto been the case. The degree of resistance to the relinquishing of a more-than-contingent characterization of sentence meaning (vs. utterance meaning etc.) is vividly illustrated in some remarks of Rorty's, critiquing the "against theory" position of fellow pragmatists Knapp and Michaels (1982). For Knapp and Michaels, authorial meaning and textual meaning are always one and the same thing, and there is never — genuinely as it were, as distinct from within the contrivances of theory — a separateness of the one from the other for analysts to explicate (for fuller treatment of Knapp and Benn Michaels's position, see chapter 3 below). This Rorty sees as an ill-judged rejection of the foundational distinction, accepted by Grice along with many others, between sentence meaning and utterance meaning. Supporting Grice, Rorty claims that the distinction opens up a logical space — "the space in which one asks the traditional interpretive question 'Granted that the sentence means such and such, did its author use it to mean that on this particular occasion?' " (Rorty 1985: 460). And that, for Rorty, is a "useful" question and indeed is of a piece, he implies, with "Grice's handy distinction between more and less familiar contexts in which to place words" (p. 461) and a distinction between two sets of intentions, "the ones normally had by users of a sentence and some special ones had, or possibly had, by an individual user" (p. 464, n. 4).

An immediate doubt must concern whether the three distinctions that Rorty upholds here (sentence meaning vs. utterance meaning; more familiar vs. less familiar; normal intentions associated with use of a sentence vs. special intentions) are all of quite the same kind. But in any event, in their rejoinder to Rorty, Knapp and Michaels declare themselves if not more pragmatist then at least less rationalist than he is: his "logical" space between sentence and utterance is for them purely empirical.

> In our view . . . normal intentions are just frequent particular ones. The "space" between these two sets of intentions is not logical but empirical. A text means what its author intended it to mean whether or not other authors on other occasions use the same marks (or noises) to say the same thing. What people normally mean when they shout "Fire!" might well be that something is burning. On some special occasion, however, someone might shout "Fire!" and mean by it "Discharge your weapon." In the first case, the speaker has an intention frequently had by other speakers on similar occasions; in the second case, not. Indeed, there could be a third case in which a speaker might shout "Fire!" and mean by it something that no one had ever meant before or would ever mean again. But in all three cases the relation between meaning and intention would be the same: the sentence would mean only what *its* speaker intended. (Knapp and Benn Michaels 1985: 469)

Minor adjustments to the foregoing formulations could be proposed (to emphasize that no one can actually shout the written form "Fire!" but only sounds that might be transcribed as "Fire!" and to suggest that "sentence" is

Knapp and Michaels's shorthand way of referring to a situationally embedded use of language), but in large part this account accords with an integrational linguistic view. At the same time, the integrational approach concurs with Rorty's idea that distinctions such as the sentence meaning/utterance meaning one are "useful" and "handy," but it denies that they are appropriate as axiomatic foundations of language theory.

The conclusion that examination of particular cases of utterance interpretation invites (and, in the last analysis, it is supposedly as idealizations from a range of such particular cases that our abstract categories derive their status) is that both of the terms *literal meaning* and *metaphoric utterance* are precipitations from authorized uses and have no other more permanent grounding, no foundational status in some autonomous and transcendent system we call "the language." Literal meanings of utterances that we metalinguistically term *words* or *sentences* are the most established and authorized uses of expressions. It just so happens that, within these historical conditions and given such and such distributions of power to signify authoritatively through the language, such and such uses have become accepted, recognized, established, habitual, and codified in dictionaries as "literal meanings." Equally and contrariwise, uses of expressions in ways that are in no way established or habitual are potentially (creatively) metaphoric, and creative metaphoric meanings compose a subset of such nonhabitual nonaccepted uses, where the expression is used in a way that is seemingly or actually unique. In chapter 6, more will be said about a central integrational linguistic tenet, which is the invariable uniqueness of every speech event and the impossibility of repetition as a first-order *realia* of experience with language. At the immediate level of language use, then, uniqueness is argued to be pervasive. Accordingly, there might appear to be a clash between this view and the claim here that metaphoric utterance or meaning stands out, vis-à-vis literal and habitual meanings, in its seeming uniqueness. But the point to emphasize here is that the entire system of categorization explored in this and the following chapter, in terms of the literal, the metaphoric, words, sentences, etc., is thoroughly metalinguistic. It is at this culture-reflective level of metalinguistic characterization that we can contrast literal meaning as authorized and established, with metaphoric meaning as uncodified use. And words that the dictionary records as n-ways polysemic are words with n literal meanings.

At least two caveats should be entered here, however summarily. One is that established use does not necessarily correlate with most frequent use: a certain expression may be used in a certain way by those who lack power or influence in verbal matters (beyond a local influence) with little effect on what the acknowledged and unacknowledged verbal legislators judge to be the literal meaning. Another is that the set of words that we think of, metalinguistically, as constituting a language is not a set without internal groupings and organization: along with established individual words and established uses come established groupings of words, established language games and practices, collocations, schemas, lexical sets, and so on. All the latter are fertile ground for the growth of idiom, dead metaphor, and systematic or conceptual metaphors (all the interrelatable established uses around the claim that "time is money" or "life is a journey" etc.).

In fact, considerable empirical evidence has emerged in recent years that questions the foundational role that literal meaning has been assumed to play in the interpretation of utterances. In particular, the assumption that understanding so-called nonliteral language use — metaphors, indirect requests, idioms, irony — is invariably based on a step-wise computation that begins with the literal meaning of whatever utterance has been used seems to have been disconfirmed. Thus, on the basis of empirical tests of reaction time to sentences presented in either a literal or a metaphoric context, Ortony et al. (1978) found that metaphors are interpreted more or less directly, without prior recourse to the literal meaning as a stage in the derivation. And, in empirical tests of rapidity and manner of interpretation of utterances containing indirect requests and idioms, the work of Gibbs (1983, 1986) also argues for a "direct interpretation" of these forms, without intermediate recourse to literal meaning.

Such a finding in relation to idioms is perhaps not wholly surprising: idioms have long been recognized as more like "long words" than decomposable sequences of words. As a result, psycholinguistic researchers have tended to hedge their bets as to how potentially idiomatic strings are interpreted. Swinney and Cutler (1979), for example, concluded that, although hearers processed idiomatic phrases like *kick the bucket* more rapidly than the necessarily nonidiomatic *lift the bucket*, yet they ordinarily processed both the literal and the nonliteral meanings of idioms during interpretation. Experiments by Gibbs (1986) and others have measured the time taken, by subjects primed on either an idiomatic or a literal sentence, to respond to a target sentence that is either a literal or a nonliteral paraphrase. Even when subjects read literal prime sentences, there was no priming on the literal target sentence: subjects responded marginally faster to the nonliteral targets than the literal ones, following a literal prime. The experiments support the view that people have a strong bias or preference for interpreting even literal uses of idiomatic expressions conventionally, as idioms, more promptly than deriving their intended literal meanings. And Gibbs has similar findings as to the nonsalience of literal meanings in his tests of subjects' processing of indirect requests and sarcasm. However, very recent research suggests that the broader picture is more complex and that less familiar and more analyzable idioms are processed less "directly" than familiar unanalyzable ones such as *kick the bucket* (Titone and Connine 1994). The general picture seems to be one in which literal meaning is not simply bypassed in idiom interpretation but is accessed by the interpreter at least to the point that it delays idiom construal. This is entirely congruent with the integrational position presented here: literal meaning is not an irrelevant category; it plays a role in utterance construal, but it has no foundational role and is not logically and interpretively prior to other supposedly derived meanings (as assumed in traditional theories of metaphor comprehension) but influences interpretation in that it often encapsulates a familar and well-established usage.

Integrational Linguistics

As indicated above, both standard semantic and pragmatic approaches hold to the theoretical importance of the notion of literal or conventional meaning in the comprehension of conveyed meanings. This position is an orthodoxy that pervades the literature and has been widely taken up in neighboring disciplines. Clark and Lucy (1975), for example, writing from a background in psychology, propose the following three-stage model (reported in Rumelhart 1979: 82) for comprehension of indirect requests (and here we should remember that most requests — in fact most speech acts — are indirect by this definition):

A person must: (a) determine the literal meaning of the utterance (presumably by a simple composition of lexeme meanings); (b) compare the literal meaning so determined with various contextual and conversational rules to decide if the literal meaning could also be the intended meaning; (c) if the literal meaning is determined inappropriate, apply additional rules to determine the indirect, or conveyed, meaning.

The integrational linguistic response to this would take the form of close consideration of the stages of interpretation postulated above. Although skeptical of any secure boundary between the literal and the nonliteral of the kind

45 Inscribed or Literal Meaning

assumed in stage *a*, that stage might be passed over and attention focused on the phrasing and assumptions of stage *b*, for here the difficulties inherent in so many such "step-wise" accounts of comprehension is displayed. A first but minor complaint is that stage 2 asserts that we *decide* if the literal meaning *could be* the intended meaning of the utterance: this is misleadingly tentative, for by definition literal meaning is always a possible reading of an utterance. The major complaint follows from making what seems to be an inescapable assumption, namely, that what the authors mean to say here is that we in fact decide if the literal meaning *is* (not "could be") the intended meaning. They do not specify how we decide this question, but, were they to attempt to do so, it would soon emerge that any such decision would rest on a comparison: a comparison of the computed literal meaning with a prior understanding of what the utterance, in context, meant. Without some such prior understanding, the implicit task specified by these stages simply could not be undertaken, whether it is phrased in terms of comparison or appropriateness or reconciliation of anomaly; but, if we do have that prior understanding, these stages are superfluous.

The integrationist does not deny a role for principles of comparison and appropriateness in the ordered and incremental rational determination of utterance meaning in context. What is contested is whether these roles amount to a simple and routine manipulation of fixed form-meaning pairs in a way that is delimitable without consideration, as more than a secondary modifying component, of context. Indeed, rather than referring directly to context, the interpreter in Clark and Lucy's account is said at stage *b* to invoke "various contextual and conversational rules." These rules are not specified, nor is it clear how an interpreter would know which ones to invoke. In short, the account is given as unworkable. With Rumelhart, it is assumed that an adequate theory of language comprehension will be able to deal equally directly with conventional meanings, metaphor, irony, and other so-called indirect utterances, rather than promoting a dichotomized account in which one set of meanings (metaphor, irony) must be calculated via a core (literal meaning): "The processes involved in the comprehension of nonfigurative language are no less dependent on knowledge of the world than those involved in figurative language. Any theory rich enough to generate the meanings people actually assign to nonfigurative language is rich enough to deal with figurative language as well" (Rumelhart 1979: 84). Integrationists tend not to express the comprehension process in quite the psychological terminology of Rumelhart, who talks of the hearer selecting and verifying some configuration of schemata (from, presumably, an open set of such schemata) that offers a sufficient account of the situation. But they share his contention that a standard bottom-up view of meaning construction, with nonlinguistic knowledge coming into play only after language-based determination of possible meanings, seems to receive no confirmation in interactional practice. For one thing, that view operates on the illicit assumption that the world is already and definitively categorized into domains recognizable as "linguistic" and "non- or extra-linguistic."

In an integrational linguistic spirit, then, and quite counter to the compositionalist position noted earlier, I suggest that we learn and store lexical items, and even whole utterances, with contexts attached. In such expression-cum-context learning, the norm will be for a range of contexts to be associated with any particular expression and a range of expressions to be associated with any particular context. The likelihood of different speakers of a language having identical combinations of expressions and contexts, to be invoked in their determinations of what is meant by any particular situated utterance, is consequently very slim: this picture relates difference in language understanding directly to variation in life experience and memory. Clearly, this suggestion addresses only the first assimilation, as it were, of new experience (linguistic or otherwise). We have every reason to believe that these relatively "uninterpreted" interactional memories are subsequently sorted, matched, backgrounded, and virtually forgotten or foregrounded into mental models, schema, scripts, notions of genre and grammaticality and contextual appropriateness, etc., etc., with the passing of time and the development of interactional (including linguistic) proficiency. Speculations concerning these kinds of ranking and sorting, concerning the architecture of memory, cannot be developed here, nor need they be: the crucial and initial premise, in rejection of reliance on a notion of literal meaning, is that learning the meanings of expressions should scarcely be called a learning at all but should rather be understood as an experiencing. And, again, that experiencing is not one of meanings of expressions but an experiencing of expressions integrated within particular occasions of use. Whatever sorting and extrapolation occurs occurs after the fact and is performed by the reflecting, thinking, language-using individual; it is in no way given in or by the language. What is undoubtedly given, by other language users rather than the language, and what will thus be experienced and added to the individual's mental modelings, is abundant feedback and example as to how the language is ordinarily used. One influential cognitivist proposal that may be viewed as just such a normative pressure is prototype theory, a theory that in addition might seem to sidestep some of the problems that attach to a standard notion of literal meaning.

Prototype Theory

In the last twenty years, an ingenious and seemingly empirically based account of normativity in concept interpretation has emerged from cognitive psychology: Rosch's prototype theory. The way this theory has been elaborated, however, and the tendency — among some psycholinguists — to assume a collective agreement on the degrees of typicality attributed to particular exponents of any given word or concept are indications of the power of the notion that in language there are given basic meanings. For Rosch's part, it should be noted that her later papers have withdrawn some of the more speculative but problematic claims of earlier papers in favor of a more guarded position: she argues, for example, that, rather than there being prototypes as such, what her research has actually displayed are "judgments of degree of prototypicality" and various prototype effects; prototypes "do not constitute any particular processing model for categories . . . [or] a theory of representation for categories" (1978: 40–41). These qualifications notwithstanding, Aitchison (1987a) is representative of others in endorsing Roschian prototype theory in the course of her inquiry into the nature of the mental lexicon. She agrees that there is no great oddity in our use of the term *tiger* to refer even to tigers with only three legs, lacking stripes, and so on. Similarly, there is nothing that defies explanation in our use of the verb *see* in cases where, apparently, the mind fails to register what the eyes focus on (as in "I've seen that picture a hundred times but never noticed it"). These are simply non-prototypical instances of tigers and seeing. We use fuzzy-edged words all the time, the argument runs, in situations where one or another such "typicality conditions" (such as, of tigers, that they have stripes) is broken.

But the danger of this way of representing matters lies in the apparent assumption that the prototypicality of tigers, seeing, etc. stays intact and is inviolable and that somewhat secondary typicality conditions are what are met or flouted in extended uses of words, metaphors, and so on. The prototype is often characterized, in the literature, as the best exemplar or central member of a category, with the implication that the "centrality" of this exemplary type inheres in its having one or more critical attributes (not attributes that all members of the category must necessarily bear, but nevertheless ones that are focal or central to the category). Similarly, Lakoff invokes Wittgenstein's notion of "family resemblance" but casts this as "the idea that members of a category may be related ... without all members having any properties in common that define the category" (1987: 12 and passim). In both cases, it looks as if an attempt is being made to have one's cake (category membership is not a matter of category-wide sharing of specific properties) and eat it too (categories are well defined and structured relative to a core or central exemplar that bears exemplary attributes). Notice the awkwardness of the scope expressions in Lakoff's gloss of *family resemblance*: "Without all members having any properties in common." This reflects Lakoff's wish (which is likely to be shared by any cognitivist theorist of prototypes) to cling to the idea that *most* category members will share *some* properties. It may also invite the following kind of inference:

Although it is not the case that all members have any properties in common that define the category, still it is the case that *some* members have properties in common that define the category.

But a more radical gloss of *family resemblance* would be simply to the effect that, in such categories, no properties are shared by all members and that none of the properties shared by only some of the members defines the category.

The implication is that there are certain core typicality conditions that necessarily apply whenever the word *tiger* or *see* is invoked. But where does prototypicality come from, except from normatively constrained usage? A reification similar to that which turns literal meaning into an unchanging given is in danger of extending to prototype theory also. Thus, Aitchison asks, of the sentence *The price of mangos* went up: "Is *went up* a metaphor, since the price did not literally travel up a hill? Or is this simply the use of *go up* with a typicality condition broken, since *going* typically involves travelling between two physical points, and covering the distance in between?" (Aitchison 1987b: 144–45). Whether Aitchison seriously intends these explanations to be disjunctive is unclear since earlier she states that the basic mechanism behind metaphor "is simply the use of a word with one or more of the 'typicality conditions' attached to it broken" (p. 144). (This would seem to make the explanation offered in the second sentence quoted a precondition for the applicability of the explanation given in the first, not an alternative to it.)

But it is with the premise here that objections begin: the premise that *went up* is not typically used to refer to increase. The one word signally absent from discussion of prototypicality, which is instead characterized in terms of cognitive grasp or modeling, is *use*. The role of use, and frequency of use, continues to be undervalued even in conspectual studies (e.g., Lakoff 1987) that invoke aspects of the later Wittgenstein's thinking. Thus, Lakoff notes that Rosch's prototypicality findings do not force the conclusion that membership of categories is ordinarily gradable so that, for example, a penguin counts as a not-very-birdy bird; rather, the findings are still consistent with the idea that categories are rigid and that a penguin is fully a member of the bird category. Yet, Lakoff adds, "that category must have additional internal structure of some sort that produces these goodness-of-example ratings" (1987: 45). One is bound to ask why additional internal structure must be involved; a perfectly adequate alternative account would point to the role of use and habituation (the frequency, especially in conventional situations, of reference to robins and robin-like birds in all matters to do with birds and the relative rarity of reference to penguins, ostriches, etc.) together with, in the case of color naming and recognition, neurophysiology. The ease with which we make sense of talk of prices rising or going up, of people "coming out" of comas, or of teenagers being "under" age may chiefly be a reflection of the frequency with which these phrases are encountered used in just these ways. In that case, the reification called *semantic prototype* has no more work to do than that called *literal meaning*. When Aitchison claims that "*coming out* typically involves physical movement, and *under* typically involves a physical position underneath" (1987b: 145), it looks increasingly possible that prototypicality is simply newfangled literalism — the literalism of historically oriented dictionaries that report that the earliest written uses of expressions like *come out*, *under*, and *go up* were to denote various physical movements and locations. The breadth of historical development of expressions from originally concrete and physical uses to (even predominantly) abstract and derived ones is a rich field (see Traugott 1985; and Hopper and Traugott 1994), but the historical linguist's perspective is not that of the ordinary language user, for whom the use of coming, going, up, down, etc. as physical denominators may not be so typical as to be more prominent or core than various other common uses.

Concluding Remarks

The purpose of this chapter has been not only to resist the notion of literal meaning as an essentialist delusion or an instrument of enforced communication but also to consider in detail what the notion entails, and what consequences follow, for one's view of language and agency. I have argued that literal meaning is always a controversial abstraction from linguistic (and, particularly, written language) behavior; while heuristically and pedagogically useful, it remains ontologically and epistemologically suspect, if not misleading. It is a myth, as Rommetveit notes, and so is not to be dismissed lightly: "The myth of literal meaning addresses the basic semantic riddle of how the Many may become One. It tries to explain how language can bring about a spiritual union of the Many, how one state of intersubjectivity or "shared meaning" is attained by linguistic means in encounters between different subjective worlds" (1988: 13). One function of the myth is to act as a bulwark against the inroads on the sociocultural order that continued reflection on Lockean uncertainties about intersubjective communication might cause. And, as Rommetveit also emphasizes, literal meaning is an important myth since in our highly literate societies it is "a *reality lived* by enlightened laymen under subtle influence from *stories told* by prominent scholars of semantics" (p. 15). We can and should extend the burden of responsibility, however, beyond the ranks of prominent scholars of semantics — particularly if we keep in mind that literal meaning is simply, as it were, the quintessence of more widely invoked authorized abstractions, namely, conventional meanings. The representing of the world in the terms authorized by conventional meanings and their most ossified forms, literal meanings, is something we are all implicated in. But, like Orwell's egalitarian animals, some are undoubtedly more authorial and implicated than others (lexicographers, editors, publishers, advertising copywriters, media stars, journalists, guardians of "good" English, writers, teachers) just as some activities are more authorial and implicating than others (composition classes, word games, news bulletins, editing, lectures, the discourses of the more influential professions, and so on).

Literal meaning is an important myth particularly within literate societies with developed traditions of legal, literary, and linguistic studies recorded in written language. While it is a myth, it is also real, with large consequences for the conduct of various societal functions. However, the ontological status of literal meaning, this chapter has argued, is not of that foundational order. Literal meaning is not essential to the very emergence of language, in the way that standard linguistics (and legal studies etc.) requires and, under the compulsion of that requirement, presupposes.

But, if literal meaning is real but contingent or nonfoundational, still care needs to be taken over how one understands and invokes the principle that there is "no such thing as literal meaning" — to use Stanley Fish's phrase,

51   Inscribed or Literal Meaning

from the sentence at the head of this chapter, out of its context. As in the view here, Fish regards literal meaning as itself a construction, not independent of perspective but "a product of perspective" (1989: 185). But in a chapter critical of Booth's (1974) foundational approach to irony, he seems too ready to treat literal meaning as therefore plural, reconstructable, and contestable; taking such a line underestimates the very real powers of the literal meaning category. The case that Fish cites is that of singer Randy Newman's controversial song "Short People." The lyrics of this song begin by declaring 'short people got no reason to live,' and proceed to "rehearse in detail the shortcomings of short people" (Fish 1989: 180). It wasn't long before groups of short and otherwise physically challenged people were lobbying Newman's concerts and campaigning against the song as offensive, demeaning, and so on. Of course Newman pleaded that there had been a misunderstanding and that his purpose had been to display and ridicule the prejudice and intolerance that his lyrics, using irony, had articulated. But many protesters remained unpersuaded. Newman's responses parallel those of Salman Rushdie over the violent reception of his *Satanic Verses*, discussed in chapter 5. In both cases, authorial protestations necessarily failed to resolve the issue.

Fish cites the Newman case to show, contra Booth (who claims that much literary irony is demonstrably stable), that irony is risky and uncertain and contestable and that no principled separation can be maintained of, on the one hand, the stable meaning of sentences preexisting their discoursal use and, on the other hand, the contingent significance or local uptake of those sentences in particular situations of utterance. In this I believe Fish to be correct. But at this point he goes on to claim that, "in fact, the dispute over the song is a dispute *about* its literal meaning" (1989: 185), suggesting that the sentence

Short people got no reason to live

has at least two literal meanings. One of these, a negative judgment, I shall not bother to spell out (and I take it as significant that there is likely to be general agreement that no spelling out of this interpretation is needed). The second literal meaning, Fish suggests, is that, "because of the indignities and inconveniences they suffer, [short people] have nothing to live *for*" (p. 185). On this reading, the sentence is, literally, a complaint and one made as if from the perspective of embittered short people themselves (the connections with free indirect discourse, the veiled projection within a narrative of a character's words, are also relevant; see the discussion in chapter 4).

A defender of literal meaning is likely to point out, however, that Fish has identified only two different illocutionary forces with which one might use this meaningful sentence, namely, dismissal of short people and protest on behalf of short people, but that prior to and independent of those forces is the stable meaning of the locution itself. And, on either reading, that stable meaning amounts to a negative description of the quality of life of short people. This seems to me correct and entirely in the nature of literal meaning: that is, it strongly privileges (outside of exceptional cases, of polysemy — and Fish is not here arguing that the sentence is polysemic) just one interpretation as normal and standard and reasonable. (Compare Bredin [1992: 72]: "A verbal expression has a literal meaning whenever that meaning is both univocal and conventional.") Furthermore, the protest/complaint interpretation of "Short people got no reason to live," namely, as a protest on behalf of short people, is harder to sustain in view of the repeated lines of the song's chorus, "Don't want no short people 'round here," and in view of the song's contrastingly lyrical "protolerance" middle section — "Short people are just as good as you and me" — not mentioned by Fish. Positing two literal meanings for the sentence acquits Newman too easily and renders the song far more bland than it was evidently taken to be; it is a failing to acknowledge the tenor of risk and confrontation embedded in the song to which its admirers and detractors alike are evidently responding. It is rather as if a critic had footnoted Swift's *Modest Proposal* with the claim that alternative meanings of a cluster of propositions to do with eating, boiling, fricassee, and so on had to do with educating and nurturing Irish babies and that these senses should not be overlooked. The partiality and normativity of literal meaning cannot be exposed by denying, against the weight of the evidence, that a single literal meaning obtains for a particular sentence such as "Short people got no reason to live"; it can, however, be revealed in its constructedness as soon as one demands the literal meaning of, for example, *short*, whereupon a highly contextualized and relational "definition," impossible of general application, will be the best that a semanticist can offer.

On Fish's interpretation, the song is for some listeners literally a string of cruel remarks, possibly ironically intended, while for other listeners it is literally a protest against such abuse and rejection. This presents an implausibly divided audience for the song, separated into sharply contrasting interpretive camps. And, if one of those camps comprises those who hear the song as literally cruel and insulting, not ironic, then surely those listeners are entirely and unqualifiedly justified in feeling abused and damaged and equally justified in securing any forms of redress available? It would be no defense for

Newman to protest that they had misunderstood the song's meaning, for, if the Fish pluralism is allowed, the song's meaning for those insulted is simply different than but equal with the song's meaning for Newman. None of this, however, is, to use a keyword of the new pragmatism, persuasive. Reactions to the song were divided, but the divisions were not over the likely, established, and authorized meaning of the utterances within the song: what some were uncertain about was what Newman *meant* by saying those things; while others, assuming the ironic intent, wondered whether that intent had been sufficiently signaled. We seriously underrate the power of literal meaning, and relatedly undermine the possibilities of ironic exploitation of that authorized categorization of sentences, if we make the claim that literal meanings are ordinarily multiple. I take the view that Newman's song does have a single set of literal meanings, his intent was ironic, and he was misunderstood by his detractors. To argue otherwise, for multiple literal meanings, tends to nullify irony and the instructive and moral challenges that it presents. At the same time, however, none of these claims can be proved logically, and none of these controversies can be settled permanently.

At the heart of all linguistic communication — not just in the use of creative metaphors — lies risk: the risk involved in attempting to get one's interlocutor to see the same picture of some aspect of reality that you, the speaker, believe you see. This element of risk is of course troubling, especially to the telementationally minded, who would wish that language "at its most precise and unambiguous" might shuttle ideas from mind to mind in a flawless, friction-free manner. On the other hand, and from outside the telementational mind-set, the risk involved is part and parcel of genuine linguistic creativity: language can genuinely go wrong only when one is genuinely remaking language as one goes along. A proper respect for the indeterminacies of language should help us see the importance of interactional risk, as Derrida has noted: "Does the quality of risk [or infelicity, voided performative, through shift of context/ circumstances] admitted by Austin *surround* language like a kind of *ditch* or external place of perdition which speech could never hope to leave, but which it can escape by remaining 'at home,' by and in itself, in the shelter of its essence or *telos*? Or, on the contrary, is this risk rather its internal and positive condition of possibility? Is that outside its inside, the very force and law of its emergence?" (Derrida 1977b: 190).

A final point for reflection must be the hidden theoretical momentum carried by the word *literal* in the phrase *literal meaning*. In the struggle between the discoursal modes of speech and writing, a range of commentators has explored ways in which the academy and its theorists have tended to privilege the latter while paying lip service as it were to the former. The tradition begins with Plato and in recent years has included Lord, Havelock, Goody, Derrida, and Ong. It has been commonplace, too, to note linguistics' protestations of the primacy of speech and yet its continued reliance on written data, written transcriptions, and, as the norm, the analysis of written language. Only very recently, in contributions from Harris and Love, has there been radical commentary concerning the reliance of literate societies on scriptist modes of reflection and analysis. Part of that argument is that the coming into written language that any largely literate society has experienced triggers a quantum leap in reflexivity of analysis of such activities as use of language. It enables, in an unprecedented way, the abstraction of language from its natural ongoing contexts into the removed medium of writing, in turn making possible a radically decontextualized metalinguistics. Love has an elegantly simple example of our dependence on writing for the ways we tend to think and speak about language. He reports how in Downes (1984) the idea of sociolinguistic variation is introduced. By way of illustration, Downes cites the dialectical variation that exists in the pronunciation of the word *butter* by native speakers of English. This is displayed by means of use of IPA transcriptions; the pronunciations that Downes records are [bʌtə], [bʌdə^r], [bʌʔə], [bʌʔə^r] and [bʌdə]. In standard orthography these might be rendered as butteh, budder, bu'eh, bu'er and buddeh; several other pronunciations of the word are also to be found. Straightforward as this seems at first glance, it veils a significant enigma, namely, that "there is no superordinate pronunciation which is the pronunciation of 'the word itself,' as distinct from one of its phonetic variants" (Love 1990a: 16). There is no Platonic, prototypical pronunciation of *butter* in existence anywhere for the five transcribed pronunciations to be versions of, yet sociolinguistic theory holds to the assumption that the five transcribed pronunciations are indeed variants of a single something. Maintaining the assumption is immeasurably assisted by the possibility of transcription and its use in such examples as Downes's. Among other things, transcription appears to make possible a full linguistic representation, in script, of speech; from the other direction, moving from writing to speech, it may even foster the illusion that it can represent "the pronunciation of written words," such as *butter*. What ties the five transcribed variants together, and makes it possible for one to see them as variant tokens of a single type, is not a phonetic entity at all, but a written one, the written type *butter*: "A stable and consistent analysis of utterance-tokens in terms of the types that they instantiate would be impossible without the assistance afforded by writing in the form of a phonetically neutral notation with which to identify types" (Love 1990a: 16). Standard writing, in English at least, is "phonetically neutral" in an unrestricted sense: it simply excludes phonetic variation, along with all the local specifities of interpretation that this might introduce, so as to promote the illusion of stability and consistency: there is a single word, *butter*, with a stable meaning or set of meanings, regardless of differences in typefaces and handwriting. Mutatis mutandis, a similar situation applies to literal meaning, typically understood as the standard meaning of written words and utterances — or of spoken utterances tacitly treated as written ones. And a similar kind of awkwardness arises when one tries to describe the filtering out of variation that goes on:

The potential diversity of local contextualized significances of (what in written language would be treated as a single utterance — e.g., "My feet hurt") seems wholly marginal by comparison with the seemingly incontrovertible givenness of a stable standard meaning underlying all the different spoken uses of (the single written utterance "My feet hurt").

Certain sections in the above formulation are bracketed at just those points where, as in the lack of a phonetic archetype for *butter*, we lack a spoken-language representation of the alleged core substance of the written utterance "My feet hurt": there is no such spoken type, and our immediate recourse is to the written form, allegedly its faithful counterpart. In the phonetic case, the concern is to get back to a level of putative invariant typicality of form (the "supertype" pronunciation of *butter*); in the literal meaning case, the concern is to get back to a level of putative invariant typicality of meaning (the "supertype" meaning of utterances that we might write as "My feet hurt"). In both cases, the glaring absence — since they are impossible — of such supertypes for spoken language is not recognized as an impediment to the theory but becomes rather a pretext for radical context shift to the more conducive mode, writing.

2

Metaphor

Metaphor as neither Process nor Thing but the Name of a Practice

When, on the chilly January morning of his inauguration as president of the United States, Mr. Bush announced that a new breeze was blowing, how did his audience know that he wasn't commenting on the weather? And wasn't he, in a sense, commenting on the weather? What kind of knowledge concerning the meaning or use of the word *gestapo* is needed in order that an addressee can understand a sentence such as *The customs officers in that country are a gestapo*? Is there really a departure from literal meaning in the sentence *John is an utter swine*? Is it possible for a word to retain a literal meaning that, in practice, is almost never used?

This chapter addresses questions like the foregoing. In broad terms, it argues that metaphoric language does not differ in kind from nonmetaphoric language, although, in the case of fresh metaphor, it often entails greater interpretive effort than conventional utterance would. It endorses Kittay's view that the literal-metaphoric distinction needs to be relativized rather than erased absolutely (Kittay 1987: 20). Although not different in kind from other language, metaphoric language is argued to be most revealing of conditions and resources that are always a potential in language. In recent years, the conviction has become more widely held that "metaphor is deeply engrained in cognitive processes, social acts and verbal usage, that metaphor in fact is a constitutive factor of all mental constructions and reconstructions of reality" (Dirven and Paprotté 1985: x). Where metaphors are a source of indeterminacy, that, too, is only a highlighting of the indeterminacy in signifying generally. Commentaries not infrequently draw attention to the "perversity" of metaphor, its fanciful and egregious way of communicating something that might have been expressed more straightforwardly; or they draw attention to the "outrageous" way in which a metaphoric utterance conveys something evidently other than what its constituent words are ordinarily taken to mean. But I will argue that metaphor should seem no more perverse or outrageous a proceeding than that of a tennis player who attempts to win points by means of exciting but risky shots — spins, lobs, run-round backhands, soft shots when he or she could have hit the ball harder, and similar deviations from normal strokes — rather than by invariably "playing safe." Conventional utterance, in one aspect at least, is like percentage tennis (as long as we add the proviso that, unlike tennis, interaction is often not a contest with a winner and a loser). This chapter develops the view that metaphorizing is risky and provocative, entailing aliveness to the creative possibilities of language. And the risk carries rewards: metaphor may be mind expanding, intimacy enhancing, contributory to new explanation of known or newly encountered phenomena, at the leading edge of our practices of language change and renewal.

In Bhaya Nair, Carter, and Toolan (1988: 21), we argued that

> The interpretation of metaphor operates not on words as meaning-types in a fixed decontextualized lexicon, but on utterances in context, as context exploitations of the lexicon integrated with a potentially diverse range of other speech-event dimensions: stress, intonation, phonaesthetics, deictic orientation, syntax, encyclopaedic or background knowledge, and so on. While this means that, in principle, "anything goes" in determining the import of a metaphor and the criteria by which it is arrived at, we maintain that in normal practice this is not the case, that there is rather a mutual attending to a cluster of particularly salient linguistic clues or cues.

From an integrational viewpoint, this does not go far enough. For example, it appears to accept the proposition that somewhere in our heads there exists a mental dictionary of vocabulary items known to us. We should not be too ready to assume that Random House–type dictionaries have a hidden mental counterpart, random-access-type dictionaries. The assumption is nurtured in Western culture by a related lay assumption: that it is natural for a proper language to have a dictionary — an assumption not so culturally remote from the view that it is natural for a proper nation to have a standing army. Various naturalizations and equivalences are posited and interwoven in such assumptions. Their interrelations will not be explored further here, beyond the suggestion that such exploration should keep in mind that such notions as "*a* language" and "*the* English language" encourage us to abstract and naturalize in the ways indicated.

The printed and published dictionary may be an aid to clarity and standardness of usage and offers partial descriptions and explanations of how a language has been used; but, on the other hand, no language requires a dictionary. Conversely, the mental dictionary conceptualized by linguists is not an optional aid to actual performance but necessary in some form to the coherence of the theory. Multicopy dictionaries are widespread today — perhaps more widespread than ever before in history — and institutionalized forms of respect for and consultation of dictionaries are equally well entrenched; nevertheless, the integrational linguist is skeptical of the existence of that rather different postulated entity said to be in the head of every speaker of a given language, the mental lexicon.

There is therefore an element of equivocation in the formulation quoted above, to the effect that knowledge from the lexicon is "integrated with" a diverse range of other phenomena. That is still essentially a segregationalist approach to the question, in which ingredients assumed to be originally and theoretically separate (lexicon, intonation, deixis, background knowledge) are then brought together in metaphor production or construal. There are no grounds for assuming that, originally, essentially, and theoretically, these so-called ingredients or dimensions are ever strictly detachable from the integrated unity of a situated speech event. How, analogously, could one detach one dimension from a three-dimensional figure, let alone two? Similarly, how can any spoken utterance in English properly be an utterance at all "with the intonation removed"? It is simply impossible to conceive of a spoken English utterance that lacks intonation (it should not be imagined that, e.g., the level monotone of computerized voice simulation constitutes an absence of intonation). Equally, utterances without stress, phonaesthetics, deixis, syntax and — inexplicably relegated to the rear of the train in the quoted passage — background knowledge are impossibilities. The condition of being an utterance is that the *materia* has or evinces stress, intonation, deixis, syntax, background knowledge, and so on, although there is no knowing which of these attributes may be most attended to by participants on any particular occasion. Finally, the reference to "mutual attending" in the last sentence of the quoted passage above must be sharply qualified: as will be argued in chapter 5, no assumption of mutuality of the kind perhaps hinted at here is strictly possible or necessary.

A further set of recurrent assumptions about metaphor will also be put in question in this chapter. Discussions of metaphor in the literature are often grounded in an explicitly relational comparison or contrast of metaphoric utterances with nonmetaphoric ones as of crucial importance. Some seem to highlight perception of contrast: "Anomaly provides the basis for one of the most versatile and widely used foregrounding devices, metaphor" (Traugott and Pratt 1980: 207). However, others see a relation of similarity rather than incongruence as the essence of the comparison: "One important consideration with respect to metaphor is that it is, perhaps, too much to ask of a pragmatic theory that it should actually give us an account of what is clearly a perfectly general and crucial psychological capacity that operates in many domains of human life, namely the ability to think *analogically*" (Levinson 1983: 159). These are two examples from among many: for numerous theorists, metaphor is bound up with the perception of either anomaly or analogy. What is most interesting about these views is not their seeming mutual contradictoriness but the fact that in both cases an underlying assumption of the differentness of metaphoric utterance, vis-à-vis nonmetaphoric utterance, is assumed. It is taken to be uncontroversial that metaphors differ in kind from ordinary or conventional language use, although whether the difference is negotiated by means of perceiving analogy (substitution or comparison) or anomaly (interactionism, also termed "perspectivalism" [in Kittay 1987]) remains disputed. Again, integrationists side with a minority view that questions whether metaphors are indeed different in kind from language use in general and pursues the question of what might be entailed in treating metaphor production and construal as not involving — in any uniquely distinctive way — powers of perceiving either analogy or anomaly.

Interwoven with characterizations of metaphor in terms of either analogy or anomaly, it has become customary, following Black (1962), to regard three rival but sometimes overlapping theories of metaphor as dominating the discussion: substitution, comparison, and interaction theories (see also Levinson 1983; Ortony 1979). In each theory, an effort is made to specify the relations between a phenomenon (the metaphor) judged to be substantially different from routine usage and that routine usage that is taken to be the condition of its emergence.

One of the more interesting parallels to this theorizing, and the general preference for some version of the interactionist alternative as the least restrictive of the three on offer, may be that which is found surrounding the phenomenon of free indirect discourse (see also the discussion in chapter 4), for there, too, notions of substitution, comparison, and interaction are invoked, in roughly parallel ways. Thus, conventional direct and indirect discourse are sometimes viewed as straightforwardly substitutional: from within a given speaker's context of utterance, the words or thoughts of another individual — possibly remote — are relayed; and the substitutionary switch from the present speaker's voice is highlighted — in written language — by quotation marks, or indentation, or tense or pronoun shifts, or some other means. By extension, even free indirect discourse is essentially, although less overtly, substitutionary (Fehr [1938] terms it "substitutionary speech and thought"). But precisely because free indirect discourse seems to involve more than an application of the "insert and format" procedures that might be said to apply in canonical direct and indirect discourse, other theorists regard an account in terms of substitution as inadequate. Thus, it is argued that comparison between the quoted speaker's voice and views and those of the quoting speaker is always implicit and significant. Or it is insisted that *comparison* is a misnomer, for in free indirect discourse what is actually encountered is a problematic merging or calquing or clashing of voices and values: in short, some form of "interaction." The intention here is not to deliver summary adjudication of these views of free indirect discourse but simply to note how they parallel the theoretical discourse surrounding metaphor and to suggest that the adoption of a particular stance toward one of these phenomena is likely to entail a similar stance toward the other.

The integrational perspective on language asserts that novelty in language use is the norm; in doing so, as indicated in chapter 1, it resists the binarism (so compelling when viewed from within componentialist or truth-conditional semantic or Searlean pragmatic perspectives) that posits a clear distinction between word and sentence meaning on the one hand and utterance meaning on the other. Previous experience, including linguistic experience, is acknowledged to be relevant to the interpretation of any particular utterance in context, but priority is given to the "current communication situation" itself (Harris 1981a: 186). There is some congruence here with Black's view of metaphor as creative (not deviationist) interactionism. Black argues that to assume that a metaphoric utterance presents something as what it plainly is not — or to assume that its producer really does intend to say one thing while meaning something else — is disablingly to beg a fundamental question by accepting the misleading view of a metaphor as some kind of deviation or aberration from proper usage (Black 1979: 22): "Somebody seriously making a metaphorical statement — e.g., 'The Lord is my Shepherd' — might reasonably claim that he meant just what he said, having chosen the words most apt to express his thought, attitudes, and feelings, and was by no means guilty of uttering a crass absurdity." Rather than the speaker being culpably unaware of the conventional (namely, authorized) meaning of *shepherd*, he chooses not to accept such standardized usage as wholly determining of his own usage. It seems probable that some speakers are habitually more metaphoric than others, using more metaphors than other speakers do, in some or all domains.

Being more metaphoric then entails, inter alia, being less iterative or reproductive of the conventional usage. All utterance is intentional, but there are degrees of individuality of intentionality reflected in one's degree of adherence to — or departure from — the conventionalized intentions that a community attaches to particular utterances and recorded uses in dictionaries, phrase books, and language textbooks.

Indeed Black (1962, 1979) has provided some of the most provocative commentaries on metaphor, particularly in his claim that metaphor is a distinctive mode of achieving insight. He suggests that certain powerfully implicative metaphors (e.g., in social or scientific theories) may facilitate or even constitute a conceptualization of the field that surpasses anything available by recourse to extant or conventional descriptions. An example often cited here is that of the metaphoric explanation of atoms as miniature planetary systems: this once-novel metaphor made available a larger and quite new way of seeing and understanding the atom (in terms of masses, gravitational pull, orbits, and so on). More recently, and intended in part to displace that now-familiar but mechanistic metaphor, it has been suggested that the movement of the electron within the atom is (like) a butterfly in a cathedral. If, as Black argues, a single metaphor reverberates through two entire conceptual fields, then this suggests that a simple nonmetaphoric utterance will, for its part, reverberate through one entire conceptual field. One branch of lexical semantics has explored these notions extensively; Jakobson's emphasis on *equivalence* is relevant here and, before him, Saussure and his still incompletely developed theory of associative relations. Contemporary developments of those early proposals can be seen in the work of systemic linguists on lexical collocation; Lehrer (1974), Kittay and Lehrer (1981), and Kittay (1987) on semantic fields and their relevance to the structure of metaphor; and Lakoff and Johnson (1980), whose thesis is that the metaphors we routinely use structure our worldview, the way we conceptualize our worlds, and the way we link certain ideas together in mental schemata. This cognitive linguistic perspective is discussed later in the chapter.

Making Contextual Sense of Metaphors

A fundamental question to be asked about metaphors is the following:

Why and how do we make metaphoric expressions relevant (to the ongoing discourse) in just the ways we do, as speakers or as addressees?

The first thing that needs acknowledging is that anything can mean anything, in particular circumstances. As a result, addressees proceed in interpretation probabilistically. In the following account of metaphor interpretation, it should be noted, the terms *use*, *sense*, and *meaning* are used interchangeably and without apology, in line with the contextual and integrational picture of meaning introduced in chapter 1. All three terms should be understood as abbreviatory references to a language user's recourse to their categorized memory of previously experienced language encounters (form-context pairings) — a recourse that is never interpretively conclusive since aspects of the present encounter (the present form-context nexus) may always be overridingly different from past encounters, however seemingly similar.

Having decided on what the frame or topic of "comment" is, on the basis of adjacent talk, syntactic, and textual organization, intonation, etc., an addressee proceeds to interpret any so-called metaphoric elements by first invoking (i.e., taking as applicable) their conventional, "core" uses (as publicly established, and insofar as they know those official uses) and seeing how, if at all, such core uses can be made relevant to a description or commentary on the topic. Here the terminology of Sperber and Wilson (1986) may be useful: always seeking to derive significant contextual effects from the utterances they encounter, the invoking of conventional meanings is a "least processing effort" strategy to be gone beyond only when the need arises — that is, when this yields no interesting contextual effects or only palpably bizarre ones (e.g., when Mary has declared, "John is a guinea pig," and none of the conventional contextual effects of this claim seem relevant in the assumed environment or context). If it seems that these normative senses cannot be made relevant to the topic, then the addressee is likely (but not obliged) to consider more peripheral or extensionist senses of the interpretively opaque expression. Sometimes — and these are characteristics actively sought in the writing and reading of literature — metaphors are combined, conflated, and mixed to the point that the interpreter is no longer confident as to the presence of a prior, established literal tenor as topic. In such cases in particular, but in the more pedestrian ones of the "John is a bear" variety too, there seems a great deal that is unsatisfactory with current theories such as the comparison and interaction ones, with their tendency to ordain that interpreters enforce a reductive assimilation on the complex information coming in.

The view of metaphor taken here is compatible with Rorty's arguments for a nonteleological view of the history of language and of intellectual history — a view that itself, in Rorty's phrase, "chimes with" Nietzsche's definition of truth as "a mobile army of metaphors." Rorty adds:

63 Metaphor

But in order to accept this picture, we need to see the distinction between the literal and the metaphorical in the way Davidson sees it: not as a distinction between two sorts of meaning, nor as a distinction between two sorts of interpretation, but as a distinction between familiar and unfamiliar uses of noises and marks. The literal uses of noises and marks are the uses which we can handle by our old theories about what people will say under various conditions. Their metaphorical use is the sort which makes us get busy developing a new theory. (Rorty 1989: 17)

As Rorty notes, Davidson pursues this line of thinking by asserting that metaphors should not be thought of as having meanings — in the sense of a determinate place in some language game. If we go this far, we should proceed to point out that thinking of any utterances (so-called literal or metaphoric) as having (fixed) meanings is a risk taking (admittedly of lesser degree) that does not differ radically, in kind, from the uncertainty involved in interpreting metaphor, for the meanings that we there take nonmetaphoric utterances to have are simply the standardized, authorized uses of those forms, to which we have become habituated. Rorty notes how Davidson rejects "the thesis that associated with a metaphor is a cognitive content that its author wishes to convey and that the interpreter must grasp if he is to get the message." But he goes on to say things about metaphor that are clearly more his own view than Davidson's. Thus he writes: "Tossing a metaphor into a conversation is like suddenly breaking off the conversation long enough to make a face, or pull a photograph out of your pocket and displaying it, or pointing at a feature of the surroundings, or slapping your interlocutor's face, or kissing him" (Rorty 1989: 18).

Striking though these comparisons are, they may misrepresent the integratedness of language and action, out of which the analyst separates strands to be named *literal* and *metaphoric* speech. The situations that Rorty sketches may be misleading in taking for granted the perceptibility or manifestness of the shift — the "breaking off" — from the routine to the metaphoric, from the conversation to the slap, kiss, or face pulling. In the relevant conversational circumstances, such integrated elements as a slap, a kiss, or a face pulling may be entirely routine and unsurprising: where, and on what basis, can a line be drawn between "sudden breakings off" and routine conversational components? As a Briton in America, I am more than natively aware of the frequency of what one might call "the elbow squeeze" taking place in the course of conversations even between nonintimates; for me, those elbow squeezes are nonroutine breakings off from the normal development of the conversation, although they are apparently a quite routine and integrated component for many Americans. What constitutes a sudden breaking off then, of the kind metaphor introduction is said to be akin to, may often be contingent on the specific expectations of participants in a particular situation. Metaphor may be nothing like so overt a shift from the ongoing activity, nothing like so announced a phenomenon, as the above analogies might suggest. It might be better thought of as the removal of the routinely assumed footing (to use Goffman's phrase [Goffman 1981]), without specifying the new footing, and perhaps without even being able to specify it. In this respect, the uncertainties that come to the fore in metaphor construal again point to a parallel with the complexities involved in the interpretation of indirect and free indirect discourse, where a similar transformation of the footing must often be identified (for recent interesting discussion of "footing" and the complexity of participant roles in discourse, see Levinson [1988]).

Creative Metaphors as Interpersonal Venture

One influential paper on metaphor concludes by suggesting that most metaphor works "by reference to analogies that are known to relate the two domains" (Rumelhart 1979: 89). For example, in

> Encyclopedias are gold mines

Rumelhart suggests that the process of comprehension involves applying the schema suggested by the predicate term to the subject term (the term *predication* itself, as standardly used, implies that characteristic properties of the predicate concept are to be applied to the subject concept). In the present example, there is only a partial fit of those characteristic properties (e.g., "containing hidden riches" fits encyclopedias, "subterraneanity" does not); indeed, such "unevenness of fit" is a key ingredient of metaphoricality, Rumelhart suggests:

> The interpretation process, I believe, is no different here than for literal predication, the outcome is simply different. We say that a statement is literally true when we find an existing schema that accounts fully for the data in question. We say that a statement is metaphorically true when we find that although certain primary aspects of the schema hold, others equally primary do not hold. When no schema can be found which allows for a good fit between any important aspects of the schema and the object for which it is said to account, we are simply unable to interpret the input at all. (Rumelhart 1979: 80)

Rumelhart's picture rests on an implied contrast (not absolute, but only of degree) between relatively institutionalized schemata and relatively creative or fresh ones. The integrational approach to metaphor is broadly congruent with this, provided a qualification is added concerning the notion of "characteristic properties." By the *characteristic properties* of an expression must be meant, I have argued, those associations, in remembered form-context situations, that the expression "calls to mind" to an individual. *Characteristic properties* cannot denote anything so psychologically unreal as, for example, the conventional meaning definition of an expression as supplied by a dictionary.

The chief difficulties of any sharply delimited notion of semantic properties, such as a defining set of semantic features postulated as present or absent in items in the lexicon, are pinpointed in Cooper's critique of the traditional semanticist proposals of Cohen and Margalit (1970). Cohen and Margalit discuss how a metaphor might be "released," from within the domain of the literal meaning that ordinarily conceals it, when certain semantic features of the words in a particular combination are "dropped" (Cooper 1986: 61–66). On this account, while we may have thought of metaphoric meanings as extras, they are in fact internal to the standard semantic profile of terms; but they come to the fore only when more prominent semantic features of that profile are, in metaphor production and interpretation, tacitly canceled. Metaphoric meanings, on this view, are more a residue than an extra: "So, one meaning of 'baby,' as in 'baby airplane,' is 'very small of its kind.' This is what is left over when we drop such features as being human and being very young" (Cooper 1986: 62).

But as Cooper notes the proposal fails, even with Cohen and Margalit's own examples, such as that of "the poor are the negroes of Europe" (there is nothing intrinsic to the semantics of the word *negro* that entails that its referents be characterized as exploited and oppressed). Or, in the case of Wittgenstein's curious remark where he asserts "the vowel *e* is yellow," what semantic features of yellow are left, to make sense of the metaphor, when the feature of color is dropped? These counterexamples strongly suggest that a reconfiguration of the defining semantic features of a word — with some major ones canceled, other perhaps secondary ones foregrounded — is not what is involved in using terms metaphorically. More generally, a reliance on "a semantic hypothesis," constituted from defining semantic features, seems misplaced. If, however, semantic hypotheses about words are much more open sets, schematic categorizations containing established semantic attributes, associations, and connotations, then it may be possible to sustain a picture in which using a word metaphorically involves setting aside many prominent attributes usually associated with the word and foregrounding others (often, characteristics that are vividly distinctive, although not defining). But this certainly entails a noncompositional contextual semantics unlike that adopted by Cohen and Margalit.

Both constructivists and nonconstructivists (to use the labels proposed by Ortony [1979]), from Searle to Cohen, tend to say that, in a metaphor, speaker S intended X but said Y and meant the hearer to compute X by means of seeing the underlying congruence of (aspects of the sense of) Y. The alternative view proposed here is that in a metaphor the speaker intends Y when she says Y but, aware that a nonconventional sense of Y is being invoked, is aware also that she has taken a calculated risk. Speakers, as creative improvisers, locally managing their meanings, are aware of conventional usage but free — should they feel so inclined — to depart from conventional usages in all but the most frozen and ritualized settings. The point is summarized thus in Bhaya Nair, Carter, and Toolan (1988: 27): "[Creative] metaphor is a creative risk-taking with the less conventional or usage-enshrined associative possibilities of the language — risky because your addressee may not 'get' your metaphor, may merely think you a liar or an idiot or needlessly obscure." The risk is motivated by commensurate rewards: the subtlety of indirect informativeness is often appreciated by intelligent addressees; in appropriate circumstances it may be entertaining and carry more influence: "These various rewards are perhaps united in involving an increased identification or affinity between speaker and addressee(s). Risky metaphor that 'hits it off,' 'gets through' from speaker to addressee, effects a more-than-everyday intersubjective accord and intimacy between the parties" (Bhaya Nair, Carter, and Toolan 1988: 27).

One way or another, metaphors frequently carry rhetorical clout. The last thing intended in creative metaphors is a bald on-record speech act; but, when they are successfully understood, perhaps the first thing effected is an on-record display of interpersonal affinity. The situation is quite complex since to use a creative metaphor is to assume a more-than-everyday level of speaker-addressee understanding, and the metaphor itself, insofar as it is a good metaphor, make available to the addressee a richer understanding of the framing subject matter than would ordinarily be possible. Enhanced affinity or understanding, then, I propose to be the chief motive of metaphor. This proposal is somewhat parallel, although distinct in detail, to Cooper's emphasis (discussed below) on "intimacy" through metaphor and Tannen's view that repetition enhances "involvement," which is discussed in chapter 6. If affinity is the privileged engine of creative metaphor, then we should expect to find the latter absent from situations of genuine hostility and conflict, such as direct insult. Indeed, it is hard to find or construct examples of creative metaphor used in specifically direct insult of an addressee (by vivid contrast with both abundant use of conventional or dead metaphor in such situations of direct address and frequent use of creative metaphor in derogatory commentary to a third party and rhetorical, less-than-genuine insult, such as medieval flyting), for it would entail respecting one of the addressee's faculties (his or her intelligence or like-mindedness to self) while simultaneously denigrating the same faculty or others: a sending of contradictory signals.

The risk-taking aspect of creative metaphor is pertinent to its abundant use in literature. The category of literariness seems to carry with it a safety net for the protection of metaphoric risk taking. Or, rather, although not in its nature a safety net, literature nevertheless is a kind of language use in which a safety net seems almost invariably in place. The safety net is the interpretive principle, of respect and deference, that people standardly bring to their reading of literature: that the unexpected and hard-to-interpret expressions therein are not defects but fresh and difficult characterizations that it is incumbent on the reader to work at understanding.

One important claim in the account of metaphor and metaphorizing presented so far is that the nonconventional is not interpreted by means of "calculating" back to or out from the conventional. The paired terms *conventional* and *nonconventional* tend to promote that mistaken view, rather in the way that *standard* and *nonstandard* can cause problems in sociolinguistic description, for, similarly there, there is no intrinsic need for nonstandard speech to be interpreted by charting a path back to standard dialect, no matter how handy such a path may be for "outgroup" members. In fact, the paired terms *standard/nonstandard* and *conventional/nonconventional* are largely synonymous: "standard language" and "conventional meaning" are two aspects of authorized and sanctioned usage. Whenever we are the recipients of a creative metaphor, we are in the position of familiars of conventional language faced with an unconventionalism. This is similar to the situation of most of us, familiar with a standard dialect, confronted with local instances of interpretively opaque dialectalism. What seems not to be the case is that familiarity with the standard dialect or the conventional expression gives us any direct interpretive help in our understanding of the outlandish expression, for the simple reason that it is impossible to see how it could. Very much after the fact, we may paraphrase the exoticism in standard or familiar language, but no such paraphrase can confirm, disconfirm, or otherwise assist the interpretation of the nonroutine expression — an interpretation that will in fact have preceded the formulation of the paraphrase. Hence, for example, the interpretive uncertainties experienced by readers unfamiliar (or not "fully" familiar) with Northern Irish dialects when they encounter the comment that "Trillick is claner nor a man kicked to death by savages fornent his childer," said by the character Dinny to a Royal Ulster Constabulary police officer in Eugene McCabe's short story "Cancer" (set in the Northern Ireland of the 1970s). Whatever standard English gloss the reader proposes for *fornent*, that gloss will not have *helped* them arrive at an interpretation of the dialectal word but is rather a reflex of *having* considered a particular interpretation.

If the metaphoric is not interpretively dependent on the conventional or nonmetaphoric, any more than a nonstandard dialect is interpretively dependent on any standard one, then there is no reason to assume that the latter has to precede the former in language development. In his memoir of the congenitally deaf student Massieu, the Abbé Sicard noted what happened when, very belatedly, the young man was introduced to language (the memoir is quoted in Sacks [1989]). The first signs that Massieu learned, at the late age of fourteen, were signs for nouns and names; he then forged ahead in devising propositions that used these, without benefit of adjectives: "Massieu did not wait for the adjectives, but made use of names of objects in which he found the salient quality he wanted to affirm of another object.... To express the swiftness of one of his comrades in a race, he said, 'Albert is *bird*'; to express strength he said 'Paul is *lion*'; for gentleness, he said 'Deslyons is *lamb*' " (p. 49). Thus, in this categorically restricted language, Massieu used metaphoric forms almost from the first — and before nonmetaphoric utterances ("Paul is strong") became available to him.

Clearly, it would be dangerous to generalize without qualification to normal language development from the practices of a socialized fourteen-year-old who clearly has a developed sense of the distinctness of people and things in the environment and of the goal orientedness of activity. Nevertheless, Massieu's example does suggest that the following developmental sequence both is possible and in his case actually did occur: first, the names of certain individuals or kinds were learned (*Albert, Paul, bird, lion,* etc.); subsequently, names were used not merely to name but to evaluate by means of the conjunction of two names, with a clear topic comment or tenor-vehicle structure and with the optional use of a copula verb. (Insofar as the topic-comment order is inviolable, here also is a rudimentary syntax.) Support for the idea that metaphoricality may precede literalness comes from a very different quarter in Muhlhausler's (1985) hypothesis that literal meaning is a fixed and narrowed usage, derived from the prior metaphoric norm. Muhlhausler argues that we may in practice derive the literal from the metaphoric — as reflected in studies of child language and creolizing languages — and not, as usually assumed, the reverse. Relevant, too, is Freud's distinction between primary thought processes (productive of dreams, neurotic symptoms, and creativity) and secondary ones (literal thinking, logicality), mentioned in Kittay (1987: 120). As Kittay observes, literal language, and its referential and logical impetus, is a "pruning" of the multifunctional expressivity of which language is capable.

Psycholinguistic Approaches

Some of the most important work on metaphor in recent years has come from experimental psycholinguists. The starting point of many of these studies has been a dissatisfaction, as strong as that of integrational linguists, with the standard approach to metaphor. That approach, heavily influenced by the philosophy of language and pragmatics, assumed a "stage theory" of metaphor interpretation (those cited as proponents include Searle [1979]; Miller [1979]; and Davidson [1978]). Onishi and Murphy summarize the ordered stages thus: "(1) Recognition of incompatible truth conditions or selectional restrictions in the literal meaning, (2) reconstruction of possible meanings, and (3) proper interpretation of the utterance" (Onishi and Murphy 1993: 763).

Crucially, the stage theory entails that literal meaning is derived first. An abundance of psycholinguistic studies show that account to be unsupported (see, e.g., Gerrig and Healey 1983; Gibbs 1990b; Gildea and Glucksberg 1983; Glucksberg and Keysar 1990; Keysar 1989; Onishi and Murphy 1993; Tourangeau and Rips 1991). Some of the richest counterproposals are to be found in the important article of Glucksberg and Keysar (1990), who argue that rather than treating metaphors as implicit or covert similes — so that, it is conventionally claimed, the metaphoric utterance *Men are pigs* is first "glossed" as *Men are like pigs* — construal is on a quite different basis. Specifically, nominative metaphors are (and are received as) class-inclusion statements, with the added twist that the class or category intended to be denoted by the vehicle term is one of which that vehicle is a prototypical exemplar. Furthermore, rather than metaphors being implicit similes, it is the case that similes are implicit metaphors. Metaphor involves a likening of unlike things; and most similes too, perhaps surprisingly, involve a likening of unlike things also. It is only with certain kinds of simile, often of the more frozen and conventional kind such as *The state is as flat as a pancake*, *It's like an oven in here*, and so on, that a likening of like things occurs. The fact that creative similes are implicit metaphors has a quite general relevance: recasting metaphors by insertion of *like* or postulating similarity affords the interpreter no assistance in the interpretive task. This in part explains why an addressee confronted with the observation that

> Life's but a walking shadow, a poor player
> That struts and frets his hour upon the stage,
> And then is heard no more (*Macbeth*, 5.5.24–26)

is given scant assistance by a recasting of Macbeth's figures as similes: "Life is like a walking shadow . . . etc." Thus, whether a speak uses the metaphor

> My job is a jail

or the simile (in Glucksberg and Keysar's terms, a metaphoric comparison)

> My job is like a jail,

in both cases the speaker uses *jail* as prototypical exemplar of a nonce category, which is striking for two reasons: the category is novel and usually very temporary; and the category is superordinate to the term that actually creates it (*jail*) and thus, in a sense, is more productive. In the given example, the nonce category invoked might be represented as Glucksberg and Keysar suggest, as "entities that confine one against one's will, are unpleasant, and are difficult to escape from" (1990: 3). Clearly, these properties constitute an open-ended set, so that some interpreters of the given metaphor may place more weight on other superordinate-category features — such as "experience intended as punishment" — than those listed above. But the principle of class inclusion, which clearly entails a hierarchical relation between tenor and vehicle, is crucial to the theory and compelling. Among other things, it entirely rejects any assumption that nominative metaphors (such as *You're the blackcurrant juice in my granita*) are identity statements (and, as philosophers are quick to add, almost invariably false ones at that). Glucksberg and Keysar note that the idea of a prototypical term doing service in place of a superordinate term is well documented in American Sign Language, classifier languages such as Burmese, and American Indian languages such as Hopi. And in English there are intermediate versions of the same potential, in the use of brand names such as *Hoover*, *Xerox*, and *Kleenex* to designate whole classes of entities, although admittedly not in the absence or to the exclusion of superordinate terms such as *vacuum cleaner* and *photocopy*.

Glucksberg and Keysar's proposal is attractive also in its orientation to the open-ended creativity of fresh or fresher metaphors. As they note, Ortony's theory concerning the pronounced semantic asymmetry in metaphoric comparisons (i.e., that certain features of the vehicle term are far more salient to construal than features of the tenor term) does not, finally, render that "salience imbalance" theory very different from other "matching models." In all matching models, ultimately, it is assumed that interpreters undertake a "search" for properties of the vehicle that may be matched with properties of the tenor. But, in all nonroutine metaphor utterance, interpreters find that properties of the vehicle become contingently salient that would never ordinarily be ascribed to the tenor, so that matching is not the issue (ironically, matching may well be relevant in literal comparisons — such as *A health visitor is like a social worker*). Instead, what is involved is the selective attribution of properties. There is situation-relative class inclusion and selective attention to properties of that superordinate nonce class: "By creating a new categorization, [metaphorizing] also creates new variants of both the topic and vehicle: The vehicle now refers to a category of things that it also exemplifies. . . . [The topic] now has the complex of properties entailed by membership in that category" (Glucksberg and Keysar 1990: 11).

The difficulty that attends such a postulated "new categorization" is that it seems impossible to make a definitive listing of what are and what are not the complex of properties that it entails; a systematic and intentional vagueness prevails. But this difficulty may be seen not as an inadequacy of the theoretical description but as part of the very point of metaphorizing. It speaks to the increasing tendency, even among more traditional linguistic treatments of metaphor, to portray metaphor as involving interaction between tenor and vehicle rather than merely transfer or resemblance. There are parallels between Glucksberg and Keysar's account and that of Kittay and Lehrer (1981), which relates lexical items to their semantic fields and sees the structure of the "donor" field, that of the vehicle, restructuring, even if only temporarily, the recipient field of the tenor. As Thompson and Thompson (1987: 84) comment in their discussion of Kittay and Lehrer, in poetic metaphor (where, as it were, every tenor carries some potential for vehiclehood), the reconceptualization often seems to be bidirectional, with both tenor and vehicle reconfigured. In this way, nominative metaphor is exemplary of linguistic change and renewal, for it is a contingent — and, although usually temporary, potentially longer-lived — renaming, or new naming, of a reconfigured experiential terrain. On some of these issues, Glucksberg and Keysar find support for their views in the proposals of Barsalou (1987), concerning the instability and context dependency of concepts; also relevant here is Tourangeau and Rips's (1991: 459) suggestion that critical to metaphor construal are " 'emergent' features, features not ordinarily seen as characterizing either the tenor or vehicle." For critical reaction to Glucksberg and Keysar's theory, however, see Gibbs (1992).

Numerous issues, clearly, remain to be better understood, including how it is that property attribution is guided or constrained (insofar as it seems to be) and how it is that people recognize when a metaphor is intended at all. Consider, in relation to the latter issue, and by contrast with

(1) My job is (like) a jail,

utterances such as

(2) San Quentin is a jail

and

(3) Monroe Detention Center is like a jail.

What prompts an interpreter to process the first of these via a process of nonce class inclusion and not to do so in the latter two cases? It may be germane that in (2), as in attributive intensive clauses generally, class inclusion, as distinct from identity, is involved. That is, (2) does assert that San Quentin is a member of the class *jails*. What then is distinctive about nominative metaphoric utterances like (1) is that *two* levels of inclusion are advanced, in moving from the tenor to the vehicle — an "indirectness" of the order of two categorial magnitudes.

Glucksberg and Keysar comment briefly on the difficult issue of metaphoric aptness, suggesting that aptness may well depend on the (proto)typicality of the member used as category-creating vehicle. They cite the following set of metaphoric variants in support of this, where all four are metaphorically possible but only (a) seems apt:

(a) Not even Einstein's ideas were all gold.
(b) Not even Einstein's ideas were all platinum.

(c) Not even Einstein's ideas were all silver.
(d) Not even Einstein's ideas were all sapphires.

In relation to this issue, in Bhaya Nair, Carter, and Toolan (1988: 36–37), we noted the productiveness of basic-level terms in everyday metaphor, by contrast with the unusably general nature of superordinate terms and the unusably specific nature of subordinate terms. We went on to suggest that in more creative metaphors — that is, ones considerably more creative than those contained in the Einstein sentences — prototypical exemplars would be less likely to be used. A newspaper review of a new novel is more likely to describe the author's insights as "uncut topaz gleaming in a bed of jet" than as diamonds or rubies.

The other most important findings that seem to be emerging with increasing clarity are (1) that literal meaning cannot at this stage be dismissed wholesale from accounts of utterance interpretation and (2) that certain kinds of metaphoricality do indeed take longer to interpret, and may be more memorable, than literal or conventional utterances. The latter finding is particularly interesting in view of claims in the recent past, counter to "stage theory," that comprehending metaphoric utterance is no more difficult, time consuming, or indirect than conventional utterance and that therefore postulating that "extra work" is involved in metaphor construal is incorrect (Gibbs, 1990b). Very soon, however, researchers began finding cases in which metaphor construal did take longer. For example, Gibbs (1990a) and Onishi and Murphy (1993) found that "metaphoric anaphors" seemed to take longer for judges to process than nonmetaphoric ones; that is, metaphors used referentially, and involving an intersentential link rather than merely an intrasentential one, took longer to comprehend. Subjects were presented with a brief story about a scheduled boxing event involving a notoriously cowardly boxer and ending with one of two parallel sentences. Judges faced with the ending *The fighter didn't even show up* apparently took less time to process that information than those given the ending containing a metaphoric anaphor: *The cream puff didn't even show up*. On the other hand, when such metaphors were merely predicative and intrasentential, that is, when some judges were shown

> That boxer is a cream puff

while others were shown

> That boxer is a fighter,

the contrast in processing time disappeared, and the metaphoric version seemed as "easy" to process as the literal one (Onishi and Murphy 1993). It would seem, then, that the parallelism of processing between literal and figurative utterance may hold only for figurative utterances of the more conventional kind, while more creative metaphor does indeed involve more time and possibly more "effort," "work," or attentiveness. Titone and Connine (1994) have recently found just such an effect in relation to idiomatic expressions — about which there is now widespread recognition that the label covers a range of more and less frozen usages. They found that a literal-like rapidity of comprehension of idiomatic expressions occurred with highly familiar and unanalyzable idioms but that this was less apparent with less familiar or conventional ones. Furthermore, delayed comprehension seems to be influenced in some circumstances more by the status of the interactants than by the degree of indirectness of the utterance. Thus, Holtgraves (1994) has found that subjects processed conventional indirect requests (*Could you fill the water jug, please?*), whether between equals or addressed by a superior to a subordinate, in the same time; interestingly, the subjects processed requests via negative statements (*The water jug is nearly empty*) when these were addressed by a superior to a subordinate equally rapidly. By contrast, when such negative-statement requests were presented as between equals, processing took significantly longer than in the three other conditions. Thus, Holtgraves found two tendencies active and interacting with each other: the tendency for less conventional requests such as negative statements to take longer to process than conventional ones; and the tendency for some kinds of discourse to take longer to process when between equals than when between unequals.

On the Comprehension-as-Process, Interpretation-as-Product Dichotomy

As implied above, findings currently emerging from the lively field of psycholinguistic research into metaphor and indirect utterance are a valuable empirical enrichment of integrational linguistic thinking. At the same time, there are some differences in assumptions and goals that need clarification, particularly since there may be a tendency otherwise for psycholinguists and linguistic theorists to be characterized as committed to essentially just two contrasting orientations. That misrepresentation seems to appear in a conspectual overview of different perspectives on metaphor, published by Gibbs in 1990, which begins by asserting a fundamental distinction between psycholinguistic and philosophical-theoretical approaches to metaphor (Gibbs

1990b). The psycholinguists are said to be concerned solely with the processes of metaphor comprehension, while the philosopher-theorists are said to conflate those processes with the products. Among the latter theorists Gibbs groups (alongside Searle, Pulman, Traugott and Pratt, and Levin) the paper to which I contributed to in 1988, Bhaya Nair, Carter, and Toolan. For Gibbs, the philosophical-literary theorists are all mistaken in contending that metaphor construal requires "extra work."

But there are deep differences among the latter accounts. In particular, in Bhaya Nair, Carter, and Toolan (1988), we argued that metaphor does not differ in any essential ways from other uses of language and does not involve "extra work" in the particular sense implied by some of the other theorists whom Gibbs cites (i.e., relatively more inferential steps, beyond a sentence's literal or conventional meaning); as Gibbs does, we rejected the thesis that a stepwise computation from the literal meaning is involved. On the other hand, as the recent psycholinguistic research reported above indicates, psycholinguists themselves are finding that, in more creative figurative utterance, something suspiciously like "extra work" seems to be involved. We used the phrase "extra work" (p. 24) of the interpretive challenge set by creative metaphors, at the same time emphasizing that the work involved was not a matter of supplementary stepwise inference. Our primary claim was that, although metaphors are the prime example of language used unconventionally, they should not be characterized as language used anomalously. They involve greater communicational risk than other standard uses of language — risk that what was intended will not be approximated by what the addressee understands. Metaphors are, as argued above, risks taken — taken in view of the possibility of the reward of a commensurately unconventional and more-than-ordinary degree of achievement of rapport and mutuality.

We also asserted: "A creative metaphor is a foregrounded exemplum of what is inherent and problematic in all normal interaction" (Bhaya Nair, Carter, and Toolan 1988: 23). And we suggested that "creativity" itself might usefully be conceptualized not merely as departure from previous descriptions of terms (cf. Pulman 1982) but as the process of "successful selection of appropriate paraphrase" (p. 27). That is to say, the creativity lies in selecting a plausible reading from among innumerable potential candidates rather than in "creative" projection beyond a "default" conventional reading. Seen in the light of both Glucksberg and Keysar's 1990 class-inclusion hypothesis and Grice's (1975) conversational maxims, creative metaphors permit a greater multiplicity of properties (from among those associated with the superordinate item that the vehicle prototypically picks out) to be adduced as relevant, by comparison with conventional expression, while at the same time the speaker continues to observe the manner maxim of brevity and, at least in prima facie terms, continues to observe the quantity maxim.

Among other claims, Gibbs asserts that "metaphor requires precisely the same kind of contextual information as do comparable literal expressions" (1990b: 67). But "same kind" may not mean "same degree." An integrational approach proposes that, while metaphor construal draws on the same kind of contextual information as nonmetaphoric language, it involves additional inferential work of that same kind. Again it is important to emphasize that the focus of attention is creative or literary metaphor, as reflected also in the title of Gibbs's (1990b) article. That a variety of writers on metaphor have had considerable difficulty dispensing with the notion of "extra work" in their accounts suggests that herein lies an abiding enigma. Is it possible to be more specific about what is meant by such terms as *work*, *extra*, *distinctive*, and *contextual information*? Gibbs (1990b) elaborates a contrast, quite widespread as a theoretical discriminator in the psycholinguistic literature, between those interested in the process of metaphor comprehension, on the one hand, and those interested in the products of metaphor recognition and interpretation, on the other. In fact he sees four distinct stages in the reception of metaphors, stages that are claimed to be distinct in time and are witness to the way in which, as literary commentaries might put it, metaphors unfold through time.

It is because psycholinguists want to give proper recognition to the developmental and temporalized aspect of metaphor reception that tensions embedded in their assumptions are the more apparent. If the developmental approach is taken seriously, and if, equally, metaphor is treated as "an event in time [not an object]," then a metaphor is, in its entirety, a single continuous process, and there are no firm grounds for segmenting that process into parts. For experimental psycholinguists, however, this cannot be the case: for empirical research to proceed, there must be some sense in which the comprehension process may be probed; this entails, in turn, that there must be valid ways of representing the comprehension process as comprising distinct phases — products — within and constituting the process. Gibbs states the case in this way:

It is the different temporal points at which theories propose that a metaphor has been understood, ranging from the first milliseconds of processing to long-term reflective analysis, which distinguish rival accounts of metaphor. This continuum of temporal moments is best reflected in different theorists' attempts to explain either metaphor comprehension, recognition, interpretation, or appreciation. Comprehension refers to the immediate moment-by-moment *process* of creating meaning for utterances. Recognition refers to the *products* of comprehension as types (i.e., determining whether the meaning of an utterance is literal, metaphorical, metonymic, and so on). Interpretation refers to the *products* of comprehension as tokens (i.e., determining the specific content of the meaning type). Appreciation refers to some aesthetic judgment given to a *product* either as a type or a token. Metaphor understanding begins from the first moments with comprehension processes and proceeds in time to the later moments of recognition, interpretation, and appreciation. (Gibbs 1990b: 76)

There are, according to this account, four temporally disjunct stages in metaphor understanding: one process (the focus of psycholinguistic research) and three products (the foci of literary and philosophical commentaries), tabulated below:

comprehension	(a process)
recognition	(a product)
interpretation	(a product)
appreciation	(a product)

But what is it that renders comprehension uniquely a process while recognition etc. are all products? Or, conversely, on what grounds are the three later stages to be thought of purely as products while comprehension is acknowledged to be a process? All nominalizations such as *comprehension, recognition*, etc. are potentially ambiguous between uses that denote an ongoing process and uses that denote a complete state or product. In the quoted passage, that ambiguity seems to have been arbitrarily resolved, in each case, along just the lines convenient to the larger psycholinguistic theory: comprehension is reserved as sole process; other stages are handed on, as products, to the theorists and critics.

The parity of these four putative stages of understanding is doubtful more generally. In particular, recognition stands apart as a rather trivial metalinguistic task, one that it is not at all clear is regularly or even infrequently performed. It is widely noted that informants readily understand utterances of all sorts without giving any indication, at the time or in subsequent tests, that they are at all concerned with categorizing those utterances as literal, or metaphoric, or metonymic, etc. Almost as peripheral to the process of understanding is appreciation, wherein aesthetic judgment "is given to a product."

What specifically is entailed at this stage of aesthetic appreciation is not clarified by Gibbs, but it is treated as subsequent to the essential stages of understanding: in much nonliterary metaphor, it is implied, the earlier stages of understanding are sufficient on their own. Thus, the four stages divide into two major and obligatory ones, comprehension and interpretation, and two minor and optional ones, recognition and appreciation. Setting the latter aside, the following remarks are directed to considering what there is in the way of evidence for a sharp distinction between comprehension ("the immediate moment-by-moment *process* of creating meaning for utterances") and interpretation ("the *products* of comprehension as tokens [i.e., determining the specific content of the meaning type]" [Gibbs 1990b: 75–76]).

What a psycholinguist like Gibbs may be expected to be relatively specific about is the stage of understanding that he terms *comprehension*, the stage said to be the particular interest of psycholinguistic studies of metaphor. In practice, psycholinguists attempt to probe whatever might be going on at this putative stage by meticulous timing of subjects' performances on controlled tests. For example, subjects are presented with sentences potentially interpretable either literally or idiomatically (e.g., *She finally spilled the beans*), but verbal or visual context is also supplied so that only one of those two interpretations is reasonable. The judge is then presented with a comprehension-checking paraphrase of the target sentence, designed to reveal whether the judge has derived the literal or the idiomatic interpretation — for example, either

> In the end she dropped the food

or

> In the end she blurted out the facts

— and is asked to record whether the given paraphrase is true or false by pressing one of two buttons as promptly as possible. Assuming that difficulties to do with cultural bias, adequacy of supplied paraphrases, plausibility of literal versus idiomatic contextualizations, acceleration of response with growing familiarity with the test (or deceleration of response with overfamiliarity), etc. can be surmounted, it is hoped that such tests reveal something substantive about ease of processing expressions open to either literal or idiomatic readings. Just in relation to this literal versus idiomatic contrast, for example, Gibbs has found that judges generally respond faster to idiomatic uses of *spilled the beans*, *kick the bucket*, etc. than literal ones. If the experiment is made more elaborate, so that judges are timed responding to a literal use of a phrase after exposure to a use of that same phrase in a passage where it is used idiomatically, the same trend emerges. In fact, even when judges are asked to acknowledge a literal use of a phrase after exposure to ("priming" by) a passage in which it has already been used literally, that judgment is slower than in the cases of idiomaticity recognition. From these facts, Gibbs concludes that literal meaning cannot be the "default" or "baseline" interpretation of words and sentences, invariably invoked first in processing words and sentences. The average differences in speed of response to literal versus idiomatic uses may appear slight — around a quarter of a second — but they are often statistically significant. Gibbs comments: "Such reaction-times are thought to tap into the 'click of comprehension' phenomenologically suggested by one's experience when understanding metaphor. Average differences of 200–300 milliseconds in the comprehension latencies of sentences in different experimental conditions may appear to be negligible in terms of normal reading, but such differences *can mark* important variations in the sequences of mental processes used in understanding different sentences or the same sentence in different contexts of use" (Gibbs 1990b: 68–69; emphasis added).

It must be said, however, that these observations represent hopes rather than experimentally supported conclusions. What has actually been tested has been (rapidity of) a particular kind of performance, on a particular kind of test ("Is this sentence a reasonable paraphrase of that one?"). Even to infer from such findings that conventional, idiomatic readings of potentially idiomatic expressions are more immediate, more direct, or more easily accessible than their less-expected literal interpretation already seems a substantial hypothetico-deductive leap. At the same time, if one measure of "work" is the rapidity with which a task is completed, then Gibbs's findings might be taken as confirming a "less work/more work" hypothesis of the kind he wishes to deny: quite explicitly, and of crucial importance for Gibbs's thesis that literalness is no interpretive "first preference," literal-utterance processing takes longer than idiomatic-utterance processing. There is no warrant for assuming that this finding holds across all cases where literal and metaphoric readings can be compared; but a variable, if not of "less work versus more work," then certainly of "shorter work versus longer work," is crucially demonstrated as applying in the given cases. This is a challenge to Gibbs's broader implicit thesis, that one type of utterance — be it literal, idiomatic, or metaphoric — involves no more processing work than another. Gibbs's own findings, then, may be interpreted as support for the view that certain kinds of utterance — literal and nonconventional uses of expressions more commonly encountered in idiomatic use (e.g., *spilling the beans, hitting the deck,* etc.) and creative metaphoric expressions — involve more work and more risk for addressers and addressees. Relatively speaking, they are more arresting, draw more attention to themselves, and are less immediately associated with the well-established mental schemata or modelings that we seem routinely to invoke, as summarized foregrounded memories from our capacious memory stores.

A great deal hinges on the question of how much may be inferred from rapidity-of-response tests. Strictly speaking, on the basis of tests of latency timings of the kind outlined, beyond observations of quicker response time versus slower response time, the analyst cannot logically go. In particular, measurement of just that kind of difference in just that kind of performance shows or proves nothing about "important variations in the sequences of mental processes used in understanding different sentences or the same sentence in different contexts of use" because we have no clear-cut evidence that "sequences of mental processes" exist. As noted, Gibbs hedges the claim by saying that comprehension latencies "can mark" important variations, where both the modal of possibility and the verb *mark* (meaning here only "reflect"?) qualify the degree of commitment to the claim that the latencies *display* the different sequences of mental processes. But that there are variable sequences of mental processes is presupposed. Yet we have no way of knowing that these exist independently of psycholinguistic discourse that hypothesizes that they exist and points to latencies in paraphrase-recognition performances as confirmations of the validity of the hypotheses. In short, "a particular sequence of mental processes" is treated as an unfalsifiable entailment of "a particular latency in paraphrase-recognition performance." The claim that the latencies can mark something is incontestable, but we have no way of knowing whether they mark any particular thing. Allusions to variation in the sequences of mental processes are metaphor of a highly risky kind; from Louise Rosenblatt or other poets, that would be perfectly appropriate, but here the high-risk metaphors are presented as low-risk experimentally confirmed realist modeling, that is, as hard science.

A further point to make about psycholinguistic tests is that they need always to be recognized as directly to do with performance; in relation to competence, conceived of as an underlying knowledge, their relevance is invariably controversial. All psycholinguistic tests, no matter how "unnatural" the experimental conditions (latent responses to subliminal words heard through one ear while other material is heard in the other ear, measurement of pupil dilations in response to seen or heard language, etc.), remain tests of performance. Whatever the conventional claim might be, to the effect that how individuals perform under such and such conditions gives us insight into underlying competence and mental processing, what is invariably examined — and cannot but be examined — is performance. And all that can be certainly derived from these performances — in the integrational view something well worth deriving — are reports about performances. The psycholinguistic tendency is to convert and embed reports about performances into claims and hypotheses about competence, by definition a theoretical extravagance.

Insurmountable difficulties, then, seem to face any claim that psycholinguistic probing of comprehension (by measuring particular kinds of performance) is distinctly different from the stage of interpretation characterized as "determining the specific content of the meaning type." It is unclear how an informant might arrive at a position from which he or she could pass judgment on a subsequent sentence as a reasonable or inappropriate paraphrase of the target sentence, without having already determined the specific content of the meaning type. And it is equally unclear how "creating meaning" (said to be the work of comprehension) differs and can be shown to differ from "determining content" (said to be the work of interpretation). Positing a contrast in terms of "immediate understanding" and "later understanding" will seem merely rhetorical, unless independent means can be found of showing that such a contrast has some psychological basis.

The simplest arguments against the view that even literary metaphors can be understood immediately and automatically, that at some allegedly "basic" level of comprehension they are unproblematic, must be ones from experience. I have shared the following poem by Sylvia Plath (1981: 235–36), with many college students of literature. Their reactions to the poem reflect the quite commonplace diversity of interpretive response triggered by metaphoric poems even when, as in this case, the title and first stanza seem to give us something in the way of a "literal grounding" (i.e., expressions used relatively normally, in line with established conventions):

CUT

What a thrill —
My thumb instead of an onion.
The top quite gone
Except for a sort of a hinge

Of skin,
A flap like a hat,
Dead white.
Then that red plush.

Little pilgrim,
The Indian's axed your scalp.
Your turkey wattle
Carpet rolls

Straight from the heart.
I step on it,
Clutching my bottle
Of pink fizz.

A celebration, this is.
Out of a gap
A million soldiers run,
Redcoats, every one.

Whose side are they on?
O my
Homunculus, I am ill.
I have taken a pill to kill
The thin
Papery feeling.
Saboteur,
Kamikaze man —

The stain on your
Gauze Ku Klux Klan
Babushka
Darkens and tarnishes and when

The balled
Pulp of your heart
Confronts its small
Mill of silence

How you jump —
Trepanned veteran,

> Dirty girl,
> Thumb stump.

This is surely not, by literary standards, a particularly obscure poem. Certainly, Plath is not regarded by literary critics as difficult or esoteric in her metaphors or in other respects, in the way that Pound and Stevens are. Yet discussions of this poem in literature classes indicate that many literate readers have the greatest difficulty "getting" the poem at all, until "nudged" in particular interpretive directions. In addition, rather different understandings, both of individual lines and phrases and of the point or scenario of the poem as a whole, are reached by different readers. At the level of local comprehension, for example, rather different readings emerge for the lines:

> Little pilgrim,
> The Indian's axed your scalp.
> Your turkey wattle
> Carpet rolls
>
> Straight from the heart.
> I step on it,
> Clutching my bottle
> Of pink fizz.

Many — but not all — students see that the deep red flesh depending from a turkey's throat may be not unlike the thick, clotting blood that glitters below a cut thumb; also, if familiar with American culture, many can imagine the mordantly ironic train of thought by which the speaker juxtaposes the first, harmonious turkey-eating Thanksgiving, of Indians and pilgrims, and later scalpings. But few are aware that "turkey wattle" is (as I have been informed) the name for a style of deep-red pile carpet. Similarly, many see the speaker, clutching their own bleeding thumb, as thereby clutching a bottle of pink fizz. But it tends to be American students who interpret the pink fizz as the consequence of applying peroxide disinfectant to the cut; and it tends to be British students who see that, as a colloquial name for champagne, "pink fizz" becomes relevant to the "celebration" declared in the following line. Incidentally, fewer still are the students who notice that there is a careful chronological ordering of these allusions to some of the major bloodlettings in American history (a chronology that perhaps significantly does not include the Civil War). These are local differences of reading and seem fairly clear-cut, so to speak; but cumulatively they contribute to rather divergent conclusions. And there are also interpretive differences in response to seemingly straightforward lines, devoid of associative invention, such as

> I step on it.

Stepping on the red carpet of your own blood strikes some readers as more than a little self-destructive and, taken with other evidence — "I have taken a pill to kill"; "kamikaze man" — is used to support the conviction that the speaker is talking about a self-administered abortion. Masquerading as the tenor, the thumb is on this reading merely a vehicle — for the true tenor, the aborted fetus, "O my homunculus."

There is great danger in dismissing this evidence as of minor significance, as retelling the story of "diversity of interpretation" that has been told thousands of times over since the work of I. A. Richards and long before him too. There is also danger that the evidence will be dismissed by psycholinguists, on the grounds that tests conducted under properly controlled conditions with objective instruments such as timers and videocameras are the only suitably sterile environment for conducting biopsies on mental processing. These reported variations of interpretation may be dismissed as predictable contributions to the language game of "talking about what poems mean. But how does that language game differ, in essentials, from the language game of identifying a paraphrase for the potentially idiomatic "straight from the heart"? And what, conversely, are the grounds for assuming that conducting and reporting exercises of comprehension and recall, of reaction times and pupil dilations, are not language games of the same order of validity (rather than, as assumed, "master" games with a much higher order of explanatory power)? And, as a final question, how has it come to be the case that teachers of literature — particularly at the college level — so generally accept with equanimity that even single lines of poems are interpreted, even by cultural affines, in strikingly different ways? For several decades now, diversity of interpretation has been widely embraced, by academics, as one of the glories of literature rather than its downfall: ambiguity, polysemy, and contradiction have been acclaimed as perhaps the only essential condition of literature, rather than a weakness. Yet, in another part of the wood, many students and readers of literature, of all ages and walks of life, despite endless assurances that "there is no single, correct interpretation of any poem," remain troubled and disturbed by the fact that even a short poem entitled "Cut" is understood in such varied ways by different readers — and hardly understood at all by others again. For these perfectly normal and intelligent readers, this state of affairs makes no sense.

As is often stressed, creative metaphors are a kind of riddle (see Bhaya Nair, Carter, and Toolan [1988] on similarities between metaphors and riddles). If this is so, then to say that such metaphors present no difficulties, different in degree from those presented by less creatively unconventional language, amounts to saying that riddles are no harder to understand than conventional utterance. The implausibility of such a position is further grounds for attesting that metaphor processing does differ in degree (of something: if not of "effort," then of cognitive distance or risk to be negotiated or of relevance-theoretic "costs") from the processing of conventional language.

The reason for exploring the ambiguities in Gibbs's representative account at some length has not been in the expectation of "finally getting the facts about comprehension straight." The point rather has been to highlight important ways in which a psycholinguistic account of metaphor that is presented as coherent, orderly, and experimentally confirmed in fact contains arbitrary assumptions. There is no immediate prospect of finally getting the facts and stages of metaphor understanding sorted out; we do not know, and may never know, quite what the brain processes are that are brought to bear on any given metaphoric utterance. The discussion is not significantly advanced by questionable segmentations of understanding into postulated domains labeled *comprehension*, *recognition*, *interpretation*, and *appreciation* when the psychological validity of such compartmentalization remains unproved. On the other hand, we know a considerable amount — and can learn more — about how individuals use and understand metaphors in their lives.

Living by Metaphors: Lakoff's Cognitive Linguistics

According to Lakoff and Johnson (1980), we live, largely unconsciously, by and through a number of pervasive conceptual metaphors that structure both our language and our thinking. But for Lakoff and Johnson this is explicable only if an "experientialist" view of language and cognition is taken, in contrast to the "objectivist understanding" they see as enjoying wide influence. Among other things, objectivist accounts are said at least to imply that

    a) there are no metaphoric concepts or meanings (so that *digesting an idea* and *digesting food* are simply instances of polysemy;
      b) metaphor is a matter only of language, not of meaning;
      c) there is no such thing as literal/conventional metaphor;

d) metaphor merely aids (and does not *revise*) understanding through making us use objective similarities based on objective meanings and inherent properties (ideas are inherently to be consumed and absorbed, and this the verb *digest* merely highlights).

Against this subordinating characterization of metaphor, Lakoff and Johnson adumbrate an experientialist view, in which certain widely used and culturally central metaphors are seen as instrumental to our everyday understanding of our world. Such metaphors are ontological since they impose a shape or an organization on parts of our cultural world: "To use a set of ontological metaphors to comprehend a given situation is to impose an entity structure upon that situation. For example, LOVE IS A JOURNEY imposes on LOVE an entity structure including a beginning, a destination, a path, the distance you are along the path, and so on. Each individual structural metaphor is internally consistent and imposes a consistent structure on the concept it structures. For example the ARGUMENT IS WAR metaphor imposes an internally consistent WAR structure on the concept ARGUMENT" (Lakoff and Johnson 1980: 219).

Although Lakoff and Johnson's theses are relevant to an understanding of the normative underpinnings of much everyday discourse and reasoning, it is clear that such ontological metaphors are different from those uses of language called *fresh* or *creative* metaphors. For one thing, all sense of risk has drained away from the now-banal thought or observation that love is a journey (or any of its derivatives). At least, there is no sense of personal risk in such routine classifications: it might well be argued that there is a society-wide risk (and misperception) in equating time with money, for example.

Relatedly, the terms of such dominant cultural metaphors are themselves so general (or are set at such a general "value" over the period of time and number of contexts of use in which they take hold) — love and journey, war and argument, time and money — that they cannot very easily be shown to be inappropriate. Given the innumerable ideas and uses associable with *love* and *journey*, how can *love is a journey* fail to apply in some degree or respect? But, by the same token, how can such conventionality of utterance succeed in applying interestingly? As Lakoff and Johnson note, the conceptual systems to which our ontological metaphors give rise are less interesting and fallible in what they include than in what they leave out. It is what is neglected or remains hidden in these metaphors of our complex and inconsistent experiences that requires analytic attention. Some of these lacunae are reflected in the way a single concept may be incorporated, in seemingly noncongruent ways, into different overarching metaphors (we metaphorize love as a journey but also sometimes as "stillness," or "arrival," or "a dance").

The view of cognition — even reason itself — as experientialist or embodied is further developed in Lakoff (1987), which focuses on human categorization processes. In particular, reason and categorization should be understood not as objectivist, abstract, and in correspondence with an objectively structured world but as emerging out of "experiential realism," which, for humans, is essentially bodily or embodied: we live in and through our bodies, and that bodily experience, in all its physical and mental aspects, informs the conceptual structures (often imaginative, holistic rather than atomistic, and ecologically efficient) that we have developed.

In a sense, Lakoff summarizes a new solution to the body-mind problem, which has been emerging from a number of cognitivist-oriented disciplines in recent years. But it is clear that his rejection of abstract objectivism is in no way a rejection of collective categorization itself but rather as emphasis on different roots of categorization (experience, in the body) and a different kind of categorization (prototypical etc. rather than absolute). As a shared mental framework, categorization is crucial to the revision. A degree of sharedness of mental categorization is assumed even if, as Rosch came to argue, prototypically judgments and effects are not directly expressive of that mental categorization. In fact, Lakoff presents "basicness in human categorization" very much as if it is analogous, for things in the world, to what Chomsky's universal grammar is claimed to be for natural language syntactic structures: "Basicness in categorization has to do with matters of human psychology: ease of perception, memory, learning, naming, and use. Basicness of level has no objective status external to human beings. It is constant only to the extent that the relevant human capacities are utilized in the same way. Basicness varies when those capacities either are underutilized in a culture or are specially developed to a level of expertise" (Lakoff 1987: 38).

Support for the notion of prototypes as "cognitive reference points" has come from various tests. These include ones in which members of a category are rated as "good" exemplars of a category (both robins and turkeys are in the bird category, but judges find the robin a much better exemplar), or reaction times to "a penguin [robin/turkey/pterodactyl] is a BIRD" are compared, or asymmetry in similarity ratings is uncovered ("A penguin is similar to a robin" is accepted more rapidly than "A robin is similar to a penguin"). Basic-level distinctions are the most useful, Lakoff observes, since they are "characterized by overall shape and motor interaction and are at the most general level at which one can form a mental image" (1987: 49). Relatedly, the basic-level categories are "human-sized": "They depend not on objects themselves, independent of people, but on the way people interact with objects: the way they perceive them, image them, organize information about them, and behave toward them in their bodies" (Lakoff 1987: 51).

Lakoff's book reports revisions as to what counts as "membership of a category" (i.e., what the criteria are); it does not take the radical step of confronting the possibility that "membershipping" (categorization) is contingent, varying from case to case according to criteria that may differ from case to case (as adumbrated in the discussion of Glucksberg and Keysar [1990] above). Thus, Lakoff's and Rosch's experientialism does not allow imaginative sense-making creativity such free rein that categorization itself becomes provisional (i.e., to a point where what counts as a type and what counts as a token cannot be determinately specified and is subject to the local ratification of each situated speech event). In these important respects, then, prototype and experientialist cognitive theory is less thoroughly responsive to the potential of situated meaning than an integrational linguistic perspective requires.

Intimacy without New Meaning: Cooper and Davidson

Why do we resort to metaphors at all? This section focuses particularly on the answers given by Cooper and Davidson to this question and on the extent to which these are congruent with the account of metaphor presented so far in this chapter.

For Donald Davidson, a metaphor has no meaning beyond the literal meaning carried by the utterance. A metaphor has nothing in the way of a distinct cognitive content, over and above the literal meaning, that it is necessary for the addressee to grasp. Whatever is metaphoric in an utterance does not involve the addition of a new meaning for that utterance or the creation of a new meaning by or in the speaker, even though, no doubt, metaphors may be the basis of recipients' illumination, "dream work," insight, or "special notice." Davidson writes:

Where [various theories] think they provide a method for deciphering an encoded content, they actually tell us (or try to tell us) something about the *effects* metaphors have on us. The common error is to fasten on the contents of the thoughts a metaphor provokes and to read these contents into the metaphor itself. . . . If what the metaphor makes us notice were finite in scope and propositional in nature, this would not in itself make trouble; we would simply project the content the metaphor brought to mind onto the metaphor. But in fact there is no limit to what a metaphor calls to our attention, and much of what we are caused to notice is not propositional in character. When we try to say what a metaphor "means," we soon realize there is no end to what we want to mention. If someone draws his finger along a coastline on a map, or mentions the beauty and deftness of a line in a Picasso etching, how many things are drawn to your attention? You might list a great many, but you could not finish since the idea of finishing would have no clear application. (Davidson 1978: 439–40)

Davidson argues here for identifying metaphors not as the containers or carriers of "meanings" but as uses of language where the receiver is invited or even compelled to notice a relation or resemblance (and some of the provocative implications prompted by seeing such a resemblance). Metaphor does not involve retrieving or deducing a meaning or cognitive content beyond the unerasable literal meaning of the sentence encountered.

The passage from Davidson is striking also for local turns of phrase, too, such as the categorization of theories of how metaphors mean as attempts to devise methods for deciphering what is assumed to be "an encoded content." Davidson's rejection of the idea of metaphoric meaning as "encoded content" is most striking here since it may be taken as a precursor of his more wholesale questioning of encoded content in his 1986 essay on malapropisms and the idea of a shared language governed by antecedently learned conventions. That later essay is the subject of further discussion in chapter 7. It is mentioned here to support the suggestion that, while Davidson's essay on metaphor is correct to deny the existence of a specifiable meaning in a metaphoric utterance, beyond the literal meaning of the sentence, it does not go far enough. Nor does it supply, or pretend to supply, a commentary that approximates explanatory adequacy. One pressing question that his discussion provokes is the following: What precisely are these mysterious "illuminations" that we are said to get from metaphor if we are not to call them meanings? What Davidson says is the case in metaphor may be extended to all uses of language: in no uses of language is there a fixed content or meaning to be retrieved. The further step needed, then, is denial of the decontextualized existence of a shared, coded, convention-governed first or literal meaning belonging to any sentence, when the most that can be expected is convergence of disparate prior theories, postulated by different interpreters, as to what a sentence may mean. That further step seems to be taken in his 1986 essay.

One general contrast that can be made concerns the different general effects of fresh metaphors on the one hand and so-called dead metaphors on the other. The latter usually give rise to no striking illumination or intimations and are not rich in fresh implicatures, unlike the former. Indeed, *dead metaphor* is often something of a misnomer — even if, as Cooper (1986: 47) notes, it sustains an ambiguity as to whether the phrase means "an expression which is no longer a metaphor" or "an expression which is metaphorical in only the feeblest way." As Fowler (1965: 359) notes, such well-worn turns of phrases can often have their metaphoricality revived: they are dormant, not dead." Furthermore, as Lakoff and Johnson's work shows, very many such stock metaphors compose networks centered on matrix metaphors that seem to be cultural mainstays (time is money, argument is war, etc.). Davidson's "burned up" just as much as Searle's "Sally is a block of ice" arguably spring from a single matrix notion, that "strong passions are hot." As Lakoff and Johnson emphasize, all such metaphor networks powerfully habituate their users to these received ways of encapsulating the world: they provide "standard" illumination as it were and rehearse the received implicatures. Stock metaphors of this kind are palpably derived from a parent sense that remains as a necessary underpinning in the systematic and wholesale application to the new domain. Given their systematicity, their power to generate further stock-metaphorical utterances of the same kind, and their low illuminative effect, Cooper urges — as urged in this chapter also — that metaphor networks and dormant metaphors be clearly distinguished from creative metaphor. He suggests that only in the latter case does the speaker "produce a metaphor"; in the former cases one is simply speaking metaphorically. He argues that we can speak metaphorically without uttering (actual, distinctly separate, countable, and analyzable) metaphors just as we can behave symbolically (e.g., in dancing) without using or producing discrete/overt symbols (Cooper 1986: 137).

For Cooper, following T. Cohen (1979) and Sperber (1975), the chief effect of uttering metaphors is the enhancement of intimacy:

In what might be called a "full metaphorical exchange" — the utterance of a metaphor, its appropriate interpretation by hearers, and a capable assessment of that interpretation by the speaker — the intimacy between the speaker and hearers presupposed by the original utterance will be reinforced. . . . The very fact of uttering a metaphor instead of something more explicit presupposes — justifiably or not — a further intimacy. The intimacy in question is constituted by that attitude or viewpoint which the speaker must take his audience to share (or appreciate) if his use of the metaphor is "justified." (Cooper 1986: 158–59, 163)

The reason metaphors often defy adequate paraphrase, Cooper goes on to suggest, is that the assumption of a particular attitude or viewpoint is crucial to the metaphor's effectiveness but that attitude cannot figure in a paraphrase of the metaphor, only in remarks that might accompany such a paraphrase. More questionably, Cooper argues that the intimacy thesis is not about practitioners' intentions (whether they intend intimacy is said to be irrelevant) but about "what sustains a practice" (1986: 170). Against this last disclaimer, however, it should be acknowledged that speakers of metaphors are not entirely unaware of the intimacy of interests and background, and expected recognition of attitude, on which the effectiveness of their metaphors depends. The speaker of a metaphor may not have the intention of "cultivating intimacy," but he or she surely wants to obtain, and relies on there obtaining, those factors for which "intimacy" is shorthand (such as ties of background and grasp of the implicitly adopted attitude).

Returning to the issue of stock or dead metaphors, an issue of some interest is the way a number of words — not always affiliated with a Lakoff and Johnson–style network — seem to appear far more often in their dead-metaphoric use than in any literal use: words such as *swine, beast, prickly* (as in *John is very prickly today*), *shot* ("ruined, worn out"), and *cool*. Here, an explanation in terms of polysemy seems appropriate, notwithstanding the weaknesses of appeals to polysemy in most situations. But the added paradox is that, if *swine* is polysemous, the primary sense to be recorded in a dictionary ought to be the dead-metaphoric one ("vile person"), with its formerly established sense now distinctly secondary.

In relation to those of our conventional dead metaphors that refer to animals (*John is a tiger/gorilla/elephant/jackal/rat/dog/swine/pussycat/wolf*), it is interesting to speculate on how these may be affected by the spread of animal liberationist thinking. It has long been recognized that the dead-metaphoric use of *tiger* and *gorilla* invokes associations (e.g., of gorillas, ferocity) that are not characteristic of actual tigers and gorillas. Blackburn (1984: 173, n. 14) remarks: "People may think of these features although they do not believe gorillas to have them. But in a population which comes to realize this, the metaphor will begin to die out, or degenerate into an idiom."

If dead-metaphoric *gorilla* does become mere idiom, it would be of an atypical kind, being a single word in length. By a curious twist, those who might contribute to the gradual atrophy of *gorilla* to the status of dead metaphoricality or obsolescence — objecting that as a genuine metaphor the term is ill suited since gorillas are not in fact rough, fierce, violent, etc. — are likely to be met with the challenge, from those who find no fault with the established usage, that they are being too literal minded. Advocates of the status quo might deplore revisionists' "wrenching" of the language and assert that of course the term *gorilla* does not, in the relevant situations, have anything to do with real gorillas. The argument here is parallel to the defence of the status quo with regard to the use of generic *he* in English: the use of *he* in such contexts is said not to denote exclusively male individuals. Furthermore, a similar chain of usage reactions could in the future apply to the worn-out idiom *kick the bucket* — if it were still used — if speakers examined its literal provenance more closely. By an ironic twist, it was only on reading Sadock's (1979) essay that I learned that the idiom derives from circumstances that once accompanied the slaughtering of horses. If enough speakers were apprised of these facts, a movement against the continued use of this newly inhumane expression might develop. From the perspective of such speakers, an idiom, just as much as an established metaphoric system such as the *is an animal/a gorilla* type, can in Lakoff and Johnson's words "lead to human degradation" (1980: 236).

Conclusion

We resort to creative metaphors, this chapter has argued, for purposes of enhanced expressivity, rapport, and understanding — in short, precisely the reasons for using language generally. Metaphorizing is using language, only more so — in view of what seems to be a lack or loss of expressivity, rapport, or understanding in the established, well-worn, overfamiliar values and language games that constitute established usage. Moving from conventional language to the use of fresh metaphors is like the transition from silence to conversation with a stranger on a train, for example. Here Shelley's remarks are germane: "Language is vitally metaphorical; that is, it marks the before unapprehended relations of things and perpetuates their apprehension, until words, which represent them, become, through time, signs for portions or classes of thought instead of pictures of integral thoughts: and then, if no new poets should arise to create afresh the associations which have been thus disorganized, language will be dead to all the nobler purposes of human intercourse" (Shelley 1967 [1840]: 1073). Interestingly, Shelley's understanding of metaphor did not preclude his own occasional failures of metaphoricality. As Kittay notes (1987: 287–88; the poem is also discussed in Kittay and Lehrer [1981]), his poem "Song to the Men of England" is a palpable failure in those lines where an industrial underclass and overclass are metaphorized as worker bees and exploitative drones, respectively:

> Wherefore, Bees of England, forge
> Many a weapon, chain, and scourge,
> That these stingless drones may spoil
> The forced produce of your toil? (1967 [1819]: 1019)

Bees in chains that they themselves have forged simply is not the kind of "outrageous falsehood" that makes for successful metaphor: what little revised understanding through metaphoricality is achieved is overwhelmed by the stronger sense of incongruity.

Part of the reason that the "bees and drones" fails, in Shelley's discoursal context of plowing, smithing, and so on, may be that the metaphor is not one that, in the context, "goes on." That is to say, it is not one that prompts consideration of further respects in which lords and laborers are drones and worker bees. Just such an emphasis on extendability in several directions is evident in the paradigmatically model-bearing metaphors that Black has discussed. These are of the kind that Aristotle called "proportional"; what seems to distinguish them is that they permit the inference of not just a single analogy or isomorphism but a whole set of them. Successful proportional metaphors (such as the idea that the electron within the atom is not a planet circling a sun but a butterfly in a cathedral) feed the imagination with a rich array of pointers as to how one might go on. It is possible that some fresh metaphors do not have these attributes of proportionality and extendability, but most would seem to. Another aspect of the infelicity of Shelley's metaphor would seem to concern the particular discoursal situation postulated, namely, something approximating a voiced ("Song") direct address to the English working class, the situation of "a man, speaking to men and women." As in the school student's reaction to Mark Antony urging the Romans to lend him their ears, contexts of direct address "overheard" by the reader as third party frequently seem to entail the risk that metaphors will be rejected as predominantly incongruous. One source of resistance to the bees metaphor, then, seems to relate to Shelley's rhetorical or political purposes in using it in the first place, in an effort to reach out, in an exceptionally striking way, to a working-class mass readership.

In this chapter, it has also been proposed that in the explanation of linguistic communication it is useful to invoke notions of distance and risk (compare, in relevance theory, the emphasis on effort). Distance or remoteness is involved in the processing of creative metaphors, where it is often necessary to identify a reference, an allusion, or an inferential conclusion that is remote from the metaphoric term's conventional associations. Situated utterances vary in their immediacy of comprehension or uptake. The activities within which particular utterances are integrated vary in their routineness, noticeableness, and difficulty (e.g., compare the activity of buying a bus ticket and that of explaining to a child why you do or do not believe in an afterlife). This means also that individuals' activities can be loosely ranked on a cline of routineness or backgroundedness (relative to which buying a bus ticket is quite backgrounded and routine, unless one is new to the ticket-buying system). And, if situated utterances vary in immediacy of comprehension or uptake, then that variation in immediacy of uptake must be relatable to interactionally relevant criteria. In the case of the notions of distance and risk, these seem to be as much social normative as mental. The senses of distance and risk (involved in attributing some remote inference as that which the speaker intended to be derived) are constructed by those social normative pressures that establish other understandings and inferences as immediate, likely, very low risk, and so on. The risk is "mental" rather than merely social insofar as we know that these patterns of the habitual and routine, and thus "unpatternedness" of the nonroutine, exist. By the same token, it is normative (rather than a compulsory "given" of mental processing) to say — as discourse analysts and psycholinguists routinely do — that previous utterances in a speech event or text play a specially prominent role in guiding interpretation of presently encountered text. Nothing requires that this be the case, although it routinely is so: the claims for previous utterances as crucial cotext are underwritten by a normatively constructed category just as powerful as that of the sentence, namely, the category *text*.

For integrational linguistics, the general linguistic tendency to conceptualize metaphor in terms of resemblance, comparison, transfer, or some other implied pairing of one expression as really meaning, or interpretable by, another is a theoretical misdirection. The integrationist argues that resemblance and comparison are no more (nor less) intrinsic or defining of fresh metaphors than they are of dead metaphors, idioms, or conventionally used language. Resemblance and interaction may be involved in metaphor production and understanding, but to argue that they are categorically involved there, by contrast with their defining absence from so-called nonmetaphoric utterance, reflects a view of language substantially shaped by a fixed-code thesis, for, as Cooper (1986: 25) notes, the notion of, for example, the transfer of expressions from the sensible to the nonsensible realm "requires a distinction between the physical vehicles of meanings and certain nonphysical entities, the meanings themselves," that is, "terms" and their "senses" (the distinction is deconstructed by Derrida in "White Mythology" [1974]).

Just as the notions of resemblance or transfer are of limited application, so too is that of paraphrase. What does a paraphrase of a metaphoric utterance supply? There seem to be no good grounds for assuming that the act of paraphrasing displays either the superfluousness or the compositional roots of a metaphor — that paraphrasing shows that metaphor is supplementary or a transfer. On such an assumption, the paraphrase reintroduces "that which was supplemented or transferred or resembled." Overvaluing paraphrase is analogous in important ways to the overvaluing of repetition, explored in chapter 6. Overvaluing repetition takes the form of setting aside its logical status as an extrinsic metalinguistic abstraction and casting it instead in an empirical role — vital to orthodox linguistic theory — as an intrinsic and first-order linguistic phenomenon. Paraphrasing is an important language game, but it is not a procedure occupying an autonomous position outside all language games, as if it underwrote or monitored them. The paraphrase of a metaphor is not equivalent to that metaphor. In Davidson's words, a paraphrase is "an attempt to evoke what the metaphor brings to our attention" (1978: 440) and within those limits has its uses; it is a valued tool of literary criticism and the teaching of literature: "The legitimate function of so-called paraphrase is to make the lazy or ignorant reader have a vision like that of the skilled critic. The critic is, so to speak, in benign competition with the metaphor-maker" (Davidson 1978: 440).

Yet another version of the same divide-and-explain strategy, akin to the "source and resemblance," "original and transfer," and "target and paraphrase" bifurcatory accounts noted above, is the privileging of simple predicative metaphors of the kind focused on by Searle and others: the "S is P" strategy. To do this is to reduce the phenomenon to be explained to an overly simple paradigm; too often, in addition, such "S is P" metaphors are not true metaphors at all but dead ones not far removed from new conventional meanings. Nöth (1985) offers interesting commentary on the processes by which metaphors are conventionalized and caused to be dead — on how, by frequent use, a lexicalized metaphor (as in *bottleneck*) may become an opaque one (as in *radical*, lit., "from the root") and finally a dead one (as in *news magazine*: originally *magazine* meant "storehouse"). But the most important phenomenon remains live metaphorically, at the preconventionalized stage.

For one thing, explaining the birth of a live metaphor involves the most direct confrontation of questions of meaning *versus* use and mention *versus* use. According to one traditionalist view of metaphor, established metaphoric meanings such as that *rat* can mean "nasty, vicious person" present no great explanatory problem since the established metaphoric meaning may be treated as one of the several established senses of *rat*. In broad terms, I am sympathetic to this view, although I have qualms about the traditionalist's scheme in which meanings, rather than uses, are or are not to be associated with expressions. Those qualms are justified, it seems, in view of what Cooper (1986: 46–55) sees as a crippling difficulty for the traditional view, the "ontological problem" of indicating how and when meanings get established. His point is that indicating how and when *rat* came to have the meaning "large rodent of the type *Mus*" or "nasty, vicious person" and even of how and when *grass* came to mean "cannabis" etc. is not impossible in principle. Clearly, these became established meanings at some time and in some way or other. In such cases, the idea that subsequent uses of *rat* to denote humans are mention-like uses dependent on an authorized established use has at least some plausibility — although I shall revise it in later chapters.

But, if we turn to a fresh metaphor such as Hofmannstahl's description of our minds as "nothing but dovecots," we at once have the problem of specifying how and when *dovecot* came to have that meaning–when it is quite evident that it never had such a meaning. The task is impossible. Fresh metaphors are precisely the clearest illumination of why thinking in terms of fixed meanings, possessed by words, rather than situated meanings, contingent on interactants' specific purposes, is the wrong way to proceed, for, if the ontological questions were simply about the emergence of particular uses rather than the emergence of fixed and non-situation-specific meanings — that is, if we were always concerned with charting the occurrence of situated meanings, such as how and when *dovecot* came to be used to describe the mind's ceaseless motions — then the fresh-metaphoric instance would be back on a par with other cases. Indeed, it would become the practice whose roots would seem to be the easiest to trace, not the hardest, for we need only refer the inquirer to Hofmannstahl's text. Hofmannstahl seems to have staked an incontestable claim to have produced the first and fathering use of the *mind as dovecot* metaphor.

The likely objection to this supplanting of fixed meanings by variable uses is that appeal to uses is not properly explanatory, that it disingenuously pretends that uses emerge without motivation, when in fact they emerge only because of a prior motivation — namely, that particular words have particular meanings. But, if that were really true, we would never have truly innovative usage (usage not already established) at all or any sense of the cognitive and cultural possibilities that we can retrospectively label *fresh metaphor*.

3

Intentionality and Coming into Language

Linguistic Proficiency: Rapid, Effortless, and Unconscious or Slow, Effortful, and Learned?

Generative linguists' most basic assumptions about the psychobiological basis of language are succinctly reflected in the following introductory observation from Lightfoot: "[Children] come to be able to speak and understand speech effortlessly, instantaneously and subconsciously" (1982: x). Compare the scarcely more qualified claims of Fromkin and Rodman, in probably the most widely used introduction to linguistics: "Five-year-old children are almost as proficient at speaking and understanding as are their parents.... In a parallel fashion [to their effortless mastery of language], a child can walk without understanding or being able to explain the principles of balance and support" (1993: 4). Commenting on Lightfoot's assertion, Love notes that, even allowing for the idealization that brackets off all "noise in the channel," one must in addition presume that it is not intended to address all the everyday situations where there is a knowledge gap between speaker and addressee. The doctrine of effortless instantaneous understanding so obviously "fails to apply to all those numerous communicational exchanges where, roughly speaking, the speaker tells the hearer something he does not already know" (Love 1990a: 14) that, presumably, a further distinction must be being assumed. Something similar evidently underlies Fromkin and Rodman's claim: although they have appeared to say that understanding is as unconscious and automatic as the ability to walk and that five-year-olds almost match their parents at it, they don't really intend us to draw the conclusion that infants could flood the professions any day now, but for our ageist restrictive practices.

The yet-to-be-declared further distinction is between the language in use and the language as such (*langue*, competence). The theory of language as a competence, a finite, determinate, and user-autonomous rule-driven system frankly sets aside all questions of variation and difference as so much interference potentially diverting the theoretical linguist's attention from the sharp lines of the underlying framework. But, once one conceptualizes language in the dichotomous terms of competence and performance or system and application, then the further task of accounting for how users effect the connection between the two, for example, how they harness competence to specific instances of production or comprehension, has to be addressed. One widely endorsed proposal designed to provide the necessary interface between fixed-code competence and the multiple diversities of actual language use has been the idea of mutual knowledge and degrees of shared background, which are discussed in chapter 5. Related proposals aimed at accomplishing parts of the same repetitive task (a task created, integrationists argue, by the parent theory's restrictive view of language) include speech-act theory and indirect speech acts (see the discussion later in this and in the following chapter), Labov's variable rules (Labov 1972), and even Hymes's model of communicative competence (on problems with which, see Harris [1990b]).

All such proposals reflect the compelling promise of prevailing assumptions about language. But, to begin with, it must be noted that the latter term, *language*, is also usually understood in a restricted sense, as meaning "a particular institutionalized language, for example, Spanish." Language in this sense is tacitly understood as a fixed-code pairing of graphic or phonic images and meanings, autonomous rather than dependent on other cognitive faculties, and as the means of telementational communication (the "faxing" of thoughts), mastered by individuals genetically endowed with a mental device that comes to generate, at a remarkably early age and with limited experiential input, a rich range of sentences conforming to the grammar of that ambient language. To understand why, for all their compelling promise, those assumptions are mistaken (and why, concomitantly, proposals that "bridge" from those assumptions about the language as system to the language as such are fragile), we must return to the most basic questions about what is involved in using language and about how language could conceivably come into existence. To speculate about the origins of language is not idle fiction making but a necessary scientific hypothesis building, appealing to imagination and reason. And whether we theorize about the beginnings of language in the species or in the individual makes for a difference in degree, not kind. Misunderstandings about one, in orthodox linguistics, match misunderstandings about the other, and a clearer sense of what is centrally involved in both will lead to a clearer sense of what is invariably central to language: "It is quite illusory to believe that where language is concerned the problem of origins is any different from the problem of permanent conditions" (Saussure 1983 [1916]: 240).

Condillac, Tree Felling, and Intentionality

Fundamental to the use of language in interaction is intentionality. Speculating on the likely origins of languages is a tendentious and unfashionable pastime, but if one considers the various putative sources of the emergence of a symbolic sound system — cries denoting warnings and threats, an inventory of grunts to accompany and help coordinate certain physical tasks, or to express emotional affiliation, or to assist in the hunting of animals for meat, or to describe and express various aspects of the environment — the auditory or visual signals involved all seem united in being simple means for the expression or display of distinct intended meanings. For instance, if the grunts of a group of early humans working to fell a tree trunk and drag it close to the settlement are not the random noises provoked by strenuous effort but are indeed a simple language with different sounds associated with different meanings, then it is axiomatic that the speakers are aware of, and oriented to, the associating of different meanings with different grunts (even if they are aware only at an unconscious level). Observation of the cognitive or behavioral development of early humans is not possible today, but, setting aside important differences, situations that parallel the one outlined above are plentiful. Consider, for example, the vocal signs produced by a group of one-year-old children working together on some task in a sandbox, their unconscious use of nonrandom noises accompanying distinct stages or evaluations of the project.

It is a crucial starting-point to recognize that there are no guarantees, in either the tree-felling or the sandbox scenario, that the same sounds will be associated with the same meanings by every participant. The language will have arisen out of no such blueprint of certainties. It will have started with a spirit, not a form or set of forms: a spirit among these primitive grunting laborers (if we focus on the former example) of trust or belief that another's patterns of grunts, observed as a constituent part of certain activities or states, are not just a random accompaniment but are reflective of the different purposes they do so accompany, in some patterned way, vaguely understood (on which, see the further discussion below). If the different grunts are not treated as part of the expression of distinct purposes, distinct intended activities, then they are not language.

The picture of coming into language sketched above and to be enlarged on below contrasts in important ways with accounts of the birth of language, often deeply if indirectly influential on present-day lay and linguistic assumptions about language acquisition and development, elaborated in earlier centuries. One of the most widely considered of those accounts is that offered by the Abbé de Condillac, the eighteenth-century rationalist philosopher whose reflections on language began almost as a respectful appendix to Locke's *Essay Concerning Human Understanding*. Over the following decades, Condillac's views developed into a picture rather at odds with Locke's conventionalism and his skepticism about the "double conformity" of words to ideas and ideas to things.

For Condillac, in their natural state, primitive people were endowed with faculties of will and reflection, but in rather restricted senses of those terms: the will instinctively motivated humans to meet their basic wants (*will*, in Condillac's writings, does not denote free will but instinctive drive); and reflection enabled them to compare and associate sensations (raw perceptions). But, in the primitive condition, this process of reflection was not voluntary or active but passive and spontaneous. As Taylor (1989: 290) puts it, Condillac's primitive human is burdened by "an original disjunction" of his two primary faculties, so that reflection lacks willed direction and the will lacks reflective control. Condillac's notion of the original will is significantly less ample than Locke's: for Locke, the exercise of free will would develop with the growth of understanding through experience.

To begin with, Condillac distinguishes three types of signs: accidental signs (which are rather like Proustian associations); natural signs (allegedly physiological universals for, e.g., expressing pain or joy); and institutional (or artificial) signs (those voluntarily adopted and used by humans). Only the last of these are particularly significant for cognitive growth or knowledge, for it is through institutional signs that humans are said to come to exploit the as-yet-deficient faculties of will and reflection with which they are originally endowed. Of the previous two types of signs, it may be worth pointing out here that since these signs represent entirely spontaneous and involuntary behavior, primitive humans do not use these signs at all (the signs are not controlled instruments); rather, the signs use the humans. Like Locke before him, Condillac also made a sharp distinction between two kinds of association of sensations (or "ideas," as he termed them): one type was passive and involuntary mental connections; the other was voluntary mental reflection, aided by artificial signs. Taylor notes that, for Condillac, such a set of artificial signs — language — is an institution quite independent of human will and understanding, even though voluntarism is involved in the creation and use of such signs: the sign itself is not an act of will, for the will operates instinctively and so has no power to control signification voluntarily. In the broader terms of this chapter, Condillac champions language as independent of the will, quite as autonomous as Saussure's *langue*, intrinsically removed from socially embedded intentions.

The great conundrum that Condillac failed to solve, and that is surely insoluble within the set of conditions that he specified as those of primitive humanity, is how the individual or the group could ever create institutional signs or artificial language. Charles Taylor (1985) notes that, in his *On the Origin of Language* (1772), Herder was one of the first to object to Condillac's account, in the *Essai sur l'origine des connaissances humaines*, on the grounds that it presupposed just what needs explaining: "The problem is that Condillac presupposes that his children already understand what it is for a word to stand for something, what it is therefore to talk about something with a word. But *that* is just the mysterious thing" (Taylor 1985: 227). The *Essai* repeatedly leaps beyond this cognitive lacuna, when, for example, it argues that, once in possession of a few artificial signs, the primitive individual can use these at will (if we bear in mind that their use is distinguished by voluntarism) to order and review past sensations, acts of will, natural signs, and so on and can do so in the orderly linear fashion that institutional language entails. But the really difficult terrain has been overcome by the time the language maker is in possession of even a rudimentary system of stable artificial signs: the lofty pinnacles of organized memory, ordered thought, and detailed linguistic categorization of the world are not far over the horizon. The problem stage lies earlier: how can the first faltering steps possibly be made by Condillac's passive, driven, sensation-storing hominid? Lacking free will or powers of selective attention, there seems to be no way that he could ever make the cognitive leap from natural cries of pain to, for example, controlled cries of warning, from having (and sensing?) signs using him to having himself use signs. For this picture to be possible requires — far beyond "bootstrapping" — something akin to miracle. The account displays its own contradictions stylistically, in the way the individuals depicted are treated at one moment as animals subject to the power of brute nature and the next moment as eighteenth-century gentlemen intellectuals, able to recall signs at pleasure (*Essai*, 2.1.1.3):

> And yet the same circumstances could not be frequently repeated, but they [early humans] must have accustomed themselves at length to connect with the cries of the passions and with the different motions of the body, those perceptions which were expressed in so sensible a manner. The more they grew familiar with those signs, the more they were in a capacity of reviving them at pleasure. Their memory began to acquire some sort of habit, they were able to command their imagination as they pleased, and insensibly they learned to do by reflection what they had hitherto done merely by instinct. (Condillac 1971 [1756]: 173)

In short, Condillac's narrative of language phylogenesis simply fails at the level of logical plausibility. Yet narrative is deeply involved in the origins of language, both in the motivation of its emergence and in our present attempts to construct plausible metalinguistic accounts.

Condillac's discussions of language center around two crucial theses (Harris and Taylor 1989): the emergence of artificial signs (language) by means of which humans can control and enlarge their linguistic activity and the dependence of the growth of the human mind, of intellectual progress, on the emergence of a linearly structured language as an essential tool of mental self-analysis. Of particular interest are his thoughts on the former of these theses, which is at once the more promising and the more important of the two.

In Condillac's view, certain axiomatic factors precede and underpin the emergence of artificial signs and the growth of human knowledge; they are that humans are social, rational, and attuned to sense experience. These are the endowments or preconditions that were harnessed in an unprecedented way, according to Condillac, in the emergence of language: "Language is man's greatest and most decisive artificial creation, and it is in turn the foundation of human knowledge" (Aarsleff 1980: 286). Concerning the nature of those artificial signs, however, it is of the greatest significance, as Harris and Taylor emphasize, that Condillac's apparent assumption of their arbitrariness in the *Essai* is considerably altered by the time of later writings such as the *Logique* and the *Grammaire*. For the later Condillac, it is crucial that such signs are not arbitrary but are related naturally, no matter how distantly or by what obscure intervening processes of analogy, to the real phenomena in the world that they represent (*Grammaire*, chap. 2): "It is a mistake to think that in the first creation of languages men could choose indifferently and arbitrarily which words were to be the signs of which ideas. If this had been the case, how could they have understood one another?" (Condillac, 1970 [1782]: 365–66, trans. Taylor).

In this important respect, then, Condillac came to side with the naturalists rather than the conventionalists in the great eighteenth-century debate over language phylogenesis. At the level of both signs and grammatical structures, any seeming arbitrariness is an aberrant growth away from the natural language of cries and gestures that was their (natural) origin. Now, artificial signs are reconnected (across the cognitive gulf of intentionality) to natural signs: "For those signs [in instituted languages] to have been understood when they were first invented, they must have been analogous to other signs already in existence, which leads to the conclusion that all signs, in all languages, must be able to be linked by a chain of natural analogies to the original natural gestural and vocal signs" (Harris and Taylor 1988: 131). In effect, the later Condillac deconstructs the sharp categorization into natural and artificial signs on which his earlier account of the origin of language had rested, for, with arbitrariness as an essential feature of neither natural nor artificial signs or languages, an essential difference between these kinds of signs has been withdrawn. Now all that distinguishes the artificial sign is the voluntariness with which it is used. Artificial (linguistic) signs are essentially voluntary rather than reflex; other, nonlinguistic signs are by contrast entirely involuntary.

However, even this claimed distinction of voluntariness has problematic aspects if the scope for volition and intentionality in the use of natural signs is reconsidered. If it is granted that cries of pain when one is bitten, or hit by a rock, are spontaneous, directly tied to that occasion of pain, and of limited control, how does the transition take place that permits the development of more complex signifying cries? At the same time, although cries of pain appear at first glance to be a reflex reaction to an experienced stimulus, even such "natural" cries can rapidly develop artificial aspects. Thus, the person who cries out in pain may often *intend* to do so, may choose to do so rather than suffer in silence, believing, for example, that he will as a result garner greater sympathy from those who can hear the cries; or he may believe that submitting oneself to a bout of unrestrained moaning may be cathartic and therapeutic.

Condillac's fundamental distinction between involuntary and voluntary actions, as instanced in natural and artificial signs, respectively, is suspect as soon as one considers the ways in which volition or intention can shape the supposedly natural and physiologically determined. The cries of a newborn baby are a good candidate for the category of wholly natural, physiologically determined cries. But it is clear that, within a few months of birth, these natural noises begin to be designed to win attention and sympathy by their increasingly alert and attentive source. Almost from the moment that an action is sufficiently distinct to be singled out at all, from the moment that a natural sign has become sufficiently distinct as to be noticed as any kind of sign, the possibility of some voluntary or controlled dimension in its production arises. The core of the paradox is that, while a "natural cry/artificial sign" distinction seems self-evident to us, the distinction is one that can be made only by those used to manipulating artificial signs: it is a classification achieved by artificial sign users who, contemplating certain kinds of sign-like behavior (cries, laughter, etc.), relegate those signs from the linguistic class to the "natural" class on the grounds that voluntariness and control seem absent. In short, the concept of artificial signs is a necessary precursor to the creation of natural signs (singly and as a class). Yet Condillac's picture stipulates that natural signs preexist artificial ones and make them possible.

Neither arbitrariness (since both natural and artificial signs are arguably "motivated") nor voluntariness (intentional control) will serve to draw a firm line between supposedly natural and artificial signs, and one is prompted to reconsider the issues involved from first principles. One of Condillac's first assumptions, for example, is that first there are signs, which may then be divided into natural signs and artificial ones. But, when the stage that something is functioning as a sign and is known to be functioning as a sign has been reached, then language has already emerged. The crucial stage is logically earlier, when some integral part of the ongoing activity is picked out and assigned a more than everyday expressive, representative, or instrumental value and is treated by an individual (and, potentially, by the group) as "worth remembering."

Clearly, this is rather a vague principle, given that everything may, in a sense, be worth remembering, and given also that nothing, in another sense, is necessarily totally forgotten. But the human brain is no less finite than other human resources, and an entirely rational tendency of humans is to represent to ourselves only the most pressing and salient aspects and elements of past experience and predicted future experience, while purposely removing from consideration and attention all sorts of experienced details that are treated as trivial, ephemeral, and literally insignificant. When, over a series of lessons, I learn ways to express greetings in German, all kinds of details of those lessons, the settings, the actual participants, will be neglected in favor of a kind of foregrounded résumé of what I take to be the salient situational, gestural, and verbal elements. But, as noted above, treating some part (e.g., some sounds or gestures) of the ongoing activity as particularly worth remembering is only half the story; the other half is that the part singled out is also judged to have a particular importance (expressive, representative, or instrumental) in performing the larger activity. The cognitive process involved here, against a backdrop of memory and rationality, is essentially metonymic—seeing a whole as separable into parts, and having the confidence to pick out a particular part of the activity (again, e.g., a sound) as signifying the whole. (Here it may be important to stress that this ability to see a whole "as separable into parts" is rather different from any postulated ability to see "that a whole comprises separate parts"; in the former case the parts "belong" to the perceiver, while in the latter case they belong to the composite entity.) The signifying sound or gesture is not strictly expressive of or representative of the whole: those are ways of putting the matter that too much suggest a "stands for" relation, as if signs "stood for" the referents and actions in a substitutionary manner. (Similarly in routine metonymy today, it is less the case that a metonym truly represents the whole than that, in context, the metonym evokes the whole.)

Like Locke's doubt about linguistic intersubjectivity, Condillac's grappling with the notion of arbitrariness provides a thought-provoking contrast between an eighteenth-century tempering of speculation with doubt, on the one hand, and a twentieth-century mentalist overriding of doubts, on the other. Discussions of arbitrariness in modern linguistics often founder in confusion. Whatever contemporary commentators might mean by *linguistic arbitrariness* needs to be set beside the clarity of that section of the *Cratylus* in which it is emphasized that a word cannot possibly be a copy of the thing it represents (outside of Laputian absurdities as in *Gulliver's Travels*, where the words-as-copies assumption is taken seriously and the men of that country accordingly opt to avoid words and their attendant misunderstandings altogether, instead carrying with them accumulations of all the things that their words would be copies of). If the simple point in the *Cratylus* is correct, talk of the nonidentity of the forms *pig*, *schwein*, and *cochon* as demonstrating the arbitrariness of the sign tells us nothing—or at least nothing more than is demonstrated by pointing out that the forms *pig*, *pig*, and *pig* are not a natural expression of either the concept or the animal itself.

Let us imagine a group of men, from a small settlement of hunter-gatherers, working together to fell a tree and bring the trunk back to the settlement for

107 Intentionality

firewood. The members of this group may not be social equals. Possibly one individual will be older and of greater authority and expertise than the others. Now, felling and dragging trees is something these men are good at. With their simple stone axes, wooden crowbars, and brushwood carrying devices, they can almost do the job blindfold. They all know, pretty clearly, that there is a set and preferred sequence to the maneuvers that need to be performed for the most efficient completion of the task.

It is in just such circumstances that the older man, the man of authority, may have come to accompany certain maneuvers with certain noises, almost as spontaneously as certain of those maneuvers (e.g., lifting the felled trunk) might come to be accompanied with other particular physical actions (e.g., bracing of the feet and leg muscles). Over time and many occasions of tree felling, the association of noises and maneuvers may become quite established and noticeable. Indeed, these associations *must* become noticeable for language to arise. A certain kind of noise comes habitually to accompany the completion of the trunk-chopping phase, a different kind of noise habitually accompanies the tree's fall, a third kind of noise "goes with" the lifting of the felled trunk, and so on. The grunt that accompanies the actual toppling of a tree is never quite the same as on any other occasion of tree toppling, just as no two trees topple in quite the same way; but the rough matching of a type of grunt and an aspect of the tree-felling activity begins to develop, as an extension of the noticed near sameness, across a number of occasions, of the other phases of the tree-felling exercise.

A few words are in order concerning the isolation and segmentation of the tree-felling and vocal noises adopted here. The segmentation of the flow of grunts — if we want to think of it as a segmentation — largely depends on how the group has come to segment its tree-felling activity. That segmentation, in the example, may appear naturally given; but we should not generalize this or overstate it: it is hardly a "natural given" that men will chop down trees in the first place. Nevertheless, some degree of reflexive self-consciousness must obtain among these primitive people as a precondition for mentally registering that felling a tree is not just an indistinguishable part of the stream of "life going on" but is — and can be remembered as — a particular current or wave in the stream, a particular routine. Here begin genres, language games, and convention-shaped activities. Once it is thought of as a particular routine or task, physical or rational considerations may well assist in the development of a sense of that routine as an ordered sequence. Thus, you won't attempt to carry the tree away before you have felled it (and the tree won't fall unless you chop away at its trunk), and awareness of this fosters a sense of "felling, then carrying" as the appropriate sequence; and you are unlikely to take the trouble to lop off the higher branches until the tree has been felled, so that felling precedes lopping, as a fitting order. Further, since side branches interfere with carrying the trunks, a set three-stage sequence may emerge: felling, lopping, carrying. What is emerging here, or rather what is reemerging here in the linguistic representation, is an important narrative dimension, which we could also call a grammar for the activity of tree felling. The basic grammatical pattern in this imagined community is that tree felling (TF) comprises felling, (F) then lopping (L) then carrying (C), or

$$TF \rightarrow F + L + C.$$

An equally valid grammar, in some other community with perhaps a different kind of tree, would be

$$TF \rightarrow F + C + L.$$

The activity itself, of felling a tree and bringing it back to the camp, constitutes a narrative. Here, via simple signs (perhaps simply three noises, in sequence, expressing tree felling, branch lopping, and trunk carrying) that narrative is recast in a linguistic medium. And, if this example is representative, a narrative dimension may be taken as common in the earliest linguistic activity of human beings: it may be said to give rise to, and also be reflective of, the linearity that is defining of language.

The segmented order of (linguistic and nonlinguistic) activities described here, an order relative to what participants see as reasonable in the situation, has been seriously neglected in linguistics, although it was partially reinstated by early work in ethnomethodology by Garfinkel. Situated reasonableness of order is evident at numerous levels, including the immediately textual. This is reflected in the jarring effect of attempting even a seemingly minor rearrangement of coordinate phrases in a famous declaration:

I pledge my allegiance to the Republic of the United States of America, and to the flag that stands for it. . . .

This can be compared with the "naturalness" of the actual sequence:

I pledge allegiance to the flag of the United States of America, and to the Republic for which it stands. . . .

Yet, to return to the tree fellers, it is not the case that the growing reflective impression of a patterned integration of particular stages of tree felling and particular kinds of grunts really makes much difference, at first: with or without the grunts, the trees would get felled. But noticeability has its own consequences. It may be that, over time, a certain ritual value is attached to the performance of the grunts: they become part of "the way to fell trees." But it is unlikely that the idea will soon emerge of these grunts having any particular relevance outside the specificities of this particular activity; they may remain, for an indeterminate length of time, a practice allied to the business of actual tree felling, not even extrapolated so as to refer to past or future tree fellings. The "displacement" often thought defining of human language could not have been present in its origins; rather, the principle of cotemporality (Harris 1981a), the spatiotemporal integration of speech and other behavior, would have been particularly evident. Cotemporality is, however, not the converse of displacement but a more foundational principle that enables the latter to arise.

As noted above, initially the gruntings that accompanied the tree felling would have been somewhat irrelevant to the task of moving the trees. One can well imagine a rudimentary gestural language preceding the emergence of such vocal language, so that at first the vocal language elements might have constituted "the *'paralanguage,'* much in the way that at present, manual gestures are the paralanguage, and are dispensable under some conditions" (Hewes 1984: 53). But over time irrelevant grunts would become established as relevant signs, probably with ritual significance first, and long before acquiring the force of counting as, for instance, an instruction from the senior man that the other men perform a particular task. Malinowski's distinction between what he calls the "pragmatic" and the "magical" functions of language fits these assumptions exactly. The magical function is that in which language is used for the purposes of, in Malinowski's famous phrase, "phatic communion," where "ties of union are created by a mere exchange of words." In phatic communion, words "fulfill a social function and that is their principal aim, but they are neither the result of intellectual reflection, nor do they necessarily arouse reflection in the listener" (Malinowski 1935: 315).

In the scenario sketched above, it is suggested that language emerges first with a magical — or at least ritual — function and that this is gradually transformed into a pragmatic one. In fact, a more fundamental division in kinds of language, for Malinowski (1923: 312ff.), is one between language as a mode of action (comprising three major function types: speech in action, free narrative, and phatic communion) and language as a means of thinking (science, poetry, literature). In broad terms, the former would seem to long predate the latter in most cultures, and there is a strong sense of a speech versus writing opposition in Malinowski's chosen examples. Be that as it may, it seems incontestable that, ontogenetically and phylogenetically, language as a mode of action begins, even if it does not reach full development, before language as a means of thinking does: the latter is a more complex, reflexive, situation-detached, and objectifying faculty. The tree-felling language scenario exemplifies, I suggest, language as a mode of action; and, within that mode, the use of language is phatic first (ritual) before it becomes speech in action (pragmatic).

This view is clearly at odds, to some extent, with Malinowski's claim that phatic communion is "deprived of any context of situation" (1935: 313) — at least insofar as the term *deprived* might imply some kind of removal of context. It seems nearer the mark to suggest that phatic communion fits or can fit any context of situation — for the point of the tree-felling example is that, gradually, the phatic utterances are taken as fitting that logging context rather specifically, so that what was once phatic becomes now pragmatic. By contrast, Malinowski views the three types evinced by language as a mode of action as forming a hierarchy, from the simplest and most immediate (speech in action) through free narrative to the more complex and disengaged (phatic communion). For him, the typical unit of phatic communion seems to be the casual conversational sentence, whereas here I have suggested that some of the simplest cries, taken as expressive, can also be seen as phatic or even protophatic. The difficulties encountered here in adopting Malinowski's arguments wholesale may have their sources in what Wolf (1989) interestingly argues are two conflicting conceptions of context — and its relation to word meanings — to be found in Malinowski's work: context as situationally variable and context as culturally categorized and fixed.

Two further points need to be stressed about the hypothetical tree-felling scenario. The first concerns intentionality: the fact that it is only over time that the grunts come to signify and come to have a speaker's intentions should in no way suggest that these men were ever without intentions. On the contrary, the business of felling a tree for firewood is shot through with intentions, whether expressed in a language or not. It is action for a purpose and, in the scenario depicted, collaborative action for a purpose. What is absent at first and emerges with language is the promotion of particular vocal noises as empowered to testify to those intentions. Gradually, they may come to be thought of as being (or as to be included as part of) the performance of an action, to borrow Austin's description of a performative utterance (1962: 60).

111   Intentionality

The coming into intentionality of the patterns of grunts constitutes also their coming into language.

The second point concerns just how problematic and protracted the coming into language of the patterns of grunts might be: it might take generations. And, over that span of time, as the randomness of gruntings gradually settles into perceived patternings, and as their role as ritual accompaniment is then enlarged so that they can come to operate as seemingly freestanding directives, there can be no recourse to metalinguistic methods of clarification. The qualification of *freestanding* by *seemingly* is important: the appearance of autonomy and isolatability of the verbal material of an interaction is an illusion, fostered by our intensely reflexive examinations of our language and our ways of talking about language.

Some sense of the uncertainties that attend coming into language is highlighted if we imagine the elder of the tribe taking out some trainees on a wood-gathering mission. When, in what for him are the appropriate circumstances, he issues the grunt that accompanies raising the felled log to shoulder height and half the newcomers lift it to waist height only and are puzzled by the senior man's apparent displeasure, there will be no easy correction of the misunderstanding. The older man cannot shout — even if he wanted to — "Not like that, you idiots"; the youngsters cannot ask, "Do you want it this high or that high?" But then, in the circumstances, the older man may well not have such a rigidly stipulative and prescriptive attitude as to correctness in the matching of linguistic and nonlinguistic actions. What would likely happen would be a return to the nondisplaced mode, with grunts as nonessential cotemporal accompaniment of the tasks they had come, for the older men, to be a signifying part of.

A related point that this picture should serve to emphasize is that, even in the collaborative world of tree felling, every individual is to a considerable extent on his own when it comes to developing a pattern of grunt signs or perceiving a pattern of grunt signs. The elder who comes to use the grunts as directives cannot return to the campfire in the evening, turn to his friends, and say, "Hey, have you noticed how I always go 'Earnnh' as the boys lift the trunk to shoulder height?" The trainee tree feller cannot turn to his peers and ask, "Hey, does 'Earnnh' mean lift the trunk to your left shoulder or your right, or doesn't it matter?" One danger in today's linguistic theorizing lies in an uncritical assumption of what such metalinguistic checking questions can do — in particular the mistaken assumption that such questions are an accurate and unproblematic means of confirming the true nature, the objective meaning, of utterances and intentions. Instead, all those involved in the emerging language system depicted have no other resources than their own personal memories of their world to fall back on as they individually come to postulate a nonaccidental, ultimately intended pattern. The essential enabling condition for the perception of such patterning, and the postulation of such intentionality, is the spirit of "orientedness to other": a faith that, because of and in spite of the impossibility of certain knowledge of another's thoughts and feelings, each community member is foundationally concerned to surmount that barrier and to assert and act out a sharedness that can never be proved. This seems to be what lies behind some thought-provoking remarks about faith in communication voiced by Halliday some years ago: "We may not in fact understand each other but we have to keep up the pretence, since it is a faith in communication, rather perhaps than communication itself, that marks our claim to social interaction" (Halliday 1967: 14).

Nevertheless, this orientedness to other may not necessarily take the form of a utopian cooperative mutual nurturing of interactants' needs. It might instead operate within a ruthlessly authoritarian social system — feudalism and the police state are, in their use of surveillance and regulation, intensely oriented to other. But police statism, and any kind of panoptical control such as that depicted by Bentham and analyzed by Foucault, is more an exploitation than an application of other orientedness. In such conditions, orientedness to other (to the center, the metropolis, the authority) is compelled and enforced to an unusual degree, and all significant traces of orientedness to self must be expunged or suffer penalty. A police state or totalitarian community, in general, is one in which the individual member is without power directly or indirectly to change or contest the terms and conditions under which he or she lives. As one part of this, the linguistic part, language totalitarianism obtains where the individual is without power to change or contest the linguistic terms and conditions under which he or she lives.

But, without some such other orientedness, some intuitive, more-than-rational, creative trust that others are as concerned as we are to resist and overcome the separateness from others that physical and mental separateness — individuality — entails, it is hard to see how innovative language development could ever get started. Our earliest linguistic ancestors, like ourselves, must have been propelled into language practice by the same paradoxes that underlie Locke's disquiet about the possibility of true intersubjectivity.

A further requirement for coming into language must be that there is, over time, a nearly appalling repetitiveness in human activity, a sameness over and over again of tree felling, or tree felling and grunting, such that other-attentive, remembering individuals begin to perceive those samenesses and actively use them as a sense-making resource (cf. Tannen [1987a] and the papers in a special issue of *Text* on repetition [Johnstone 1987]). But is this the same thing as what Derrida calls *iterability*? I will argue in a later section of this chapter, and in chapter 6, that it is not.

Mother-Child Interaction; Language Emergence as Metonymic

Alongside the "work-related" account of linguistic innovation sketched above, we should set a more domestic but equally representative version of the same gradual process: for example, language development in the interaction between a mother and baby; that is, a scenario in which nurturing, rather than directed work, is the primary motivation. Both scenarios are representative of what coming into language entails, and both, ultimately, are kinds of other-attentive caregiving.

Again, Malinowski's reflections are germane. Szymura summarizes Malinowski's views on practical meaning ("the pragmatic use of speech within the context of action," to be distinguished from phatic, magical, and narrative meaning) thus:

The author of *Coral Gardens* emphasized that the operational nature of language is connected with the fact that the uses of utterances are learned during collaborative actions, when we strive to react properly to verbal signs. They cannot be learned otherwise than by observing the effects to which they lead, or through active participation in activities aimed at these effects.

Taking care not to draw hasty conclusions as to the phylogenesis of speech, Malinowski nevertheless devoted some space to reflections on its ontogenesis. He pointed out that words in the language of a child function originally only as tools. More or less articulate sounds produced by the infant are always the natural expression of physiological states and needs connected with these states. Adults, employing the method of trial and error, establish the relation between a particular sound and a particular need. Such a sound becomes a sign for the parents who have learnt to interpret it. The skill of interpreting enables them to satisfy the child's corresponding needs. The child, in turn, perceiving the efficacy of sound, begins to use it purposefully as a tool; by this means — with the help of the adults — he brings about desired changes in his environment. In the course of using the tool its form, worked at by both the child and the adults, becomes perfected. Invariably the meaning of the form has to do with bringing about a desired effect, rather than expressing thoughts. (Szymura 1988: 122)

I offer the following seven propositions as ones that can and should be taken as givens or resources, and as aids to an incremental communicational sophistication, in the first stages of mother-child linguistic interaction, both today and in the earliest human eras:

1. In the first months of life, there is typically a near-total dependence of the baby on the mother.
2. There is a natural bond between mother and child.
3. Both mother and child are endowed with natural human other orientedness, which in part takes the form of a quite fundamental interest in getting a reaction or response from one's environment.
4. Babies cry, in some cases a great deal, sometimes owing to apparent natural causes (hunger, cold, tiredness), but very often absent such evident causes. Even the "natural" cries of a baby tend to be quite patterned and repetitive (understood as perceived similarity—not identity—between multiple instances of crying), and this perceived patternedness suggests that, although natural, the cries are neither random nor arbitrary. As a result, the cries tend to prompt a patterned set of responding sounds, gestures, and actions from the mother; in turn again, the mother's patternings serve to encourage patternedness in the baby's behavior. The other orientedness noted under proposition 3 above will tend to encourage a mother's "repeating" of sounds or gestures (in a spirit of emphasis, confirmation, and recycling). As Aitchison (1987b: 135) remarks: "At first, children may learn off whole chunks of sound, which are simply ritual accompaniments to particular actons." But, at first, children familiarizing themselves with the sound chunks that are part of particular activities will possibly not distinguish between nonvocal actions and vocal accompaniments.

It should be emphasized that repetition as such, on the part of mother or child, is not a prerequisite for the success of the developments sketched above. In particular, there is no assumption that the baby begins life repeating noises and knowing that he or she is repeating noises. What is assumed instead is that humans are, at a profound level, oriented toward pattern and perceived repetition. This predisposition may be akin to the power of analogy, and analogizing, singled out by Condillac (with the difference of emphasis that here the analogizing must be creatively performed by the individual). I take orientedness to pattern to be a foundational human mental attribute, part of our genetic resources for rationality and sense making, and of general relevance rather than specific to language learning.

5. No two babies cry, laugh, feed, or gesture identically; this assists the differen-

tiation of particular babies' patterns of behavior (of which cries and gestures will be a part).

6. Comparatively coarse-grain, aggregative signaling between mother and child may be what each is first aware of. For example, a multifeatured performance by the child conveys hunger, or pain, or unhappiness, or tiredness; an equally "gross" or holistic performance from the mother is intended to reassure, to accompany feeding, to make the child happy, or to soothe him or her to sleep.

7. A development that is in a sense metonymic proceeds from the stage described in proposition 6: the established sense of trust of each other and the rational human interest in economy of effort may lead to a metonymizing of the multidimensional performances of demands for goods and services or supplyings of them. That is to say, the performance evolves into an abbreviated and focused version: for example, the mother gradually and unconsciously trains her growing child to be reassured that food is on its way, not by supplying the full panoply of gestures, noises, patting, etc. (in whatever way "fullness" might be defined), but by just vocal noises — and, over time, relatively simple noises at that. The vocal noise to which "offering feeding reassurance" is reduced is noticeably different from the simplified vocal noise expressing "giving love and affection." Such distinct noises, associatable and performative of distinct situated actions, could be called *behavioremes*. The time scale involved in coming to these metonymic simplifications of "natural" behavioremes may span very many generations. In a sense, the process is still going on and is an essential dynamic of language change (see Hopper [1987b] on emergent grammar). Finally, it is reasonable to assume that the simplification of each behavioreme facilitates, and is in part prompted by, a concomitant multiplication of the number of distinct behavioremes.

Although both scenarios sketched above are hypothetical, they seem more realistic and plausible than Condillac's. Part of the problem with Condillac's account of humanity's progression from natural signs (such as cries of pain) to artificial or institutionalized signs (language) is that he brings the mind into the account, as if it were a distinct and distinctly conceptualized faculty, prematurely. The tenor and assumptions of Condillac's descriptions of humans developing reflective control over the powers of their own minds are far too rooted in the eighteenth century rather than a protohuman period. The scenarios sketched above of language development in contexts of work and nurture try to be properly integrational. The integrated phenomenon to be understood is the intelligent, attentive, adaptive, incipiently linguistic behavior of primitive hominids, instinctively aware that they need covering and shelter from the elements, that without food comes misery and death, that risks are everywhere but sometimes worth taking — instinctively aware of these things and now beginning to be more reflectively aware of them.

In particular, integrational linguistic assumptions require that in the tree-felling scenario, for example, it be postulated that signs emerge from an established, routine, ritual, and valued social activity. The emphasis on emergence is important and is congruent with Hopper's concept of "emergent grammar," noted in chapter 6. There is no preliminary stage at which there are signs (e.g., natural cries) and phenomena (lions, hunger) existing independently and separately, to be followed by a miraculous stage at which children or geniuses discover that they can use the natural cry for fear of attack to refer also to past attacks or to possible attack on an addressee rather than themselves. That amounts to a picture in which the sign user sees signs and the world as already quite distinct and sees also that signs can be yoked together in "the routine ways" and then, by contrast, in nonroutine ways. That is part of Condillac's misconception, an adoption of a segregationalist stance at the outset: here the cries, there the phenomenon. The tree felling is an integrated, purposeful human activity, familiar, routine, and ordered, and is no doubt long experienced as a single, integrated activity. It is hard to see an intrinsic reason why those involved should at first trouble to analyze it into parts and adopt a scientific stance toward it.

The holism of, for example, the tree-felling activity and the signs embedded within it has prompted the introduction of further revisionary proposals. Chief among these, perhaps, is the suggestion that language may have begun not at all with discrete signs, and certainly not with detachable discrete signs, but with simple sequences of activity-embedded nondetachable signs. Thus, language begins, not with what we think of as individual words, but with what we think of sentences or, better, simple narratives serving as commentaries as part of (and only later as accompanying, and later still as detachable from) simple activities. Long before early men and women had repertoires remotely resembling what we today call a language ("a system"), they had locally relevant sentences, in the form of simple narrative sequences.

But in at least one respect the speculative phylogenetic scenarios offered above are rather like Condillac's, namely, in their supposition of a naturalness in the form and substance of whatever signs gradually emerge. At least, at the inception of these signs, the emergence of a potentially detachable signification of just these noises or gestures, their potential for arbitrariness, and their availability for change and enrichment via artificiality are not foregrounded. In form and substance, these signs are quite natural in the way that, say, raising the felled trunk to one's right shoulder must have seemed quite natural. This is a naturalness, however, that is rather different from the naturalism asserted by Condillac when in his later writings he espouses a linguistic naturalism that amounts for him to a genetically shared endowment, without which, he believes, speakers could not have understood one another.

It has also been suggested here that the emergence of authorized signs in some area of semiotic activity (tree felling, mother-baby language) may be usefully thought of as metonymic. The point of laying emphasis on metonymic relations is to promote a part-whole integrational way of thinking about language, rather than a segregational and surrogational one in which language is set over against "reality" or "thought." Along these lines, language is metonymic and evokes a larger whole; it does not represent any such larger whole. At first glance, this view seems similar to that of Slobin (1982: 131–32) who writes: "A sentence is not a verbal snapshot or movie of an event.... Language *evokes* ideas; it does not represent them. Linguistic expression is thus *not* a natural map of consciousness or thought. It is a highly selective and conventionally schematic map. At the heart of language use is the tacit assumption that most of the message can be left unsaid, because of mutual understanding (and probably also mutual impatience)." But, despite the apparent similarities with integrational thinking, it is important to identify the ways in which Slobin's position remains logocentric and surrogationalist. For him, a sentence is not a verbal snapshot; implicitly it is some kind of abbreviated verbal sketch; language does not represent ideas, but it does evoke them. The formulation in terms of metonyms (*the bench*, a baby's cry) evoking wholes (the judiciary, a baby's hunger and wish for food) is significantly different from the surrogationalist notion of language evoking ideas: the latter implies that language and ideas differ in kind, whereas metonyms do not differ in kind from their wholes. And language is still a map, for Slobin, albeit a schematic or abridged one: it maps *some thing* (compare the integrational view: language is *part* of the terrain that it evokes). And, finally, language use is abridged and abbreviated, for Slobin, because mutual understanding enables us to fill in the unsaid background. But, insofar as mutual understanding is conceptualized as a determinate background body of knowledge, as prerequisite for the swift computation or processing of abbreviated utterance, that emphasis is questionable.

Further critique of linguists' appeals to mutual (background) knowledge will be pursued in chapter 5; my general counterthesis is that orientedness to other (mutuality, but not mutual or shared knowledge) is the pertinent prerequisite for coming into language, which is also to say coming into understanding. In the present case, for instance, in the hypothesized development of communication between mother and baby, what mutual knowledge precedes their earliest interactions? If we accept that mutual knowledge is not present at the outset, prior to interaction and the beginnings of communication, at what point shall we say that it does become implanted (and, crucially, *mutually* implanted)? If communication between mother and child, using signals, does indeed develop without benefit of mutual knowledge, it is clear that such mutual knowledge is not, here at least, a prerequisite for understanding semiotic activity. What I will argue are prerequisites are just the kinds of especially (but not solely) human attributes alluded to above: other orientedness, trust, pattern receptivity, rationality, imagination, "trainability," and memory.

Some of the principles posited above as foundational to language are highlighted by their nonappearance or disrupted appearance in the behavior of those who suffer some kind of linguistic deprivation or restriction. Some examples may be taken from the anecdotal observations of Sacks (1989), who writes of Joseph, a boy who showed considerable intelligence in the visual medium but whose deafness was diagnosed late, when he was already four years old. When observed at age eleven, Joseph's only language was the beginnings of American Sign Language, which he was belatedly acquiring. Sacks writes: "Joseph longed to communicate, but could not. . . . He looked alive and animated, but profoundly baffled: his eyes were attracted to speaking mouths and signing hands — they darted to our mouths and hands, inquisitively, uncomprehendingly, and, it seemed to me, yearningly. . . . He had, as yet, almost no idea of symbolic communication. . . . I was partly reminded in a way of a nonverbal animal, but no animal ever gave the feeling of yearning for language as Joseph did" (p. 39).

Joseph's case is unlike the tragic one of Genie (who, after rescue at the age of thirteen from a life of terrible deprivation, was found to be language-less and subsequently acquired only very limited speech). Abuse and mental retardation are likely contributors to Genie's limited command of language, but Joseph's virtual languagelessness had nothing to do with a lack of intelligence. Apparently, everything needed was present in Joseph, except "the idea of symbolic communication." Most particularly what is palpably present is the required "orientedness to other" that underlies all language and without which it is hard to see why or how languages would ever take hold. Relatedly, implicit in the following observation is a recognition of the crucial role of sequentiality in language — and the absence of such a concept of sequentiality in Joseph. By *sequentiality* I mean a sense of orderly chronology much richer than a narrow conception of linearity as "one sign at a time, one after another"; the sequentiality of language is instrumental in creating individual and community-wide chronologies, narratives, and histories: "Joseph was unable . . . to communicate how he had spent the weekend — one could not really ask him, even in Sign; he could not even grasp the *idea* of a question, much less formulate an answer. It was not only language that was missing: there was not, it was evident, a clear sense of the past, of "a day ago" as distinct from "a year ago." There was a strange lack of historical sense, the feeling of a life that lacked autobiographical and historical dimension, the feeling of a life that only existed in the moment, in the present" (Sacks 1989: 40). One can mark time, in a rudimentary sense, without benefit of language; but that really is only marking time, in both senses. Without the deictic and referential eloquence that language enables, no fuller reflection on time, change, and the changing self is possible.

Nearly two hundred years earlier, the Abbé Sicard had taught an equally languageless fourteen-year-old, Jean Massieu, how language supplied names for all the things in the world. Massieu was overjoyed, gripped, by this revelation. Why so? Sacks asks. "What is naming *for*? It has to do, surely, with the primal power of words . . . to allow mastery and manipulation" (Sacks 1989: 48). For Sacks, orthodoxly, naming is empowering; it enables the namer to manipulate, generalize, speculate, imagine, and so on. But, before all these instrumental applications, naming expresses and performs an enactment of solidarity or convergence of experience, of fate, between the name teacher and the name learner. Over and above displays of affection and sympathy, naming is in effect a declaration that those things you perceive all around you are indeed the same things I perceive all around me and that we experience them similarly — at least, we do so insofar as we converge on a public system of naming them.

Beyond the crucial question of how a child starts to use signs loom others, such as how and why momentum "up and out" toward standard adult language is maintained. This is one of the questions that Brown (1973) asked, at about the same time that Halliday was considering how it is that a child learns to mean. Brown asked how the child comes to improve on his or her language, "moving steadily in the direction of the adult model [*sic*]." Specifically, what drives the expansion of the child's early primitive morphosyntactic system, given the seeming communicational effectiveness of children's stage 1 language systems, at which all sorts of grammatically required morphemes are at best intermittently present, so that there is "a seemingly lawless oscillating omission of every sort of major constituent including sometimes subjects, objects, verbs, locatives, and so on"? For example, since parents seem to have no difficulty glossing a child's uninflected generic verbs as (intended as) now imperative, now past time reference, now present progressive, etc., why does the child advance to the adult-style grammaticalization of these meanings? The parents' encouragement or pressure, in Brown's view, was not the cause: "In general, the parents seemed to pay no attention to bad syntax nor did they even seem to be aware of it. They approved or disapproved an utterance [from their child] usually on the grounds of the truth value of the proposition which the parents supposed the child intended to assert" (1973: 412). That is to say, parents valued and demanded honest content much more than grammatical form. On the other hand, Brown acknowledged that there was some overt monitoring by parents of children's speech: "From inquiry and observation I find that what parents generally correct is pronunciation, 'naughty' words, and regularized irregular allomorphs like *digged* or *goed*" (1973: 412). Such interventions are not as insignificant as Brown and a generation of subsequent language-acquisition researchers have tended to assume. They impress on the child a lesson that he or she is unlikely ever to forget: that in speaking there is a right and approved way of doing things and wrong and disapproved ways — or, at least, that in speech there are ways that we (the family, the preschool, the peer group) like things to be done and ways we do not like things to be done. That impression is significant irrespective of the effectiveness or otherwise of such caregiver corrections.

What Brown did not find, however, was parents correcting, for example, *wh*-questions with noninversion of subject and auxiliary: *Why the dog won't eat?* (the kind of format that is also common in some varieties of second-language English). He concluded, somewhat surprisingly, that there was as yet no strong evidence of "selective social pressures of any kind operating on children to impel them to bring their speech into line with adult models" (1973: 412). Brown's basic criterion for selective social pressure was thus overt correction of a child's linguistic productions, and no consideration was given to the effect of the continual exposure of the child to the language behavior of older speakers, consistently using standard format *wh*-questions in real contexts (and equally consistently never using such formats as *Why the dog won't eat?*). Why there should be such neglect of instruction by observable example and induction from the behavior of those taken as models is not at all clear. Proper attention to such factors might discourage premature recourse to explanations in terms of innatism, rules, and mental programs. None of the latter seemed to be involved when, for the first time and without overt instruction, my eighteen-month-old daughter was observed attempting to put on her lace-up shoes by herself. She had had her parents or caretakers put her shoes on her on countless occasions, had seen us putting shoes on the older children, and had seen us putting our own shoes on too. She could have passively waited for us to do the work for her, as always in her past. What prompted her that day to strike out on her own, at once brilliantly but inexpertly, other than the same faculties and drives (of attentiveness and memory, rationality, creativity and self-expression, of struggled for independence within an other- or group-oriented framework) that underpin her present and future language activities?

The motivation for the development of vocal signs (as in the tree-felling activity or in infant behavior) should be thought of less as the development of the wish to communicate, or the development of intentions or goals, than as the adoption of a more efficient means to an already-emerging end. The developing vocal signs are a means that more reliably and efficiently display that which could have been communicated by other means. Similarly, the development from cries, to holophrases, to "two-word" utterances, to sentence-like fragments is only in part a matter of "making what was inarticulate, unformed, etc." articulate and explicit. It can be this only up to a point since we know that, in fact, it is impossible to specify—outside a particular context of utterance—the optimally articulate and explicit linguistic proposition. Sometimes, as far as articulacy and explicitness are concerned, a gesture is worth a thousand words. So at least as important in our explanations of the motivations for the development of spoken language should be the impulse to *display* those goals and reactions previously grasped and internalized.

Speakers' Intentions as Hearers' Intention Attributions

In recent years, an intelligently argued critique of anti-intentionalist critical theories has been presented by Stephen Knapp and Walter Benn Michaels (see Knapp and Michaels [1982, 1987] and a collection that includes responses to the earlier of these essays [Mitchell 1985]). They argue that, contrary to the assumptions—in their view, the enabling assumptions—of most contemporary theory (which they understand as "the attempt to govern interpretations of particular texts by appealing to an account of interpretation in general"

[1982: 723]), there is no gap between authorial intention and textual meaning for theoretical explanations to fill. The meaning of a text or an utterance is simply and solely what the author intended it to mean. Despite the reactionary sound of this, it merits close consideration, not least since, in their denial that there is any gap or gulf for theoretical explanation to fill as a necessary supplement, their argument is strikingly congruent with those that can be invoked in an integrational linguistic account of literal meaning and metaphor. Of interest, also, are their brief remarks on interpretation as facilitated, not algorithmically, but via verbal "clues." While Knapp and Michaels's arguments for the identity of authorial intention and textual meaning are essentially correct, there are nevertheless important aspects of the discussion of intentionality and theorizing that merit fuller attention — specifically, the role of intention attribution by the addressee/interpreter and the misconceptions underpinning Derridean iterability. The following remarks review Knapp and Michaels's arguments particularly in relation to these two aspects and propose integrational linguistic amendments.

Knapp and Michaels begin their argument by suggesting that language, to be seen as language (in Harris's terms, not merely audible or visible but hearable or legible [Harris 1981a: 178–79]), necessarily involves intentionality. Noticed marks, shapes, noises, must be categorized, by human beings, as either the work of some intending agent or the work of random or mechanical processes: this choice is inescapable and has the effect of categorizing those marks as either language or nonlanguage. To treat marks as intended, as language, is thereby to assume an intending author, regardless of their evident absence. And the basis for deciding whether marks are authored, intended, and language or accidental, unintended, and meaningless, Knapp and Michaels stress, is empirical rather than theoretical: an empirical assessment must be made as to whether the marks were authored, guided by past empirical experience and the larger present context. It is regrettable that, in response to criticisms, Knapp and Michaels qualified their position to the point of accepting that physical features of marks "intrinsically determine" whether those marks are a token of a sentence type in a given language. As Searle notes (1994a: 650–52), such acceptance of intrinsic determinations of sentencehood in a given language undercuts all their other claims. An integrational explication of the earlier Knapp and Michaels position would, by contrast, assert that sentencehood and wordhood are secondary and contingent on the prior identification of marks or sounds by a recipient as intentional utterance. And it would add that, contra Searle (1994a: 652), it is not the case that a text's meaning can be examined in two ways: either in terms of authorial intentions or in terms of the linguistic meanings of the words and sentences of which it consists. As indicated in chapter 1, the integrationist rejects the Searlean faith in the latter approach and its assumption of stable and invariant word and sentence meanings.

Knapp and Michaels's contention is that "the meaning of a text is simply identical to the author's intended meaning" (1982: 724). Indeed, this is the basis for their rejection of the doomed Hirschian pursuit of intention as (in Hirsch's view) the only valid grounding for interpretation. Once authorial intention is seen to be the meaning of a text (and not, as in Hirsch, some form of "hidden basis" for that meaning), then there is no longer a categorized dualism (meaning vs. intention) or any coherence to the idea of getting to one via the other. Once you have one, you have the other.

The point of Knapp and Michaels's critique is not at all to privilege the text as pure, simple, and autonomous but rather to reinstate the author. Their objection is to the tacit assumption of the autonomous identity of the text, which they see in both the interpretive methodology of hermeneutics (whether Hirsch's or Ricouer's) and the interpretive nonmethodology of deconstruction (whether De Man's or Derrida's). The assertion of the autonomy of the text leads to either the unlimited textuality of deconstruction or the delimited textuality of hermeneutics, and both are incoherent. Both wrongly assume that a text can mean something other than what its author intends.

In all this, Knapp and Michaels argue powerfully for the shaping role of the author as, in effect, responsible agent. Where their account still seems lacking is in not considering the degree to which attributed intention (on the part of some reader/addressee) rather than actual — and uninspectable — intention is what is involved in textual meaning. Indeed, there is a general neglect of the reader/addressee in Knapp and Michaels's essays, although they do show their own commitments by implication when they characterize the views of those who treat the text as autonomous thus: "The text is what it is, no matter what meaning is assigned to it by its author and no matter how that meaning is revised by its readers" (1987: 50). While they mount an effective attack on the notion that "there can be any plausible criteria of textual identity that can function independent of authorial intention" (p. 50), their implied alternative notion is correct but incomplete. Their alternative notion is that textual identity and meaning are related to (indeed, identical with) authorial intention and that therefore absolutely no theoretical machinery is needed in order to "get back to" authorial intention (the strategy of hermeneutics) or to justify disregard for it (the position of deconstructionists): what we say the text means is, without refraction of any kind, what we say the author intended it to mean. The chief qualification that this requires is a noting that it is incomplete in making no mention of the addressee's intention (purposes, goals) in relation to which any particular assessment of authorial intention/textual meaning will be made. Both author and addressee, sender and receiver, are essential participants in any linguistic communication, although there is no merging of their positions, no "negotiating" of some intermediate or compromised textual meaning. There is monological embedding rather than dialogical conjunction: the situated, interested, and intention-driven recipient of a text or communication makes a current and provisional assessment of the sender's intentions in the course of and by virtue of making a current and provisional assessment of the meaning of the text.

An example of Knapp and Michaels's neglect of the interpreting recipient of a text is evident in their brief remarks on irony. They discuss irony since it might appear to be one case where, contrary to their thesis, authorial intention and textual meaning diverge: "Is irony a case where intention and meaning come apart? After all, the utterance only counts as ironic if the speaker's meaning is not simply the conventional one. At the same time, however, the utterance only counts as ironic if the speaker *intends* that both the conventional meaning and the departure from conventional meaning be recognized. Since both aspects of an ironic utterance are equally intentional, irony in no way frees the meaning of the utterance from the speaker's intention" (1987: 56). Their counterargument holds for intended speaker irony; where it fails to apply, it does so not because their claim about the identity of meaning and speaker meaning is faulty but because they neglect the role of the addressee (in postulating irony and in postulating meaning generally). Their observations do not address those cases of verbal utterance that give rise to unintended irony. These are a kind of situational irony, but, unlike typical situational irony, they depend directly on verbal utterance for their effect. Thus, they are distinct from both typical verbal irony (in being unintended by the speaker) and typical situational irony (in that verbal utterance is required so as to create the irony, whereas situational irony is typically nonverbal).

In unintended utterance-based irony, what is important is the mismatch between what the recipient takes to be the speaker's intended conventional meaning and the encompassing circumstances (circumstances to which the recipient is apparently more alert than the speaker). The objection here is not to the claimed identity of intention and meaning but only to the primacy accorded the speaker in creating irony. In both intended and unintended irony, the speaker's intended meaning and the textual meaning are one and the same. In intended irony, the textual meaning is the entertaining intended double perspective comprising both the conventional meaning of an utterance and the inappropriateness of that conventional meaning; in unintended irony by contrast there is an unintended double perspective comprising the intended conventional contextual meaning of an utterance and its unnoticed inappropriateness. But none of these determinations, including the decision as to whether a text is a case of intended or unintended irony, is in the gift of the speaker; they are the responsibility of the recipient. That is why Knapp and Michaels are wrong to say of irony that "the utterance only counts as ironic if the speaker's meaning is not simply the conventional one." In cases of unintended irony, the utterance counts as ironic precisely because the speaker's meaning—in the recipient's estimation—is simply the conventional one. Thus, Knapp and Michaels's quoted counterargument, to the supposition that textual meaning diverges from speaker meaning in the case of verbal irony, holds for intended speaker irony. Where it fails to apply, it does so not because their claim about the identity of meaning and speaker meaning is faulty but because they neglect the role of the addressee—in both the postulation of irony and the postulation of (speaker) meaning generally.

In Knapp and Michaels's view, the actual identity of authorial intention and textual meaning vitiates even so persuasive an account of meaning as that of Gadamer in *Truth and Method*. Gadamer writes: "The real meaning of a text does not depend on the contingencies of the author . . . for it is always partly determined also by the historical situation of the interpreter and hence by the totality of the objective course of history" (Gadamer 1975: 263). This, they note, is an ontological claim about the text rather than merely an epistemological one about understanding. Elsewhere, Gadamer talks of adapting the meaning of a text to each new concrete situation (p. 275) and of judges interpreting law as supplementing that original meaning of the text (p. 305). Again, as Knapp and Michaels see it, the misrepresentation in these remarks lies in thinking of a text as having an original, presitutational meaning, which must then be adapted, applied, or supplemented in particular subsequent situations. The integrational linguistic alternative, which Knapp and Michaels might accept, is that meaning is always "now," a present determination of what textual meaning and authorial intention are. Subsequent historically situated interpretations of texts are not an overlaying of new contingencies on an established original meaning but a thoroughgoing reformulation (not a revision in the sense of a correction) of what the original meaning is.

Knapp and Michaels exemplify this principle by reference to a problem for judicial interpretation. A cyclist has been arrested for riding in a park, much frequented by joggers, in which the following law restricting traffic applies: "No vehicle shall be permitted in the park." A judge must decide whether the cyclist is guilty as charged and specifically whether the law applies to bicycles, even though bicycles are not mentioned in the law. Now, although Gadamer and many others seem to believe that what is involved is some sort of revisionary enlargement of the law, some supplement to the law that will enable it now to apply to bicycles, skateboards, golf carts, and all manner of vehicles unimagined by the legislators, no such adjustment of meaning or going beyond original intention is involved. What is involved is a currently relevant determination of just what the original meaning and intention were. Knapp and Michaels write: "The judge didn't mean to go beyond the legislators' intention but only to decide what that intention was; when they said 'vehicles,' the judge decided, they meant dangerous vehicles" (1987: 52).

The first half of this sentence is irreproachable, the second half more contentious. Applying laws to particular cases does indeed involve decision ("decision, rather than discovery," as Harris [1981a: 193] has emphasized) as to what the intentions or purposes of a law were and are. Purposes do not change; only our determinations of what they are do. But whether a judge is obliged to focus on the question

What sort of things did the legislators mean to refer to by the term *vehicles*?

rather than on the broader question

What sort of purpose did the legislators have in mind when they declared, "No vehicle shall be permitted in the park"

is at least debatable. My assumption is that the broader question, addressed to a proposition rather than simply a word, must be much more influential. As in the similar case of a drunk man wheeling a bicycle (discussed in Harris [1981a: 191–92] and here in chapter 4), the point is not so much that a judge must decide whether bicycles are invariably dangerous vehicles but rather whether, in the given circumstances, the individual riding a bicycle in the park was behaving in a way that the legislators intended to prohibit. Other cases, involving cyclists wheeling bicycles with or without flat tires or where the "carriage" is a baby carriage or roller skates (two vehicles?) are extraneous to the particular case and must be resolved independently, on their own merits. As for the influence of the rules of the language and of dictionary definitions, in deciding such issues, Knapp and Michaels comment: "How are [the rules of the language] relevant at all? They are relevant not because they provide a range of possible meanings but because they provide clues to the meaning the author intends. The dictionary definition of 'vehicle' is useful not because it determines the range of possible meanings 'vehicle' can have but because it provides clues to what an English-speaking author might mean by 'vehicle' " (1987: 57). The dictionary definition(s), let it be said, may not be particularly good clues to the intended meaning, and other sorts of clues may be more readily invoked: one source of clues will be a speaker's memory of past contextualized uses of the word, a source championed by Gardiner (1932), among others; another source of clues will be the interpreter's assessment of the purposes of the current communicational encounter in which the word is embedded.

Against Iterability

The second part of "Against Theory 2" (Knapp and Michaels 1987) turns to Derrida's views on intention and iterability, as set out in "Signature Event Context" (1977b) and "Limited Inc abc" (1977a). Knapp and Michaels are perhaps unfair to Derrida in suggesting that he implies that meaning cannot be determined by context since Derrida does acknowledge that local determining goes on all the time and is inescapable — he just denies that there is any timeless logical basis for such determinings. Derrida's general point seems to be that convention is irrelevant and original intention uninspectable.

Knapp and Michaels are right, however, to identify Derridean iterability as the basis of the deconstructionist distrust of intention and intentionality. And they even agree with Derrida that intention cannot govern the scene of utterance: "Even if . . . intention determines meaning, there can be no guarantee that the intended meaning will be understood" (1987: 61). But such misinterpretations are not what concern Derrida, they argue; rather, it is the possibility of *citation*, of detaching an utterance from its original authored context and recontextualizing it such that the originally intended meaning is subverted or lost. For Derrida, iterability and citationality are two aspects of a single intention-flouting property of signs: their repeatability.

Unfortunately, the radical attack that Knapp and Michaels need to mount on Derrida's position at this point does not surface, for Derrida's entire thesis of intention-obscuring iterability rests on the plausibility of his notion of the sign and the claim that the sign is, by definition, repeatable. But both the notion and the claim are wrong; ironically, they are also theses that entirely conform to the assumptions of Saussurean linguistics (of which, elsewhere, Derrida is so critical). Derrida begins by saying that for a sign to be a sign it must be readable beyond its original context, but he rapidly comes to the conclusion that this entails iterability — the second occurrence of a sign must be identified as the same sign as occurred before, in a radically different context. This Saussurean doctrine of the autonomous sign as the essential unit of linguistic analysis is the chute down which Derrida slides when he recasts readability (definitionally part of any sign) as iterability. And in saying that iterability itself is "the positive condition of the emergence of the mark," (1977a) thus a feature of the condition of being a mark from the outset and by the same token an intrinsic undermining of a mark's intentionality, Derrida is making the same mistake of privileging the epiphenomenal (marks taken as "the same" marks) over the phenomenal (new marks in new situations as clues to new intentions) that is incorporated into a theory of language by code-oriented linguists. It is not iterability that is the positive condition of the emergence of the mark; the positive condition of the emergence of a (signifying) mark is that an intelligent actor takes notice of it, as a purposeful part and exponent of a purposeful activity — that is, that intentionality is attributed to its source.

Renewed emphasis on intentionality, on the part of the addressee or recipient of an utterance, as definitional of language activity is a necessary corrective to some notions that have emerged from Derridean deconstruction concerning the "freeing of the signifier." In a widely read guide to deconstructionist thought, Culler (1983) summarizes the Derridean arguments for the iterability of the sign and the displacement of an utterance from any specific grounding origins or speaker's intentions in this way:

Iterability can be shown to be the condition of any sign. A sequence of sounds can function as a signifier only if it is repeatable, if it can be recognized as the "same" in different circumstances. It must be possible for me to repeat to a third party what someone said. A speech sequence is not a sign sequence unless it can be quoted and put into circulation among those who have no knowledge of the "original" speaker and his signifying intentions. The utterance "Ris-Orangis is a southern suburb of Paris" continues to signify as it is repeated, quoted, or, as here, cited as example; and it can continue to signify whether or not those who reproduce or quote it have anything "in mind." This possibility of being repeated and functioning without respect to a particular signifying intention is a condition of linguistic signs in general, not just of writing. (Culler 1983: 102)

One of the more problematic claims here is that implied in the fourth sentence, where Culler specifies what he regards as necessary for a speech sequence to be something "extra," namely, a sign sequence. This implies that there can be speech sequences that are not sign sequences. However, the very decision to characterize an extent of vocal sounds or noises as a speech sequence is thereby to treat it as a sign sequence, as language. Seemingly a harmless mistake or a trivial point, the implication that there are detached speech sequences that preexist application in particular contexts of signification is a theoretical maneuver favored by theorists in general, as Knapp and Michaels (1982) suggest. The corrected account threatens the job-creation schemes of all textualist theorists: if to identify a stream of vocal sounds as a speech sequence is thereby to identify it as a sign sequence (i.e., if a speech sequence is simply one kind of sign sequence), then the initial procedure — not a secondary applicational one — is that of treating vocal sounds as signs. And to treat sounds as signs is to treat them — again, from the outset and not as some kind of appendix — as the expression of signifying intentions. To treat sounds or marks as signs is to attribute signifying intentions to their imagined or attributed source. But all this undermines the Derridean textualist account in which signs can somehow still be signs and yet remain free to acquire new and unforeseen sources and intentions.

This brings us to the second and related misrepresentation, the idea that sign sequences are "put into circulation" like coins of the realm and, like coins, have values and uses without being tied to any particular use, purpose, or controlling source. Analogies with monetary economics are common in linguistics and have their uses when used to exemplify the fluctuation of value. But in other respects they can be distracting. Thus, I use coins and notes every day without considering for a moment, for example, that the quarters in my pocket are authored or intended or that they can or should be associated with any origin. The coins are just there, devoid of individuality by virtue of being stamped from a common mold. They are there to be used by the situated participant in the economy.

True as all this may be, it is no demonstration that we are ever free from attributing intentions to the user of coins or, mutatis mutandis, to the user of signs. It is hard to conceive of speaker A quoting speaker B without intending to quote speaker B, and it is equally inconceivable that coins are put into circulation without the agent who performs that act intending to do so. The Derridean argument shows no interest in that kind of permanent intentionality and focuses instead on the banal point that, in A's quoting of B's utterance, B's intentions may well not be preserved or carried over. This is no more surprising than the fact that the circulating dollar that you used yesterday to buy a hotdog may today be used to buy a latté. In passing, one cannot help suspecting that this analogy of freely circulating coins alludes uncritically to a world of monetary affluence; the analogy ignores the fact that, in every society where coins are used, there are large numbers of people who have great difficulty getting their hands on sufficient "freely circulating coins" to permit civilized life. The analogy is nevertheless initially plausible since for the rest of us a picture of steady getting and spending seems utterly commonsensical. But our coins do not circulate freely, no more than free market economies operate freely (if by *freely* is implied "randomly, arbitrarily, without purpose, interest, and control"). To analogize as if they did is to adopt a capitalist mystification in the service of a linguistic one.

Like most linguists, Derrida chooses to ignore the fact that to talk of linguistic repetition is already to talk at a level of considerable abstraction, removed from the empirical instances of the noniterated. But Derrida's purposes are different from the linguists'. He passes off a theoretical abstraction — the iterability of language — as if it were an empirical fact of language and then uses this "empirical" fact of iterability as a basis for arguing the logical detachability of a speaker's intentions as a factor that is potentially remote and unrecoverable. But, on the contrary, the empirical and logical facts are that in language there is never absolute repetition and that it is our assessments of speakers' intentions (in given contexts of utterance and situation) that determine the sense we make of the unrepeated signs we encounter.

The more general reaction to Derridean iterability must be first to note that much of this is neither new nor exceptionable: the observation that language carries the potential for "iteration without inherent signification" is adumbrated in Locke, who titled a section of the *Essay Concerning Human Understanding* (3.2.7) "Words Often Used without Signification." But the radical reinterpretation of this notion, to the effect that utterances "can continue to signify whether or not those who reproduce or quote [them] have anything 'in mind' " (Culler 1983: 102), seems to reflect a conceptual confusion. The confusion is one sponsored by the adoption of Saussure's fixed-code theory of a language. Within that theoretical perspective, recurrent signification is simple and unproblematic. The meaning of any expression of the language is determinate, underwritten by the fixed form-meaning associations of that language. Accordingly, reproduction of any expression is guaranteed to trigger the same signification as previously, regardless of a change of speaker, circumstances, and so on. Such guarantees, it is claimed, are the necessary condition for describing a language as a sign system.

In the integrational alternative, no assumption of assured, fixed-code reproduction of signification is made. Indeed, the noniterative nature of language behavior is made one of its hallmarks and essential characteristics. The reverse of iterability is assumed: namely, that we can never be sure that signification remains constant from one use of an expression to the next use of the "same" expression. It is no accident that, in the extract quoted above, Culler refers to "Ris-Orangis is a southern suburb of Paris" as *an* utterance and talks of *it* being repeated, quoted, and used over and over. But Culler's singular entity is a linguist's or theorist's abstraction, representing a multiplicity of actual utterances; it denotes a type, not a token, in the objectifying ways devised by literate cultures, almost impossible in purely oral ones. When a language user encounters, on three occasions, the utterance that Culler's sentence represents, then they encounter three utterances, not one. If utterances are examined closely enough, similarities can be found between the two expressions in many respects — those respects privileged by orthodox linguistics. But we will also invariably be able to find dissimilarities too; with such variation between the two expressions, why assume identity between them or their significations? If the remark about Ris-Orangis is enunciated by one speaker with final rising or questioning intonation and then by another speaker with final falling or declarative intonation, nonrepetition is as important to the sequence as repetition. In general, for integrationists, signification is not assumed to be constant across "repeated" expressions from a single speaker; equally importantly, it is not assumed to hold constant between a speaker and an addressee.

It is as much due to this rejection of telementation (the picture of language as a conveyance of invariant contents between senders and receivers) as to the rejection of fixed-code constancy that an integrational perspective entails a different notion of signification from that adopted by Derrida and Culler. The integrational picture is at least dual, if not plural: signification is (following Locke) an association made by a language user between the expressions she uses or encounters and ideas in her mind (in effect, an association made between present ideas and past ideas). If I revise the terms here and speak of signification as an assessment of intended meaning made by a speaker or hearer on the basis of supposed or hazarded likeness between a current form-context pair and previous remembered pairings, then the essential point remains unchanged. The essential point is that signification pertains to the individual language user, without possibility of verification that such private signification is iterated, repeated, or reproduced in the mind of any other language user.

Here lies the basis of the integrational objection to speech-act theories, which undertake to resolve the tension created by attention to two conflicting theses, namely, that language is fundamentally intentional and fundamentally conventional. Speech-act theories attempt to contain this paradox; they are theories about how intentions are channeled, conveyed, and recognized via an apparatus of conventions. But the very idea of conventionalized intentions borders on the contradictory, as many commentators from Strawson on have noted. It might be argued that the status of spontaneous intentions as expressive of the unique goals and purposes of the unique speaker is diminished to the extent that those intentions become "reduced" to the simple classifications of conventional conditions and linguistic encoding devices described by Searle (1969). The upshot would be — and arguably is — that in the machinery of speech-act theory we can have a model only of the standard intentions and conventional practices for constituting and recognizing those standard intentions. Because of this, the speech-act machinery has its own kind of prescriptive pressure on linguistic analysis, such that nonstandard behavior may be rendered invisible or aberrant trivia of performance. The speech-act model is introduced to specify and explain what linguistic and extralinguistic conditions count as constitutive of a promise; but, once such a grammar of promises is adopted, it encourages us to identify as promises all and only those situated speech acts that its felicity conditions and linguistic conventions ratify as constituting promises.

In language (interaction, reading) there is always an unpredictable meshing of distinct significations rather than the sharing or exchange of a single signification. It is not simply that an expression can continue to signify whether or not those who reproduce it have anything in mind: that is always a possibility, although the Culler formulation focuses solely on the speaker/author of the utterance, signification according to speaker, which is always only half the story. More importantly, and regardless of what a "reproduced" utterance signifies for the speaker, regardless of what she actually has in mind, that utterance does not signify at all for the addressee/listener unless that individual does attribute some intended message, something in mind, to some assumed or hypothesized producer of the utterance. The simple truth argued for at length by integrational linguists is that language in all its diversity and contextual embeddedness cannot reasonably be characterized as a closed system of endlessly iterable fixed signs — in short, as a code. Any theory of language that implies closed systematicness also implicitly endorses a primarily conventionalist view of language, and vice versa. In subscribing to the conventionalism that underpins "iterability," Derrida is, oddly enough, not at odds with the speech-act theory of Austin and Searle that he purports to deconstruct.

Speech-Act Theory and Marrying

When Knapp and Michaels themselves turn to speech-act theory, however, some strained arguments surface, seemingly caused by the same overemphasis on the speaker and neglect of the audience noted earlier. Thus, they puzzle over how a performative analysis would cope with the case of a speaker who follows all the appropriate conventions in the appropriate circumstances for performing the act of marrying (saying "I do" before a registrar, with witnesses, etc., etc.) — but who happens to be married already. The question, in Knapp and Michaels's view, is:

> How can "I do" mean (roughly) "I hereby marry [the aforementioned party]" in cases both of successful marrying and of void attempts (when the speaker is already married)? Suppose we paraphrase "I do" in the following way: "By the sounds I am now making I am entering into marriage." The paraphrase holds both for the case in which the speaker says "I do" and succeeds in marrying and for the case in which the speaker says "I do" but doesn't. What, then, is the difference between these cases? The meaning of "I do" is the same in both; the only difference is that, in the first case, what the speaker says is true because the speaker *is* getting married, while in the second case, what the speaker says is false because, as it turns out, the speaker isn't getting married. Saying "I do" when one is already married is indeed an example of failing to perform the conventional act one intended to perform, but it is not an example of failing to perform the *speech act* one intended to perform. (1987: 62–63)

Even allowing for the likelihood that Knapp and Michaels intend the term *speech act* in a nonconventional sense at odds with the standard usage associated with Austin and Searle, still there seem to be needless complications in their discussion of saying, intending, and successfully performing the speech act "I do" but failing to marry. Among the relevant circumstances of a plausibly contextualized "I do" is the fact that in the marriage ceremony it is a response, one given to a public and institutionalized question as to the addressee's current purpose. Indeed, that question is an official formulation of that purpose, a displaying on public record and in advance of the purpose and nature of the commitment that the addressees (*sic*) are about to undertake. In such circumstances, unless some impropriety is pointed out, then the marriage takes effect, and the individual becomes a happily married bigamist. Possibly, at some later date, she or he may be found out — but that would be to adduce new circumstances in a new situation, and in that new context the meaning and intention of the disputed "I do" would presumably be reformulated. At the now at which the second marriage takes place, Knapp and Michaels mention no such salient public considerations, simply remarking that "It clearly is possible for such an act [of saying "I do" and getting married thereby] to fail: if, for example, I am already married and am thus excluded by convention from marrying again" (1987: 62).

Perhaps the chief problem here lies with the word *thus*, as if there were something intrinsic to the condition of being already married that automatically cuts across the effective performance of another act of marrying; as a matter of law this may be the case, such that a bigamous marriage is, in law, no marriage at all. But it is unclear why the legal perspective should prevail here, determining success and failure, unless it is specifically invoked. A similar objection applies to the introduction of truth and falsity, in the earlier extract. Truth and falsity, as Austin insisted, are simply not very relevant to performative utterances — how can "I hereby marry X" be true or false? — where what is important is whether the action goes through or not. In such ways, Knapp and Michaels weaken their own case for the inescapability of intentionality by paying too much attention to the (one) speaker and neglecting the highly conventionalized public understanding of ritualized utterances and actions that underpins the form of life we call marriage ceremonies.

They are much nearer the latter perspective when they turn to Culler's example of the newlywed who reveals, after due completion of the marriage ceremony, that he had been pretending. Should any such denial of having had the proper intention "be understood as cases where the intention is irrelevant to determining what speech act has been performed?" Not at all, they say. "The reason a speaker who pretends is nevertheless taken seriously is not that his intentions don't matter but simply that he is held to have had the intention that in these circumstances ordinarily goes with these sounds. The point of holding someone to the intention that ordinarily goes with certain sounds in certain circumstances is not linguistic but social" (1987: 63).

One reason that Knapp and Michaels can successfully protect their thesis that the speaker determines the meaning of a speech act is the fact that they confine themselves to relatively simple speech acts — the person who says "I do" but is only pretending in a marriage ceremony, or the car passenger who says "go" to the driver but means "stop," and so on. What happens when Fred wants to apologize to Alice for making some unkind remarks last night about her weight problem, wants to tell her that he still finds her attractive but that he would still like her to lose a little weight, although he doesn't want it to become an issue between them? Those are Fred's intentions. They determine the meaning of whatever speech act(s) Fred comes up with, in the sense that Fred really intends these intentions. But will Alice "get" all and only what Fred intends and means? The answer must be maybe, with Alice's subsequent behavior as the chief and inconclusive evidence available. This example rehearses our everyday risk of communicational failure, one of far greater importance than the risks mentioned by Knapp and Michaels: "You meant to produce a sound but didn't, or you meant to produce one sound and produced another instead" (1987: 65). Ordinarily, people are far too busy with their immediate purposes to worry about producing the right sound; what concerns them is producing the intended effect. Fred's intention determines the meaning of his speech act, but what he means may not be what Alice, assessing his intentions, takes him to mean. Since language is not a fixed code of endlessly reproducible signs, this uncertainty as to how intentions are taken up (intentions that are cued by the norms of linguistic behavior) is a permanent dilemma and resource.

The Searlean Critique of Literary Confusions

Interestingly, on all the foregoing issues, of speaker meaning, intentionality, iterability, and so on, John Searle has recently once more taken up the cudgels on behalf of orthodox linguistics and the philosophy of language, chastising principally Derrida and Knapp and Michaels for their alleged misunderstandings. The cudgeling takes the form, first, of a rehearsal of the foundational coordinates of Searle's conception of language theory. He begins with a brief notice of his ideas about the background and the network and the nonsharpness of various theoretical distinctions, then moving on to reiterating the importance of the following distinctions: types versus tokens; sentences versus utterances; uses versus mentions; and sentence meaning versus speaker meaning. In each case, as I indicated in chapter 1, the integrational response is not to question that such distinctions exist at all (as Derrida often seems to do) but rather to question the level at which any of them may be said to exist. For instance, consider types and tokens — the notion that particular occurring words are usefully thought of as instantiations of abstract types, so that "if, for example, I write the word 'dog' on the blackboard three times . . . I have written one *type* word, but I have written three different *token* instances of that word. . . . The token is a concrete physical particular, but the type is a purely abstract notion" (Searle 1994a: 642).

The real issue, however, is not whether linguists and even lay language users on occasion typify usage in this way but rather what role such categorizations play in actual language use. What is the evidence that language types govern language tokens in a speaker's production of utterances or a hearer's interpretation of them? Or, to put things another way, is there any principle of priority in the type-token distinction such that knowledge of the type must precede production of tokens? The integrational objection to type-token theorizing is precisely that it typically does assume just such a relation of precedence and that such an assumption utterly fails to characterize the level of innovation and change in language use where, to depict the situation using these problematic terms, new tokens precede typification, with the result that — contrary to the definitions of these categories — it is impossible to state what type such tokens are tokens of.

This is particularly evident if we turn from writing to spoken language — just as we saw in relation to literal meaning in chapter 1. If we imagine Searle within a nonliterate oral community, uttering (sounds that I here represent as) *dog* on three adjacent occasions, where can we find encoded or represented the type of which he would claim those three utterances were tokens? Caught in the web of speech, he would be able to specify the putative type of those three tokens only by uttering the sounds for *dog* a fourth time; but in doing so he has produced a further token — "the token is a concrete physical particular" — rather than something "purely abstract" and of a quite different ontological status. This example reveals again the importance, for language theorizing, of attending to speech — or sign — as the more natural of "natural languages." In signed and spoken languages, we are obliged to look at language in use in "concrete physical particular" situations, whereas in written language we can be misled into imagining that we can escape those to a para-realm of the "purely abstract."

Searle (1994a) ends his commentary on types and tokens by noting "further distinctions" within the type-token distinction, giving by way of example Hemingway's novel *The Sun also Rises* as a new type "of which your copy and my copy are two further tokens" (643). Again, this is a resolutely Western example, which makes sense relative to a background of literacy and multiple-copy typeset printing. But that background is a contingent background — it is not one that all language-using humans must have to qualify as language users — and this in turn suggests that, rather than being foundational to the nature of language, the type-token distinction itself is also contingent. Furthermore, since it is in the nature of tokens to be nonidentical with each other — as Searle notes, "actual physical tokens are precisely not iterable" (p. 643) — it may at first seem odd that Searle calls copies of Hemingway's novel, which when taken from a single printing would seem to be as close to identity as we could imagine, different tokens. If iterability is valid anywhere, it will be in cases involving mechanical reproduction — multiple copies of books, photographs, and so on. But is the person who uses again the word *dog* in speech or writing operating on anything like the basis of the device that creates multiple copies of a book or photograph? Finally, the "origins" question is again germane: Where did the type of which our copies of *The Sun also Rises* are said to be tokens come *from*? Searle is obliged to assert that, at the outset, Hemingway "produced a token, which inaugurated a new type, his novel." But what was that initial token a token *of*, and how — and why — would one produce a token that is not a token of a known type? To elide those questions and assert that a particular token inaugurates a type is to invert the foundational logic of type-token theory. If, however, in writing his novel Hemingway was not instantiating a given type — and he surely was not — then it seems more coherent to say that what he created was neither a type nor a token, and in that respect what he did was exactly equivalent to the situated innovativeness of utterance that is common in everyday language use.

In the course of a thoroughgoing rejection of Knapp and Michaels's sometimes confused arguments to have speaker intentionality govern all instances of language, Searle restates the "autonomous mechanist code" view with startling clarity. He wishes to emphasize that sentences are rule-conforming structures with compositionally based meanings quite apart from any contribution of speakers and their intentions and their use of sentences in particular speech acts. As far as sentencehood is concerned (as distinct from the speech acts that particular utterances might perform), this is for Searle a property that is achievable unthinkingly — by a parrot, say, or a computer or a cat: "Suppose my cat wanders over the keys of my computer keyboard and out comes a perfect English sentence: 'The chair is made of wood.' By any of the standard criteria this is a sentence of English" (1994b: 680).

Nothing more succinctly demonstrates the remoteness of the standard criteria and accounts of sentencehood, "from Frege to Chomsky" as Searle emphasizes (1994b: 679), from the contextualized study of real language. Animal lovers, taking into consideration that any cat belonging to John Searle is likely to be exceptionally articulate, may wish to keep an open mind as to whether the feline wanderer is intentionally communicating in English. But most observers are unlikely to make such generous attributions. In any event, the observer's crucial judgment, in this case exactly as in Knapp and Michaels's case of language-like marks found on the beach, will be to decide whether the observed *materia* constitute an intended utterance (language) or an accidental configuration (nonlanguage). Only if the former choice is selected would reflections on the utterance as a sentence become an issue. If, alternatively, we maintain the "standard" thinking upheld by Searle, then we are saying that it is in the nature of English that it may be produced at random, unexpectedly, and unconsciously by cats, parrots, the action of waves on the beach, patterns of fallen trees in the forest, and so on. There is a kind of trickery involved in all these scenarios where cats produce English sentences and waves inscribe poems; they trouble the observer in the way the liar's paradox may or even the magician who appears to saw a victim in half. Observing the latter, which we assume to be an illusion even if real blood is thrown about and the victim expresses pain and anguish, remains a fundamentally different experience from observing a real torturer sawing a real victim in half. By comparison, in the case of the cat on the keyboard, the observer must make a similar judgment as to whether he or she is observing genuine communication, that is, whether the cat is really writing in English, or whether he or she is witnessing only an extraordinary illusion, an uncanny appearing to communicate. Commentators are sometimes rather too quick to add that "obviously" the cat, parrot, or waves are not really communicating in English, thereby denying rather than addressing the degree to which such scenarios would surely half convince us that those individuals *were* communicating. Similarly, it is a poor magician about whom we are entirely confident, throughout, that he obviously isn't actually cutting the victim in half.

Searle would have us agree that, if a cat wanders over a keyboard leaving behind on the screen *The chair is made of wood*, our first reaction would be that here was an English sentence. He has nothing to say about the cat itself; in particular, if we regard the animal as extraordinary in any way, then this is mistaken or irrelevant from Searle's point of view. If, for example, we speculate that the cat really is trying to communicate with us, this is sheer foolishness from Searle's point of view, foolishness that will tend to damage the status of the screen message as a fully formed English sentence, without author or intentions. But I would suggest that such "foolishness" would be entirely natural in the circumstances: we cannot plausibly continue to regard the screen message as an English sentence without, however perplexedly, casting the cat as its intentional author. If we refuse to promote the cat in that way, then, ultimately, we do not accept the screen text as an English sentence, notwithstanding appearances to the contrary: it becomes no more significant than the jumble of characters that appears if I rest my forearm on the keyboard. It is important to note in this regard that it is perfectly possible for an observer initially to treat marks as intentional utterance and a sentence in a language and later withdraw that assessment and reevaluate the marks as merely random. Searle's perspective cannot see or address this: for him, once a sentence, always a sentence.

Ultimately, however, scenarios in which unintending parrots and cats appear to use perfect English are diversionary. It is no accident that they have no interest for linguists of any tradition (on the other hand, Bonobo chimpanzees trained to use keyboards are of interest to linguists, but just such cases are rarely addressed by philosophers such as Searle). The scenarios are of no interest to linguists, even if they involve sentences according to formal definitions of the latter, precisely because they have nothing to do with real language by virtue of having nothing to do with communication. The key question is, What relevance does Searle's "English sentence"–producing cat have to students of language or language theory (compared, say, to the situation in which the given sentence is uttered by a five-year-old child)? The answer is that the cat sentence is of no relevance whatsoever, beyond showing us that a particular tradition of analytic philosophy has wrenched the notions of sentencehood and "sentence of English" to the point where analysts interested in the role of language in communication can use them only couched about with bizarre qualifications.

4

Further Principles of Integrational Linguistics, or, On Not Losing Sight of the Language User

> In every single person's mind there lie, thrust into the background at the moment, many memories of previous linguistic experiences: what is meant by saying they "lie" there, is for the psychologist to explain: the rest of us take memory as a fact we cannot get away from. — Otto Jespersen, *Mankind, Nation and Individual from a Linguistic Point of View*

On the Relevance of Memory Limitations and Shifts of Interest

It was Saussure's view that the only vantage point from which a language could be studied scientifically, as a synchronic network of interrelated signs, is that of the language user. In the twentieth century, this view has been cherished in theory but often abandoned in practice, as is clear even in parts of the *Cours de linguistique générale* itself. Besides, the claim that linguistics must adopt the perspective of the language user immediately prompts the question just what kind of (presumably representative) individual best merits designation as *the language user*. The essence of the most influential answer in contemporary linguistics, it will be argued below, is partial and theory laden. In itself this is no surprise, for anything in the way of a nonvacuous answer is likely to be theory laden; but the nature of that partiality merits scrutiny. This is undertaken in the first part of this chapter, after which, at greater length, an alternative specification of the language user and his role in linguistic communication is presented.

The standard linguistic view of the language user, accepted with little in the way of qualification, is most influentially characterized in Chomsky's 1965 description of the "ideal speaker-hearer." (The fact that in more recent writings Chomsky seems to have modified his picture of the language user and of what a language and a grammar are is a separate issue.) In Chomsky (1965), the ideal speaker-hearer is introduced as a necessary abstract idealization of the kind of speaker theorists must have in mind if their account of linguistic competence is to be properly delimited. But this necessary idealization has no bearing on the noncognitive complexities of language in social contexts, Chomsky emphasizes: the "ideal speaker-hearer" has at best an indirect relation to actual speakers and hearers and is rather an abstract construct necessary for an orderly study of linguistic competence as a cognitive faculty (regardless of how, in actual linguistic performance, scrutiny of that competence may be obscured by individuals' errors, social "noise," and so on). This being noted, the characterization of the "ideal speaker-hearer" may more safely be rehearsed. This abstract individual "is a member of a completely homogeneous speech-community, who knows its language perfectly and is unaffected by such grammatically irrelevant considerations as memory limitations, distractions, shifts of attention and interest, and errors (random or characteristic) in applying his knowledge of the language in actual performance" (Chomsky 1965: 3).

This characterization is one of considerable complexity, and it is important to be clear about some of the distinct claims it makes. For example, it does not directly assert that memory limitations and so on are irrelevant to language performance, only that limitations and distractions are grammatically irrelevant—that is, of no bearing on the complex structural knowledge that underpins language. However, and notwithstanding the insistence that a theory-internal entity and no real speaker of an external language is the focus of concern, it has to be said that from an integrational perspective all four of the considerations dismissed here as grammatically irrelevant—memory limitations, distractions, shifts of attention and interest, and errors—may be deeply relevant to an account of what is involved in knowledge of a language. Two of these will be of particular importance, however, in a revised model of language: memory limitations and shifts of attention and interest. A subtype of a third allegedly irrelevant consideration, characteristic errors, is also ripe for revaluation. Thirty years after Chomsky's famous postulation, one is struck by the confidence of the dismissal of crucial considerations concerning the psychological and interpersonal or sociological pressures on the nature and design of language. But so compelling is the Saussurean paradigm of autonomous language study that many linguists have been willing to regard memory and shifts of attention and interest as peripheral to language, as simply parts of an enabling (or disabling) background. By contrast, reaffirming the tradition that runs through Malinowski and Firth, integrationists argue that there is nothing more foundational to language than shifts of attention and interest. Without the human ability to shift attention and interest from one part of the flow of experience to another and to attend self-consciously to those very shifts of attention and interest aided by finite powers of memory, human language in all its complexity could not have developed. That is one of the essential points of chapter 3.

An integrational approach prompts the question, Can there be a practice (of language using) without a single set of rules and without a single model or theory? The answer is largely in the affirmative, although more will be said about rules in chapter 7 below (and, here at the outset, we must distinguish the question, Can there be language use without unified rules? from, Are there languages (English, French) without unified rules?). Language use is a practice that does not require a (single, community-wide) model, although it is not a practice without modelings. Each speaker of the language has his or her own remembered and revisable modeling of how to use language, how to do what things with what words in what circumstances. This modeling (which really comprises innumerable submodelings for the innumerable language games that speakers play) is provisional and open ended since, besides being a guide to doing known things with known words in known circumstances, it must have room for, and not render impossible, new experiences in which unforeseen things are done with new words in novel circumstances.

Indirect Speech Acts

The provisionality of speakers' modelings of how to use language is the source of objections to the more prescriptive reaches of speech act theory and its attendant parts. The foundation of speech act theory is an effort to specify the calculation of the illocutionary force and perlocutionary effects of so-called indirect speech acts. A typical example of an indirect speech act is saying "The door is open" (i.e., apparently making a statement) but intending to convey the request or command that the addressee close the door. This is taken by speech-act theorists, some pragmatists, and linguists generally as indicative of an ellipsis and indirectness that is assumed to be pervasive in

143 Further Principles

language performance. The view taken is that situated utterances are refracted tokens (refracted by ellipsis, indirectness, etc.) of the actual forms, sentences, and meanings of the language system proper, which is a system of unrefracted and invariant types.

But there are difficulties with such theories of ellipsis, incompleteness, and indirectness in actual utterances — theories of a sentence-to-utterance "gap," which the speech-act theory or other pragmatic model is intended to fill. The difficulties concern explanatory sufficiency. Either such theories fail to go far enough in spelling out just what will count as, for example, a promise or a warning, often declining to specify the particular words needed (the locutionary act) to perform the given act; or they go too far, spelling out just what sequence of words will count as, for example, a promise, in ways that can be readily found wanting, via counterexamples where the given locutions did not, for the interactants involved, count as promises or where quite other locutions than those specified counted as promises. Or, as Levinson has summarized matters: "Any theory of speech acts is basically concerned with mapping utterances into speech act categories, however those are conceived. The problem then is that either this is a trivial enterprise done by *fiat* (as by LFH [the literal force hypothesis]), or an attempt is made to predict accurately the functions of sentences in context. But if the latter is attempted, it soon becomes clear that the contextual sources that give rise to the assignment of function or purpose are of such complexity and of such interest in their own right, that little will be left to the theory of speech acts" (Levinson 1983: 278). The conclusion would seem to be that no general pragmatic grammar of all and only the linguistic and extralinguistic conditions for performing (for example) promises is possible — or indeed necessary. Searlean discussions of background conditions (constitutive rules) are a useful generalized ethnography, but there is no guarantee that these will be of direct relevance to situated occasions of warning, promising, threatening, and so on (see, e.g., Kreckel 1981; Rosaldo 1982; Pratt 1986). The conceptual conditions of all acts of promising may be specifiable, but the discourse-grammatical ones seem not to be.

Conversational analysts and speech-act theorists tend to assume that utterances like "There is a bull in the field," and "How old are you?" (said by a therapist to a patient who has said that she cannot go out to work because her husband doesn't want her to) are in themselves incomplete (see the discussion in Harris [1981a: 199–200]). They are an abridged or indirect formulation of what the particular speaker in particular circumstances intended, and the task of pragmatics has been taken to be the "bridging" of the gap, back to a full expression of the intended communication (cf. Ross's "underlying performative" hypothesis or more recent alternatives). Pragmaticists have not been slow to see that, once the versatility of such so-called indirect speech acts as "How old are you?" is represented as a problem to be solved (the problem is to specify which illocutionary application is intended and how), then a vast undertaking has been launched, for, if indirect speech acts require ingenious explanatory reconnection to underlying full expressions, so too must one-word sentences like "Yes," referring expressions ("Mary," etc.) that stand in for full propositional-form replies ("That girl's name is Mary"), and all utterances containing deictic expressions. By definition, the specific references of deictic expressions can be determined only by recourse to the particular context of utterance in which they are anchored. Similarly, metaphor and irony are also typically characterized by pragmaticists as a strategic indirectness and incompleteness in need of explication by calculating back to the full and direct paraphrase.

As Harris has argued (1981a: 201–2), there is no end to the task that pragmaticists (or other analysts) set themselves if they undertake to provide definitive explication of the bridge between "indirect" utterances and definitively full and direct underlying sentences. If the exercise is conducted scrupulously, there will be no logical stopping place: there are no definitively explicit sentences, ideally determinate in form and meaning, that might be identified as the terminus of inquiry. If *There's a bull in the field* is an incomplete exponent of *I warn you that there's a bull in the field*, the pursuit of the fully explicit version must justify now asking, "But what do you mean by *warn* [or *you*, or *bull*, etc.]?" Once we assert that speakers do not say what they mean and argue that they produce oblique formulations of unambiguous underlying expressions, any formulation purporting to be that exact and full expression can itself be subjected to analytic reformulation.

The response provoked by this attempt to promote "full paraphrase" into a scientific branch of linguistic pragmatics hinges on paraphrasability itself: not on whether it is possible (it clearly is) but on what it is that paraphrasing does. An integrational linguistics accepts and insists on the paraphrasability of (contextualized) "Yes," "How old are you?" and so on as a permanent possibility. The possibility of paraphrasing is part of the resources for understanding that belong to everyday linguistic practice. But that possibility does not mean that we should ordinarily take these utterances to be incomplete or inadequate and in equally invariable need of referral to some fuller underlying form. On the contrary, it is these utterances' ease of paraphrasing in context that highlights the irrelevance, to a theoretical explanation of their workings, of any paraphrase-supplying maneuver. Ordinary speakers do not ordinarily need to do it (because they can do it, ordinarily, so very easily and redundantly); why should the theory? As Gardiner remarks of speech, "Words are chosen with a shrewd calculation of their intelligibility" (Gardiner 1932: 50).

If everyday linguistic behavior is any guide, there is no "incompleteness" in so-called elliptical utterances, indirect speech acts, one-word replies, and so on — except in relation to a linguistic theory that assumes the preeminence of a certain kind of grammatical sentence. The pursuit of full direct sentences underlying incomplete and indirect utterances is a theoretical misdirection, prompted by a prior theoretical commitment to the idea of a general determinacy of meanings and forms. The "filling-in" maneuver is an unnecessary reminder of the (most normatively plausible) parts of the background of previous sanctioned contexts of use — of previous associations — in relation to which any present use will in part be seen. But the more germane factor in relation to which a present use must be seen is what interactants severally take to be the larger purposes of each interactant in the particular exchange: what each participant is after. Literal meanings of words and sentences are typical of such reminders of an authorized background. But rejecting a binarist model in which elliptical utterance in the foreground is interpretable relative to a full and invariant background, we need to consider the ways in which utterances are actually understood relative to plural but present communicational purposes and plural presently remembered patterns of use. A better term than *background* to use here might be *context*, although this term is also unfortunate in some ways since it is so commonly thought of as a detachable counterpart to *text*.

While I am arguing against the idea that linguistic meaning essentially resides in the heads of competent speakers of a language, the seemingly counterposed view also needs to be avoided: that, in ordinary circumstances, meaning is (and is assumed to be) unproblematically present and unremarkable for all competent participants in everyday interaction. A prominent feature of the opposed view is that, far from being reflections of lay ignorance and misunderstanding, commonsense lay statements and questions such as "I don't understand this sentence" and "What do you mean [by x]?" are in fact the best kind of guides available in the uncovering or display of meaning and understanding. But, equally importantly, the content of lay statements about meanings of words and sentences is varied and divergent, as the conditions vary within which those statements are made. Accordingly, from an integrational viewpoint, there is no single "thing" that we can call meaning to be found either in speakers' heads or in public practices. If we are to talk of meaning at all, it must be in the plural: interactants bring and take their own meanings to and from every linguistic experience they undergo. Language users do not find meanings; they make sense. Rather than meanings (as if these belonged to words and sentences) being "accessed" by speakers and found by hearers in the course of interaction, sense is made by each party, as attentive and oriented communicators.

The view that meaning is not essentially in heads but is displayable in everyday interactions seems to underlie a simple social experiment devised by the ethnomethodologist Garfinkel. Garfinkel asked his students to record what happened when, in the course of their everyday lives, they responded incomprehendingly, via some form of comprehensive echoic question, to the routine conversational contributions addressed to them by friends or family. As a constructed example, imagine a friend bidding you good-bye on Friday with "Have a good weekend" and your responding, feigning incomprehension, "What do you mean, 'Have a good weekend?' "; your friend's discomfort and irritation are likely to emerge rapidly. The experiment seems designed to highlight the ordinarily "unquestioned" nature of everyday conversational understanding. Interactants understand each other ordinarily and assume that this is unremarkable, to such an extent that it simply is not acceptable to put that understanding in question by implying one's own failure to understand. In a real instance reported by Garfinkel, a family member, S, announced one evening that they had had a flat tire that day. E (Garfinkel's student and a family member) promptly responded, "What do you mean, you had a flat tire?" Garfinkel continues: "She (S) appeared momentarily stunned. Then she answered in a hostile way: 'What do you mean, "What do you mean?" A flat tire is a flat tire. That is what I meant. Nothing special. What a crazy question!' " (Garfinkel 1967: 42). Clearly, E's claimed failure to understand what is meant by saying that one has had a flat tire is not accepted by S, who infers that some kind of lack of face-attentive orientedness to other is being displayed by E toward S (gratuitous hostility, lack of sympathy, or similar).

As noted, part of Garfinkel's point seems to be that speakers do not ordinarily go around putting understanding in question by prefacing responses with "What do you mean . . . ?" nor could they reasonably do so. However, the experiment also strongly suggests that the "What do you mean . . . ?" routine has an established place in some of our language games. To use the

"What do you mean . . . ?" format to preface an echo of a question or remark that is believed by its speaker to be nonobscure and nonproblematic, where that speaker is someone with whom one has an established affinal relationship, invites being heard as unsympathetic or hostile.

By the same token, "What do you mean . . . ?" is indeed the known and familiar format, used because it is an established means of indicating that a previous remark is in some way obscure or difficult to understand or respond to. If E had believed that S had not traveled by car that day, or if E is four years old, E's question becomes much more reasonable: it combines orientedness to other with display of problematicity. Between adults who are fluent speakers, however, much of the inference of hostility derives from the holistic questioning of such a response: an entire prior proposition is, it is implied, problematic (and not just the idea of "flat tire–ness" but even of "having" and "I-ness").

It is a mistake, then, to assume that asking a question like "What do you mean, you had a flat tire?" constitutes acting — as Garfinkel's experiment pretends it does — as if one did not understand what had been said. In ordinary circumstances, that is, ones in which interactants can reasonably claim that text and situation are "nothing special," such a question more normally constitutes acting obtusely, if not hostilely. In fact, Garfinkel knows this quite well — so well that he feels warranted in supplying a prefatory gloss to S's reply, reporting hostility of manner: "Then she answered in a hostile way: 'What do you mean, "What do you mean?" ' " How did Garfinkel know that there was hostility in S's reply (or "What do you mean 'she answered in a hostile way'?")? Perhaps S was enrolled in another section of Garfinkel's course and had been set the same assignment as her interlocutor. Evidently saying "What do you mean?" in response to either "I had a flat tire" or "What do you mean?" in circumstances that are "nothing special" will ordinarily not be taken merely as a report of nonunderstanding.

Gardiner and Knowledge of Past Speech Events

In the discussion of literal and metaphoric meaning, it was proposed that, in interpreting texts and utterances, every speaker of the language draws not on a shared knowledge of a shared code but on his or her unique memories of past experience and the various encounters with verbal forms, in contexts, recorded therein. It was suggested that speakers store words "with contexts of their previously encountered use attached." There are affinities between this view and those of Alan Gardiner, an Egyptologist and linguist who had considerable influence on British linguistic theorizing in the period between the world wars (he was roughly contemporary with Malinowski and Firth), although he is now largely forgotten.

In Gardiner's major work of theory, *The Theory of Speech and Language* (1932), knowledge of language is characterized as, at foundation, simply knowledge of past speech events "formed through countless individual experiences of purposeful acts of speech" (Taylor 1988: 134). In important respects, however, Gardiner's account reflects the dichotomized view of language most compellingly presented in Saussure's *Cours*. The terms in this dichotomy are *language* and *speech*, although these are used somewhat differently from Saussure's *langue* and *parole*. For Gardiner, language is the intensely individualized aggregation of experiences of speech events that a speaker has stored away in memory and draws on in the reasoned interpretation of a present speech event. By contrast, speech is in essence social and interactional, with each speech event a unique occasion on which prior knowledge of the language may be brought to bear. Language is diachronic or historicized, speech is synchronic or momentary. *Language* is thus something of a cover term, for Gardiner, for the potentially quite diverse languages that different speakers have come to know through experience. A speaker's language amounts to a mental model, derived from past experiences with speech, of various patterns of usage. This personalized model is invoked, together with an assessment of the present context of situation and more general reasoning powers, in the production or interpretation of any particular instance of speech. Since language is only a modeling derived from speech, priority must be accorded the latter. Study of a language must begin with proper study of particular concrete acts of speech, a language being only a personalized stored abstraction from countless experiences of such concrete acts of speech. A major enigma not fully explained by these assumptions is how language relates to *a* language: how the individual's speech-derived language relates to the kind of social object known as a language, such as English.

Related to the separation of speech from language, and again in partial contrast with Saussurean theory, the sentence is for Gardiner the crucial unit of speech performance, while words are merely a unit of language, with 'copies' of stored words used in speech events. On the other hand, Gardiner's concept of the word seems entirely matched with that of the Saussurean sign (see esp. Gardiner 1932: 69, 88–89), words being units of the language that are "utilized" in speech and are "not easily altered" by the individual. As a result of this combination of Saussurean and individualist-contextualist (or Malinowskian) principles, Gardiner's account of speech communication includes some interesting contradictory tensions.

Meanings are the aggregated records of the uses of each word (part of language), while sentences (part of speech) do not strictly have anything so abstracted and "virtual" as meanings at all: rather, any sentence, embedded in a speech event, gives rise to a unique and situation-specific "thing meant." By the locution "thing meant" Gardiner sought to reinstate the human purposiveness that he saw as inherent in the use of language to mean particular things. That human purposiveness or intending, in his view, was somewhat obscured "when it began to be said that words 'mean' this or that" (Gardiner 1932: 102). Ways of thinking that were "esoteric" and "altogether baneful" (p. 100) began to emerge: "Perhaps the words could now be conceived of as constituting and creating the very substance of the things meant by them. Just as a house is a 'building,' so perhaps the things meant by words might be a 'meaning.' Certainly some such fallacious conception appears to underlie the terms often employed to indicate the thing 'meant' by a sentence" (Gardiner 1932: 102). Calculation of the "thing meant" of a sentence involves the speaker or addressee in a selective adducement of parts of the remembered past meanings of the words composing the sentence. While intuitively attractive, much remains to be clarified in Gardiner's account — in particular, how it is that a speaker or listener adduces a part of a word's meaning and discards the remainder, in the determination of a particular "thing meant."

Gardiner elaborates an example of how a situated "thing meant" is rationally derived, in a given context, from the clue(s) of word meaning. James and his wife, Mary, are sitting indoors reading and have planned to take a walk later, weather permitting. Mary is in poor health, so, if it rains, the walk must be postponed. At some point, James hears the sound of raindrops on the window, looks up and finds his suspicion confirmed, concludes that the walk must be put off, and decides to apprise Mary of the situation. He addresses the sentence "Rain!" to Mary. Mary identifies the sound she hears as the word *rain*, the use of which she has encountered in the past for a number of different purposes (it helps, here, that James did not announce "Rain, dear"), and goes on to see that James intends her to notice that it is raining and indeed that he intends quite a lot more besides (the full "thing meant" of James's utterance).

First Gardiner acutely points out, concerning Mary's response to James's utterance, that in the given circumstances of private reading Mary is not expecting to be addressed. She has not been designated as addressee and yet at once becomes one in the process of understanding James's utterance as addressed to her: "This readiness to attend is an important and almost invariable feature in the operations of speech, though I shall not allude to it again. It arises, partly from the general recognition of speech as a source of mutual advantage, partly from the habitual courtesy which social life has engendered" (Gardiner 1932: 76). However, Gardiner moves on from this crucial phenomenon, namely, Mary's need and ability somehow to judge James's outburst as a remark addressed to her — and not simply a clearing of the throat or a self-directed comment provoked by his reading matter. And the turn that his account of Mary's processing of the speech event takes is toward Saussurean abstraction. The auditory sensation that she experiences, Gardiner states, "is immediately identified by Mary as a familiar word. But which word? The sound of *Rain!* is very ambiguous, embracing all the possibilities of *rain* and *rein* and *reign*" (p. 77).

For the integrationist, a more interesting question than "which word?" must be directed to Gardiner's own assumptions: Why is it assumed that identifying James's utterance as a word, and then as such and such a word and not others, is a necessary preliminary step in the first place? This implies that interpretation of the thing meant of James's utterance cannot proceed until it is "typed" in relation to the autonomous system of units known as words of the language: only with a cognitive conversion of utterances into words of the language, Gardiner implies, can grasp of the thing meant be achieved. But just how such a conversion of utterance into word is achieved remains unspecified. To be sure, Gardiner goes on to say that Mary "does not doubt that *rain* (and not *rein* or *reign*) has been meant" and that "solely the first of these possibilities" occurs to her. But this does not so much downplay the putative process of word identification as serve to reassure the reader that, in context, it proceeds without a hitch. Yet, given Gardiner's descriptions elsewhere in the book of how the individual's linguistic knowledge is steadily built up from accretions of remembered uses of speech in past situations, this compromise with the Saussurean notion of the language as a uniform structured system, on the basis of which verbal communication is achieved, is unjustified. It was, however, perhaps inevitable from the moment Gardiner opted for a number of paired theoretical concepts, of which the most significant are the word and the thing meant. Either one of these concepts, when its implications are examined in detail, leaves the other with a considerably diminished role to fill in a theory of language communication. Just how thoroughgoing and natural seeming is the kind of compromise that even Gardiner made is shown by the fact that speaker, listener, uttered words, and thing(s) meant are singled out by him as the four chief factors involved in the typical act of speech.

At the same time, Gardiner's many observations of relevance to contemporary pragmatics should also be acknowledged. In addition to his insights on the crucial role of politeness, reflected in earlier quotations, he formulates the grounds for Mary taking James's "Rain!" as indicating rain in terms now familiar in relevance theory: "Since the possibility nearest to hand suits the situation, she has no reason for looking further afield" (1932: 77). And, also common in pragmatics today, he often characterizes the role of words in actual speech as that of clues. Thus, James's thing meant, what he intends Mary to see, is a far more complex state of affairs involving the rain, the walk that cannot now take place, and the disappointment entailed. The word *rain* is only a clue, which James intends Mary to use in reasoning out the intended thing meant: "If, then, I wished to explain what was meant by the sentence *Rain!*, I should have no hesitation in recounting the whole course of James's reflections from the moment when he first perceived the rain down to the actual instant of articulation. . . . To omit, for example, his fears for Mary's health would be to omit the very thing which provided him with a motive for speaking" (1932: 80).

Here Gardiner insists on the cotemporality of linguistic behavior with the rest of human behavior. He also insists on an account of language that denies that it is essentially nomenclaturist or designatory. James's "correct" designation of the meteorological precipitation by "Rain" rather than, for example, "Snow!" or "Music!" is only a small part of the complex thing meant; more important is the performative or demonstrative effect of this integrated use of language, its part in acts of recognizing (the rain), informing, showing concern, and regretting. The orthodox linguist's complaint that all these things cannot possibly be part of the meaning of "Rain!" can be answered by the argument that meaning only strictly ever arises in the local determination of a speech event's thing meant—which is to say, in the determination of what a speaker intends to convey or what a listener takes to have been intended.

Given Gardiner's protointegrational views of language and speech, it is interesting to consider what he regarded as a legitimate and coherent enterprise for the linguistic analyst to undertake. In particular, since Gardiner treats each occasion of speech as sui generis and the sentences occurring in each occasion of speech as equally unique, one is drawn to ask whether a generalizing system-oriented linguistic study of sentences was possible. Taylor frames the question thus: "Do Gardiner's views of the irremediable individuality, context dependence, and creativity of the sentence mean that he thought it could not be an object for linguistic study?" (Taylor 1988: 143). Gardiner's answer is in the negative, for although the sentence qualities derivable from the rational consideration of the interaction of sentence form and situation relative to any given sentence are numberless, the types of sentence forms that can be used in this computation are limited in number; specifying the types of sentence forms becomes the linguist's task. Here, habituation and expectation are most important since, whenever we encounter a sentence form, we bring to our assessment of it certain expectations of use based on how we have habitually found the form used in the past.

In this picture, constant repetition is needed to form a habituation or an expected use and to transcend somehow the unrepeatability that characterizes any single occurrence of speech. Somehow, single instances have no effect on the established pattern of expectations, but, when sufficiently reiterated, they do. There are Saussurean shadows lurking in the following sentences summarizing this position: "Because sentence-quality is invariably unique — dependent as it is on the particular features of the situation — the particular and unique means by which any specific sentence-quality is communicated does not influence our expected habits of use: that is, our knowledge of language. All that is creative and situation-dependent in speech is *ipso facto* non-repeatable and so cannot through experience become a part of our habits and expectations. It is only at the highest level of generality that there is repetition of sentence-qualities" (Taylor 1988: 144). Here we see Gardiner take the wrong turn waiting in advance for him owing to his own bifurcation of linguistic activity into language (and its words) and speech (and its things meant). In discounting the effect of individual situation-dependent acts of speech, he repeats Saussure's tenet concerning the impossibility of acts of *la parole* impinging on the collectivity of *la langue*. Revising the penultimate sentence of the quoted passage, the integrational position is as follows:

All that is creative and situation dependent in speech is, strictly speaking, nonrepeatable; nevertheless, the sense that we make of innumerable such specific situated speech acts is the only source of our linguistic habits and expectations.

Free Indirect Bakhtin

Fascinatingly, Gardiner's example of the couple sitting indoors communicating via the single word *rain* can be set alongside a passage from a 1926 paper

153 Further Principles

by Volosinov (see Volosinov 1983) on a remarkably similar theme. Here again, a couple are sitting in a room, and, disappointed by a deterioration in the weather, one says to the other "Well!" and nothing more. Volosinov's point is that the sense and significance of this exchange are not remotely adequately discovered by inspecting "the purely verbal part of the utterance," for this neglects the nonverbal context of the word — the interactants' spatial purview, common knowledge, and understanding and their common evaluation of the circumstances:

> At the moment of the exchange both individuals glanced at the window and saw that it was snowing. Both knew that it was already May and long since time for spring, and finally, that they both were sick of the protracted winter. Both were waiting for spring and were annoyed by the late snowfall. The utterance depends directly on all this — on what was "visible to both" (the snowflakes beyond the window), what was "known to both" (the date was May) and what was "similarly evaluated" (boredom with winter, longing for spring); and all this was grasped in the actual meaning of the utterance, all this soaked into it yet remained verbally unmarked, unuttered. The snowflakes stay beyond the window, the date on a page of the calendar, the evaluation in the mind of the speaker, but all this is implied in the word "well." (1983: 10–11)

In his discussion of this passage (Pateman 1989: 209), Pateman suggests that ideas similar to those in this remarkable passage were not seriously developed anywhere until the advent of Gricean pragmatics in the 1960s. But, as we have seen, extraordinarily congruent reflections appear in Gardiner's book of 1932. Furthermore, Gardiner's explication does not move beyond the "purely verbal" part of utterance only, as here, to become bogged down in questionable assumptions about shared knowledge. But in making this appeal to shared knowledge, as Pateman notes, the Volosinov of 1926 is indeed the neglected ancestor of Grice and, beyond him, of Sperber and Wilson, and, like the latter, is distinguished by the Chekhovian richness of implicatures he confidently derives from a simple remark about the weather.

For it has to be said that Volosinov's gloss of the exchange is mildly absurd: what we are granted insight into is not — despite his protestations — the extended covert part of the meaning of the word *well* as understood by the couple in the scene but an account of Volosinov's own interpretation of the covert meaning of the word *well* in that scene. It is an omniscient narrative report, not an analytic clarification, for all its other similarities with the Gardiner scene. In that respect, Volosinov "goes too far," while in attributing such a wealth of interpretive commentary specifically to the word *well*, representing it as the word's meaning, he fails to go far enough: that is, despite the eloquent testimony of his own extended reading of the scene, he fails to set aside the doomed notion that *well*, or any other isolable chunk of language, has a meaning. Where the Gardiner narrative is credible, this one is illicit, perhaps most specifically in the erasing, even in a picture predicated on particularity, of all differences between the two individuals involved. They are "a couple," repeatedly referred to by the word *both*: both glanced, both knew, both were waiting for spring, and so on. No such presumption of commonality is insisted on in Gardiner's picture: like Volosinov's couple (and Sperber and Wilson's couples too, as we shall see in the next chapter), his couple know each other well, but it is never assumed that they certainly both know anything.

Elsewhere, however, the many-voiced Bakhtin/Volosinov espoused positions that either are consonant with integrational linguistics or can form the basis for constructive dialogue with it. For example, the issue of the potential revisability of meaning determinations over time and with change of situation is drawn into his concept of *intertextuality*: "The life of a word is contained in its transfer from one mouth to another, from one social collective to another, from one generation to another generation. In this process the word does not forget its own path and cannot completely free itself from the power of these concrete contexts into which it has entered" (1981: 270). By *word* here Bakhtin evidently means *utterance*; and we may question both the personification of the living utterance that "does not forget" but "cannot completely free itself" and the attention exclusively to the broad categories of collective and generation. But, insofar as this quotation emphasizes that language exists only in its "transfer," its endless variable use, this is an important premise. Equally important are Bakhtin's allusions to "the loophole of consciousness and the word" (1981: 313): the option—particularly in speech, it is claimed—of retaining for oneself "the possibility for altering the ultimate, final meaning of one's own words."

The phenomenon that Bakhtin seems to have in mind here is the opportunity for repair, reformulation, and alteration of meaning or effect that always remains open to a dialogue participant up until the closure of that dialogue (there are numerous studies of such procedures in the conversation analysis and psycholinguistics literature). Thoroughgoing dialogism or integrationalism, however, asserts that such a potential for revision applies beyond specific dialogues to all occasions of language use, on the assumption that proprietorship of meaning is always local in the first instance, provisional, and relative to the interactional purposes of the parties involved. The final meaning of utterances in spoken dialogue is not open to alteration in some unique way since all language remains open to revision and no revisions are final. By contrast with speech, the writtenness of writing appears to guarantee permanence and fixity of meaning: "The fiction of a word's literal realia promotes . . . the reification of its meaning" (Volosinov 1973: 80; see also Goffman 1976). Writing gives the impression, partly justified but partly misleading, that it is immeasurably more *inspectable* than speech — indeed, that it is *definitively* inspectable.

Bakhtin wrote frequently and celebratedly of the dialogical in language: "Linguistics studies 'language' and its specific logic in its *commonality* as that fact which makes dialogical discourse *possible*, but it consistently refrains from studying those dialogical relationships themselves. . . . Dialogical relationships are totally impossible without logical and concrete semantic relationships, but they are not reducible to them; they have their own specificity" (Bakhtin 1973: 151–52). Of this Rommetveit shrewdly comments: "This passage from Bakhtin sounds as if he might very well endorse the kind of pure semantics of literal meaning proposed by Katz . . . as some sort of prerequisite or base for his own literary or 'metalinguistic' analysis of dialogical relationships. Even Vygotsky and Bakhtin as well as Habermas, it seems, are thus somewhat and in certain respects constrained by the myth of literal meaning" (1988: 22). Accordingly, Pateman's conclusion, if not all of his implicit approval, seems justified: "In the end, I think Volosinov (and Bakhtin) hold back from an ultra-Wittgensteinian contextualism ('meaning is use') in favour of something closer to an orthodox distinction between semantic and pragmatic aspects of meaning, distinguishing what a sentence means from what a sentence-in-an-utterance means and does" (Pateman, 1989: 208).

Perhaps surprisingly, it is the writing attributed to Volosinov, among that in the Bakhtinian oeuvre, that is the most radical and provocative in linguistic-theoretical terms, particularly in its nearly contemporaneous critique of Saussure, long before the latter had become orthodoxy, for Volosinov's argument with Saussurean homogeneity and coherence and with the idea of language as a form "où tout se tient" (where every element holds its distinct place in complementarity with all other elements in the whole) is developed in a thoroughgoing consideration of quasi direct discourse or what is now commonly termed free indirect discourse (for an introductory treatment of which, see Toolan [1988: 119–37]). This widely discussed technique seems to have its natural home in the novel, where it can be used to embed a representation of the thoughts or words of a character within the standard narratorial frame (commonly, this frame is past-tense, third-person narration). Thus, alongside such sentences as

> He said, "Look the little monkey has scrawled all over my proofs, here, and again here"

and

> He said that his child had spoiled several pages of the proofs,

we might find, in free indirect discourse, and merging the subjectivity of direct utterance with the objectivity of report:

> Look, the little monkey had written all over the proofs, here, and again here. *Now* what was he going to do?

Free indirect discourse is most at home perhaps in literary narratives, but it crops up in newspaper stories and is also to be found in literature for children, which is more versatile and challenging than we sometimes imagine. The following extract, from A. A. Milne's *The House at Poor Corner*, goes one better than a modulation to free indirect discourse: within a single sentence, it moves from narrative, to direct discourse, and back again: "So then Rabbit said he'd go with them; and Tigger and Eeyore went off together because Eeyore wanted to tell Tigger How to Win at Poohsticks, which you do by letting your stick drop in a twitchy sort of way, if you understand what I mean, Tigger; and Christopher Robin and Pooh and Piglet were left on the bridge by themselves" (1961: 46). Here, some at least of the sequence *which you do by letting your stick drop in a twitchy sort of way, if you understand what I mean, Tigger* is evidently Eeyore's direct speech to Tigger; as in many of the most skillful modulations, the boundary here between narration and direct speech (does the latter begin with the word *which*, or *twitchy*, or *if*?) is somewhat indeterminate.

Besides being of general interest for its ambiguities and problematic amalgam of voices, free indirect discourse is of particular interest here since it constitutes perhaps the strongest kind of threat to the deictic anchoredness, the cotemporal situatedness, that the integrational stance takes to be inherent properties of language. The "threat of unanchoring" is perhaps captured by the following formulation (itself a modified quotation from Pateman [1989]):

The incorporation of the represented speech of the other into the representing narratorial discourse necessarily transforms it.

Contemplating this verdict, the reader may well ask, With what is the final *it* coreferential? Which entity is it that gets transformed? Is it "the represented speech of the other," "the other," "the representing narratorial discourse," or, even, "the incorporation"? To this, free indirect discourse gives the sphinx-like reply, "Yes," for any or all of these may undergo sea change once free indirect discourse's subtle recyclings of projected representation are entertained. Free indirect discourse produces an unanchoring effect. This is evident in the great difficulty of imagining a situation where

> Look, the little monkey had written all over the proofs, here, and again here

might actually be uttered by someone in direct interaction with an addressee (i.e., by an experiencing "I" commenting to a copresent "you," as distinct from an "I" telling or reconstructing via performed narration of the kind that free indirect discourse itself promotes). Reflecting that unanchoring, Banfield (1981) has dubbed such text "unspeakable sentences." For her, however, the category of unspeakable sentences extends to include all sentences of narration, counterintuitively grouping what is a routine and pervasive phenomenon (narration) with a rarer and much more provocative strategy.

But to say that free indirect discourse puts integrational assumptions about deictic presentness and cotemporality to the test is not to concede that the strategy flouts or refutes them. It is rather the case that free indirect discourse exploits the inevitable deictic cotemporality of any language act in a particularly sharp way, invoking two contexts of utterance and situation simultaneously. It does so in such a way that no definitive adjudication (e.g., this part is representing discourse, this part represented discourse; or here the narrator tells, from the narrator's deictic center, while here the character speaks, from his or her deictic center; etc.) can be made. All the helpful binarisms — a self and an other, speaking and reporting, showing and telling, using and mentioning, transcription and interpretation, repetition and reformulation, past and present, empathy and irony — have their contingency and provisionality highlighted, for none apply to such discourse unproblematically. The thrust of integrational linguistic thinking, however, is that such contingency, such only local and provisional determinacy (of what is use and what is mention, of what is empathetic and what is ironic, and so on), is the permanent condition of language. In the simplified discourse traditionally analyzed by linguists as perhaps in many ordinary linguistic circumstances, this permanent condition of language is backgrounded; it is in free indirect discourse — and metaphor and irony — that the condition is richly foregrounded.

Situationally Relevant Determination

In place of the overly determined context and overly optimistic assumption of shared attentiveness entailed in the notion of mutual manifestness, an account of the resources that interactants draw on in their interpretation of dialogue must begin with the minimal factors that each participant will ordinarily assume:

> When I intend and attempt to communicate with another person, I assume that we are to some degree oriented to each other, have faith in the possibility of communication, and have memories of similar past interactions (perhaps even of past interactions with each other).

These assumptions affect how intentionality is conceived; specifically, it is not understood as a recognition by a hearer of the information and evaluation that a speaker intended to convey. Intentionality, in an integrational perspective, concerns the intentions that a hearer attributes to a speaker. These intentions are attributed without hope, possibility, or need of confirmation by the speaker of the attributed intentions' accuracy, prior to the hearer's involvement in some interactional response. Speaker A has recourse to various means of trying to display to hearer B that the latter's understanding of what A intended by her previous turn seems to be mistaken — including the bald "No, that's not what I meant at all." But none of this can logically occur before B has hazarded and made some sort of display of his attributions and his (mis)understanding.

The immense variety of strategies that speakers develop to try to make noticeable their sense of the kinds of misunderstanding their interlocutors seem to hold deserves to be a major branch of linguistic inquiry in itself. A rich field of behavior lies behind activity that is too often glibly summarized as "the negotiation of meaning" or — even worse — "repair." And the growing awareness of this possibility in language activity, the possibility of revising an addressee's seeming misunderstandings by recourse to further signifying activity, must be one of the most exhilarating discoveries in a child's language development.

Intentionality is always a matter of attributed intentions, done "now," in a language user's historicized present, and is never a matter of specifying telementationally conveyed speakers' intentions. The distinction drawn in Harris (1981a) between hearability and mere audibility is germane to the discussion (the same contrast holds between legibility and mere visibility). Harris makes the point that orthodox linguistics has chiefly attended to audibility (and visibility), a property conducive to treatment with a mechanistic descriptive apparatus of determinate units, rules, and criteria. However, "When *A* speaks to *B*, the prime communicational concern which both share in common is not just the audibility but the hearability of what is said; as when *A* writes a letter to *B* the prime communicational concern is not just the visibility but the legibility of what is written" (Harris 1981a: 178). Harris pursues the discussion of hearability and legibility via interesting examples of the indeterminacy of form in each domain. He considers the bases of interpretation of a sound transcribable as [zaaaa] produced with a falling intonation, uttered by a bowler in situationally appropriate circumstances in a game of cricket, and the parallel interpretation of a scrawled figure, in a letter, that might possibly be the word *and*. In the latter case, he writes: "We say, for example, of some dubiously legible word in John's letter, 'It looks like *and*' — as if we were engaged in an actual process of comparison between the scrawl on the paper and some imagined copperplate prototype, whereas what we are in fact trying to do is to determine how the scrawl is most plausibly interpretable in its context, in such a way as to make sense of John's communication" (1981a: 178–79).

We ordinarily tend to take visibility and audibility for granted; we take for granted that signs will almost invariably be adequately differentiated, as far as substance is concerned. But consider a student of German confronted by Gothic script for the first time. Or — more startlingly — the assumption of Stokoe and others that, in Sign, there was just one sign for both the verb *sit* and the noun *chair*; only more recently (Supalla and Newport 1978) has it been shown that a subtle gestural difference separates the two signs involved. Given Stokoe's expertise in Sign, his pioneering demonstration that Sign was a language with syntax and structure at a time when many Signers themselves doubted this (Stokoe 1960), a third possibility must be considered: that in the years intervening between Stokoe's and Supalla and Newport's studies, two morphologically related signs have been derived from a single source. In all such uncertainties about substance (here, over visibility), the situated resolution of the uncertainty is guided by the more salient criterion of legibility (i.e., of *how* one judges the sign was intended to be understood). In the case of signing *sit* and *chair*, the addressee's situated assessment of whether the signer intended to communicate "sit" rather than "chair" (or anything else) is what is crucial, so whether there are two gestural configurations or just one here is distinctly secondary.

To take another example, imagine that I wish to write Roy Harris's name on the whiteboard at the front of a classroom containing forty students and am contemplating two ways (among innumerable) of proceeding: (1) writing the name *Harris* in six-inch-high letters, but neglecting to dot the *i*, or (2) writing the name *Harris* in a flawless script, but each letter only a half-inch high. Despite involving failure to conform to the established form of one of the letters, the former procedure easily crosses the crucial legibility threshold; although the latter procedure leads to visible text and flawless orthographic form, it fails the legibility test for those students who have forgotten to bring their opera glasses. Thus, one aspect of legibility is "contextually appropriate size of script": legibility is essential to writing, appropriateness of size is always required, but no decontextualized and generalizable prescription as to what the appropriate size of script might be is possible. This is just one of the respects in which, for language to function as language (I can write the name *Harris* in half-inch-high letters all the way around the whiteboard, using it as a decorative motif, but such small script remains unworkable — in the given situation — as language), it must be seen and assessed within its context of use.

If we emphasize legibility rather than mere visibility, then, as an essential element in interpretation, we must also remember that legibility is to be understood as a matter not of what a written form "is permitted to be read as" but of what it "can be, and is, read as." Harris proceeds to demonstrate the unhelpfulness of any assumed reliance on a prototypical *and*; prototypicality cannot give an *and* in the reading task:

> In some respects the scrawl will be similar to the prototype, and in other respects it will be dissimilar. What we need to know is which similarities matter. But the prototype itself cannot tell us this. It does not incorporate in its own visual contours the criteria relevant for matching it with every other written shape. All we have done is to substitute one problem for another. Furthermore, the substitution leads us nowhere. For we now have to decide in which respect the scrawl would need to be like the prototype in order to determine whether the scrawl is indeed "like *and.*" The answer will be that the relevant respects are precisely those in which the scrawl is legible as *and*. If we can determine that for the scrawl, then we do not need the prototype at all. If not, no amount of visual inspection of the prototype will help. (1981a: 179)

Harris's chief target here is the fixed-code assumption that there is a prototype form of *and* in the written language (or of *How's that* in the spoken language) that would somehow "tell" the language user whether a particular encountered form was an instantiation of that prototype, that is, whether the encountered item was an imperfect token of the authoritative and preexisting type. On the contrary, Harris argues, there is no warrant for assuming that such prototypes exist, and, even if they did, they would not be able to resolve the question of whether a particular encountered form was a token of the posited type. That crucial question can be resolved only (provisionally) in the perceived circumstances of an experienced communication situation. At the same time it is clear that *perception of similarity* plays an important role in the local determination of whether some scrawl is an *and*, that is, in deciding what a particular shape or sound "counts as." Readers' and listeners' procedures of comparison and judging similarity are a crucial part of language comprehension and interpretation. Even to supply the metalinguistic commentary "It looks like *and*" is to identify the speaker as an inducted member of a language community, with memories of previous uses of the word *and*. As Harris remarks: "No one supposes that two individuals can somehow achieve instant communication on the basis of words neither has used or heard before. The question is whether it is correct, or useful, or even plausible to represent their past linguistic experience as standing in relation to their present communication situation as the rules of a game to a particular episode of play" (1981a: 186).

But not only are these makings of comparison not performed on stored prototype forms of verbal items; more importantly, they are not performed on abstracted forms at all. We can perform a comparison of instances of the same abstracted forms, of course—printers, for example, do this frequently—but this is a very different task, really only a visibility task, from that undertaken by an involved language user. The visibility task of comparison performed by a person setting movable type who compares two *m*'s, for example, is rather like that of a house framer who lines up two eight-foot-long two-by-fours to see whether they are sufficiently similar in length for his framing task; this is a comparing of like with like. But legibility tasks involve comparing like with unlike, involving assessments of relation within a localized economy. When a carpenter framing a house grasps a piece of lumber of whose dimensions he is unsure and lines it up beside two pieces he knows to be a two-by-one and a two-by-three, respectively, and on this basis is able to judge the mystery piece to be a two-by-two, this is a simple assessment by relation of the kind involved in the interpretation of forms generally.

In the case of the reader of scrawled *and*'s and the hearer of distorted [hawzðæt] appeals, it is not that such addressees have no memory of previous encounters with diverse expressions interpreted as *and* and appeals against the batsman, respectively. Nor is it reasonable to deny that the language user will have some form of mental grasp — an abstracted and schematic grasp — of the typical graphic shapes of an *and* and the typical phonic sounds of the cricketing appeal. Such schematics undoubtedly underpin interpretation and communication; they do not, however, govern those processes in a relation of prototype and instance. To assume that they do is to attend to diachronic assessments of visibility or likeness to the neglect of crucial synchronic relational assessments within the experienced developing situation of integrated activity — whether that is reading John's letter or playing (or watching) a game of cricket. In the former case, judging a particular scrawl as *and* will depend considerably on how other scrawls in John's letter are read, on whether *and* seems to fit, and so on; that is, signs are interpreted first and foremost on the basis of the relation they seem to maintain with co-occurring signs in the local integrated economy that the language user is actively negotiating. By the *local integrated economy* I mean here something approximating to what Wittgenstein calls "a form of life" (or, potentially more misleadingly, "a language game"), or what Firth called "restricted languages" (Firth 1968: 105), or what Levinson (1979) has termed an "activity type."

Firth invoked the idea of restricted languages, local linguistic ecologies for specific kinds of language use, in discussing the work of the descriptive linguist at its best. When the linguist is confronted with such a language, he claimed, "The material is clearly defined, the linguist knows what is on his agenda and the field of application is sufficiently circumscribed for him to set up *ad hoc* structures and systems." But what suits the descriptive linguist applies even more immediately to the situated language user. Firth continues: "Such restricted languages would be those of science, technology, politics, commerce, a particular book, a particular form or *genre*, a characteristic type of work associated with a single author or a type of speech function with its appropriate style. A restricted language can be said to have a *micro-grammar* and a *micro-glossary*."

All the key terms here are relevant to the present argument, including the acknowledged provisionality implicit in Firth's adoption of the term *ad hoc*, the recognition of the need for "sufficient circumspection," and the formulation in terms of particularity, characteristicness, associatability, and appropriateness. And the significance of the final reference to a microgrammar and a microglossary is not so much that, for the participant language user (here does lie a difference from the position of the descriptive linguist), any such microgrammar can be definitively written but rather that *some* such microgrammar and microglossary, rather than a macrogrammar guiding production and construal of all forms and meanings in all contexts, is the more immediately relevant guide to the language user.

The crucial point about our encountering of the expression roughly transcribable as *zaaa* is that we do not, directly and immediately, attempt to match it with a single, one-entry-for-all-purposes lemma in a mental lexicon, which supplies one or several possible meanings for the heard form. That is the essence of mistaken biplanarity. We do not live in language that way. Between forms and interpretations lies a categorization so experientially and ontologically different from those of form and meaning as these are standardly characterized in linguistics that it makes little sense to call it a third or additional level, lying between them and of the same kind as those others. It is, rather, a socioculturally informed act of assessment of just what kind of activity is going on here, now, in the course of which this *zaaa* has been uttered, seemingly intentionally. We have names for many of the more familiar and established activities: playing softball, apologizing, getting married, sharing a meal, participating in a committee meeting, making travel arrangements, going to the doctor, buying a car, making a promise, writing an epic, declaring war, laying tiles, sailing a boat, playing computer games, and so on. But, even if this list went on for several pages, it would not begin to be adequate because each of us is familiar with many more established activities, locally recognizable contexts of language use, than there are established names for. One could make an effort at setting out a "map" of such activities, in the form of some sort of branching diagram, but such a mapping is likely to be endlessly fallible: there seem to be few if any firm grounds for establishing hierarchical relations among the activities, and, unlike a syntactic phrase marker, the branches of this diagram can cross at any point. Therefore, if we set out playing softball, getting married, apologizing, appealing, and writing an epic as if these were five distinct and equivalent activities with complementary distribution, we do so only provisionally; we know well enough that apologizing can take place within softball or getting married, that playing a game of softball with someone may conceivably count as an apology, and that, if it has not already happened, then the future may hold occasions on which marriages take place in the course of softball games. Nor need a linguistic event be seen as geared to only one or two recognized activities: it may blend numerous otherwise-distinct activities in ways that defy prediction from outside the ongoing exchange.

Those within linguistics and literary theory who have long accepted the idea that language must be understood within the context that has shaped its emergence may feel here, as perhaps elsewhere in this book, that integrationalism is old news or a pushing at an open door. But that may be to underestimate it. Having cited Firth above on restricted languages and microgrammars, it is only appropriate to note Halliday's influential treatment of register, in which he has proposed that categories he calls the "field," "mode," and "tenor" of the discourse clarify and build on Firth's brief remarks. Within linguistics, systemic-functional linguists like Halliday and Hasan have been some of the most attuned to the significance of genre, and there seems nothing inherent in the definition of *field*, *mode*, and *tenor* to preclude interpretating each of them as open sets of semiotic possibility.

At the same time, however, the practical application of those categories in standard treatments of language variation is often at odds with the more radical direction in which the principle of "provisional situated determination" would take the analyst-participant. Since field, mode, and tenor are language-wide dimensions or parameters and are thus three universal gauges in relation to which every instance of discourse can be tagged, some language-variation discussions have tended to imply that, despite registral or generic difference, all texts relate back to the same single lexicogrammar, variously put to work relative to just those three dimensions. But integrational linguists reject the idea that any three parameters will invariably locate or explain the multiply variable forms and meanings that co-communicators put to work. And they are willing to consider the picture that emerges if it is *not* the case that seemingly various discourses can be projected from or traced back to a single community-wide language via the prisms of field, mode, and tenor: in their picture there is no such unitary, uniform, biplanar, community-wide language in the first place. Perhaps this is at base a difference of perspective between comparativist-variationists (who always, ultimately, characterize particular instances relative to other comparable, synonymous, equivalent, or parallel instances — hence always first and last assume underlying commonality) and integrationist-contextualists (who wish to give full theoretical recognition to the potential for newness, unpredictability, and the primarily local grounding or sense of interactions, such that comparison with past interactions, the established language or record, is theoretically secondary). The critique of field, mode, and tenor here is not that of, for example, Crystal and Davy (1969), who suggest that these three categories are incomplete, imprecise, and inadequate; the integrational stance is that, given the potential in language for innovation and local determination, whatever categories we postulate are bound to be incomplete.

Significantly, where activity types or forms of life have been paid much attention at all within linguistics, they have been so in a noticeably restricted or conservative way, by focusing chiefly on a very few highly institutionalized genres or language routines: the Russian folk tale (Propp), or nursery tales (Hasan), or service encounters (Ventola, Gumperz), job interviews, news or political interviews, and so on. All the work in these genres and subgenres of language use are relevant to integrational linguistics, but the tendency within the standard linguistic studies that are committed to the twin levels of form and meaning and the triple pillars of phonology, syntax, and semantics is that the "grammar" of service encounters has no place alongside the autonomous, context-transcending grammars that we need to formulate for phonology, syntax, and semantics. The general assumption has been that service encounters, compliments, and cricketing language, for example, are each merely "one kind of use" of the core resources of the language and that the latter can be given extensive characterization independently of such individual cases. What biplanar linguistics makes every effort to avoid contemplating is the fact that *every* use of language is "one kind of use" of language and that, if a particular *zaaa* is not read through the framework of expectations created by treating the embedding activity as one of playing cricket, it is only because it is being read through another framework of expectations.

Fires and Bicycles

The arguments in the previous section concerning the interpretation of a barely legible *and* were aimed in part at the infatuation with forms and types, to the neglect of interactants' situated purposes, to be found in linguistic discussions of interpretation. But the argument was a rejection neither of abstraction per se nor of the role of type-token relations in sense making (on which see also chapter 6). Rather, the point was that the comparative task is more complex and involves more unconstrained intelligence than is sometimes suggested. The task involves both comparing presently encountered form-context material with remembered form-context material and assessing the differential and mutually defining relations between elements (cries, scrawls, gestures) within the unitary language-using event.

Talk of comparing a present scrawled *and* with previous instances of *and*, it was argued, misrepresents what is actually involved in reading barely legible words. What is actually involved is a comparison of a present integrated use with previous encountered occasions of seemingly similar use. But even this broader comparative task is only part of the interpretation process. At least as important a role is played by our situated assessment of what a presently encountered utterance or written form is intended to communicate — an assessment that is creative and rational rather than blind and routine. The local relevance of such assessments always has a place for the creative and rational in meaning determination. And it is possible to cite any number of examples where, in circumstances sufficiently pressing, the potential (but usually disregarded) controversiality of just what may reasonably be taken to be meant by such everyday words as *fire*, *carriage*, and *souvenir* has come to the fore. Those pressing circumstances almost invariably involve the threat, to some participant, of loss of face or of property, that is, loss of spiritual or material capital, summarizable in the single word *damage*. Accordingly, the participant at risk claims, sometimes in a legal setting, that his or her understanding and use of the word or words in question are reasonable and ordinary and is grounds for some redress from an opposed party, who, of course, claims that his or her own contrasting understanding and use of the words are reasonable and ordinary.

But indeterminacies of meaning do not continually give rise to feelings of misrepresentation, wrongful damage, and imposition in ways that others continually find are worth contesting; to the extent that they do not, the credit should perhaps go to the community of language users rather than to the words themselves. The evident potential for differences in meaning interpretation supports a conception of utterances of all kinds (including words such as *fire* and — see below — *carriage*) as by nature double or multivoiced in the Bakhtinian sense. A bicycle is and is not a carriage, at the same time, depending on your point of view; when a pair of trousers is scorched and ruined by a hot iron, this does in a sense constitute fire damage, depending on the encompassing circumstances; and so on. In fact, the lessons to be learned from the case of the fire-damaged trousers are particularly compelling. As Harris emphasizes in his discussion of this real case, in which an insurance claim for compensation of "fire damage" was filed and then contested (Harris 1981a: 187–89), at least two contextual circumstances are absolutely crucial to the whole exercise of establishing whether the scorching of the trousers be termed a *fire*. Those contextual circumstances (which we may easily see as culturally rooted) are, first, that the damage was regarded by those who suffered it as not inconsequential (for, had the loss been inconsequential, the detail of its correct linguistic description would have been, literally, not worth discussing) and, second, that the owner of the trousers had an insurance policy that purported to protect him from fire-caused damage. Strictly within the context, striving — and succeeding — in having the damage ratifiably called a fire made sense. It is clear that quite distinctive concepts of damage and restitution now obtain within middle-class Western culture, interwoven with entrenched habits of materialist consumption, commodification, and warranties. In earlier times, damage and loss would have been far less routinely associated with compensation; today, particularly in middle-class America, it seems that compensation is such a strong corollary expectation whenever damage is suffered as to be coming close to becoming an entailment of it.

In (ordinary) circumstances of politeness, deference, and mutual respect, disputes as to how a situation or entity is to be described and, conversely, how it must not be described arise infrequently. Clashing interpretations rarely surface in any full-voiced form. But, where important needs and wants are perceived to be at stake (*face* is not nearly strong enough to subsume questions of interest ranging from the petty pecuniary to the politico-ideological), that potential multivoicedness may be actualized — in arguments, rows, court cases, and wars.

Returning to the humble bicycle, Harris cites the case of a British defendant charged under section 12 of the Licensing Act (1872), which deals with persons drunk while in charge of a carriage on the highway: the defendant had been caught pushing his bicycle along Broad Street, Ilfracombe, while intoxicated. Rejecting the defense's contention that the defendant was not guilty as charged since in popular usage a bicycle is not a carriage, "Lord Goddard held that what the word *carriage* meant might vary from one Act of Parliament to another, in some cases being taken to include bicycles and in other cases not": "What governed the application of a term was the purpose of the relevant section of the act [Goddard contended], which in this case was clearly the protection of the public and the preservation of public order. A drunken man with a bicycle was no less a threat to the public and to public order than a drunken man in charge of any other vehicle. In this context, therefore, the term *carriage* was to be interpreted as covering any kind of vehicle, including a bicycle" (Harris 1981a: 192). As Harris goes on to stress, what is significant about all this is that, rather than being any sort of "special case," it is simply a bringing into the foreground of the locally relevant issues of meaning determination that are always implicit; the case "lays bare to an unusual degree the procedures and the rationale which underlie a determination of 'what is meant' " (p. 192).

Two points in particular need stressing. The first is that the determination of "what is meant" is contestable and procedural rather than an automatic and invariant deferring to a definitive dictionary in or out of the head; we have a rich array of strategies and devices and routines to invoke in the course of such determinations, ranging from the raised eyebrow and the double take to appeals to higher courts and letters to the newspapers. The second point to make is that, although not a special case, the "drunk man with a bicycle" incident remains a case and every new incident involving language is in a sense a new case, meriting, in principle, a fresh and independent determination of its sense and purpose. What is possible in principle may be radically curtailed in practice, given our limitations of time and energy, our judgment that the linguistic specifics of innumerable everyday instances of indeterminacy are simply not worth more than fleeting attention, that longer review — often called quibbling — would be downright unhealthy, a privileging of the verbal aspects of interaction at the expense of other important aspects, such as the purposes and feelings of interactants. For the ordinary person to become preoccupied with the verbal material of interactions to the neglect of speakers' purposes and feelings would indeed be to have the tail wagging the dog. Accordingly, language users have a host of devices and constructs that serve to keep the potentially troublesome indeterminacies of language in check: dictionaries, thesauri, grammars, the ideas of literal meaning and idiom, denotation and connotation, the standard sense, and standard usage. All these are reflexes of the centripetal forces of a normativity that we, in varying degrees, often welcome and sometimes resist.

In everyday life, the principle that today's communicative activities will bring new cases to be relevantly resolved is accepted without question. Similarly, whatever we may think of Lord Goddard's powers of reasoning or of his authority to punish the inebriated, we rarely question the idea that, where disputes over word meanings arise, some sort of contingent resolution of the dispute is both possible and desirable: our everyday practices embody a recurrent demonstration that arguing to the contrary and casting doubt on the plausibility of local meaning resolution make little sense. We need to see the continuity between court cases involving word-meaning disputes, everyday language use, and Scrabble, despite the different procedures and routines of local resolution that these activities invoke and the different orders of magnitude of the stakes involved. As Harris goes on to say, the resolution of semantic uncertainties in every case "involves decision rather than discovery; and ... is indefinitely revisable" (1981a: 193). It is no more the case that the last word has been said on carriages, fires, or souvenirs, that we *now* know the true and proper nature of a carriage, a fire, etc., than it is the case that our culture has seen the ultimate and definitive achievement in the *design* of carriages, fires, and souvenirs. Knowing this to be the case, we typically use the word *definitive* itself to mean not "the best and absolute" but "the best so far": "the Longman edition of Milton by Fowler and Carey was for many years the definitive one; but now...."

It is because Lord Goddard has passed judgment in a particular case, that of the bicycle as carriage, that objections along the lines of wondering what he would say of a drunk man "in charge of" a shopping cart or a walker are somewhat beside the point since these circumstances were not part of the case at hand. That is to say, as speculations about varied circumstances such questions are unexceptionable; but as objections (to the situated determination of a particular case) they are simply invalid. They may legitimately imply dissatisfaction with some aspect of the procedures invoked, but they cannot plausibly question the reasonableness of coming to a decision. And, if we feel that there is something a little casuistical about calling a bicycle a "carriage" or a hole burned by a hot iron on a pair of trousers a "fire," this may be because language myths of code fixity and predeterminately correct and incorrect meanings have led us to give casuistry a bad name. But casuistry has a long and distinguished history and is currently enjoying a positive revaluation in the United States (see Jonsen and Toulmin 1988). It is a method for the practical resolution of moral issues that sets great store by the specificities of each particular case. Every case issues in a unique and contingent determination, and every determination may be influenced by previously determined cases. Casuistry emphasizes the local determinations of morality. It should not be remarkable that this is congruent with the case-specific sense making recognized by integrational linguistics, for in an important sense this perspective sees language behavior as a branch of morality.

Meaning, Mind, and Use

If integrational linguistics owes a debt to Wittgenstein's philosophy of language (particularly in the later works), still there are numerous distinct interpretations of those philosophical investigations, tending to divergent conclusions. Some may challenge the emphasis, here, on intentionality, on linguistic meaning as an individualized, memory-enabling filtering of countless experiences of integrated language-in-context occasions, and on individualized mental modeling as still too mentalist. My account wishes to give room to both (mental) intention and public use; but some Wittgensteinians emphasize use and everyday or commonsense practices with the language while remaining deeply skeptical of the need to speculate about mental processing in relation to what, for them, is an entirely public activity. Speculations about brain activity or mental processes as, or as if these were, the crucial underpinnings of language behavior amounts, in the latter view, to a disastrous category mistake.

A standard case posed as a counterargument to mentalist intentionalist theory is the later Wittgenstein's commentary on individuals' use of the word *pain*. A person may declare that he has a certain pain, but, it is argued, there is absolutely no way in which any other individual can adequately inspect that pain, let alone feel it or know it in its specificity. Just what the mental or body-internal activity is that goes on within the person such as to prompt him to describe it by saying "I have a pain" is beyond the reach of others. What is within the reach of others, however, is the person's use of the word *pain*, in expected contexts, accompanying standard symptoms, and so on. Those are the everyday criteria by which we judge whether a person is using the word *pain* correctly (i.e., appropriately) and, by extension, the criteria by which we judge whether she or he knows the meaning of the word *pain*. The meaning of the word *pain* is revealed in its appropriate or nonproblematic use, monitored and backed not only by dictionaries but also by off-the-cuff paraphrases in context and other in situ means of displaying that the appropriate use of a word is known. Appropriate or nonproblematic use is the best criterion of correct understanding. The most glaring problem with this view, however, is that it is no sooner formulated than it self-destructs: the phrase *appropriate or nonproblematic use* advertises its own roots in collectivist homogeneity, in which each knows the (single, determinate, code-like) language perfectly. In practice, all these homogenized singularities strive to conceal pluralities. There is almost never a single appropriate and nonproblematic use of any particular word but always a great number of ways of using it appropriately or inappropriately, problematically or nonproblematically. And, on each distinct occasion of use, it will be some of those endlessly varied judgments of appropriateness that will be displayed by interlocutors in situ. To invoke dictionaries in support of the singularist view of appropriateness is merely to increase the huffing and puffing, to pull rank in a situation where this may seem effective only because rank and source of authority were the issue all along.

These caveats notwithstanding, the radical corollary of the thesis that meaning is displayed in established public use is that all commentary on the mental machinery, associations, and effects sometimes claimed to be going on in the individual, behind or beneath the actual public inspectable use, is redundant and distracting: in Wittgenstein's analogy, it is a wheel that turns without engaging with the rest of the mechanism. What we mean by the meaning of an expression is essentially a paraphrase — typically a representation, as one or more propositions — of what we judge to be the use to which that expression is or has been standardly put. And here the tendency to treat stretches of linguistic activity as abstractable and recurrent items — *expressions* — has a deep influence (see further in chapter 6). So too has our tendency to judge that our own use of any expression is only a tiny part of the bulk of uses of the expression throughout the speech community; as a result, there is a strong impulse for individual language users to subordinate their own uses and meaning paraphrases of expressions to ones that are more widely established.

Extensive attention to normative tendencies in language use is therefore a significant need, from an integrational linguistic point of view. What get abstracted and labeled *utterance meanings* are constantly, and with good reason, a function of community judgments about how those utterances are used and to be used. The fact that there are indeed foundational public understandings of utterances like "I have a pain" is confirmed by the variety of activities in which we frequently engage that appeal to that understanding.

Although Wittgenstein's example of *pain* is one in which uninspectability of private mental response is particularly dramatized, the larger point is that, mutatis mutandis, the same uninspectability — and the same alleged irrelevance of private response to meaning, when the latter is construed entirely in terms of evident appropriate use — applies to much less speaker-internal language. By *less speaker-internal language* is intended language that purports to refer to phenomena potentially in plain view of the speaker and addressee, such as observable physical events, states, and entities. Thus, even language with humdrum external reference, as in such utterances as "I have two feet" and "Seattle is rainy," the same verificationist issue — or misdirection — can arise if we let it. And that verificationist issue concerns the inspectability of the actual mental activity that might underlie the declaration "I have a pain" in the one case and "Seattle is rainy" in the other. Although the distinctly different verificationist issue of whether in fact the speaker is in pain and whether in fact Seattle is rainy is clearly more or less easy to resolve in particular cases, it is not the focus of interest here. What is of interest, as indicated, is the nature of the putative mental activity accompanying particular utterances, particularly when those utterances make reference to private and seemingly uninspectable experiences, for in those cases we are tempted to judge that the fittingness of the utterance itself depends directly on the occurrence of a particular kind of accompanying mental activity. The mental experience of pain — and this alone — seems to be the wheel engaged with the machinery so as to warrant the public utterance "I have a pain." But the temptation to travel, qua linguists, along this theoretical cul-de-sac must be resisted. To so travel would be to subscribe to a version of "communicational skepticism" and in the face of this to require "a mental criterion of understanding" (Taylor 1990: 132); in themselves, neither of these moves is warranted, and, if adopted, they are soon found to bring neither theoretical relief nor resolution.

The questions, What is meaning? and, What is linguistic meaning? are problematic from the outset — as I have hoped to show from chapter 1 on. It is not evident that they can or should be answered prior to consideration of arguably more foundational questions such as, What is language? and, How does language emerge, function, and change? And it is these latter questions that have been my implicit focus. When in chapter 1 it was argued that individuals derive meanings of utterance partly by recourse to extensive but schematically ordered memories of past situations in which they have encountered language embedded within purposeful interaction (memories in which, then, linguistic forms are remembered as they were experienced, integrated within specific contexts), the whole argument was geared not to the subordinate question, What is the nature and function of literal meaning in language communication? but a more comprehensive one: What has been assumed to be the nature and function of language communication, such that a characterization and role has been assigned to literal meaning within it?

Nevertheless, many social-normativist theorists want to preserve — at all costs, it sometimes seems — the sensibleness of such everyday remarks as "What does *egregious* mean?" "I bet you don't know what *egregious* means," and "What's the opposite of *egregious*?" All these straightforward uses of language would become problematic, they suggest, if meaning had no singulary existence at all and was at best a reflex of complex reticulations of diverse and uninspectable private knowledge in the minds of individuals. While accepting the Wittgensteinian argument against private language as an argument against the notion that language meanings are in the mind/brain, they are unwilling to abandon the notion of shared meaning itself. If shared meaning is not sourced "in" the individual, it is concluded, it must be established, shared, and sustained by the community.

But to invest such absolute power in the community is to escape cognitive-mechanist determinism only to become enmeshed in social determinism. A social-determinist view of language asserts that what is said and what is meant by what is said are factors fixed in advance for the entire community and binding on all members. By virtue of being a member of that community, you necessarily use the community's language, into which you have been inducted, in just the ways that prevail. What such social-determinist accounts have no explanation for is the fact that an individual's experience of language use is nothing like this. Our experience as individuals is that what we say and how we say it and what it will mean or be taken to mean varies with each succeeding case and that, when we use language, it is first and foremost on our own behalf: each of us is individually responsible and accountable for what he or she says. The importance of the various everyday language games in which we quiz each other over word and sentence meanings needs acknowledging; but, despite the charm of their everyday commonsensicality, these are a potentially misleading activity. They are misleading, that is, if they are taken to constitute adequate grounds for theorizing about language. Distinct from the extremes of both cognitive and social determinism, then, is the kind of local determination, negotiated by individual speakers and hearers (and subsequently potentially ratified by other language users), emphasized here.

The course being charted, between the Scylla of mentalism (mental "hardware" as the source and basis of communication in a language) and the Charybdis of collectivist imposition (the language as socially given facts), highlights some seeming paradoxes concerning such "natural" and foundational parent-child language games as questions and answers about words. Consider the case where a child asks "What does *intoxicated* mean?" and the parent answers or where these roles are partly reversed and the adult asks a "teacher's question." Such activities are quite common throughout childhood and would appear to lend support to views of language and meaning as publicly verifiable phenomena. If word meanings are not real and available for public display, how is it that the child's question seems to make sense and affords a coherent and corrigible answer? Indeed, how could the child have come to frame her question in quite the way she did unless she had assumed that word meanings were real and publicly inspectable?

The short answer to these questions is that, within and beyond such language games, words are indeed treated as having meanings, which meanings are constituted by good multipurpose paraphrases. But the child who asks "What does *intoxicated* mean?" is already using language at a level of considerable sophistication, a level of abstraction at which sequences of sounds can be detached from the flow of interaction and "displayed" for identification or correction by a reliable informant (i.e., *intoxicated* is mentioned more than used here). In short, the child is using language reflexively or metalinguistically rather than simply experiencing it phenomenally. Nor should we assume that metalinguistic reflection on their own language begins in children only with such formulations as questions like "What does *intoxicated* mean?" Certainly, if so-called rich interpretations of children's early gestures and noises is allowed, metalinguistic awareness of particular situation-embedded sounds as repetitions and nonrepetitions, or as occurring as expected or not occurring as expected, begins to appear in the first few months of life. As has been argued in chapter 3 and will be elaborated in chapter 6, almost at the birth of language, with the onset of the grasp of a semiotic linguistic faculty, comes the metalinguistic possibility of inspecting, reviewing, and playing with that faculty. If intentionality precedes linguistic semiosis, using language qua language can never have been without the potential, at least, for reflexive metalinguistic inspection. At the same time, clearly, at the beginnings of coming into language in early hominids or in infants that potential for metalinguistics seems to be logically strictly limited.

At this point, a word more needs to be said in correction of the assumption made above concerning the "natural" or foundational character of parent-child language games. To describe such games as *natural* and *foundational* wrongly invites the inference that those games or procedures are essential, basic, and a permanent grounding. But, in fact, *foundational* here may be understood only as applying in a restricted sense: it may be glossed as "what is established" but not as "what is essential." It is perfectly possible to become fluent in a language without benefit of the particular game for eliciting word meanings described above. By contrast, the other term applied here, *metalinguistic*, does seem applicable without reservation or restriction: the potential to proceed metalinguistically, the possibility of metalinguistics, is, arguably, a permanent and essential feature of human discourse, of *homo signans*. By the time a practice has become sufficiently established to become

175 Further Principles

a recognized practice involving language (e.g., by the time the tree fellers described in chapter 3 have become aware of a simple patterned sequence in the noises to which they have become accustomed to respond in the course of felling trees, have become accustomed to regard the directives as being as much "in" the distinct noises as "in" the older man producing them), the potential ability to develop metalinguistic reflections has also emerged. The development of practical methods and of perceived need to engage in metalinguistic reviews, however, may come only later; arguably, these undergo enormous and irreversible expansion with the invention of writing. Relatedly, the adult-child "What does x mean?" game may be compared with the tree fellers portrayed in the previous chapter, who are never able to ask "What does 'Earnnhh' mean?"

As an answer to the substantive question, How can understanding of meanings be corrected if meaning is private? a single answer with two aspects must be offered. That part of meaning that is the mental storage of remembered prior situations of use of a word cannot, in ordinary circumstances that do not extend to brainwashing, be corrected by "us"; that part of meaning that consists in the appropriate use of the word is corrected, of course, just when the child consistently uses the word in the preferred ways. And the ways in which "we" intervene to achieve such changed use by the child are, directly or indirectly, by providing that child with alternative contextualized uses of the given word (with associations deriving from those uses attached, sketchily or richly filled in) to remember alongside or in preference to those previously stored.

Language games about word meanings, then, need to be recognized as to some degree metalinguistic — taking, for example, *intoxicated* away from its contextualized uses, calling it a word (perhaps, even, an "adjective"), holding it up in detached splendor to see if others can recontextualize it properly. This is a kind of police work, not unrelated to other such police work noted elsewhere in these chapters. In addition to being metalinguistic, but almost certainly related, such everyday checking for correctness is highly normative, disciplinary, and centripetal. It is an important part of the ongoing maintenance of the language in a seeming steady state, preserving the status quo, received practice and opinion. In very large measure, the degree to which such metalinguistic activities of corretion (of grammar, word choice, pronunciation, etc.) take place in a culture reflects the degree to which that culture accepts that there is an established "common sense" of the language and particularly of a form of that language regarded as standard. Clearly, however, such cultural acceptance and commonsense standards demand more thorough scrutiny: it is a truism that common sense of the kind implied here is almost never owned in common, and the metalinguistic corrections from a position of assumed authority routinely fail — or decline — to consider the differences of power and resistance within practices, as if, in being "what we've always done," practice were self-justificatory and self-explanatory.

Language games of the "What does *egregious* mean?" variety are subsequent to a division of interaction into the linguistic and the nonlinguistic, an arbitrary and judicious (certainly so in pedagogical contexts) separating out of certain material then designated "strictly verbal" and submitted to a sophisticated analytic description (as words, sentences, parts of speech, etc.). But, in our theorizing about language, we have no grounds for assuming that such a division is natural or self-explanatory, when in fact it is a contrivance facilitated by the emergence of writing. What is natural, rather, is our constantly onward-moving experience of situated interactions within which language is embedded and our interpreted memories of those interactions and the uses of language that they contained. There is merit in the reminder that all such memory work is like a cog that turns no machinery until such time that it (remembered meanings) gets displayed in publicly inspectable use. On the other hand, this does not compel the conclusion that anything whose existence is postulated, other than the observable use, may be safely ignored. Much of this book implicitly considers just this question: What is the role of memory, given that language is understood as an integral part of situated interaction?.

Emphasizing memory in this way also requires that a contrast be highlighted between how it is here assumed to contribute to present linguistic interaction and how memory is conceptualized in, for example, Turing's famous paper of 1950. There, as Harris (1989) notes, Turing characterizes computation done by humans as a process involving the following of fixed and inviolable rules, the actual calculations being done either on paper or in one's head. Calculations in the head are made possible by the fact that, according to Turing, we are endowed with a mental counterpart to paper: memory. In fact, memory is used in both the mental "setting out" of the calculation and for the storage of rules or procedures that govern the calculation; and the whole enterprise works because human beings "really remember what they have got to do" (Anderson 1964: 9). It should be clear from the various commentaries in the chapter so far that an emphasis to the effect that humans "really remember what they have got to do" is profoundly misleading: for much of the time, and beyond the grosser abstractions, humans have not "got to do" anything; and, insofar as what they end up doing has not yet been done, there is no way in which they can remember this. Memory, contra Turing, should not be contextualized as an enormous memo pad reminding us what to do when in what circumstances because it is always the case that the specifics of what, when, where, how, why, etc. have yet to emerge.

In addition to memory, we must also invoke imagination. At one point in their book on relevance, Sperber and Wilson write: "A child drinking from a glass with a straw is a stereotypical event which we assume, as do most other people working on the organisation of memory, is recorded in the form of a single chunk, stored at a single location in memory and accessed as a single unit" (1986: 186). What difference would it make if a particular individual had no such "chunk" in memory, only in his imagination? What is the difference between "a child drinking etc." as a chunk in memory and as a "chunk" imagined? For integrational linguists, the key mental facilitator is not memory (of or for past words or contexts or scenes or schemata) but imagination. Memory is important to interaction, but not always in the most expected ways: perhaps its most important function is that it records the ways imagination has been successful, in the negotiation of meanings in context, in the past. Imaginative powers enable us to make rational assessments of what — given our awareness of the present circumstances and present agendas of interactants, together with awareness of how perceptibly related gestures, signs, and effects have been interpreted on past occasions (i.e., memory) — might possibly be going on in a current situation.

A first step in questioning the privileging of the coherence of everyday language games such as "What is the meaning of *egregious*?" must be to ask whether this is not to fall into the kind of trap about which Wittgenstein warned theorists, a thinking about our language practices naturalized by what he called the "deep structure" of the language. Wittgenstein emphasized that what is required by way of a description, or concerning adequacy of meaning paraphrase, or as regards scrupulous accuracy, is not all laid down once and for all but varies from case to case. In one situation it may be sufficient, as a means of displaying understanding of the word *soporific*, if the questioned party supplies the simple and somewhat inaccurate substitute *drowsy*. On another occasion a great deal more may be required to be said, so that the "meaning" of *soporific* in the particular context can be made clear. Imagine that a parent is speaking on the telephone to the pediatrician, shortly after his child has fallen off her bike and banged her head. In his anxiety the parent remarks that the effect of the fall seems to have been "soporific" (for the child is now lying drowsily half asleep on the couch). It is surely appropriate that the pediatrician inquire further as to what is meant by *soporific*. In doing so, the pediatrician is not at all interested in monitoring the parent's use of *soporific* for dictionary correctness; rather, she seeks a kind of correctness that may have altogether more urgent consequences. For mutually beneficial purposes, the doctor is concerned to get a fuller picture (to be matched against countless now-schematized remembered situations in which she has had a worried parent telephoning about a child rendered lethargic by a bang to the head) of the situation in which the parent has been prompted to use the word *soporific*. There is mentalism here, but no Saussurean *circuit de parole*, only and simply the cycle or cyclicity of life. It may be protested that this is a particular constructed situation and not the standard use of *soporific*. But that is no weakness of the argument; rather, it is its point: one can always think up situations in which just what *soporific* means will have to be adjusted to the specificities of the situation within which its use is embedded.

The appeal for a place for mentalism (in the sense of memory and imagination) in theorizing about language can never finally be adjudicated by methods of proof or disproof; it is finally about commitments and varieties of faith. Social-determinist language theorists subscribe to the view that the collective language-shaping forces of the community are incontestably sovereign. Cognitive determinists locate an equally fixed and uniform program controlling language competence within each individual's mind-brain. The view here has tried to give due attention to cognitive factors that, at the very least, can be said to be hard to conceive of as purely determinist — particularly the faculties that we summarize as memory and imagination. Those cognitive factors, it is argued, work in conjunction with aspects of an individual's reaction to and use of language that are unquestionably nondeterminist, no matter how constrained they may on occasion be owing to societal pressures to conform. The individual's active and reflective part in language use is characterized by speakers' unequivocal habitual sense that they are personally and severally responsible for what they say and for the effects that their uses of language have. Moral judgment is directly involved in language use, then, including, as it were, the morality of using language publicly in a way that diverges from established social norms. Morality is involved since, in practice, language is always in use within human purposeful activities, and those are inescapably value laden, choice implicating, preference and assumption reflecting, reflecting and articulating judgments about what is right and wrong, desirable and undesirable, correct and incorrect. Part of the standard linguistic depiction of the language user has entailed a theoretically absolute separation of this value laden–ness, this concern for correctness, that is implicit and explicit in everyday language use from "the language proper," "the language itself." But this contrived separation of the language itself, "as a system," from language in use, shaped by unpredictable group and individual preferences, prescriptions, prejudices, and affiliations, continues to unravel as the allegedly autonomous structural-systematic "core" is reexamined. If speaker intuitions — one of the preferred instruments of autonomous linguistic theory — are to be trusted, where lies the boundary between the autonomous core and the normatively shaped, value-expressive supplementary specifics? Where can we place a border between the purely structural and the partly functional? Is it even coherently conceivable that a sharp transition exists between two components or levels of such intrinsically distinct character?

The integrational perspective also rejects the idea that linguistic meaning is a real object, whether that object is claimed to be a psychologically real object or a socially real one. For integrationalism, from the point of view of the situated language user, language and meaning are never objects — to be found, accessed, or retrieved — that preexist the yet-uncharted interaction. In actual interaction, meaning is not antecedently objectified in this way: it cannot exist prior to or outside the conditions of its own emergence. And, when meanings do emerge in speech events (as understandings, kinds of affect and support, and commitments), these remain provisional and contingent on the surrounding circumstances in ways that entail that those "meanings" can never transcend the local conditions of their emergence. Yet it is clear that linguists and nonlinguists, team players and keepers of the social order, all have desired and continue to desire such a transcendent possibility, which contains the idea that particular determinate forms might be the vehicles of particular determinate meanings, sine die and without danger of corruption. It is perhaps a Lacanian desire that becomes invested in language. And the upshot of this yearning, in part, is the metalinguistic, abstractionist, and autonomy-asserting turn in linguistic studies of "meaning" and the language user. In the process, words and word meanings (and sentences and sentence meanings) are cast as indeed capable of transcending the specific conditions of particular cases within which, alone, those things that we abstractedly characterize as words and meanings ever arise. So the wish for context transcendence and autonomy of forms and meanings is powerful enough to sustain a reciprocity of wishes and goals. Among other effects, this causes dictionaries to be received not as contingent historical descriptions but as timeless definitive authorities: "The central indeterminacy of all communication is indeterminacy of what is meant.... [For orthodox linguistics, setting aside exceptions and hard cases,] what the words themselves mean ... is held to be determinate for the linguistic community" (Harris 1981a: 167).

Indeterminacies are bracketed off by procedures of abstraction: various conflicting judgments of word use, utterance interpretation, and so on can be set aside on the grounds of dialectal difference and situationally driven variation. At a deeper, abstract level, it is asserted, there is a core of denotational meaning inherent in every determinate expression. Standard linguistic theorizing proceeds on the assumption that there is such a core, and, although the group of individuals said to share an identical set of such expression-meaning pairs is sometimes abstracted to the theoretical limiting case of one, namely, the ideal speaker-hearer — in which case, clearly, no *sharing* is involved, no *group* or linguistic *community* is being characterized — still the general assumption is that identity of expression-meaning pairs, a sharing of a common *langue*, can be predicated of several if not many individuals (hence, a community). But this foundational assumption is a theoretical necessity for standard, biplanar linguistics rather than simply a reasonable inference or assumption. Underlying determinacy of meaning is a stipulative precondition for such linguistics, and the role of this tenet in linguistic theorizing is a classic case of deriving an is from an ought.

5

Relevance in Theory and Practice

Sperber and Wilson's (1986) account of relevance and its foundational role in linguistic communication has generated considerable interest within and beyond pragmatics. Their model of communication is in some respects an elaboration and systematization of Grice's crucial insights on the logic of conversation and nonnatural meaning (Grice 1957, 1975). In other respects it is a simplifying account, in which the intended meanings of utterances are said invariably to be calculable on the basis of an overarching principle of relevance. This principle is single and inescapable, in Sperber and Wilson's view; that is, it is not an option that interactants decide whether to take up or not but a necessary adjunct and grounding of all communication. The principle is as follows:

Every utterance communicates the presumption of its own optimal relevance.

Maximal relevance is measured in terms of cognitive effects (i.e., via the strengthening or weakening of the addressee's assumptions or the introduction of new assumptions), and the theory assumes that speakers aim to achieve the most effect with the least effort. The presumption of relevance is identified as the basis for a properly explanatory account not only of straightforward speech exchanges but also of so-called indirectness of utterance, where implication or irony is involved.

Not the least of the reasons for detailed discussion of relevance theory here is that Sperber and Wilson espouse an attractively fluid notion of context, thoroughly congruent with the account of context and text proposed in my introductory chapter. There it was noted that numerous interrelated developments (including the spread of writing, multiple-copy printing, dictionaries, written grammars, discipline formation, scientism, and computers) have established the text-context distinction as a foundation of linguistic and literary studies. A powerful imaginative feat — the conceptualization of text and context as independently variable products (so that we can proceed in, e.g., language-teaching classes to "teach" appropriate routines and behavior by varying one while keeping the other constant) — has come to enclose us by the same conceptual horizons that it made perceptible.

Now Sperber and Wilson, too, reject the idea of the context as stable and given. They begin by arguing that "the context used to process new assumptions is, essentially, a subset of the individual's old assumptions, with which the new assumptions combine to yield a variety of contextual effects" (1986: 132). (Sperber and Wilson use the term *assumptions* in ways roughly comparable to the more commonly used *propositions*, and by *contextual effects* they intend the kind of inferences elsewhere often called *implicatures.*) They go on to address the question whether context is fixed and given (they argue that it is not) and the question of how, where required, context is enlarged or extended. They reject the unworkably vague and cognitively burdensome scenario that assumes that any and all encyclopedic information associated with any concept invoked in the expression of assumptions will be added to the set of assumptions making up the context used in interpreting further utterances. In place of that picture of unconstrained context extension, they argue for a relevance-governed and therefore disciplined extension of context: context can be extended by "going back in time" to adduce assumptions used or derivable from earlier cotext (p. 140), by adding encyclopedic information about concepts already present in the context or the assumption being processed (p. 140), and by adding information about the immediately observable environment (p. 141). "The selection of a *particular* context is determined by the search for relevance" (p. 141; emphasis added). They propose a complete reversal of the usual assumed order of processing, in which first context is determined and then relevance is assessed: "On the contrary, people *hope* that the assumption being processed is relevant (or else they would not bother to process it at all), and they try to select a context which will justify that hope: a context which will maximize relevance. In verbal comprehension in particular, it is relevance which is treated as given, and context which is treated as a variable" (p. 142; emphasis added).

Integrationally oriented linguistics of the kind espoused in this book has no quarrel with these principles; there seems to be a considerable degree of congruence between the theses concerning "relevance" (that it is foundational) and "context" (that it is situationally variable) supported by both integrational linguists and relevance theorists. Where these persuasions part company, however, will be over just how orderly and monological the notion of relevance can be in its application to utterance interpretation. For Sperber and Wilson, relevance, as a principle and a calculus for interpretation, is stable, given, and straightforwardly explanatory. For integrational linguists, it is *n*-ways variable. Accordingly, the present chapter raises questions less about relevance as a foundation of linguistic communication than about Sperber and Wilson's account of that foundation. For Sperber and Wilson, relevance amounts to a demonstrable given, which can then operate like a calculus in the derivation of intended meaning. Here, by contrast, it is assumed that relevance itself is often in the process of being made and remade in the course of interaction and that, although its situated use (in hazarded utterance interpretation) can look calculus-like, this should not lead us to mistake it for a calculus. Counterposed to Sperber and Wilson's neopragmatic view of interpretation (and relevance) as calculable, then, is the view here — integrational linguistic in spirit — of interpretation and relevance as probabilistic.

Notions of maximal relevance and cognitive effect are elaborated in Sperber and Wilson (1986) only after a lengthy ground-clearing discussion of the code theory of communication, mutual knowledge, and similar touchstones of orthodox linguistic theory. Of specific interest here are those points in the relevance-theoretical revisionist account that seems to remain questionable. Although they reject a code theory of communication and mutual knowledge as impossible or inadequate, Sperber and Wilson's own model remains founded on ideas of direct evidence, mutual manifestness, and ostensive behavior. The following sections turn to these issues.

Manifestness and Ostensive Behavior

> Instead of taking the code theory for granted and concluding that mutual knowledge must therefore exist, we prefer to look at what kind of assumptions people are actually in a position to make about each other's assumptions, and then see what this implies for an account of communication.
> (Sperber and Wilson 1986: 45)

The above quotation articulates an approach to theorizing about communication that is inherently attractive to the integrationist. But as relevance theory is subsequently developed, I shall argue, the approach is inconsistently maintained. In particular, the theory itself makes unwarranted assumptions about the kind of assumptions people are actually in a position to make about each other's assumptions. I shall also suggest that Sperber and Wilson are led to make those unwarranted assumptions in order to give substance to one of the foundational claims of their theory, namely, that interactants share, to a degree, a cognitive environment comprising a set of all the facts and assumptions that they do or could each mentally represent to themselves. The key and most problematic postulate here is that of "shared cognitive environment."

This is what is meant, in relevance theory, by the term *manifest*. A fact or assumption is manifest (in some degree) to an individual if they are aware of it, or could become aware of it, in their given cognitive environment. Analogous to the idea of degrees of manifestness might be the idea of degrees of visibility: we might say that an object located at some distance from a viewer is to some extent visible, but it is so to a degree that will change with increased viewer-object proximity. What is manifest, in Sperber and Wilson's terms, is what to an individual is situationally recognizable, comprising the actual and potential impingements of the physical environment on their cognitive environment (the latter will include knowledge and memory). The idea of manifestness, to be contrasted with earlier theories' psychologically unreal claims concerning background or mutual knowledge, is developed with acuity. The manifestness to an individual of any facts or assumptions does not hinge on those facts having been thought about or mentally represented or "known" in that conscious sense. Rather, the domain of what is manifest to a person includes innumerable unmade assumptions, together with one's made assumptions. For example, it is manifest to the reader that, on turning the page, he or she will not find that the present English orthography is supplanted by Japanese hiragana: this is manifest to you — it is a very reasonable assumption for you to make — although prior to the formulation of that assumption here it is most unlikely that you will have made that assumption or mentally represented the thought to yourself. Thus, a manifest assumption in relevance-theoretical terms is any assumption "makable" in the given and recognized circumstances. The circumstantial contingency of unmade but "makable" assumptions is clearly important here: that the next page will not be in hiragana script is manifest in the present situation in a way that it is not if, say, you are taking a country walk, where no books, page turning, or script is in the cognitive environment.

The notion of *manifestness* is attractive in its emphasis on potentiality rather than actuality: things are manifest to an individual if, potentially, they could be mentally represented and deemed true (this is clearly a more open set than the set of actually known and represented facts or propositions usually said to characterize "background knowledge"). A second attraction is that "manifestness" and its difficult corollary "mutual cognitive environment" seem to give proper attention in communication to what may be termed *ordinarily unreflected-on trust* rather than anything stronger and more suspect such as *known-to-be-shared knowledge*. That trust rather than knowledge is the dynamic here is reflected in the fact that, when Sperber and Wilson turn to examples of communication and its asymmetry (the primary responsibilities lying with the communicator, not the addressee), they emphasize not what speaker and addressee may or may not have noticed in the given environment but rather what the speaker can assume with "reasonable confidence" may be manifest at the appropriate time; and, in a second example, the speaker's remark is shaped relative not to any made or mentioned assumptions but simply relative to what the speaker "expects": "she expects . . . that her utterance will act as a prompt" (1986: 44).

Ordinarily unreflected-on trust is entirely congruent with the notions of confidence and orientedness to other that are foundational to communication. Here, it suffices to note that manifestness rests on trust rather than knowledge in that it denotes (inter alia) the great range of assumptions that a situated individual *could* make and might use in inferring the communicative intent of others' behavior; it is neither feasible nor appropriate that much of that unreflected-on background will be actively confirmed in the course of interaction. This has implications for the notion of *mutual cognitive environment* or, as is preferred here, *overlapping cognitive environments*. As Sperber and Wilson put it: "Peter and Mary are talking to each other in the same room: they share a cognitive environment which consists of all the facts made manifest to them by their presence in this room. One of these facts is the fact that they share this environment" (1986: 41). As implied above, just how much reliance may be placed on the claim that such a cognitive environment is *shared* is a controversial question. Nevertheless, the example does make a plausible appeal to certain kinds of fundamental sharedness and reciprocity: for example, that, in virtue of interacting as they do, Peter and Mary are each trusting that they are similar kinds of individual, are each trusting that they each trust — without reflection — that they are occupying a single or overlapping setting ("the same room"), and so on. Furthermore, they unreflectingly trust that they each trust in these kinds of overlapping of background, so that this in itself becomes a communicational resource, a fact usable in the communicational process.

Sperber and Wilson remark that, as far as cognitive efficiency is concerned, "an individual's cognitive goal at a given moment is always an instance of a more general goal: maximising the relevance of the information processed" (p. 49). It is that goal that constrains an interlocutor's procedures of sense making, which, in relevance theory, are basically the following:

1. A does something that "modifies" B's cognitive environment.
2. Presented with A's environment-modifying contribution, B chooses, from among those things now newly manifest (assumptions, facts, etc. now newly — or more strongly — makable), just those assumptions that are likely to be most relevant to B.

The above amounts to a sketch of signifying in general. Difficulties with it center on the issue of just how it is that, prior to the processing of assumptions, any particular B participant will know just which of the newly manifest material is most relevant and most in need of processing. The inescapable conclusion seems to be that, in the given situation and prior to A's doing anything at all, B's cognitive environment (and that of any participant) of known and processable information is already tagged for relevance, in some sense.

Here we may consider one of Sperber and Wilson's earliest examples, in which Peter and Mary are sitting together on a park bench. Peter is said to communicate relevantly when he deliberately leans back on the bench, thereby disclosing to Mary's view the approach of her boring acquaintance William (1986: 48ff.). It is because, at this point, William is already tagged as relevant — even if only negatively — in Mary's cognitive environment that she is inclined to proceed to make inferences on his appearance (by contrast with other less relevant newly manifest phenomena, previously hidden by Peter's torso — e.g., that there is an ice-cream vendor set up further along the path). All such past relevance assessments are always the foundation for every current relevance (and contextual-effect) assessment; seen from this perspective, the notion of cognitive environment may be alternatively characterized as the sum of multiply-categorized extant relevance assessments made by an individual, of his or her previous experience. This may not make relevance an entirely circular criterion, but it certainly means that it is an embedded one: it is always already in place, serving as a guide in the calculation of what is most significant in the ongoing interaction. Any suggestion that relevance applies just once, as it were, at a specific and fixed stage in a procedure of information processing, is exceedingly hard to substantiate in practice. Relevance assessments are continually going on, as are interpretive hazardings, in a context of likelihood and contingency rather than certainty.

This particularly needs to be borne in mind when discussing manifestness and information "made manifest." As noted above, Sperber and Wilson take care at the outset to emphasize that for things to be made manifest amounts not to their being made known but only to their being made knowable (or more knowable). Counter to ordinary usage of the term *manifest*, in this scheme *manifest* does not mean "displayed" or "evident" but only "potentially displayable or assumable." That being so, some of Sperber and Wilson's own language may give rise to misunderstandings. Thus, at one point they seem to suggest that, in the example cited above, Peter's leaning back might display to Mary that it is intended to display some information. In that case, "Peter's behaviour has made it manifest to Mary that he intends to make some particular assumptions manifest to her. We will call such behaviour — behaviour which makes manifest an intention to make something manifest — *ostensive* behaviour or simply *ostension*. Showing someone something is a case of ostension. So, too, we will argue, is human intentional communication" (1986: 49). However, it seems more strictly in accord with the previously established notion of manifestness to say that no signifying action can be said to display an intention to display (something): signifying actions can do no more than make potentially displayable an intention to make (something) displayable. There is an important contrast between these two characterizations of signifying action, in terms of the interpretive burden that remains to be managed by the addressee, and the absence of any guarantee of displayedness, proper uptake, or successful ostension. Sperber and Wilson claim that ostension carries (or implies) a guarantee of relevance and that this underpins inferential communication. But ostension ("showing someone something") is frequently hazardous and uncertain. The ubiquity of the criterion of other-attentive relevance cannot at the same time specify the respects in which a hazarded ostension is relevant; therefore, inferential communication remains more probabilistic and cultural (a warranted undertaking) than certain and logical (a guaranteed procedure). Notwithstanding the common etymological roots of the two words, a distinction is being suggested here between the relevance-theoretical emphasis on guarantee (certainty of interpretive procedure) and the present emphasis on warranty (reasonableness, in the assumed context, of efforts of interpretation).

Furthermore, manifestness to an individual is not a sufficient basis on which to build a theory of relevance: there must also be an important degree of mutuality of manifestness between speaker and addressee in order for B to take the "indirect," implicature-ridden utterance or stimulus of A and, invoking (however stumblingly) inferences retrievable from that domain of mutually manifest information, understand the relevance of A's stimulus. "Mutual manifestness" is espoused as sufficiently different from the notion of mutual knowledge to escape the charge of psychological implausibility directed at the latter; it is asserted that "the claim that an assumption is mutually manifest is a claim about cognitive environments rather than mental states or processes" (Sperber and Wilson 1986: 43). Just what the difference between "cognitive environment" and "mental state" amounts to, however, is not specified, and elsewhere it is clear that manifestness and shared cognitive environment are intended to do much the same work (under much the same assumption that certain situational elements are ostensively evident) that mutual knowledge was hypostasized so as to do. The chief contrast detectable in the shift from mutual knowledge to mutual manifestness is the idea that, while the former was claimed to be knowledge already mentally represented by both (or all) interactants, important parts of the latter are assumed to be either assumed or assumable by each party, although much will not have been processed to the stage of constituting mentally represented knowledge.

Exactly how one participant manages to draw another's attention to a particular piece of manifest information is a crucial question for any theory of communication. Sperber and Wilson's answer is an appeal to ostension: B can assume (cf. our assumption of truthfulness in interaction) that whatever information A makes manifest is, by ostension, judged by A to be relevant to B. What is most noticeable here is Sperber and Wilson's own assumption that ostension works: "The existence of ostension is beyond doubt" (1986: 48). This is surprising, since the authors are certainly aware of the arguments of Wittgenstein and Quine, highlighting serious difficulties with an overreliance on ostension. The essential difficulty is that of showing how ostensive behavior can reliably single out, to an addressee, just that particular element in the environment that the interlocutor intends to comment on or intends that the addressee use in the deriving of communicative inferences.

The authors' interim reply (Sperber and Wilson 1986: 49) adopts a compromise position, to the effect that an addresser's ostensive behavior is not overly ostensive in the standard sense at all since so many new assumptions may be displayed by a single gesture, glance, or remark; much of the work of ostension is in fact done by the addressee, who is said to have little difficulty identifying which of the newly manifest assumptions is most relevant to him or her, and who can then assume that just that or those were the ones that the addresser intended him or her to attend to. This answers to reasonable doubts about ostension, to the effect that the most that we can hope for from ostensive behavior is that the recipient will understand that the addresser is trying to show or disclose something and that that something is, in the addresser's view, directly observable. But it leaves some difficult questions unanswered concerning just how an addressee is so sure of what will be most relevant to him or her if ostension does not in fact unambiguously identify this. The model is one of interactants entering into interaction (very often, in the examples discussed, with old acquaintances) with a strong sense of what information is or will be most relevant to them. Thus armed, they can usually and safely discard all the potentially informative material "revealed" in the environment and attend to just that intentionally manifested material that answers to their already-formulated sense of what is most relevant. In this account, B's rational and all-knowing self-interest is sovereign, and the role played by the compliant interlocutor A is excessively attenuated. The model works best in scenarios in which an addressee knows in advance what will be relevant to him or her; perhaps such scenarios are overwhelmingly the norm. But it would seem to be far less adequate to situations — that is, less able to model such situations — in which an addressee is confronted with thoroughly new information, information whose relevance was not foreseen and indeed whose relevance now, in the current time of the interaction, is doubted or ill understood.

Some difficulties in the relevance-theory account are apparent when Sperber and Wilson describe how manifestness and relevance might operate in a particular instance. Consider once more the example mentioned above, in which Mary and Peter are sitting together on a park bench and Peter leans back in such a way that what is now visible or potentially visible to Mary is different from what it had been: "Here is how the inference process might go. First, Mary notices Peter's behaviour and assumes that it is ostensive: i.e., that it is intended to attract her attention to some phenomenon" (p. 50). Granted the visibility of Peter's behavior, one's first question concerns its interpretability: how can we be confident that Mary notices it in just the way Sperber and Wilson represent it (i.e., as a leaning back so as to disclose to view, rather than a leaning back so as to hide something from Mary's view, or a leaning back so as to ease the lower back pain, indigestion, or stiff neck etc. that Peter may be experiencing)? And, having noticed it, what are the grounds for assuming that it is ostensive, has a "signposting" function? Putting things the other way about, what can we safely discount as nonostensive? Motionlessness? But then are not certain kinds of immobility, seemingly displayed by interlocutors, highly communicative? If every kind of gesture, and even lack of gesture, and every kind of noise or lack of noise is potentially attention directive, is there really a basis *in the behavior itself and evident to any detached observer* for identification of the intentionally ostensive? How can certain stimuli signal their own intended ostensiveness, prior to the recipient's search for the relevance of the information that the stimulus allegedly singles out? Alternatively, might it not transpire that Peter never intended to reveal anything to Mary by leaning back — indeed, that he was not aware that he had leaned back — and that Mary's construal of events was mistaken? In summary, might not all this supposedly communicative behavior have been in Sperber and Wilson's terms merely informative, in the way that mere informativeness and not communicativeness is attributed by them to an audibly hoarse voice (p. 22, an example discussed below)? But then, if both the informative and the communicative readings remain possible, the distinction between the communicative and the (uninterestingly) informative cannot be grounded (as Sperber and Wilson elsewhere claim) in the *materia* of the stimulus alone.

Nowhere is this more clear than in the first elaborated example of fully fledged "ostensive-inferential communication":

Suppose a girl is travelling in a foreign country. She comes out of the inn wearing light summer clothes, manifestly intending to take a stroll. An old man sitting on a bench nearby looks ostensively up at the sky. When the girl looks up, she sees a few tiny clouds, which she might have noticed for herself, but which she would normally have paid no further attention to.... Now, however, the old man is drawing her attention to the clouds in a manifestly intentional way, thus guaranteeing that there is some relevant information to be obtained.

The old man's ostensive behavior opens up for the girl a whole new strategy of processing.... Knowing the area and its weather better than she does, he might have reason to think that the clouds are going to get worse and turn to rain. Such an assumption is of a very standard sort and would probably be the first to come to mind. If it were not manifest to the old man that it was going to rain, it would be hard to explain his behaviour at all. The girl thus has reason to think that in drawing her attention to the clouds, he intended to make manifest to her that he believed it was going to rain. (Sperber and Wilson 1986: 51)

This seems to rely more on stereotypes of behavior than on a freestanding account of inference-based communication. The proposed explanation of the interaction makes sense only if we imagine that someone who comes out of a building wearing light summer clothes is already oriented to weather and, in particular, the depradations of bad weather and that the girl will be closely observant of the gestures and assessments of the old man she sees. The problems begin in earnest when, we are told, the old man "looks ostensively up at the sky." "Looking ostensively," like referring ostensively, is more easily said than done (cf. Sperber and Wilson [1986: 55], where Mary "sniffs ostensively"). And here the man looks ostensively not simply at the sky but at the tiny clouds in order to convey to the girl, indirectly, that there may be rain coming. Let us grant for the moment that the man was a resident of the area and not a visitor like the woman herself, that he had noticed the woman and her light clothing and cared enough to worry about her well-being on the stroll that — granted — he somehow knows (via her manifest intending) that she is about to take in an area that he evidently knows will avail her of no sort of adequate shelter from showers, and let us grant also that the woman noticed the man's head movement. Even if we accept the possibility of all this intercalated knowledge and care, the man might yet have been ostensively intending to confirm that, because the clouds were so tiny, the weather would almost certainly stay fine, that, yes, it was a wonderful day for a stroll in light summer clothing. Or both parties might have been looking at the predominantly clear blue sky and appreciating that blueness rather than the negligible and unnoticed tiny clouds. Or, nonostensively, perhaps the man simply had a crick in his neck and was stretching.

One is compelled to conclude that a theory that relies on ostensive highlighting of the manifest aligns communication more with guesswork that is unconstrained rather than constrained. To be sure, Sperber and Wilson's "focusing" device is relevance itself — the recipient's picking out of the ostensively manifested material that is most significant for him or her. But, as in the example above, that focusing seems to operate plausibly only if certain stereotypes of the "culturally relevant" hold sway — rain on light clothes, a general preference for not walking in the rain, etc. There seems to be nothing particularly cognitive or individualized about the calculation of relevance here. And the possibilities that the woman is a meteorologist, or likes walking in the rain, or simply doesn't care either way, are not entertained. In short, example scenarios such as that sketched above suggest that the relevance presumption can help identify only *one* of the possibly intended communications in a particular case, without demonstrating that it necessarily has superior claims on the attention of the addressee.

In his discussion in the *Philosophical Investigations* of ostensive definition of names in a simplified language, Wittgenstein gives grounds for concluding that "ostensive definition can be variously interpreted in every case" (1953: 13e [par. 28]). If this is true of the defining of names, how much more must it be the case in the conveying of assumptions? Paragraph 33 (p. 16e) of the *Investigations* begins thus:

Suppose, however, someone were to object: "It is not true that you must already be master of a language in order to understand an ostensive definition: all you need — of course! — is to know or guess what the person giving the explanation is pointing to. That is, whether for example to the shape of the object, or to its colour, or to its number, and so on." — And what does "pointing to the shape", "pointing to the colour" consist in? Point to a piece of paper. — And now point to its shape — now to its colour — now to its number (that sounds queer). — How did you do it? — You will say that you "meant" a different thing each time you pointed. And if I ask how that is done, you will say you concentrated your attention on the colour, the shape, etc. But I ask again: how is that done?

Sperber and Wilson are undoubtedly aware of the problems that Wittgenstein highlights; their model of communication does not seem to circumvent them, however, despite the plausibility sometimes lent their examples owing to their embeddedness in culturally stereotyped situations. But the examples discussed so far have been gestural — pointing, leaning back, and so on — and it is reasonable to suppose that the vagueness and multiple interpretations of gestures, used in ostensive-inferential communication, are precisely why, more commonly, we instead resort to language for the purposes of communication. Is the kind of indeterminacy of gesture-based communication, which I have argued Sperber and Wilson downplay, something that equally bedevils their account as it applies to linguistic communication? Subsequent sections work toward an answer to this question.

Language and Grammar as Code

Some of the more questionable aspects of relevance theory are in fact not central to the theory itself, although Sperber and Wilson subscribe to them quite strongly. They are assumptions that could be modified or jettisoned without rendering certain key arguments of the theory foundationless. The first such assumption is that linguistic communication involves a coding process (although this is not simply a matter of code manipulation or the transfer of messages between minds), after which an ostensive-inferential stage occurs. In a given situation, with a speaker's and a hearer's given assumptions about what each already knows and about what may be mutually manifest, the speaker (S) communicates with the hearer (H) by supplying a stimulus (e.g., an utterance) the inferential interpretation of which can be expected, by H, to have sufficient effect on H's cognitive environment to be worth the processing effort. Thus, linguistic communication is said to begin with the automatic linking, in H's mind-brain, of the heard sound patterns and the semantic representation to which these give rise. That code-given semantic representation is then the input to the pragmatic stage of utterance processing, during which ambiguities of word meaning and structure are resolved, reference is assigning to referring expressions, and so on, in the movement toward a full propositional form for the utterance. Often, a further stage of inferencing and deriving implicatures is needed to achieve an adequately informative interpretation. That is, on the many occasions when something other than the standard or literal sense of an utterance is intended, the hearer will have to inferentially combine information conveyed by the stimulus with contextual assumptions already available to him or her and readily accessible (via short-term memory or perception) so as to arrive at sufficiently interesting contextual effects.

While much of this outline is plausible, an integrational perspective is bound to question the accommodation of a "coding stage" of language processing within the account. As I have argued in previous chapters, a model of language as a fixed code (or, for that matter, as a fluid code) ignores the actualities of language practice. It is significant that Sperber and Wilson devote several pages at the beginning of their book to a rejection of a code theory of communication, only to compromise with the prevailing code-oriented linguistic paradigm later on. Language is not a code, they assert, but they do allow that it does have an important code or coding stage. Sperber and Wilson's acceptance of orthodox linguistic theory is not unlike that implicit in Tannen (1987a), where repetition is treated as an automatized but widespread exception to the rule, namely, that linguistic behavior is characterized by creativity and unpredictability. Similar, too, as we have seen, is Searle's view that a cat wandering over the keys so as to produce *The chair is made of wood* on the screen has produced a meaningful sentence of English, notwithstanding the absence of "speaker meaning" in that scenario.

In order to defend the code model of verbal communication, Sperber and Wilson write, it must be shown how a speaker and hearer can come to have not only a common language but also a common set of premises to which they apply identical inference rules in parallel ways. Questioning the latter of these requirements, much of their book explores how language users are guided by considerations of relevance in their inference making. But what is of interest here is Sperber and Wilson's assumption that the first requirement, of a common language, presents no difficulties. They write:

> For language, the demonstration is fairly straightforward. The evidence suggests that speakers with quite different linguistic histories may end up with very similar grammars. Any number of different examples will do to illustrate a particular aspect of linguistic structure — say, the relative clause — so that it does not much matter which utterances of the language the child actually hears. It is also clear that after a certain point, the structure of the language has essentially been mastered, so that as new utterances are encountered, the grammar of an adult speaker will hardly change at all. The requirement of a common language thus presents no real difficulty for the code model. (Sperber and Wilson 1986: 15)

Such confidence about the existence of a common language is standard among theorists who tacitly subscribe to the fixed-code myth. But in practice demonstrating commonality, indeed uniformity, of adult grammars of a language is not something that can be done in a straightforward way. What can be explored in some detail, however, are speakers' reactions to various usages, on the basis of more and less constrained questioning and nonintrusive observation. But what is on view here is public practice, performance grammar, rather than the so-called competence grammar, allegedly uniform across a community of speakers, to which Sperber and Wilson's comments refer.

There are several controversial claims in the passage cited above. These include the assertion that "it does not much matter which utterances of the language the child actually hears," that learning a language is learning to "master" it, and that after a certain age the grammar of a speaker will hardly change at all. The most contentious is the one that is not explicitly stated at all but implicit in the use, interchangeably, of two key terms; this is the assumption that the terms *grammar* and *language* are variant terms for a single phenomenon. This is a conviction that seems to be remembered and forgotten as is convenient, but we should not be misled by Sperber and Wilson's focus on grammar in the morphosyntactic sense ("say, the relative clause") into forgetting that Chomskyan competence, and uniformity of language, must include lexical knowledge as well as the morphosyntactic. The requirement of a common language that "presents no real difficulty," then, includes the requirement that all speakers within a community also end up with very similar knowledge of words and their meanings—for example, of the words *quark*, *haslet*, and *diapason*. Thus, they assume that all members of some English-speaking speech community will have a uniform grasp of a sentence containing a relative clause, such as the following:

The thief snatched the bag that contained the haslet.

They are unlikely to find—publicly displayed via, for example, paraphrase—evidence of any such uniformity of grasp; given the absence of such adducible evidence, it would be rash to assume that the language uniformity nevertheless resides at some deeper level, in the mind.

It may seem astounding to those outside linguistics that such obvious objections and cautions should need restatement in the above manner, but such has been the power of the myths of code fixity and code autonomy, and the strength of the optimism over the possible advances in the understanding of language that they promised, that these reexaminations of first principles are necessary. From the outset, Sperber and Wilson show themselves to be very much of a kind with other orthodox pragmaticists, despite qualifications and insistences purporting to make themselves distinct. They share with other pragmaticists the view that linguistic communication is best analyzed by first granting the existence of a coded component in any sentence and then characterizing the inference-based supplementary factors involved in conveying and recognizing communicative intentions. The pragmaticist component—a theory of speech acts, or of conventional maxims and implicatures, or of relevance—is in this view a necessary companion to the codified core. Thus, they declare:

A language is a code which pairs phonetic and semantic representations of sentences. However, there is a gap between the semantic representations of sentences and the thoughts actually communicated by utterances. This gap is filled not by more coding, but by inference. . . . The semantic representation of a sentence deals with a sort of common core of meaning shared by every utterance of it. However, different utterances of the same sentence may differ in their interpretation; and indeed they usually do. The study of the semantic representation of sentences belongs to grammar; the study of the interpretation of utterances belongs to what is now known as "pragmatics." (Sperber and Wilson 1986: 9–10)

But here, what is first offered as a characterization of a language—paired phonetic and semantic representations—just a few lines later is said to be a study that "belongs to *grammar*." That is, there is the same strategic conflation of language and grammar as noted previously, a conflation of a by no means trivial or stylistic kind since it points to a deeply rooted conviction within orthodox theorizing of language, semantics, and pragmatics.

In an effort to reconcile the potentially radical principle of relevance with fixed-code linguistics, Sperber and Wilson are pushed close to some disabling admissions. Chief of these would be that a language is a code, but the code does not really work as far as communication is concerned and requires vital help from speakers' and hearers' uncoded and uncodable inferential capacities. The gap (between the tasks performed by the code and the actual communicated effects) is not filled by more coding, and the inferences are nondeductive, they say. The idea that a language is a code but that the code does not work is a theoretical incoherence that can be papered over only by shuttling between the terms *language* and *grammar*. It is worth noting that, when Sperber and Wilson discuss and reject the "code model" and the "code theory" in chapter 1, it is the code model of communication that they reject: they remain committed to a code model of a language. Parallel to Searle's two-stage account in terms of sentence meaning and speaker meaning, relevance theory assumes that there is a first stage of sheer coding in utterance processing, namely, the linking of sound patterns with semantic representations, and a second, uncoded, stage of nondeductive inferencing. The alternative, of questioning at the outset whether, despite all its codificatory tendencies, a language is in essential respects a code at all, remains unaddressed.

Critics of integrational thinking routinely deny that standard linguistics views languages as fixed codes, usually on the shallow grounds that, "obviously," dialectal and idiolectal variation exists, that no one denies this, but that such "variation" (as it is called; rarely is it termed linguistic *difference*) has no bearing on the deeper commonalities that are the subject of inquiry. What is striking in this rejoinder is the extent of supposedly superficial variation or difference that such "deep" linguistics is prepared at once to acknowledge and set aside, so as to maintain the pursuit of incontrovertibly fixed principles at the deeper level, the level of universal grammar (UG). There is a sense, then, in which UG linguists have discarded an earlier belief in code fixity — but they have done so only because their entire focus has turned away from the specificities of different language practices in situated uses. It makes no difference to them whether we talk of "English" as a language or a code or neither since all such constructs are riven with sociologically shaped contaminations. The UG linguist's task is more profound: the difficult and complex task of best representing the fundamental language-structuring principles with which we seem to be genetically endowed. Committed to that assumption, an assumption indeed of species-wide fixity (but fixity of principles, of core language-productive and -interpretive mechanisms, such as C-Command), no amount of empirical variation is likely to redirect such linguists' energies and attention to whatever factors give rise to difference, change, and potential indeterminacy. The objection is not to the UG pursuit of the deepest structure-constraining species-wide linguistic principles but to the degree to which a discipline established to pursue the systematic study of languages and linguistic ability has become intellectually dominated by that pursuit, at the expense of others.

Direct Evidence and Mutual Anything

The major stumbling blocks to full acceptance of Sperber and Wilson's (1986) relevance theory concern its overreliance on principles that are more fallible or tenuous than they allow. These include ostensiveness, the manifest and the mutually manifest, the recognition via inference of what is manifest, and direct evidence. The controversial use of the last of these notions is apparent on page 22, for example, where it is claimed that Mary's audibly hoarse voice is direct ("salient and conclusive") evidence, to Peter, that she has a sore throat. But this is not communicative in any interesting sense, the authors say, and is a method of informing that "can only be used with information for which direct evidence can be provided"; by contrast, real communication can inform the recipient "as long as direct evidence of the communicator's intentions can be provided" (p. 23).

The first objection must be to the claim that an audibly hoarse voice amounts to direct (conclusive) evidence of a sore throat; we know that hoarseness can be brought on by many other circumstances. Grice's analogous example, for what people treat as a kind of "natural" meaning, is more careful: he cites the example of people noting black clouds and saying that they mean rain. Here, the recipient takes the blackness of the clouds and makes of it good (reasonable and fairly reliable) evidence of coming rain. But there is no question of this evidence being conclusive. The very phrase *conclusive evidence* is a near contradiction, to be contrasted with the commoner phrase *conclusive proof*, which is clearly inapplicable to black clouds or hoarse voices. The fact is that evidence is never conclusive or unproblematically "direct" in matters of communication. We marginalize the kind of meaning that we get from the blackness of clouds since we do not in our culture attribute the crucial intention to communicate to those clouds — or any other entity using the clouds as a medium. But other cultures, such as some American Indian ones, might look at this evidence very differently and take it to be significantly communicative.

Conversely, one wonders how firm the grounds are for Sperber and Wilson's assumption that Mary's audibly hoarse voice is somehow unambiguously unmodulated, neutral, and unintended evidence and therefore not properly communicative. There seem no a priori grounds for ruling out the possibility that the audible hoarseness could be evidence that Mary intended to convey to Peter that she had a sore throat. That being so, any sharp distinction between implicitly trivial direct informative evidence and nontrivial evidence of intention to communicate has yet to be demonstrated. The distinction cannot be made by reference to allegedly noncommunicative hoarseness or any other kind of appeal to some factor within the communication situation said to be predeterminately trivially evidential. It is mistaken ever to assume that, in a given communication situation, particular items of evidence are preexistently "there," staring participants in the face. The term *evidence* itself is a nominalization, involving a process of construal of some data (e.g., sense perceptions) as evidence of one kind or another, by contextualized participants. Evidence is no more certainly mutual than knowledge is, however assumable it may be in particular circumstances.

Numerous critics have alleged that mutual manifestness is merely a new variant of the problematic notion of mutual knowledge; Sperber and Wilson have been accused of " 'sneaking' mutual knowledge in the backdoor of their theory of conversational inference" (Gibbs 1987: 569). For Gibbs, this points to the resilience and necessity of some properly formulated notion of mutual knowledge, which he describes as not only a result of comprehension but a "prerequisite for the comprehension of many kinds of utterances in conversation" (p. 585). The representation of mutual knowledge that Gibbs finds defensible and psychologically plausible is that of Clark and Marshall (1981), which he paraphrases as follows:

People ordinarily rely on three kinds of *co-presence heuristics* as evidence for inferring mutual beliefs. The first source is linguistic co-presence. Here the listener takes as common ground all of their conversation up to and including the utterance currently being interpreted. A second source for common ground is physical co-presence. Here the listener takes as common ground what s/he and the speaker are currently experiencing and have experienced. The final source of evidence is community membership. This includes information that is universally known in a community and can be represented by mental structures such as frames . . . , scripts . . . , and schemata. Moreover, it also covers mutually known conventions . . . , etc. governing the phonology, syntax, and semantics of the sentence uttered. (Gibbs 1987: 576)

In fact, it is hard to see relevance theorists having any objection to these claims. From an integrational linguistic perspective, too, there is much to be said for careful attention to the first two of these three bases for mutual belief. But the third basis needs further clarification; otherwise there is a danger of circularity in explicating mutual knowledge by appeal to shared experience and "information that is universally known." All three sources are described by Clark and Marshall as copresence heuristics, but that description sits well, significantly, only with the first two. None of these bases for inferring (some) mutual beliefs, however, amounts to a demonstration of the existence of mutual knowledge. What they amount to is the suggestion that apparently alert and rational interactants with functioning memories are likely to be sufficiently other attentive for that attentiveness to be used by both parties as a communicational resource in the developing interaction.

Gibbs is on this safer ground when he summarizes Clark and Marshall's initial assumption thus: "People search for evidence that they, their listener, and the objects they refer to are 'openly' present together, physically, linguistically, or indirectly" (Gibbs 1987: 576). But, with Clark and Marshall, he errs in assuming that the presence of evidence of the appropriate kind can be mutually confirmed to be present and used to infer mutual knowledge. It is the orientedness to searching for evidence, not the reliability of finding evidence, that underpins communication and understanding. We are sufficiently oriented to others to assume (or to take the risk of assuming) some degree of overlap of our knowledge and background and theirs, but trust in overlapping knowledge is a very different thing from mutual knowledge.

Commentary in line with this approach has come recently from Wright (1992: 44), who argues that communication requires a mutual *presupposition* about correct shared identification of the entities to be discussed, not any mutual *belief* in such things:

[In all communication] one begins with a mutual presupposition: that speaker and hearer have already achieved a perfect coinciding of reference upon the continuum [of entities in the world], that they have singled out exactly the same portion together.

The hearer knows well that in fact he has not: in being prepared to listen, he is preparing himself for an updating of his selection from the continuum, but the speaker could not even begin to effect that adjustment unless both he and the hearer pretended for the nonce that the very same portions of the continuum were being referred to by both of them.

Mutual presupposition, rather than belief, is "the very best way in which we can go about correcting each other about the real continuum, terrifying in its contingency, in which we find ourselves" (p. 44). In short, Wright offers a judicious and nonskeptical corrective to claims about mutual knowledge or manifestness or what he terms the *idealization of reciprocity*. In that idealization, a useful assumption is wrongly converted into a belief: "A needful *methdological* dictum has been falsely exalted into a metaphysical one," thereby "converting a faith into a dogma" (p. 49).

In practice, linguistic communication proceeds successfully without recourse — without the possibility of recourse — to mutual knowledge, shared background, a common ground, or any other such putatively determinate intersubjective foundation. There is no need to resort to such theoretical fictions except where a mistaken attempt is made to protect the notion of linguistic autonomy, of a language as a freestanding and determinate system matching forms and meanings. Theories of mutual knowledge or background sit well with code linguistics, for the former are ways of attempting to define and delimit the context needed to be invoked, in the interpretive progress that is claimed to occur, from the sentence interpretation (given in the grammar) to utterance interpretation (delimited in the mutual-knowledge-shaped context). Against the unsubstantiated claims for all such machinery, integrational linguistics avoids assuming and relying on any assumptions of mutual awareness except an awareness of mutuality itself, and here mutuality denotes that tendency (among other tendencies) within every individual to be to some degree oriented to the interests and values of others.

Ironically, in modern linguistic theorizing in general, more pernicious than overconfidence in adequate direct evidence has been its obverse, an axiomatic conviction that the direct evidence available to language uses is insufficient. This is an enabling assumption within the generativist account of language and language acquisition. (Notice that in both positions evidence is presumed to be, in its nature, direct, as if it were a body of instructions staring every speaker-listener in the face rather than, as argued here, always problematic, indeterminate, provisionally adduced by rationally generalizing and extrapolating communicators.) Thus, in the generativist argument for extensive genetic "hardwiring" of human beings with fundamental, species-wide parameters and principles governing linguistic structure (parameters and principles that are customized slightly differently depending on which natural language(s) a child acquires), much is made of the logical necessity that some such innate and structure-encoding faculty exists, given the rapidity with which native language fluency is achieved despite the "poverty" of the linguistic data encountered by an infant. In general, it is argued, five- and six-year-olds reveal an unconscious knowledge of, for example, grammatical English on the one hand and ungrammatical non-English on the other hand that far exceeds what even very alert inductively reasoning children could acquire if at birth they really started, linguistically, from scratch.

Furthermore, it is argued, not only do infants lack adequate direct evidence from which to generalize a grammar; sometimes they lack any evidence whatsoever. The kind of evidence repeatedly cited here concerns such matters as the allegedly idiosyncratic facts surrounding what is allowed to be grammatical and what ungrammatical among English *wh-* or content questions. Thus, Berwick and Weinberg (1984: 18–19) take the declarative sentences:

(1) Ronald Reagan finally issued a statement without contradicting it.
(2) Ronald Reagan finally issued a statement without contradicting himself.

and then contemplate the transforms of these when the main clause object (*a statement*) and subject (*Ronald Reagan*), respectively, are questioned:

(3) Which statement did Ronald Reagan finally issue without contradicting? [*it* omitted]
(4) Who finally issued a statement without contradicting? [*himself* omitted]

Berwick and Weinberg point to a disparity here between the grammaticality (*sic*) of (3) and the ungrammaticality of (4): the sentence-final pronominal reference to the questioned object in (3) may be omitted, but a parallel omission of a sentence-final pronoun reference to the questioned subject in (4) is disallowed. This, Berwick and Weinberg argue, is linguistic knowledge of a kind never expicitly taught to children and involves data—such as (4)—of a kind they would never ordinarily encounter. Somehow, lacking direct experience of ungrammaticalities such as that in (4), children just know that some structures fit the grammar and others would not: they know because the foundational parameters of the grammar have been genetically preset.

The first difficulty with this argument (for an alternative response, see Love [1988: 75–76]) concerns Berwick and Weinberg's own evidence. If standard or traditional grammar is to be a guide, they are simply wrong to claim that

(3) Which statement did Ronald Reagan finally issue without contradicting?

is a grammatical English sentence. Nor does the product get any closer to being standardly grammatical if (3) is framed so that it is a proper counterpart to (4); that is, by questioning a full constituent rather than simply the head of the object constituent:

(3') What did Ronald Reagan finally issue without contradicting?

Conversely, converting (4) to a +specific questioning of the subject head does not improve matters either:

(4') Which person finally issued a statement without contradicting?

(Alternatively, "Which Reagan....")

Such adjustments to the data simply highlight the fact that all four of these *wh*-questions (sentences [3], [4], [3'], and [4']), where a final anaphoric pronoun or reflexive that is coreferential with the fronted interrogative phrase has been ellipted, are ungrammatical by established standards. (This presupposes that it is reasonable to speak of an ellipted final constituent in sentences (3) and (4) — an assumption that I take to be simply a fact of grammatical usage of the verb *contradict* [as with *hit*, *admit*, *deny*, etc. and by contrast with *recant*]: that this verb requires lexicalization of the affected participant.) No doubt the information in the first sentence of this paragraph can be revised and reformulated as a description invoking constraints on the deletion of bound anaphors, followed by claims that these constraints reflect some parameter in a universal innate grammar. But explanation — rather than a linguist's description — of the standardly grammatical must be in functional terms. The functional explanation turns on everyday logic and is that you cannot both (*a*) thematize (front) and question a constituent and (*b*) ellipt reference to it elsewhere in the same sentence. Doing the former implies that a speaker has insufficient knowledge of a thing, while doing the latter implies the contrary. To thematize and question is in part to indicate "the item questioned is being treated as unknown to at least one participant in this interaction and will be new information if subsequently supplied"; to ellipt or delete an item amounts to saying that "the item ellipted is known to me (and perhaps others), is so given as not to be in need of (re)statement." It reflects Berwick and Weinberg's mistaken disregard of semantic or functional explanation, in pursuit of a purely structural logic, that they can assert that "semantically [4] is much the same as (2)" (1984: 19). Those sentences are repeated here for convenience of comparison:

(2) Ronald Reagan finally issued a statement without contradicting himself.
(4) Who finally issued a statement without contradicting?

On the contrary, it is the semantic difference between (2) and (4), concerning what is treated as unknown, that constrains the co-occurring utterance structure.

This is a simple point about the oddity (and the standard grammar pronounces it odd) of implying that you know something and do not know it at the same time. This is a matter of everyday logic, but there is no rule of logic involved here for the child either to learn or to be prewired with: children simply come to recognize (using their rationalizing mental faculties) that this makes sense, just as they come to realize that it makes sense that putting a cup behind a sheet of paper will not cause the cup to disappear and that pouring a volume of water from a tall thin beaker to a short fat one neither adds nor subtracts from the volume of water involved. We can state what it is they learn in all these cases as rules and laws, but children themselves (if indeed they reflect on these matters at all) think of these phenomena and their part in them not as bound by rules that must be followed but rather as what seems to be a sensible view of the way things are. In all these cases, they learn a more general fact or tendency, enabled to do so by their genetic cognitive endowment, which has been suitably stimulated through early childhood, and relevant experiences in the world. Only (roughly) in secondary school, where we instill in our children the codifications that have grown up around science and written language, do they get sidetracked into thinking of language like chemistry and physics, as essentially subjects with syllabi, examinations, units, and rules attached.

Some of the insistences that jar in Sperber and Wilson's account of relevance are inscribed equally firmly in the Gricean urtext, "Logic and Conversation" (Grice 1975). Thus, Grice declares: "A general pattern for the working out of a conversational implicature might be given as follows: 'He has said that p; there is no reason to suppose that he is not observing the maxims, or at least the CP [the Cooperative Principle]; he could not be doing this unless he thought that q; he knows [and knows that I know that he knows] that I can see that the supposition that he thinks q IS required; he has done nothing to stop me thinking that q; he intends me to think, or is at least willing to allow me to think, that q; and so he has implicated that q'" (p. 50). Here, notwithstanding the invocation of supposition and reasonable likelihood ("there is no reason to suppose . . ."), principles of probabilism and reasonable uptake in the assumed circumstances are not uppermost. Rather, the reasoning by which implicatures are said to be calculated is presented as primarily unmodalized and necessary; it is asserted that the inferencing must be along the lines specified and according to the assumptions specified. Thus — somehow — the speaker could not be (not "probably would not be") saying p in a cooperative spirit unless he thought q; the speaker knows (not "thinks or believes"); the hearer can (not "may") see that q is required (not "is probable, reasonable, and relevant"); and so on. As a result, the locally determined and contingent character of implicature, which cannot derive in a decontextualizably general way from the "what is SAID," is obscured in Grice, as in Sperber and Wilson. Uptake is far more probabilistic than Grice's account would suggest. This does not amount to saying that meaning or implicature is "statistical"; rather, patterns and norms of implicature invariably interact with the specific details of particular cases. At one point, Grice gently confesses that he is "enough of a rationalist to want to find a basis" underlying the facts of CP-exploiting implicature. One is tempted to suggest that, where he presents the relations between the said p and the implicated q, given the operation of the CP, as matters of necessary or obligatory inference, he is not merely enough but too much of a rationalist.

When A approaches B and explains, "I am out of gas" and gets the reply from B, "There is a garage round the corner," A's inferential sense making may be guided by an assumption that the CP is still being observed, but it cannot be guided by a set of conditional statements concerning what, if the CP holds, B then must intend to implicate. What guides A's sense making may itself be rather less of a guide to the derivation of implicatures than Grice's picture (1975: 50) suggests. In place of that picture, it may be proposed that A's interpretation of "There is a garage round the corner" will be guided by an assumption and a probabilistic question:

1. It is reasonable to assume that B thinks (and that B assumes A will assume B thinks) that his reply is truthful, informative, relevant, and perspicuous.

2. How could the reply be so?

The answer to question 2, assuming a reasonably other-oriented pair of interactants, must be along the following lines: whatever the reply does (here, it informs) must make a significant contribution to A's (or A's and B's) completion of the task or problem, or advancement toward the goal, that B thinks A has. Here, B's reply will be cooperative for A if A understands that, in informing him that "There is a garage round the corner," B is making a contribution to the solution of what he, B, takes to be A's problem (lack of gas) and goal (acquisition of gas). There is a complex background in place, as a backdrop to this little exchange, that it would be egregious or bizarre for either party at this point to recapitulate linguistically (cf. the discussion of Searle's notion of background in chapter 1). In another similar situation, there are a host of things B might offer by way of replies to A's "I am out of gas":

Oh, then your best bet is to find a garage — one that sells gas, that is (and not just one that repairs cars). There you will be able to buy gas — if you have money. Also you will need to take along a can — or borrow one, if they'll let you. . . . As a matter of fact, there is a garage round the corner.

But, clearly, all but the last of this is bizarre or downright insulting to A's intelligence, being so obviously part of the assumable background without which A's "I'm out of gas" would make little sense. Put another way, anyone in the position of being in possession of an immobilized car who, on being approached by a stranger, says, "I am out of gas," can be assumed already to know all but the last piece of information supplied above. So particular utterances do assume and rely on some degree of shared common background knowledge. Situated utterances rely on estimations about the kind and extent of background knowledge that can be assumed of interlocutors; they do not rely on the existence of mutual knowledge. And it is perfectly possible for participant A to assume, mistakenly, that his or her utterance will be interpreted by B relative to one kind of background of knowledge when in fact B invokes a different one.

Another respect in which the "working out" of conversational implicatures is uncertain and probabilistic rather than governed by guarantees and sequiturs concerns the kind of contribution that a cooperative (truthful, relevant, etc.) reply constitutes — in particular whether a response supports or challenges a previous remark. This is evident if we consider another of Grice's examples, in which B's reply is said to be indirectly relevant to A's claim:

    A: Smith doesn't seem to have a girlfriend these days.
    B: He has been paying a lot of visits to New York lately.

Grice suggests that B implicates that Smith may have a girlfriend in New York — that is, that B contributes to the goal (of "knowing about Smith") by supplying an informative that may be seen as challenging A's assumption. But, as in the previous example, part of the essential feature of such interaction is that the challenge has not been expressed in any more explicit or incontrovertible way. Furthermore, in the present case, the implicature that Grice derives is controvertible. B's "He has been paying a lot of visits to New York lately" may quite reasonably be understood as a cooperative support of A's observation rather than a challenge to it. These contrasting cancelable implicatures may be highlighted by making certain additions to B's reply (additions that, as noted above, are no actual part — covert or underlying — of the heard reply):

> A: Smith doesn't seem to have a girlfriend these days.
> B1: Not so. He has been paying a lot of visits to New York lately.
> [roughly, the Gricean reading]

> A: Smith doesn't seem to have a girlfriend these days.
> B2: True. He has been paying a lot of visits to New York lately.

Interestingly — and this would seem to suggest that relevance takes precedence over quantity in at least some situations — the potential appropriateness of either one of the B replies holds even if what he explicitly informs A of here is something (B knows) A already knows. This is evident if we insert "as you know" before "He has been paying . . ." in each of B's replies.

It may be doubted whether the observations above present any kind of difficulty for the Gricean picture, on the grounds that Grice acknowledges from the outset that conversational implicatures are cancelable. The point of the present proposed counterinterpretations is to suggest that, cancelability notwithstanding, some adjustment to the Gricean picture seems called for if his examples of implicature turn out, as here, to be "highly" cancelable, as it were. In certain kinds of familiar or generic situations, the CP and maxims are reliable resources for the derivation of implicatures without extended scrutiny of the assumed background knowledge, precisely since the content of that background knowledge is stable and stereotypical; but it is important to recognize that in very many cases derivation and interactants' goals are more various than the standard Gricean account would suggest since invoked background knowledges are more distinct than the canonical examples imply.

Irony

Turning to specific kinds of verbal communication, Sperber and Wilson have proposed interesting and influential analyses of such tropes as metaphor and irony. In particular, their evolving account of irony has attracted many adherents. Furthermore, despite their own claims to the contrary (Sperber and Wilson 1986: passim), it is doubtful whether their account of irony depends on the relevance framework in which it is embedded. The account is congruent with their other relevance-theoretical proposals, but its strengths can be assessed independently.

In an earlier influential paper (Sperber and Wilson 1981), irony was characterized as the echoic mention (as opposed to the use) of a previously occurring utterance. This view is modified in Sperber and Wilson (1986, 1989), where irony is said to involve the use of echoic utterances that display an "interpretive resemblance" to some prior utterance; irony involves, as it were, modulated near repetition, the modulation being the attitudinal variance brought by the echoing speaker to this second use of the given utterance. The 1989 article, to which most of the following remarks particularly respond, is also significant since it enlarges the scope of discussion so as to consider other literary phenomena dear to stylisticians, notably direct, indirect, and free indirect discourse.

The paper begins with a recapitulation of objections to both traditional and Gricean accounts of irony, which assert that ironic utterances intend or implicate the opposite of that which they literally convey. Only certain types of irony, notably the simple form of sarcasm, may communicate the opposite of what is said. Taking what is arguably the simplest inferential step (roughly, "formulate the opposite or converse of the proposition actually expressed, and assume that the speaker intends to convey just this") will rarely be adequate interpretive work in the derivation of ironic meaning: irony is subtler than that. Instead, Sperber and Wilson argue that irony involves a recycling or in some sense echoic use, which cannot reasonably be accepted by the addressee as intended to be taken at face value but rather must be understood as intended to convey criticism of the topic, or situation, or addressee, or some other salient aspect of the context.

Examples that they give to highlight the inadequacy of the traditional definition of *irony* include the following:

(1) When a man is tired of London he is tired of life. [said while stuck in wretched rush-hour traffic in present-day London]

(2) Ah, Tuscany in May! [said by a friend whom you have brought to Tuscany with the promise that the weather there is glorious, only to be welcomed by a torrential downpour, howling winds, etc.]

In both cases, the remarks could be ironically intended, but in neither case can we say that the opposite of what is literally said is in fact intended. In the second sentence, the exclamation, Sperber and Wilson claim that it is hard to identify a full proposition, available for negation or contradiction, at all. Strictly speaking, this is true, but, equally, it is evident that readers/listeners do (i.e., must) rapidly construct (i.e., hypothesize) a full, propositional form if they assume, as is reasonable, that the speaker of (2) intended it to represent a full proposition. Since the transcribed content of (2) is likely to be taken to constitute an expressive exclamative (Ah!) and just one argument (Tuscany in May!), a low-effort but plausible expansion of this to a full propositional form would involve supplying a copula predicate and an evaluation:

Tuscany in May [copula] [evaluation].

Here, one simple solution (in the nature of the situation, there cannot be just one solution) would link the given subject argument to an approbatory or derogatory complement via a tensed form of the verb *be*. In this case, and cued by "Ah" (cf. "Ugh," "Yuk," etc.) and an associated intonational contour, an approbatory proposition may likely be inferred:

"Ah, Tuscany in May is good."

(The temporal reference supplied by the tensing of the verb is important: past tense is one of the crucial ways that shift of situation can be indicated within the text, a point of some significance to arguments below.) Without the assessment in terms of either approbation or derogation, no irony can arise — a point about the intrinsicness to all irony of critical commentary, which I will elaborate more fully below.

But it seems to be foundationally the case that richer interpretations of utterances involving inference making and inference application (such as irony and metaphor and "indirect" speech acts generally) require that encountered utterances be grasped or cast, at the interpretive outset and guided by assessments both of what the activity type in progress is and of what more local determinations of the particular present intentions of interactants are, in proposition-like form. This applies whether the encountered utterance happens to be an appealing cricketer's [Zaaaa] (as discussed in chapter 4), or a conversationalist's "No!" or a vacationer's "Ah, Tuscany in May." Very often, the preceding and immediately following verbal context will assist in that determination of a proposition-like form, but the larger context, including specifics of the cultural context, will often be essential guides too.

While conversion to proposition-like form is a necessary first interpretive step in all cases, there is then the further requirement that this proposition-like form must be interpretable as an expression of approbation or disapprobation, in some respect, in cases where an ironic reading is subsequently derived. This is why, if the heard remark "Ah, Tuscany in May" were expanded to either of the propositional forms (which I take to be non- or obscurely evaluative)

Ah, "Tuscany in May" has a musical ring to it

or

Ah, there are many visitors to Tuscany in May,

then subsequent ironic interpretation would be difficult to derive.

Irony as: Shifted; Critical; Commentary

Returning to example (1) above, Sperber and Wilson argue that this is said not with the intention of flatly denying Dr. Johnson's aphorism but "to make fun of the sentiments that gave rise to it, the vision of London it was originally intended to convey" (Sperber and Wilson 1989: 98). It is possible to explain the irony here somewhat differently, however. The speaker trapped in modern-day traffic who reuses or recycles Johnson's comment in that context contributes to several developments:

a) Thereby, and first and foremost, they contrive to make evident to the addressee (manifest to him or her) a mismatch, an incongruity of fit, between the world and assumptions associated with Johnson's remark and the immediate context of the present utterance.

b) The addressee who notices this mismatch must now ask herself whether she takes the mismatch to be deliberate or unconscious on the part of the speaker. (If adjudged unconscious, the speaker may be deemed to have a strange and different view of London and/or not to be making a comment relevant to the immediate context of the traffic jam, etc.)

c) If, as is likely, the speaker is deemed to have deliberately contrived this mismatched commentary, then some kind of irony will be assumed — some kind of message other than what has been overtly said. Here, I would suggest, the speaker's commentary might be interpreted as

> making fun of the idea (the speaker's overtly stated idea) that the Johnsonian vision of London fits the London currently being experienced, at the time of speaking.

This formulation is significantly different from that of Sperber and Wilson, quoted above, and clarifies an important stage in their account. In the given traffic-jam situation, Johnson's vision of London is not necessarily being mocked at all, nor is it necessarily the case that in all modern circumstances the speaker would intend the utterance of (1) to be some kind of sarcastic echo of the Johnsonian original. It is simply that, in the present context of speaking, the utterance is critical and ironic. In other words, a crucial element in such echoic or "quoting" types of irony is the assumed disjunction or noncongruence between an original or established situation of use and the present one. At the same time, however, the account of the workings of irony can very easily become distorted if too much reliance is placed on the idea of a prior original use, contrasted with the current one. Just how important is it, for instance, that (1) be recognized as originally Johnson's or indeed originally *anybody* else's? It seems that something of the piquancy and literary cleverness of the irony is lost on or by the recipient, but the effect of irony itself is not lost. However weakened, (1) can give rise to irony, along the lines specified above (with perceived mismatch and critical intent as the key instruments), even where the addressee has no inkling of an echoed Johnsonian original.

It may be worth adding that, having uttered (1) in the traffic jam, it would not be impossible for the same speaker to use the same utterance at a later date, with a seemingly noncritical ironic purpose. For example, two days later, the same speaker and addressee are relaxing in the late afternoon sunshine at a café in the refurbished Covent Garden complex. They have had a wonderful day visiting galleries, an exhibition at the British Museum, etc. and are all set for the opera that evening. The speaker now "echoes," in a chastened, corrective spirit, his own previous use of Johnson's remark, possibly with emphasis on the second verb:

> (3) When a man is tired of London, he *is* tired of life.

This is surely a kind of ironic utterance, although at first glance it appears noncritical: it supports Johnson's approbatory view, and there is no sense of the speaker being covertly at odds with the proposition expressed. In this respect, (3) is strong support for the view that irony frequently does not convey the opposite of what is actually said. But notice also that (3) works as irony (as distinct from simple echoic observation) only given the known background of the traffic-jam use of the same phrase in the recent past. (3) is indeed a critical commentary (of the kind that I claim is required in all irony) on the justness of the previous negative assessment of London in these current changed circumstances. (As in the relations between [1] and Johnson's original utterance, so in the relations between [3] and [1], an important factor is the evident situational *shift* between the prior utterance and its echo.) In this way, a separate principle that (as indicated above) I will argue is crucial to the identification and production of irony can be preserved, despite the seemingly noncritical, approbatory use of Johnson's sentence in (3). The principle is the following:

Verbal irony is always in the nature of a critical commentary on some state of affairs and not merely a description of a state of affairs.

Just what counts as flagging that a remark is by way of commentary and not mere factual description will vary from case to case; it is very likely guided by a relevance-style principle that sufficient evaluative features be embedded in the utterance to prompt the addressee to assume that it is intended as more than descriptive.

The above remarks are germane to Sperber and Wilson's example, taken from Grice, of nonironic falsehood. According to the traditional definition, saying something patently false and intending to communicate the opposite should result in irony, but the following example appears to conform to that definition and yet fails to be successfully ironic. Passing a car with a broken window, you remark to a friend,

(4) Look, that car has all its windows intact,

and you intend to communicate the opposite, roughly:

(5) That car has one of its windows broken.

Clearly the likelihood is that no such uptake of (4) will be achieved. Sperber and Wilson, following Grice, comment that something is clearly missing from the traditional definition here, but they do not specify what that is. Because (5) is not triggered by reliably inferrable embedded evaluation in (4), what is missing from (5) is the element of critical commentary that I have suggested is essential to irony. Commenting on the failure of (4) to convey irony, Grice justly remarks: "The absurdity . . . is I think to be explained by the fact that irony is intimately connected with the expression of a feeling, attitude, or evaluation. I cannot say something ironically unless what I say is intended to reflect a hostile or derogatory judgment or a feeling such as indignation or contempt" (1978: 124). It is very hard to see

"That car has all its windows intact,"

when said as you pass the car with a broken window, as adequately expressive of the evaluative assessment that you may intend to convey; it seems to be a simple factual description, albeit an inaccurate one. Even if the addressee assumes that you know that (4) is false and that you have said it without intending to misinform, the intended uptake remains unclear. If, however, in place of (4) you remark, on passing a car with a broken window,

(6) That car's windows are in fine condition!

the addressee is more likely to notice the embedded evaluation (especially, the word *fine*), treat the remark as more than description (i.e., commentary), notice the mismatch, assume intendedness, and infer mocking ironic intent.

Understatement

An adjusted analysis is also possible for one of Sperber and Wilson's earliest examples of irony in the 1989 paper, an example that they take to be one of ironic understatement that, nevertheless, does not conform to the traditional view that the opposite of what is said is meant. The example is that of the prospect of a customer in a shop, blind with rage at the service he is getting, viewing whom S turns to H and remarks:

(7) You can tell he's upset.

The traditional explanation fails since neither of the standard negations of this statement is what is in fact meant (S intends to convey neither "You can't tell he's upset" nor "You can tell he isn't upset").

But is (7), as Sperber and Wilson assert, understatement? In what way is it a saying less, or insufficient, about a given phenomenon? (One standard handbook of literature — Molman's — describes understatement as "a form of irony in which something is intentionally represented as less than in fact it is" [1972: 543].) If we take the following as canonical understatements —

(8) Carl Lewis is a fairly fast sprinter,
(9) Amsterdam is a few miles away from Seattle

—then Sperber and Wilson's own example of understatement stands out by comparison since it is hard to see that it is a calculated "intentionally saying less than is reasonable" in the way that (8) and (9) are. I suggest that understatement is characterized, in Gricean terms, by quality observance but quantity breach. The quantity breach gives rise in each case to an implicature that we would not normally accept as a reasonable assessment of the topic. Thus, the quantity breaches in (8) and (9) give rise to the implicatures, respectively, that Carl Lewis is no more than fairly fast and that Seattle is no more than a few miles from Amsterdam. For addressees in the know about Lewis, Amsterdam, and Seattle, (8) and (9) might be whimsically willful misdirections, a kind of verbal play (a playful distortion of "received reality" seems to be a motivation for much understatement). But only fully *situated* understatement is likely to be amusing in an ironic sense. In the situation sketched by Sperber and Wilson, a better example of ironic understatement than (7) might be the following:

(10) He seems a little bit upset.

What unites all understatements, including the suspect (7), is observance of the quality maxim (indeed, [7] observes it the least problematically of them all). Thus, it certainly is true that Amsterdam is a few miles away from Seattle and that Carl Lewis is a fairly fast sprinter. But what separates (7) from (8)–(10) is that these latter clearly breach quantity in a way that (7) does not. The addressee of (7) is not bound to see mismatch in it, as the reasonably informed addressee of (8)–(10) will.

It may seem of little consequence whether (7) is classified as understatement or as a more standard kind of irony. But, if the utterance is indeed more an instance of the latter than the former, then this presents a difficulty for Sperber and Wilson's insistence that standard irony is invariably echoic, or an "interpretively resemblant" use, of some prior heard or imagined utterance; (7) seems to lack any of the echoism that Sperber and Wilson stipulate. As indicated, it is hard to see (7) as an "intentionally saying less" at all. Rather, it is either simply nonfigurative, a describing on record prompted perhaps by embarrassment or by a poor assessment of other onlookers' ability to assess the situation for themselves, or, conceivably, it is ironic, where intended and received as mismatched with the situation, particularly in its emphatic insistence that "one can tell . . ." where in fact no doubts about perceptibility or recognition seem warranted. The utterance—on just this reading—is ironic, but with no relation to understatement, in just the same way as is displaying an American dollar bill to a normal American adult and "informing" him or her, "This is a dollar bill."

The distinctions between irony and other rhetorical stances are touched on by a passage in Grice that immediately follows one quoted earlier (Grice 1978: 124): "I can for example say *What a scoundrel you are!* when I am well disposed toward you, but to say that will be playful, not ironical, and will be inappropriate unless there is some shadow of justification for a straightforward application–for example you have done something which some people (though not I) might frown upon. . . . Whereas to say *He's a fine friend* is unlikely to involve any hint of anyone's approval." While *He's a fine friend* is easy to imagine in contexts where it is intended ironically (indeed, it is harder to imagine it used unironically), *What a scoundrel you are!* may well be used and intended playfully but not ironically. Grice argues that the latter will be appropriate where there is at least some justification for the utterance's "straightforward application" — that is, where the quality maxim is, arguably, according to the opinions of "some people," observed rather than breached. In this respect, the playful insult can be grouped with understatement rather than typical irony — although actually the insult is closer to overstatement than understatement. Notice, particularly in the light of Sperber and Wilson's principle of echoism, that in contextualizing *What a scoundrel you are!* Grice invokes other communicators, whose "frowning" judgment the present speaker interpretively echoes: the speaker who perpetrates a playful insult is in effect mentioning the disapprobatory judgment of others but embedding it in a different use (playful in its orientaton not only to the addressee but also to those putative frowning sources of disapproval).

At this point, it should be acknowledged that the separating out of quality and quantity in the way just sketched is not unproblematic and that quality and quantity are arguably more intertwined than Gricean pragmatics suggests. Thus, some speakers of the language may find it hard to accept the idea that asserting "Seattle is a few miles from Amsterdam" is not a saying of that which the speaker knows to be false. Be that as it may, the characterization of understatement as involving a perceived underinformativeness still holds, and this feature is noticeably absent from (7).

Irony Always Echoic?

The more numerous and varied the examples examined, the harder it is to agree with Sperber and Wilson that irony definitionally involves "echoic interpretive use." We have already examined situated utterances such as (6) and (10), finding little evidence of echoism in them. Similarly, how is Jane Austen's celebrated opening to *Pride and Prejudice* (1970: 1) echoic?

It is a truth universally acknowledged that a single man in possession of a good fortune must be in want of a wife.

This can be seen as echoic only in an attenuated sense, echoic of various culture-bound frames or scripts, particularly of Austen's time and just before, in which assumptions about marriage and wealth and their interconnection were articulated.

Or — one of Sperber and Wilson's own examples from Austen — what is echoic in the following rejoinder from Emma Woodhouse to Mr. Knightley? On seeing Emma playing happily with her sister's child, Knightley counsels Emma:

"If you were as much guided by nature in your estimate of men and women, and as little under the power of fancy and whim in your dealings with them, as you are where these children are concerned, we might always think alike."

And to this she replies:

"To be sure — our discordancies must always arise from my being in the wrong." (1971: 89).

The nearest this comes to echoism is in the way that it arguably ventriloquizes Knightley (unfairly): it pretends to be a reformulation of Knightley's views. It pretends to be echoic, then, while not actually being echoic at all. Such ironic rejoinders are a common conversational maneuver and equally commonly provoke the response, "That's not what I said."

But, again, what first alerts readers to the possible ironic interpretation of Emma's reply is not echo (Emma's assertions are not remotely echoic of what Knightley has just said) but the perception of Emma's expressed view as ill matched with what might be a reasonable commentary, in the circumstances. It is not reasonable, in the affairs between two rational and civilized adults, for one of those adults to admit — insist, even — that he or she is invariably the source of error and discordance. Emma's "to be sure" and "must always" are unreasonable, and the strength of these assertions of epistemic modality is a feature of her discourse sharply at odds with the accompanying declaration of inferiority and fallibility: her righteous *insistence* on her wrongness is just the discoursal clue we need that the speaker intends that her mismatched commentary be recognized as intended mismatched commentary. Leech's discussion of an irony principle (1983: 82, 142–45), parasitic on standards of cooperativeness and politeness, is also useful here. Emma's response is impeccably polite, supportive of Knightley's face wants at great expense to her own. Indeed, it is too polite to be true (politeness is insisted on to the point where the quality maxim of the CP is flouted, in implicature-triggering ways).

Similarly, consider the following conjunction of signals, which I take to be intended ironically by its composers. This example comes from a book entitled *Signs of the Times: A Portrait of the Nation's Tastes* (1992), compiled by N. Barker and M. Parr, that comprises a series of photographs of British individuals juxtaposed with their personal choices in interior decoration and some brief comment from them on their own preferences. One page displays a photograph of a white light switch framed by gaudy wallpaper; appended to this is the following text:

"We wanted a cottagey stately-home kind of feel."

It is germane to the reader's or viewer's interpretation that someone other than those responsible for both the decor and the text has brought them together here. If a reader perceives irony here, it is not in virtue of some recognized interpretive resemblance to a prior utterance but on the basis of kinds of incongruity, beginning with the near-oxymoronic conjunction of *cottagey* and *stately-home*.

Or consider the following extract, from a feature article by Susan Whitehead in the *Guardian Weekly* (12 June 1994, 25), a parent's perspective on organized children's soccer in the United States:

The children are keen as mustard and, having got possession of the ball, they are certainly not prepared to pass it to a team-mate.

Again, echoic interpretive resemblance plays no role in any irony perceived here, which seems to be grounded particularly in the modal expressions of certainty and willingness — *certainly not prepared to* — that a reader may judge to be Whitehead's evaluative assessments of the situation, purporting to be merely descriptive of the children's own outlook; this in turn interacts with a reader's sense that keenness at soccer should, in fact, involve teamwork and passing. Two kinds of willingness — keenness at soccer and willingness to pass to teammates — are conjoined, by *and* significantly, as if the latter willingness elaborated on and bore out the claimed existence of the former kind of willingness. In fact, the additive conjunction seems crucial to the effect; it is a moot point whether any clear sense of irony remains if *but* is substituted for *and*:

The children are keen as mustard but, having got possession of the ball, they are certainly not prepared to pass it to a team-mate.

At this stage a tentative listing of the core elements of irony, that is, the core steps in the construal of irony, may be offered:

1. A preliminary interpretation of the speech event is performed, by the association of (*a*) the linguistic material and (*b*) the nonlinguistic context with previously experienced and remembered speech events.

2. A mismatch is perceived: the addressee hazards that there is incongruity in the utterance-to-context fit.

3. That mismatch is judged to be deliberately contrived by the speaker (if not deliberate, it may create either unintended irony or no irony at all — as in lying, psychotic speech, etc.).

4. The addressee judges the utterance to be more than description, that is, at least implicitly evaluative commentary on some part of the present situation.

5. The addressee assesses the degree and focus of the critical commentary in the present situation (the participants, the circumstances, the actions or state), that is, speculates as to the ways in which the speaker seems to intend that her utterance, conventionally interpreted, diverges from being a reasonable commentary on the present situation, thereby simultaneously identifying those things in the present situation that the speaker finds unreasonable, intolerable, or a source of amusement.

I have argued that irony does not invariably involve the echo of, or an interpretive resemblance to, any particular prior utterance. If the idea of "echoic-ness" is to be retained as applying to all irony, it can be done only by modifying the formulation and saying something to the effect that

irony is the echoic (interpretively resemblant) use of a voice or utterance whose original may never have been heard.

Whether this is helpful or not may depend on one's reasons for theorizing about irony in the first place, but what is quite apparent is that the formulation is unfalsifiable. This revised characterization may be compared with that of Cooper, who proposes revision of Sperber and Wilson's claim in favor of the following, much weaker assertion (1986: 192):

An irony must echo a proposition, or one suitably related to it, that someone might actually, or in some 'possible world,' have seriously stated or believed.

Of this, he comments: "So weakened, however, it is unclear that [this notion of echo] does not also accommodate all metaphors. . . . I am unclear how useful it is to describe all ironies in these terms as well."

Cooper specifies two ways in which the categories of metaphor and irony overlap: he suggests that echoic mention may be involved (but need not be) in both phenomena and that both activities reflect a "cultivation of intimacy" between the producer and the addressee (as noted, concerning metaphor, in chapter 2). But whether metaphor is commonly echoic remains questionable. Cooper's single example of echoic metaphor is presented as follows: "Some metaphors can certainly be echoes — as when I metaphorically describe the ferocious doberman next door as a wolf, intentionally echoing a child's seriously stated belief that this is what the animal is" (p. 193). The most striking thing about this example is the very lack of metaphoricality in either the child's behavior or the adult's. The child evidently actually but mistakenly believes and says that the neighbor's animal is a wolf. No metaphor is involved — and it would be bizarre to claim that in identifying the animal as a wolf the child has stumbled by accident into producing a metaphor. (When the adult hears the child call the neighbor's dog a wolf, she or he must decide whether that name is a mistake or an intended metaphor: it cannot be both.) Since there is no metaphoricality in the child's naming the animal a wolf, it is hard to see how the adult's echoic mention of that misnaming is at all metaphoric. If the adult's addressee happens to know that the neighbors have a dog and not a wolf, the adult's remark is a straightforward ironic recycling, which relies on the addressee's ability to perceive mismatch and then to see that the mismatch is achieved by means of using a conventional metaphor for a ferocious dog. But, while the adult's recycling happens to draw on a conventional metaphor, it is not itself metaphoric but ironic. On the other hand, if the adult's addressee does not happen to know that the neighbors do not in fact have a wolf, then the reference to the neighbor's wolf will not be heard as either metaphoric or necessarily ironic; the adult's allusion to a wolf will be simply an echoic recycling of a misnaming.

Interestingly, it seems that the framing and subordination of metaphoric elements by an ironizing intent holds equally when one speaker echoically but disbelievingly recycles another speaker's genuine metaphor (as compared with the child's metaphor-like misnaming). Thus, if speaker A has told B "My neighbors are a pair of Hush Puppies" and it subsequently transpires that these neighbors suffer an attempted burglary but manage to subdue and arrest an entire gang of intruders, B may comment: "Some Hush Puppies!" A famous historical instance of this kind was Churchill's response to the suggestion, early in the Second World War, that in attempting to stand alone against the Nazi aggression Britain would have its neck wrung like a chicken: "Some chicken! Some neck!" In both cases, the echoic response is ironic but not metaphoric: neither speaker B nor Churchill is speaking metaphorically, although in both cases metaphors are mentioned in the course of conveying a disparaging evaluation of the appropriacy of those metaphors. Metaphor construal is thus simply involved in understanding these remarks as intended, namely, as ironic.

These latter three examples also highlight some of the respects in which metaphor and irony are not strictly parallel modes of figurative utterance. It is not the case that, in commenting on some state of affairs, either one may speak metaphorically or one may speak ironically; nor is it correct to think of metaphor and irony as two variant ways of saying "that which is not the case." The set toward the message, to use a Jakobsonian formulation, is of a different order in the two different situations. Irony may be thought of as a creative adjustment of the set, while metaphor is a creative adjustment of the message; in Hallidayan terms, irony is primarily a part of the interpersonal function of language, while metaphor is primarily a part of the ideational function.

A distinction may also be made between the different roles played by intimacy in the two practices. In irony, intimacy is assumed and is the precondition for proper uptake of the ironic utterance: the addressee must be already "in the know," must be already aware of whatever special, private, or insider knowledge is necessary for the derivation of the intended ironic message. In fresh metaphor, only the possibility of intimacy is assumed: the actual process of grasping the metaphor puts the addressee "in the know." Intimacy cultivation is part of the process of metaphor; intimacy, as a condition, is an external enabling ground for irony. This contrast between being "in the know" before irony can work and being "put in the know" when metaphor works reflects the general tendency for fresh or creative ironies to be most centrally the expression of new evaluations, while fresh metaphors are most centrally the expression of new descriptions or new knowledge.

In view of the complexities explored above, it seems necessary to redefine the role of echo and to treat it as instrumental in only some forms of irony, not all. The following chapter includes a fuller discussion of the idea that all discourse is partially echoic of previous discourse. Whether or not that notion is valid, the question remains as to how to constrain the principle of echoism so as to specify those aspects of it that are distinctive of irony and to render the claim testable. What is needed to make a notion of echoism interestingly constrained is, for example, an emphasis that what is at work is what might be called (drawing on conversational analytic language) *displayed echoism.*

There are two relatively common situations in which displayed echoism is invoked for ironic effect: one is where a speaker recontextualizes an utterance recognizably of a particular provenance within the culture; the other is where a speaker recycles an utterance only recently used in the ongoing interaction. But, barring evidence to the contrary, it must be assumed that, while some verbal irony exploits the phenomenon of displayed echoism, much does not.

The idea of mismatch must be ranked above that of echo first on the grounds of generality. Mismatch entails comparison of a present phenomenon with some previously encountered phenomenon, which previous phenomenon is taken to be the normal case, or "normal circumstances"; but additionally mismatch entails divergence between the present case and any previous "normal circumstances" cases. The idea of the echoic, by contrast, entails comparison and similarity only, without the additional crucial feature of divergence. (Like Tannen's viewpoint, an emphasis on the echoic privileges the similarity between a repetition and its origin at the expense of the important difference between a prior event, scene, or utterance and the presently encountered one.) There is no intention here, then, to deny the important role of echoism in language — even if Sperber and Wilson's more recent label "interpretive resemblance" or my commentary in terms of "recycling of perceived-as-related material" are to be preferred as characterizations. Although projected recycling is neither necessary nor sufficient for irony, it is common therein; it is, however, criterial for another important discourse technique, that of represented discourse.

Whether one is considering represented speech or represented thought, and whether this is direct, indirect, or free indirect, in all cases it is essential that the reader/hearer identify the projected material as projected, as some form of displaced re-presentation — displaced from the putative original context of utterance — of some individual's words. That re-presentation may be seemingly neutral, transcript-like, and so most mention-like; or it may highlight its own interpretive acts of recasting and so appear very use-like. Either way, as far as addressee uptake is concerned, and as readers of the post-1800 novel — particularly — are well aware, such projections introduce a new layer of uncertainty and unreliability (or, if you like, trust) into the interpretation of discourse, an enhanced sense of the risk and contingency of our sense makings and evaluations, in which the comfort of a sharp use-mention dichotomy is most visibly absent.

By a perhaps tortuous route, these phenomena return us to a fundamental feature of language and representation, which I will simply note here. It is that the use of language in projected representation (echoism, recycling, represented discourse, narrative) is the consequence of what all introductory linguistics textbooks note is one of the few fundamental characteristics (or design features) of language: displacement, the possibility of talking here and now about (what was the case) there and then. Sometimes this is described as the possibility of effecting "deictic shift" in language, from a present orientation to some removed one; but this view of things can lead to misunderstandings. Deixis, the rootedness of any language act within the situational present of which it is a part, is fundamental to language behavior — too fundamental, as it were, ever to be fully dispensed with or suspended. *Within* the logically unshiftable deictic present of a discourse, however, there can be gestures or rhetorical contrivances of scene change and speaker change. Representation and representation as displacement are a mystery and a charm that have played through thinking about language at least since the time of Plato and his reflections on mimesis, copies, and truth.

One of the most difficult issues confronting relevance theory is that of constraining interpretation — in the theory's own terms, of delimiting the set of assumptions that the speaker intends to make manifest to the addressee. On these issues, Furlong comments:

The first task of the reader is to arrive at the intended interpretation of the text, that is, to derive an adequate subset of the assumptions made manifest by the writer.... The difference between those assumptions intended by the writer and those made manifest to the reader but not intended by the writer is crucial; the writer succeeds in her communicative act if the reader recovers an adequate subset of her intended assumptions. Her responsibility extends very little further than pointing the reader in the direction of a range of further cognitive effects; she has no control over where the idiosyncrasies of the reader's cognitive organization will lead him. (Furlong 1989: 141)

What are the implications of this account for, for example, the diverse interpretations and reactions that have greeted Rushdie's *Satanic Verses*? By the standards of relevance, are the interpretations of the novel as blasphemously contemptuous of the Islamic religion and its prophet correctly based on authorially intended manifest assumptions, or are these reactions unintended cognitive effects? Rushdie insists that any such assumptions or effects are, at most, of the latter kind, that is, unintended. But, again, by the standards of relevance theory, such unintended cognitive effects evidently may be said to be ones that "the text itself makes manifest" and are arrived at by inference that is in turn constrained only by the goal of maximal relevance. Is it the case, then, that, even if the interpretation of the *Satanic Verses* as blasphemous is beyond Rushdie's area of responsibility and control, it is nevertheless arguably inherent or licensed by the text?

The issues cannot plausibly be decided in vacuo. Rushdie will continue to protest that the text makes manifest no such hostility or disrespect, that inferring such is not licensed or reasonable, and that reading his novel as an evaluation of Islam (i.e., treating *evaluation of Islam* as the most relevant criterion by which to interpret the discourse) is simply wrong. Part of his defense will be that for a speaker or author to cite, mention, or embed utterances interpretable as contemptuous of or disrespectful to a religion (or a race or a sexual orientation) within a novel, particularly when those utterances are explicitly attributed to particular characters, is a very different thing from actually using such utterances. Others will not allow this distinction and will claim that the inference that any mention is a kind of use, however oblique, is reasonable. And so on.

The essential point is that there is no method, no delimited set of criteria established in advance that we might apply, finally to determine whether, as it were, Rushdie has a case to answer. He will always have a case to answer, just as, for those who infer no ironic intention, Swift will always have a case to answer for proposing that the starving Irish be helped from their predicament by having their babies eaten (to deny that Swift ever proposed such a thing simply begs the question). As argued in chapter 4, meanings are determined locally and case by case, and all relevance theory's promises of constraining interpretation and predictive power as much highlight as conceal certain permanent conditions of communication. These are that the only constraint on interpretation is whatever sense is relevant to the situated interactants and that the only prediction is that situated interactants will be constrained in their interpretations by their own specific interests. Since relevance theory articulates the preconditions of communication rather than specifying a method for the interpretation of specific utterances — and since, in addition, it chooses to address only the postulated second phase of interpretation, when linguistic decoding has already taken place (but see Wilson and Sperber [1993] for a recent modification of this picture) — it is hard to see how it could be used to adjudicate between interpretations. There is a sense, then, in which it has little to say about competing interpretations of *Satanic Verses* or Frost's "Stopping by Woods on a Snowy Evening." Relevance theory does not explain how certain interpretations of certain example sentences are achieved; it simply reports on some of the steps in that interpretation process.

Relevance, Pro and Con

Notwithstanding the foregoing objections, it should be acknowledged that those working within relevance theory have advanced and continue to develop invigorating and insightful contributions to a range of linguistic phenomena, from irony and indirect speech acts, to child language acquisition, intonation, and translation. As with work done under the aegis of other "strong theories," it is not always clear just how dependent the account of specific phenomena is on the supposedly framing background of general theoretical claims. Alternatively, as noted in relation to irony, the explanation of the specific phenomena seems often to be detachable from the relevance-theoretical paradigm. A representative example of such illuminating work on specific linguistic material is Carston (1993), on pragmatic constraints on the interpretation of certain kinds of conjunction. In particular, the focus is on the meanings of or triggered by *and*, when it conjoins potentially independent sentences. Compare the following, for example (the author's numbering of examples has been retained):

(8a) John broke his leg. He slipped on a banana skin.

and

(8b) John broke his leg and he slipped on a banana skin.

Why is it that "the 'backwards' causal and temporal relations possible for juxtaposed sentences are excluded when they're conjoined with *and*" (Carston 1993: 35). It should be possible to say more than Bar-Lev and Palacas do (Bar-Lev and Palacas 1980), namely, that, when *and* is used, it encodes the instruction that the second conjunct is not prior (causally or chronologically) to the first. For one thing, that "instruction" seems to apply more generally than to *and*-conjoined sentences alone: it applies also to juxtaposed sentences where, too, it is difficult to get a "reverse temporal sequence" interpretation:

(11d) He rode into the sunset. He jumped onto his horse.

just like

(11e) He rode into the sunset and he jumped onto his horse.

resists an interpretation in which the second clause temporally precedes the first (Carston 1993: 36). Furthermore, there is a distinct property of juxtaposed sentences that is not a potential property of *and*-conjoined sentences:

juxtaposition can imply or trigger a reading of the second conjunct as a reformulation or explanatory paraphrase of the first. Consider:

(14a) Language is rule governed; it follows regular patterns.

By contrast, in

(14b) Language is rule governed and it follows regular patterns.

the content of the second conjunct is not understood as merely a reformulation of the content of the first conjunct. In Hallidayan terms (Halliday 1994: 215ff.), the former of these is a paratactic clause complex with expansion via elaboration, while the latter is one involving expansion via extension; examples like (14a) and (14b) point to the robustness of this part of the Hallidayan classification of paratactic clause complexes.

Carston works toward the modest but plausible conclusion that *and*-conjoined sentences cannot be used to carry "claim-explanation" sequences, whereas juxtaposed sentences (and many other formats besides, such as main + subordinate clauses) can. A chief reason for this disallowed use, she argues, is that *and*-conjoined structures are "a single syntactic unit," by contrast with juxtaposed sentences, which "are two syntactic units." Such a proposal runs athwart both standard generative accounts of English and traditional descriptive grammars, neither of which would be inclined to see conjoined sentences as single units; and, again, there is a similarity between Carston's proposal and Halliday's long-held and much-questioned conviction that structures such as *John ran away, and Fred stayed behind* are single clause complexes. There are more pointers for further research, in this broader area between syntax, semantics, and pragmatics, in this valuable paper. Thus, while the present chapter has developed a number of criticisms of relevance theory at different levels of generality, the final emphasis should be on the fact that much relevance-theoretical analysis, particularly in its practical developments in the recent work of Sperber and Wilson, Carston, Blakemore, Clark, and others, has the potential of being quite congruent with integrational linguistic thinking. Of particular significance may be Sperber and Wilson's increasingly clear emphasis on the role of procedure — and grammaticalized constraints on procedural analysis — rather than conceptual encoding and decoding in utterance interpretation (see, e.g., Wilson and Sperber 1993: 21–23). Discourse particles and even such grammaticalized phenomena as interrogative mood do not so much express a specific conceptual representation as constrain and signpost the direction in which the utterance's relevance is to be found. One viable future direction that integrationalist analyses of situated interaction could take might well involve combining relevance-theoretical insights with those to be derived from a functional linguistic descriptive apparatus such as that of systemic-functional linguistics (see esp. Halliday 1994).

6

Repetition

> Language is perpetual creation. What has been linguistically expressed cannot be repeated. . . . The ever-new impressions give rise to continuous changes of sounds and meanings, that is, to ever-new expressions. To seek the model of language, then, is to seek the immobility of motion. — B. Croce, *Aesthetic*

Differing over Reiteration: Derrida and Searle on Signs

One of the most intriguing challenges to Searle's account of literal meaning and the conventionality of intentional language arose in the pages of the journal *Glyph* in the mid-1970s. There, in "Signature Event Context" (1977b), Derrida published a complex and multifaceted attack on some of the dualistic distinctions that appear to underpin speech-act theory as sketched in Austin (1962): literal meaning versus nonliteral meaning; serious versus nonserious language; use versus mention; and so on. Searle came to the defense of Austin by simple reiteration of the differences and distinctions on which speech-act theory depends, in an essay that is a striking example of attempting to take the higher ground, in an Anglo-American tradition of reasoned inquiry. For example, Austin's distinction between the serious and the nonserious, Searle implies, is perfectly straightforward: Derrida grossly misconstrues Austin and perpetrates disturbing confusions of basic terms and principles. In answer to this came Derrida's "Limited Inc" (1977a), a celebratedly irreverent treatment of the Searlean proprieties, in the course of which the entirety of Searle's paper is quoted within (or, in Derridean terms, "folded into") the new context of Derrida's essay and even Searle's name is reinterpreted and rewritten. Derrida dares to raid, reread, and even deride Searle's seemingly arid literal mindedness.

Despite the bizarre aspects of this dispute, it would be wrong to dismiss the exchange as of no lasting importance; as noted in chapter 3, Searle has found the claims of Derrida sufficiently persistent provocation to warrant resumed critique (in Searle 1994). Ironically, the absence of Searle's earlier rejoinder, "Reiterating the Differences" (Searle 1977), from the 1989 publication in book form of the original articles (*Limited Inc.*) misled some commentators into thinking that Searle had no continuing interest in this engagement. Writing in 1990, Norris observed, "For Searle the debate is now closed" (Norris 1990: 147); with hindsight, that declaration of closure was evidently premature. Nor should any great store be put by the characterizations of a serious Searle thwarted by a ludic Derrida; on the contrary, Derrida argues in all seriousness that the arbitrary delimitations of intentionality and contextualization insisted on by speech-act theorists are a failure to take the creative possibilities of language seriously. In what follows, I shall argue that the encounter is real and instructive and that a coherent picture of intentionality and iterability must critically address the arguments of both theorists. By the end of this chapter, I hope to have made a plausible case for saying that this section's title, "Differing over Reiteration," does not merely describe what Searle and Derrida are doing in their counterposed *Glyph* essays. If we interpret *differing* as a nominalization rather than a verb, the entire phrase ranks correctly two of the tendencies fundamental to signification. For signs to be able to signify, recurrently, they must be relatable to—taken as similar to, an iteration of—previous instances. At the same time, according to whatever criteria one invokes—whether of form, meaning, context, or some other—differences between instances can invariably be found. There is thus a conflict, in both theory and practice, concerning the theoretical weight that one should place on iteration and, conversely, on difference. Standard linguistics resolves the conflict entirely in iteration's favor; an integrational approach argues that there is much to be gained by resetting these two pressures into a state of balance and hence of productive tension. To do so, at least for the remainder of this chapter, it is necessary to emphasize the scope and range of differing, over the extent of reiteration.

Derrida begins by reviewing some of the problematic terms in which, it seems, the issues must necessarily be discussed: terms such as *communication*, *meaning*, *literal meaning*, and *context*. One of his earliest remarks is also one of the most significant for all that follows. He notes that, even to "articulate and propose" the question whether the word *communication* corresponds to a coherent concept, he has been "constrained to predetermine communication as a vehicle, a means of transport . . . of a meaning" (1977b: 172). Such double binds, constrained predeterminations of the terms and notions one wishes to reassess, are endemic in discourse on language — and not just discourse of the reflexive, self-conscious deconstructive kind, but all discourse, even of the Searlean kind. And it is perhaps Searle's failure to acknowledge such constrained predeterminations in his own discourse, more than anything else, that enables Derrida to appear the victor of their encounter.

Derrida proceeds to emphasize the openness of context: "Context is never absolutely determinable, or rather, . . . its determination can never be entirely certain or saturated" (1977b: 174). Consequently, meanings themselves can never be entirely determinate. This characteristic of speech, Derrida adds, only appears to be removed when we turn to writing, which we too readily assume to be straightforwardly representational, pictorial in fashion, and telecommunicational (in that it seems to function despite the absence of sender and/or receiver). More accurately, as Condillac and Warburton perceived in the eighteenth century, writing is a modification or supplementing of presence, Derrida claims, although we ordinarily think of it as a necessarily iterable use of a public code, which must continue to "act" even in the absence of a writer or of his or her intentions. Derrida asserts, "The sign possesses the characteristic of being readable even if I do not know what its alleged author-scriptor consciously intended to say at the moment he wrote it, i.e. abandoned it to its essential drift" (1977b: 182). Writing can always be "re-grafted" into new contexts, and "no context can entirely enclose it." Writing always has this power to break free, this *force de rupture* (p. 182). But then so also, mutatis mutandis, has spoken language or any other coded or semioticized experience: "Every sign, linguistic or non-linguistic, spoken or written . . . can be *cited*, put between quotation marks; in so doing it can break with every given context, engendering an infinity of new contexts in a manner which is absolutely illimitable. This does not imply that the mark is valid outside of a context, but on the contrary that there are only contexts without any center of absolute anchorage" (pp. 185–86).

But, while Derrida's emphasis on the infinity of contexts is unimpeachable, his treatment of the sign as straightforwardly iterable is open to challenge. He assumes that, while contexts are freely and endlessly variable (noniterable), signs or marks are not. Yet the same possibilities of variation and difference accorded to context must be extended also to the linguistic mark or sign, no matter the degree to which, in modern habitualized and normative practice, that variation in the phonic or graphic (or kinesic etc.)

nature of signs is or is not acknowledged by language users. Subscribing to the permanent and constant possibility of citation and iteration, the possibility of relocating a sign or discourse in contexts quite removed from the context in which that sign was originally intended to signify, Derrida undermines confidence in any appeal to or search for a speaker or writer's original intentions. But it is important to note that his quarrel here is chiefly with absolutist appeals to originary or foundational or true intention, not with intention per se. Furthermore — although this is not fully developed in his essay — he does not seem averse to some sort of classification or typology of "forms of iteration": "One ought to construct a differential typology of forms of iteration, assuming that such a project is tenable and can result in an exhaustive program, a question I hold in abeyance here. In such a typology, the category of intention will not disappear; it will have its place, but from that place it will no longer be able to govern the entire scene and system of utterance" (1977b: 192). The notion of a typology of forms of iteration may be compared with the later Wittgenstein's remarks on language games, systemic linguistics' and others' attention to genre structure, Levinson's outline of "activity types" (Levinson 1979), and indeed some proposals in the speech-act theory tradition with which Derrida is evidently generally at odds. In fact, Derrida's division of the components of linguistic communication into (1) iterable form and (2) unpredictably variable context asserts an analytic division at much the same point proposed by Austin, in the latter's distinction between locution and illocution.

It has become commonplace, since Austin, to recognize that speech is a kind of action, a performing of interactional tasks with words. If this is so, then, although the meaning of the locution used in any such speech act is important, more important are the conventions observed and other appropriate contextual factors, so that the locution can count as an illocutionary act of promising, or warning, or stating, or whatever. Austin's and Searle's work (the latter's certainly more systematic than Austin would have preferred) is an extended inquiry into just what the basic and universal speech acts might be and into the conventional contextual conditions under which a particular locution will (predictively) be taken, by speakers and hearers of a language intersubjectively attuned to such conventions, as constitutive of a particular type of speech act. As such, speech-act theory may be rescued from the Derridean attack based on variability of context if an acknowledgment of the local determinability of context, the provisionality of speakers' and hearers' assessments of what conditions are in force on any particular occasion of interaction, is built into the model. Just such an acknowledgment and adjustment is easily stated and seems necessary. But the more fundamental problem for speech-act theory emerges if intersubjective attunement to the conditions and conventions for performing speech acts is questioned, rather than being simply assumed (as it seems to be by Searle), and if fixed-code reliability of the meaning of locutions (claimed to be guaranteed by the linguistic system), or what Derrida refers to as "iterability," is also questioned.

The refusal to countenance any departure from fixed-code iterability and concomitant (potential) intersubjectivity clearly has much to do with a powerful tradition hostile to notions of private languages and hostile too to the problems of uninspectability and seemingly "needless" complexity that such a departure seems to promote. All our common sense suggests that we understand one another in most daily interactions, that we can correct misunderstandings, that we can identify the misuse of words in the language, and that we can ordinarily recognize when someone has promised something, warned of something, and so on. It seems only common sense to say that there must be a shared code and a shared set of conventions or rules that we unconsciously follow in order for all this to be possible. An alternative common sense, however, takes note of the fact that no two children learning "the same language" either begin with identical mental powers or learn from (encounter) identical sets of linguistic experience and that, as a result, no two fluent speakers of the "same" language have identical linguistic resources, memories, faculties, orientations, lexicogrammars, or conventions. Despite the difficulties of inspectability involved, empirical evidence suggests that different language users do indeed regularly "take" utterances in unpredictably different ways.

Language Used Nonseriously

One of the most debated moves in Austin's discussion (one endorsed by Searle but challenged by Derrida) is that where he sets aside, as unhelpfully complex cases, the language of plays and poems. Despite deconstructionists' critique of this as an illicit and revealing effort at exclusion, nothing fundamentally disabling hinges — in Austin's discussion — on the treatment of jokes, poems, and theatrical discourse as "nonserious" uses of language. I shall propose, without further argument, that the claims that poems and soliloquies etc. are cases of language used "nonseriously" in ways parasitic on its normal use and that fictional language is language used in special circumstances are simply mistakes — ones out of which Derrida and others have made far too much. For all we know, they are misrepresentations that Austin might have quite readily withdrawn — and even shown to be mistaken, in view of the theoretical position he has reached by the close of *How to Do Things with Words* (1962). In short, it is not at all clear that Austin was deeply committed to seeing certain kinds of language as serious and other kinds as nonserious.

No such uncertainty, however, applies to Searle's insistence on reiterating the correctness of Austin's earlier casual exclusions. In fact, Searle's comments are not simply reiterations: much more is at stake in Searle's insistence on the serious/nonserious division. While Austin's focus in the passage that Derrida challenges is on the *circumstances* attending speech-act performance (where it seems reasonable to argue that the contextual circumstances ordinarily attending the understanding of speech in plays are more complex than those attending the understanding of speech in direct interaction), Searle's focus is on the nature of *utterances* used in speech-act performance and reflects assumptions of simplicity versus complexity pertaining to utterance interpretation. Whether it can be shown to be or not, nonfictional discourse has to be "logically prior" (Searle 1977: 205) for Searle's larger project, in which literal meaning and the preparatory and other conditions govern the production of particular "straightforward" illocutions such as promising and govern also, in complex and derived ways, production of unstraightforward and "logically consequent" uses of language, such as indirect speech acts, irony, metaphor, and the pretend speech acts — as Searle describes them — of fictional discourse.

By way of entry into the debate over the nonserious and secondary nature of literary uses of language, Culler's rehearsal of the Derridean objection to Searle on the subject of "promises in plays" is perhaps worth quoting in full — not least since it may prompt us to revise the Derridean conclusion. Adopting a Derridean perspective, Culler writes:

In what sense is the pretended dependent upon the nonpretended? Searle gives an example: "there could not, for example, be promises made by actors in a play if there were not the possibility of promises made in real life." We are certainly accustomed to thinking in this way: a promise I make is real; a promise in a play is a fictional imitation of a real promise, an empty iteration of a formula used to make real promises. But in fact one can argue that the relation of dependency works the other way as well. If it were not possible for a character in a play to make a promise, there could be no promises in real life, for what makes it possible to promise, as Austin tells us, is the existence of a conventional procedure, of formulas one can repeat. For me to be able to make a promise in "real life," there must be iterable procedures or formulas, such as are used on the stage. "Serious" behavior is a special case of role-playing. (Culler 1983: 119)

The crucial first step in this argument is Searle's, namely, that promises in plays depend, for their existence, on the possibility of promises in real life. Deconstructionists simply reverse that dependency relation: real life promises depend on theatrical ones; if the latter did not exist, neither could the former. But why should we assume any dependency relation at all? Can we even assume that plays will contain promises, or any of the other speech acts that we seem to encounter in everyday life? Certainly there are many parts of the world in which the language and logic of literature, the "action" performed by the literary work, seems radically different from the language and logic of the community's nonliterary practices. And it would be a strange claim to make, analogous to Searle's about promises, that goddesses, green knights, and statues coming to life in plays depend, for their existence, on the possibility of such phenomena in real life, or vice versa, as in the deconstructionist reordering.

In any event, a dependency relation in either direction seems to be something that can only be asserted, not proved. And foundational to asserting either pattern of dependency is an even more fundamental assumption, namely, that there is an evident distinction between theatrical and nontheatrical discourse, reflected in expressions like *real life* and *role-playing*. If we accept such a distinction, the sorts of evidence to which we will point in support of the view will be evidence of the quite different circumstances surrounding (1) plays and (2) everyday interactions. The institutionalized distinction between plays and nontheatrical interaction rests on the complex and contrasting contexts of circumstances surrounding these different activities. However, if we reconnect these supposed "polar" discoursal opposites, we find countless intermediate kinds of discourse (therapeutic acting out, play reading in a literature class, oral interpretation of literature, street theater arguing for political causes, drama-documentaries, consumer canvassing, sales pitches, flirting, performed stories in conversations, scripted and unscripted interviews, adult-child interaction), which raise the question whether there is an essential or intrinsic difference in kind between plays and what might now be called other everyday interactions. The differences are of degree and of uptake, of locally determined intent and relevance. What applies to categorizations of language use applies also to speech-act categories: there is only local determinacy and limited generalizability of what counts as a promise, a threat, an undertaking, a denial, an acceptance, a smile, or a twitch of annoyance.

The deconstructionist confidence in iterability is therefore misplaced, and the Derridean insistence that a performative utterance could not succeed unless it were conforming to an established iterable model is mistaken. Culler asserts: "For the 'standard case' of promising to occur, it must be recognizable as the repetition of a conventional procedure, and the actor's performance on the stage is an excellent model of such repetition" (Culler 1983: 119). On close examination, however, the expression *the standard case* is a near tautology, and perhaps the scare quotes are intended as acknowledgment of this. "Standard cases" never, in fact, occur: they are normative extrapolations from actually occurring cases, deductive extrapolations that involve association and provisional matching rather than recognition in the sense that Culler implies. This follows from the fact that standards and norms are always constructed and adopted rather than preexistent. The emphasis in the theoretical discussion of standard cases needs to shift so as to focus directly on the role of perceived approximation rather than recognized repetition, on nonoriginary modelings rather than originary "models," in the characterizing of particular instances as standard or typical.

Culler's discussion of the Derrida/Searle exchange includes a footnote on the use/mention contrast full of interest in its own right. Searle had rightly taken Derrida to task for suggesting that Austin did not accept that all use of language involved iterability and went on to point out — correctly — that even the nonserious uses of language were uses, not merely mentions. Culler suggests that use/mention is another of the controlling hierarchies that attempt to characterize distinctive aspects of language's iterability as parasitic or derivative and that "a deconstructive reading would demonstrate that the hierarchy should be reversed and that use is but a special case of mentioning." But such a demonstration is not easily come by. By way of example of the alleged ambiguities of use versus mention, Culler gives the following case: "If I write of a scholar, 'Some of my colleagues think his work "boring and incompetent" or "pointless",' what have I done? Have I used the expressions 'boring and incompetent' and 'pointless' as well as mentioned them? (Culler 1983: 119).

Even to ask the question in this way — note the "as well as" — implies a lack of parity between using and mentioning: all expressed words are always mentioned, some are, "as well," used. The simplest answer to Culler's question is that, by conforming to the conventions surrounding the use of quotation marks, he has on a conventional reading indicated that the evaluative phrases so enclosed are simply mentioned by him, that their use is to be attributed to some quoted other. In the scenario that Culler sketches, one would need to know more of the circumstances surrounding the written report within which the damning verdicts of "boring and incompetent" and "pointless" are ostensibly mentioned but not used. Thus, if the report were part of an internal college review of a candidate for tenure in an American university, a report to a dean or college council, one would not have high hopes for the unfortunate subject's chances of success. No amount of "rescue work" elsewhere in the report is likely to save a candidate indirectly criticized so frankly, and you simply have to be cognizant of the norms of American academic culture (of rapturous enthusiasm and of critical caveats added in only the most oblique and coded ways) to be able to make the judgment that "boring and incompetent" would be read by an American dean as partly used and not merely mentioned. In other related cultures and situations (e.g., a report to the dean on a candidate for promotion to senior lecturer in a British university), such detractions might be less damning and taken simply as mentions, not significantly laced with use.

In short, merely to mention such words as *incompetent* in the American academic tenure-review context might suggest to those acting on the report that some degree of use valency had been intended. The qualification in the previous sentence is crucial: any particular tenure-review situation can depart from the norm of "mentioning with some intent to use" posited of *incompetent* above. Putting things within quotation marks (scare or otherwise) or asserting that you are only mentioning some utterance cannot establish, in and beyond the sphere of review controlled by the addressee, that said utterance was mere mention, not use. Similarly, there is no context-free or context-neutral way of determining that the speaker who says "I was being ironic" is not, via the latter utterance, being ironic — ironic, for example, about the way, with some interlocutors, one always has to pretend to retract the veiled criticism that an earlier ironic utterance carried.

Undoubtedly, there are real ambiguities surrounding the use/mention distinction, even if the principle that mention is displaced use, an understood projection from and attribution to the "full" use of the utterance in some other context of utterance, is relatively simple. The example that Culler gives would be less easy to adjudicate if spoken or presented without the quotation marks, and a host of uncertainties over whether particular utterances are direct uses or indirect mentions, or some troubling mixture, lie at the heart of free indirect discourse. But none of these are arguments for a wholesale dispensing with the use/mention distinction and certainly not for the privileging of mention over use. At best, as with the distinction between theatrical and everyday discourse, we may be drawn to acknowledge the provisionality and convention boundedness of having the distinction between use and mention at all. The distinction arises as an operational convenience, when a speaker wishes to produce an utterance without triggering the attribution of direct intentionality to himself or herself.

Dishonorable Mentions

All of the above debate around uses or mentions either of verdicts on a colleague's work as "pointless" and "incompetent" or of "bad language" has assumed that just those words (or spoken utterances of which these are the standard transcription) were actually uttered by the speakers to whom they are attributed. But what if that is not the case? There is a range of situations in which utterances never actually produced by their asserted source are nevertheless cast as though they were. A cover term for the utterances found in just one of these situations is *pseudoquotation*. Pseudoquotations are often prefaced by items — such as, in American English, *hey, I'm all* and *I'm like* — that help signal that what follows is an encapsulation of a viewpoint rather than a transcription of actual words (see, e.g., Dubois 1989). By contrast with a more verbatim reporting, and somewhat paradoxically, such pseudoquotations often manage both to summarize and to dramatize a speaker's viewpoint at the same time:

> Throughout his state of the State speech, the governor was like "Hey, we can beat this recession."
> He spent the whole evening talking on and on like that, and I'm all "What's this got to do with me?"
> (invented American English examples)

The grammar and usage handbook prescription is that what goes within quotation marks, in standard transcription, is just what a speaker has said. But, with the more critical scrutiny occasionally applied today and continued concern for genuine information access, it has become clear that, for example, journalists in both the tabloid and even the quality press will on occasion make considerable editorial changes to the recorded speech of a politician while retaining the quotation marks suggesting direct report. Such editorial change may go well beyond removal of hesitations, grammatical discontinuities, and repetitions, to include suppletion of pithy near synonyms, syntactic rearrangements, and other substantial changes. This is most prominent in the use of familiar, informal, and sensationalizing language in headlines ostensibly containing the direct speech of some public figure:

"Clean up your act!" Clinton warns Suharto.
"In your dreams!" sneers Dole.

where the actual remarks of President Clinton and Senator Dole, respectively, may well have been far more circumspect and formal. The tendency to rewrite or even simply invent direct speech — and still present it as direct speech, as mention, not use — seems to be quite widespread in journalism and often difficult to detect. One consequence of this is that a vast media industry now revolves around the spin control or denial of what political leaders such as President Clinton actually said, or actually meant, or actually meant to say. In a democratic Western society with a free (but commercial) press, denials and retractions are the preferred corrective mechanism of the media's overly vivid or wayward mentions; in a less democratic society with a less free press, journalists' temerity to mediate and rephrase the utterances of the powerful tends to be more forcibly suppressed. Many factors are involved here, including the narrowing — or collapse — of the power and authority differential between the subjects of news stories (e.g., politicians) and journalists. In the past, an establishment politician, allied with establishment proprietors and editors, could rely on journalists to convey deferentially what often amounted to full and verbatim mention (with the proviso that even Hansard-like verbatim record is neither ideally full nor unchallengeably pure mention [see, e.g., Short 1988; Slembrouck 1992]).

A comical instance of the interplay of concerns for accurate representation and "spin control" arose a few years ago in the United States, when lengthy excerpts from a book purporting to be the autobiography of basketball star Charles Barkley were published in the *Philadelphia Inquirer*. When he came to read the extracts in the newspaper, Barkley was so outraged at his own remarks that he tried to stop publication of the book, on the grounds that his autobiography misquoted him. Rather more serious have been several lawsuits in which plaintiffs have claimed that particular journalists willfully and damagingly invented phrases or "merged" words culled from very different contexts and presented those utterances within quotation marks as the direct speech of the individuals being profiled.

Another version of the use-mention wrangle surfaced in recent years in relation to doubts about the satisfactoriness of British police interview procedures. During enquiries into the reliability of the procedures followed in the course of mounting a case against individuals who became known as the Birmingham Six (tried and found guilty of participating in an IRA pub bombing in 1974 in which twenty-one people were killed), expert forensic analysis determined that portions of interview transcripts used in evidence were written at some other time than the bulk of the transcript. This contravenes the required procedure, which is that a statement be written down at the same time as it is given orally and that it should approximate dictation. That standard of immediately reported quotation seemingly not having been met, the reliability and authenticity of the evidence brought forward by the police was put in question, and all the original convictions were eventually quashed as unsafe. Police interview procedure is one of the institutional areas where maintenance of the use-mention distinction seems especially needed: was a particular statement, later brought forward in evidence, genuinely made by the individual to whom it is attributed (i.e., genuine use), or has it been contaminated in the process of recording, so that it has only the lesser status of a mention? But, even in this critical area of crime-interview procedure, it is noticeable that the pressure for accuracy of record has not led to a general practice of having statements recorded by the interviewees themselves. Clearly, the relations between an interview and a statement are complex. Here, it should be noted that in Britain, under the new Police and Criminal Evidence Act of 1984, all interviews of suspects must take place in a designated interview room, with audio and video recordings.

If we return to the larger debate on intentionality and iterability, the contrasting positions may be summarized in part as follows. Derrida insists on iterability and argues that the very fact of iterability puts a speaker's intentionality in question (iterability is the means that makes signification without originating intention possible). Austin and Searle equally insist on iterability, codified reproducibility, but, given other premises that they subscribe to (that speech is a means of performing action, in accordance with conventionally constituted conditions), they assert also that the speaker's intention and the hearer's recognition of the speaker's intention are foundational characteristics of speech acts. Distinct from those positions, integrational linguistics claims that both iterability and recognition of speaker's intentionality are uncertain: iterability can be asserted only by means of an arbitrary and provisional disregard of differences, and a hearer's estimation of a speaker's intentions (a required estimation) remains always an estimation and only the hearer's. In short, Searle espouses both telementation and a fixed-code model of language and speech-act constitution; Derrida deconstructs telementation (his counterpart term is *telecommunication*) but still subscribes to a fixed-code theory; integrationists wish to proceed without presupposing the existence of either.

Repetition as Abstraction

It is no purpose of this chapter to deny that repetition does in some sense exist and that it is an important factor in the language user's making sense of his or her own linguistic activities. The issue concerns the ontological level at which repetition exists, and the thesis is that, at the first-order level of ongoing situated activity, the embeddedness of language within developing circumstances subject to time means that language itself never repeats. That is, saying or hearing now what was said or heard previously is not a resaying or rehearing, although we speak in terms of "saying again" and "hearing again." In particular, what we talk of as repetition of a given utterance is not achieved by second or subsequent recourse to a single freestanding system of utterances (the language as autonomous system) that preexists any particular occasions of use (and, by extension, all occasions of use), in the way that a print compositor's desk of compartmentalized types stands waiting in advance of any particular typesetting task, the same types available for use over and over again. We know how the printer's bench and types got there; but it is impossible to devise a coherent account (a theory) of how, for example, in the mind of a child a parallel predetermined system — and indeed one effectively identical with those of all other speakers within the same linguistic community — could be implanted at a stroke and definitively, genetically or otherwise.

Integrational linguistics is not skeptical of repetition; it is, however, concerned to characterize it in theoretically coherent ways. Harris has been misrepresented on this point in a chapter by Pateman in a widely used guide to contemporary linguistics (Pateman 1987b; see also Pateman 1987a). Pateman is responding to a passage in Harris (1981a: 155) in which he argues that contextualization by succession in time means that every linguistic act is experienced, by the individual, as new and unique. Harris warns that this idea sometimes gets misleadingly glossed as "nothing that is said can be repeated." Ignoring the warning, Pateman is indeed misled into mounting a refutation of the "impossibility of repetition" view that he attributes to Harris.

In fact, Harris uses the term *repetition* in a way that presupposes that it does exist, although its true function in linguistic theory is misunderstood: "Repetition, to put the point somewhat differently, is only partial replication, and even that partial replication is context-bound by succession in time. In what respects one utterance is a replication of another cannot be assessed independently of their sequentiality" (Harris 1981a: 155). Pateman neglects this emphasis on sequentiality dependence. He takes up Harris's example of use of [zaaaa], with falling tone, uttered by a bowler at an appropriate point in a game of cricket, and intended to contribute to an appeal for lbw against the batsman. Somehow, the umpire interprets this as a version of what the rules of cricket specify as the formulation "How's that?" (see also the discussion of this example in chapter 4). It is not the umpire who is in trouble here but the linguistic theorist: how, relative to one's theory of language, is the [zaaaa] speech act best explained? In Harris's view (1981a: 176–77), the orthodox theorist is led, via choices between more or less desirable judgments, to an uncomfortable conclusion. Thus, the linguist is likely to concede that [zaaaa] is a kind of communicative English, not merely noise or foreign; thereafter, the linguist is likely to prefer an explanation that "derives" [zaaaa] from [hawzðæt] to one that simply postulates that the noise is an entirely separate and unrelated English expression. "Depth" and the hidden workings of derivational rules thus come once more to the segregationalist linguist's rescue. Unfortunately, this is not much of a rescue since [zaaaa] is only one of innumerable differing expressions that various cricketers might perpetrate, by way of lbw appeals. And, no matter how ingenious the phonologist may become, in formulating descriptively adequate accounts of their derivation from [hawzðæt], all are strictly beside the point as far as those within the cricketing activity (players, umpires, spectators) are concerned. Were contemporary anthropologists to proceed in the way the orthodox linguist is induced to here, they would secure little respect.

Pateman's response to Harris's strictures on repetition is as follows:

Harris does not put it this way, but one could say that the relation between *How's that?* and utterances of it should not be construed in terms of class and members or types and tokens; rather, the species of *How's that?* utterances should itself be treated as an individual and not as a class, and explained by a historical narrative.... (1) We may not be able to give a plausible derivation of all the utterances which have counted or would count as utterances of *How's that?* and we may be in the dark about how speakers and hearers produce and understand such utterances (2); but that they make use of some iterable form not defined by temporal co-ordinates seems presupposed by the very critique of that idea (3). (Pateman 1987b: 251; sentence numbers added)

One could begin the counterargument demonstrated that situated repetition is invariably only partial replication by considering Pateman's quotation of Harris's (1981a) argument in Pateman (1987a, 1987b). I could witness (since all these matters come down to the judgments of individuals) to how Pateman (1987a) includes only partial replication of Harris's argument (as I experienced the latter in the course of reading his book-length argument about language myths and the role of fixed-code theorizing in a segregationalist linguistics). I could add that the very similar material that Pateman (1987a) uses, where it is introductory to his own book-length thesis and more particularly looks forward to a chapter on Wittgensteinian linguistic theory, is only a partial replication of that "same" material in the very different context of Pateman (1987b), a multiauthored conspectus of major trends in current linguistics, the kind of volume one might consult in the expectation of being afforded an impartial introduction to the field.

Alternatively, a consideration of the quotation from Pateman above may be made sentence by sentence. The crucial factor left unspecified in Pateman's first sentence, where it is speculated that Harris would not countenance construal of seeming repetitions as variant tokens related to a single type, is just who is doing the construing and why, for there is a world of difference between the theorist of language treating situated utterances as tokens algorithmically related to an underlying type (an allegedly determinable, community-wide, rule-governed relation) and the situated language user — an umpire, for example — creatively construing a range of sounds (from the literalist's [hawzðæt], to [zaaaa], to untranscribable growling and roaring, to the visiting French team's *Quoi?*) as tokens of a single type or repetitions of the prototypical form for an appeal. In this case, as in every case, we have no such prototype; we only think we have.

Of these latter observations Pateman is well aware — sentence 2 makes some of these points succinctly. But they seem not to delay him from his conclusion, concerning which the chief integrational objection is to its neglect of the distinctions between theorizing about the nature of language as a first-order faculty, on one hand, and metalinguistic, after-the-fact interpretive glosses of what people think is involved (the "we" of Pateman's sentence 2 and the "they" of sentence 3), on the other hand. But notice also how Pateman's implicit reformulation here of Harris's point as

> Noniterable form is defined by temporal co-ordinates

only partially replicates Harris's emphasis. For one thing, the individual is removed from this formulation, whereas Harris's essential point is that temporal succession acts as much on the individual as on that individual's language. It is the individual's continually changing circumstances that guarantee incompleteness of replication.

All of the above is by way of suggesting that, contra Pateman, "forms like those 'abstracted' by modern linguistics (Saussurean, Bloomfieldian, Chomskyan)" are indeed "the misleading and obscuring abstractions they appear to be to the empiricist and sceptic" (Pateman 1987b: 250–51), even though, as argued in chapter 4 and elsewhere, there must be a place in our theories for psychologically real abstractions. The objection is not to abstraction per se, or to speculations about users' psychological models and assumptions, but to the sweeping abstraction that posits a fixed linguistic mechanism in the brain, identical for all speakers in a community, which acontextually generates and interprets all utterances, repetitive or otherwise.

Prepatterning and Automaticity as Interactive Resources

In Tannen (1987b), repetition is singled out as a pervasive type of spontaneous prepatterning in conversation. There seems to be a universal human drive to imitate and repeat, Tannen argues, which is of use in learning. Although a view of language as prepatterned, imitative, and repetitious might be resisted because it seems to see humans as less autonomous, Tannen asserts that, "by means of prepatterning and automaticity, speakers are highly interactive individuals who can use repetition as the basis for creativity and sense of self" (p. 217). Imitation and repetition enable and enhance interpersonal rapport, creativity, and sense of self: "Discourse is interactionally developed. . . . Individuals say particular things in particular ways because they have heard others say similar things in the same or similar ways" (p. 216).

Some such thesis might be said to be the starting point for Hopper's recent contrasting (Hopper 1987a) of two approaches to grammar: one where grammar is a set of a priori rules, logically prior to the discourse it structures, the other where grammar is seen as always emerging. The "emergence of grammar attitude" sees grammar as "the name for a vaguely defined set of sedimented (i.e. grammaticized) recurrent partials whose status is constantly being renegotiated in speech and which cannot be distinguished *in principle* from strategies for building discourses" (p. 118).

Hopper's two papers on the topic of emergent grammar (Hopper 1987a, 1987b) are, it is clear, more a programmatic manifesto than an empirical demonstration (although specific examples of the phenomenon are offered). Even in this preliminary form, however, the proposal is attractively congruent with several currents of thought about language practice in contemporary theory. A theory of emergent grammar is a theory about language change and grammar change. It hypothesizes that what became institutionalized as "the grammar" are the relatively stable discourse formulas — always in the process of emergence and disappearance, in fact — out of the sheer recurrence of which, in both powerful discourses and the discourse of the powerful, grammarians have derived a picture of the standard or most acceptable syntactic patterns of a language. Implicit in Hopper's proposal is an attention to two aspects of usage, and their effect on that subsequent institutionalized usage that we call grammar, that standard dictionaries only falteringly address: frequency of a particular usage and the prestige associated with its use or users. Inter alia, the emergent grammar hypothesis is an invitation to pursue historical linguistics focused on chunks and formulas and so on rather than, as usually, at the level of word. (There are links, too, with the diachronic study of collocation sketched in Firth's essay "Modes of Meaning" [Firth 1957].) It furthers speculation as to the effect of individual authors and language users, on the rate and direction of whatever grammatical patterns are emerging or disappearing. The lexical effect of Shakespeare's use of new or newer words in the language is not hard to see: but what of the effect of some of his stylistic tendencies at the level of phrase or clause or clause complex? Similarly, what may be the effect on our grammar of such contemporary influences as the distinctive language of machine-user interfacing? Aspects of what Hopper proposes sound remarkably akin to what some stylisticians already do: at one point he states, "The major descriptive project of Emergent Grammar is to identify recurrent strategies for building discourses" (1987b: 148). At the level of individual texts or individual authors, this has long been a goal of stylistic analyses.

If frequency of use of some recurring discoursal chunk is an important element in the making of grammar for Hopper, so is it also for Tannen, whose book *Talking Voices* (1988) considers repetition, dialogue, and imagery in speeches and conversations. For Tannen, repetition is the central linguistic meaning-making strategy, a resource by which conversationalists together create a discourse, a relationship, and a world. Tannen's book is rich in examples, transcribed data, and alertness to the implications of such phenomena as fused idioms, malapropisms, and imitations. But the sweep of references, supporting examples, and citations and the concomitantly broad conceptualization also create some difficulties. It is open to question whether the range of topics discussed — including poetic parallelisms as studied by Jakobson (1960) and Kiparsky (1973), rhythm, verbal patternings, the echoic mimicry found in both the speech of young children (see the essays in Ervin-Tripp and Mitchell-Kernan [1977]) and the "shadowing" production of aphastic patients — can all appropriately be subsumed under the term *repetition*.

Problematic also is the characterization of repetition as forms of "prepatterning and automaticity" in speech, to be set over against the spontaneity and creativity ostensibly sponsored in the generativist linguistic paradigm. Much repetition can as easily be seen as creative relatedness (not automatic identity) between a later utterance and some earlier one. All language interpretation proceeds on the assumption that what is heard or read now is partially echoic, in form and function, of what has been encountered before (and remembered). There is a grounding principle here (which is also an ecological and conservationist one) of "relative recurrence" or "perceptibly related recyclability." The local and immediate contrivance and attribution of repetition/recycling are simply the assertion of a special and local relatedness.

But the faculty of seeing similarity is no minor skill. It prompts questions, which lack easy answers, about the conditions needed to enable the perception and discussion of repetition to arise. By what means do human beings come to see that degree of similarity between utterance b in context y and utterance a in context x such that b is deemed a repetition of a? It would seem that, along with many others, Tannen sees this faculty of "treating as similar, as repetition" as the starting point for language and linguistic communication; that is, Tannen treats it as a prelinguistic enabling faculty, the means by which all the samenesses and differences that make up an entire language can hold their distinct and interrelated places. But it may be more fitting to see this faculty of "treating as similar" not as a nonlinguistic precondition but as an end-point and crowning achievement of linguistic communication. For it is an enormous cognitive breakthrough, when a community comes to treat distinct moments of (linguistically characterized) behavior as recyclings in large measure rather than as fundamentally unrelated. Here, the faculties of short-term memory and mimicry — for example, when a child immediately imitates a mother's noises, or vice versa — must be crucial prompts to a coming into awareness that "repetitions," or reuse of near-identical linguistic materials, are possible. Tannen's book is largely about the kinds of repetition, imagery, and speech reporting that we employ and the functions that these perform. But, as far as issues of language emergence are concerned, a prior question is, How do we learn to repeat? That question in turn prompts an even more foundational one: How do we realize that repetition is possible (where by *repetition* is meant "treatment of material$_j$ as a recycling of material$_i$")? The child comes to grasp that "treating material as recycled" is indeed a possibility and resource in interaction, and this constitutes a quantum leap in understanding; many other features of language activity are made possible — and relatively easy — after that discovery.

Like Bolinger (1976), Tannen (1988) urges that linguistics undertake a positive revaluation of idiomaticity and prepatterning in language (the discipline allegedly neglects such prepackaged material in favor of language that invites systematic analysis). She notes: "Although proverbs may not be routinely uttered in English conversation, idioms and other prepatterned expressions are pervasive in American speech, although their form in utterance is often only highly, rather than utterly, fixed" (p. 221). The importance of fixed phrases shows up even in our everyday real-time production of altered or fused formulas. Her examples of these include *the best of both possible worlds* and *then you can pipe in with your ideas*. She also cites the marvelous case of a speaker putting her hand on her chest and saying, "I felt so chestfallen," although this is nearer malapropism than fusing. Other examples of fusing might include one participant at a conference advising a colleague, who intends to forgo the evening's social activities so as to prepare his plenary paper for the next day, "not to burn the midnight oil at both ends." A particularly succinct example of a seemingly unintended fusion is the mocking aside "perish forbid!" which appears in an article by R. Lakoff: "The notion of testing examples on a large group of informants (or even — perish forbid! — getting examples from real, spontaneous data) was unheard-of" (Lakoff 1989: 960). In all such cases, according to Tannen, "meaning is gleaned by association with the familiar sayings, not by structurally decomposing them [sc. the nonce phrases]" (Tannen 1988: 223).

This formulation alludes to an implied contrast between the interpretation of idiomatic and skewed-idiomatic utterances on the one hand and nonidiomatic utterances on the other. Echoing the views of contemporary psycholinguists, Tannen agrees that idioms and skewed idioms are interpreted holistically rather than via structural decomposition. But the implication of this is that the rest of the time, with nonidiomatic utterance, that other means, structural decomposition, may be at work. Thus, two methods of interpretation of utterances are specified, "association with the familiar saying" and "structural decomposition," although it is not yet clear how or when an addressee knows when to apply one method as against the other or what is specifically entailed in either method. Examining these two methods more closely, and adducing arguments concerning the ways individuals might logically make sense of nonidiomatic utterances that are grammatically incomplete or malformed, I shall argue that "association with the familiar use" (rather than merely "the familiar saying"), drawing as relevant on a procedure that may be called *compositionality*, is involved in all utterance interpretation. Along those lines, idiomaticity can be seen in a new light, as routine and pervasive in language rather than incidental and occasional.

Compositionality and the Processing of Imperfect Performance

The argument can be developed in relation to a fused formula such as that cited by Tannen:

the best of both possible worlds.

The question raised by such utterances (as also by malapropisms and metaphors), raised more acutely than by nonconflated usage, concerns just how, when heard in some proper context, they are understood. As suggested throughout this book, situationally embedded utterances such as the one that is abstracted, cast into writing, and recontextualized above are interpreted in situ. But supplementing the guiding hand — for interpretation — of the assumed direction of the present talk will be each participant's ordered and schematized memories of past situated uses (form-context pairings) of what we metalinguistically call "the words and phrases constituting the expression *the best of both possible worlds.*" Beyond this, one cannot speak with any certainty for anyone else. But, for myself, given a suitable context, other related form-context pairings might come to mind: the cliché *the best of both worlds*, the Voltairean satirical pronouncement that *everything is for the best in the best of all possible worlds* (itself an ironic, interpretively resemblant echo of Leibniz), and perhaps the formal semanticist interest in *possible worlds*. None of these can be deemed necessary for interpretation of the given utterance, but then on the other hand none can be deemed irrelevant: it all depends on what the speaker expected the listener to do or know — on the basis of hearing the utterance in the given situation — and on what the listener wanted or expected to get from the interaction. In the foregoing, three form-context pairings have been picked out, as it were, by the linguistic forms used (rather than the contexts), and I have specified the contexts for each in only the most vague way (utilitarianism, formal semantics). But the logic of integrationism warns that there is no warrant for assuming that interpretation is "form driven" in the way this implies, even if numerous scriptist practices, such as focus on written representations of putative utterances, fosters that impression; rather, one situation evokes prior, imagined, and possible situations, each comprising a complex interweaving of those factors that abstraction enables us to categorize as *form* and *context*. If the context in which *the best of both possible worlds* is heard is one where A is telling B about some happy outcome for C at the end of various tribulations, interpretation is as likely to be facilitated by matching that context-form pair with other related context-form pairings that might come to mind: for example, other contexts in which difficulties have been overcome, success has been plucked from adversity, an individual has been fortunate on two different counts, and so on. Matching the present context-form with such past context-form pairings, very likely the listener — even the listener familiar with formal semantics — may not even pause to query why the speaker said *possible*. On the other hand, in some particular context of interpretation, adducing a range of remembered uses, beyond the various pairings mentioned above, may well be justified. A situated determination must be made as to whether consideration of that wider range of associations, of past meaningful interactions, is reasonable. The situation is therefore not so very different from that of interpreting poetry, where, as Sperber and Wilson (1986) note, consideration of a wide range of weak implicatures is the norm. It is this situated accessing of present relevant purposes, and the part assumed to be played by heard utterances (themselves understood in relation to an open set of remembered and imagined similar form-context pairings) in the advancing of those purposes, that justifies describing the interpretive process involved as compositional. Interpreting situations and the utterances embedded in situations entails integration and compositionality rather than analysis and decomposition. We make sense of a situation, or an utterance in a situation, or a "word" within a speech act, not by breaking complexes down into parts, as if those parts had stable and independent value or meaning, but by postulating (i.e., speculatively composing) the purposive whole of which it is a part. That, at least, is the language user's perspective. Integrationism challenges linguistics to develop descriptions that represent that perspective.

If this is the basis on which idioms and quasi idioms are made sense of, what about sentence fragments and grammatically fractured sentences? How do conversationalists make sense of the utterances directed toward them by co-conversationalists, particularly when those utterances are syntactically ill formed? What processing of the garbled "input" must an interpreter perform when presented with speech such as the following:

I've watched him for a long — longer than you have.

(Posing the question in this way, presupposing that the input is indeed garbled and *must* be "processed" in some way, begs several questions to be returned to below.) Some have argued that hearers cope with such fractured sentences by invoking a set of mental "editing rules," which serve to abridge the input until a syntactically well-formed string remains. Although elegant and simple, this argument seems to be wrong: as Taylor and Cameron (1987) show, none of the sets of "editing rules" that have been proposed work consistently on a range of speech samples so as to isolate single target sentences (see also Toolan 1989). But, while no unified procedure of "editing by reduction" seems available to occupy an interface between utterance and language system, the possibility that diverse procedures and habits of nonunified and nonautomatic reformulation are involved remains open. By *reformulation* here is meant any procedure by which, in the course of making sense of a situated utterance — such as

I've watched him for a long — longer than you have

— an addressee tacitly and perhaps unconsciously adds contextually plausible material, or deletes contextually egregious material, or rearranges the given material, implicitly treating that given material as unsatisfactory as it stands. But all such reformulations would seem to be a metalinguistic activity, one that follows rather than precedes interpretation. The fact is that, in situ, the addressee has all and only the "unsatisfactory" utterance with which to understand the speaker (self- and other repairs, requests for clarification, and so on complicate but do not undermine the situation considered here). It is on the basis of determined interpretation of the "fractured" utterance that reformulation, as an option, becomes available. Thus, in the case of treating the utterance given above as an abridgement of

> I've watched him for a long time, longer than you have,

addressees often understand what, by grammatical standards, are incomplete or fractured sentences by proceeding as if they had heard grammatically complete sentences of a kind that seem relevant to and congruent with the preceding and expected utterances and contexts. But this proceeding is posterior, not prior, to hazarded interpretation. The powerful inclination is to assume otherwise, that is, to assume that hearers "tidy up" utterances, converting them to coherent sentential and propositional form, before interpreting them. But what would constrain or control that "tidying up"? No automatic or mechanical procedure can be shown to apply so as to produce plausible results across a range of cases. Thus, if any "tidying up" is involved, it is inescapably interpretive, not mechanical: it is predicated on a prior, hazarded interpretation of the utterance rather than preliminary to it. In short, the "tidying up" is entirely after the fact; it is therefore interpretively irrelevant; often it may not occur at all. There will be those, for example, who hear "I was so chestfallen" as "I was so crestfallen," with no awareness of anomaly, no mental activity of reformulation having gone on. Similarly, there are those who read reports about terrible airplane crashes and the sad task that families have of burying the survivors, again without noticing any anomaly.

Even simply as the written representation of a seemingly problematic utterance, the example raises further interesting issues. First, as inevitably happens, the conversion of a putative spoken utterance to a standard orthographic form introduces a slantedness of its own. Thus, in the written format

> I've watched him for a long — longer than you have,

a dash is introduced that is no counterpart of the putative spoken version. The incommensurability or lack of "counterpartedness," between speech and writing is a quite general phenomenon: the interword spacing that matches no pausing in speech, the sentence-initial capitalization that has no spoken corollary, and so on. But the transcriber's introduction of a dash is, I suggest, the clearest example in the present case of how transcriptions make rather than merely find. That dash does more than simply mark a pause or period of noticeable silence: it additionally suggests that what follows is a supplement or reformulation of part of what preceded the dash — as dashes standardly do. The chosen written format predisposes the reader to accept

> I've watched him for a long time, longer than you have

as a highly plausible paraphrase of the utterance and equally predisposes the reader not even to consider

> I've watched him for a lot longer than you have

as plausible. Yet, had the actual utterance been rendered in written format without the dash, that is, as

> I've watched him for a long   longer than you have,

it might have occurred to the reader that, possibly, a performance error (anticipatory duplication of a velar nasal where an alveolar stop was intended: *long* for *lot*) and a following fleeting pause in which repair was perhaps considered but decided against was an equally plausible account. But this alternative account does not of course exhaust the possible accounts.

What is more important to emphasize is that, first, in most circumstances, no such account carries with it guarantees of its own conclusive reliability, for there can be none, and that, second, all such tinkerings with "damaged input" (spoken or written) seem to be external and posterior to understanding that input. Thus, in the "a lot longer" interpretation of

> I've watched him for a long–longer than you have,

it must be the case that, before the addressee determines that where *a long – longer* was said *a lot longer* was intended, that same addressee has considered

> I've watched him for a lot longer than you have

as a plausible paraphrase of what he understands the speaker, in the circumstances, to be saying. Whatever problems of uptake are presented by

> I've watched him for a long — longer than you have

are not of a kind that are resolved by "correcting" this to

> I've watched him for a lot longer than you have.

The blunt practical reason this is so is that, in a way quite obvious to situated language users but seemingly opaque to formalist theorists, there is scant informative difference between the "work" involved in understanding

> I've watched him for a long — longer than you have

and

> I've watched him for a lot longer than you have

and, for that matter,

> I've watched him for a long time, longer than you have.

In situated interaction, these are all much of a muchness, and the illusion that the first is significantly different from the latter two amounts to the bizarre assumption that something like careful proofreading is both an important aspect and a goal of everyday spoken interaction. But, to repeat, the blunt logical reason why correcting

> I've watched him for a long — longer than you have

to

> I've watched him for a lot longer than you have

plays no significant part in interpretation is that such corrective reformulations are possible only after, and not prior and preparatory to, uptake.

If interpreters invoke reformulations as an interpretive aid (and it seems likely that they do so intermittently rather than routinely), then these are an interpretive aid in an "echoic" sense: they "report back" to the interpreter, in the form of a hard copy, as it were, an already-hazarded compositionally based interpretation of the "uncorrected" heard utterance. Clearly, such interpretations may lack the sharp constrainedness that linguistics orthodoxly demands; but, although inelegant and incompletely constrained, this argument seems to be confirmed by discourse analytic findings. Just as *the best of both possible worlds* is interpreted by compositional enrichment, adducement of other pairings related to the given one (and not, e.g., by mentally deleting *possible* from the source expression), so interpretation of fractured sentences will involve similar matchings and associations, with the proviso that here, sometimes, it may be necessary to "fill out," in a rational way, the heard utterance. In fact, some such "filling out" is a commonplace of interaction interspersed with noise and distraction, where an utterance is discontinuously heard owing to some interruptive noise or event — the phenomenon of driving under a bridge while listening to talk on the car radio, for example. Hearers often have to make informed guesses as to the missing material; that is, they have to compose the given material.

*Fixed Expressions and Repetition: Natural, Spontaneous
Language-Acquisition Devices*

From her review of idioms and garbled idioms, Tannen concludes that "fixity in expression can encourage, rather than discourage, creativity" (1987b: 223). But proverbs, idioms, and fixed expressions are also institutionalized usage, made so by the normative pressure of the authoritative and dominant writers and speakers within a society. The institutionalization of phrases and idioms has the effect of indicating to users that, in specifiable circumstances, such and such may or even must be said or written. In some circumstances, the institutionalized utterances are rather strictly to be adhered to: wedding ceremonies; insurance documents; passports/customs declarations; loan papers, tax statements; etc. In other situations, there is more free variation: introducing guest speakers, speeches at retirement presentations, and so on. Once this institutionalizedness is in place, and not before, *chestfallen*, *piping in* (*with your comments*), and *perish forbid!* — and all other malapropisms and flubbed tokens — are noticeable as unexpectedly fresh variants.

At the same time, by their very nature as fusings and quasi idioms, none of the examples cited above (*chestfallen* etc.) are *repetitions* of the institutionalized type but variants that are recognizably related to the established usage. It is not really a question of fixity in expression *encouraging* or even enabling creative but recognizable departure from the fixed usage but rather that without some fixity of expression this kind of creativity would not be noticeable at all. The creativity of adjusted formulaic speech is foregrounded by its own contrast with the formulaic; the creativity of most speech, adapting and adjusting institutionalized usages that have not become recognized as formulaic — that is, words (or noncollocational institutionalization) rather than phrases or clauses — stays in the background.

Whether all the routines, strategies, and prefabrications that language users draw on to bring shape, pattern, and predictability to their interactions can be characterized as *repetition* is doubtful. The term applies most naturally to proximate repetitions within the same interactional encounter and often in adjacent turns of talk. These are most justifiably described as repetition since most factors in the situation hold constant between the two utterances (even if speaker and purpose change). These proximate conversational repetitions have various functions in different circumstances: for example, to highlight emphasis or agreement or for humorous purposes. But, arguably, the more challenging case is that of nonproximate usage of the "same" institutionalized verbal material, where there is usually some shift in situation, perhaps a considerable lapse of time, and so on. There is never total phonetic or graphetic identity between two instances of speech or writing; nor is there ever total identity between any two contexts of situation within which any phones or graphs arise: participants and their purposes are always moving on. In view of this, the reuse of the "same" chunks of verbal material may be better understood not strictly as repetition at all but as a recycling, one invariably involving some shift of situation and value. Nonproximate "repetition" is then better described as normativity-underwritten continuity. This is not difficult to demonstrate when a longer perspective is taken — for example, in a study of a speaker's changes in use and pronunciation of a particular phrase over several decades.

At several points in the book, Tannen seems to venture near a point of "crossing over" from orthodox linguistics to something antifoundationalist. This is most evident in her main thesis about repetition — that it contributes, as a supplement and an aid, to the achievement of speaker-addressee involvement and audience participation. At the same time, from the perspective of orthodox linguistics, "(emotional) involvement" and audience participation are noticeable, not typical and routine. Thus, a view of linguistic is implied in which the norm is rule-governed creative and nonrepetitive use of the code, in communications without any marked degree of speaker-hearer involvement or participation. To be set beside that norm, and seen functionally as an enrichment of such normal circumstances, is the use of repetition. It is only from a perspective outside the orthodox linguistic paradigm that the proper place of perceived repetition in a theory of language can be recognized. Perceived repetition is foundational to the activities of linguistic production, comprehension, connection, and interaction.

This radical perspective is glimpsed at the close of a passage interpreting conversational self-repetition, where Tannen notes: "Almost paradoxically, repeating the frame first foregrounds and intensifies the part repeated, then foregrounds and intensifies the part that is different. To quote Jakobson (from Jakobson and Pomorska 1983: 103), 'By focussing on parallelisms and similarities in pairs of lines, one is led to pay more attention to every similarity and every difference'" (1987a: 583). The reasons why it may be unhelpfully paradoxical to say that a repeated given being foregrounded has the delayed effect of making the new material more than usually foregrounded may chiefly have to do with the term *foreground(ed)*. Although *foregrounded* is both a relational term (so that not everything can be foregrounded at once) and implicitly an evaluative one, it carries no specific evaluation of whatever is designated foregrounded. A more relevant Jakobsonian term may be *equivalence*, which does carry the specific evaluation that whatever items or chunks are deemed equivalent are more than normally alike, or related, in meaning. The way in which perceived-to-be-repeated (equivalent) items or chunks are alike in meaning remains to be contextually determined, by particular attention to their present uses (now, as it were, a single joint use) and remembered past uses.

Is there a standard or invariant effect of repetition? Tannen plausibly suggests that, as a kind of standard implication of its occurrence, repetition signals increased interpersonal involvement between participants: "Such involvement may be identified with what Goffman (1967: 73), building on Durkheim's 1915 notion of positive and negative rites, called 'presentational deference,' through which 'the recipient is told that he is not an island unto himself and that others are, or seek to be, involved with him and with his personal private concerns" (1987a: 584). To contrive or to perceive a repetition, then, is to construe a local familiarity (a close or distant family resemblance), which may be glossed as above as "interpersonal involvement" or "orientedness to other." But this orientedness to other that repetition displays need not be for the purposes of conveying rapport and empathy. That is too "utopian" a reading (in the sense of Pratt [1987]), too cooperatively and collaboratively oriented an account. Repetition can equally underpin coherently dialogical or conflictual discourse and is widely used with ironic intent in echoic mentions (as we have seen in chapter 5). Privileging the function of conveying "a metamessage of rapport" (Tannen 1987a: 583) should be avoided, when oppositional purposes, from the mild to the intense, are equally likely possibilities. Repetition is the mother device of all expressive devices, the heart of rhetoric, the essence and the unmasking of language. It (or, rather, we who perceive it) has the potential to turn any use into a mention, everything natural and spontaneous into things artificial and mechanical. We experience it in small when, during a transcontinental telephone call, we hear the echo of our own words a second or so after we have produced them. In conversation, a repetition can be deeply encouraging, taken as indicating that one's interlocutor thinks along similar lines to one's self or sees the sense of your views; it can be mildly irritating, taken as a mindless echoing without interest; it can be frustrating, taken as an interlocutor's incomprehension of the point behind one's words; and it can be downright insulting, when taken as an addressee's mocking or contemptuous mimicry.

One of the most interesting recent discussions of the role of repetition in language learning is that of Peters (1987) on the role of imitation in the developing syntax of Seth, a child who is blind. On the basis of data from an intensive study of the child's language learning between nineteen and forty months, Peters argues that blind children in general may rely on various sorts of imitation — immediate, delayed, literal, and expanded — as they make sense of and assimilate the syntactic complexities of the spoken language that they encounter. A "use first, analyze later" strategy seems to be at work. This prompts the reflection that accurate imitation may be thought of as simultaneously very difficult and quite undemanding: as a physiological challenge, to match a heard production, it may present considerable difficulties; but if there is little or no requirement that the copied material be used appropriately in a new context (i.e., there is no relevance constraint beyond the fact that an imitation follow its target), then the processing burden is slight indeed. Seen in that light, imitation, mimicry, echoism, although by no means a trivial accomplishment (and at the fine-tuned standards of "exaggerated faithfulness" set by adults, a skill or gift that some display but most cannot attain), is nevertheless perhaps the simplest and least cognitively demanding form of vocal response. As Kagan (1984: 94) has argued: "Acts that are too easy or too difficult to assimilate and to perform are not likely to be imitated." He adds: "Events in the environment representing responses which are in the process of being mastered by the child function as incentives that alert or excite the child. The reaction to that arousal is the attempt to reproduce the act" (Kagan 1984: 97).

To attempt to imitate an utterance may often serve as a simplest means of "keeping structures in play" as the child struggles to comprehend them. Older language users have similar means of recycling chunks of language that they judge themselves to have processed inadequately or incompletely on the first encounter (e.g., by echoing the utterance or asking for it to be repeated). Such imitations would thus be an indicator of what Vygotsky called "the zone of proximal development." Repetition is a maintenance of the interactive vocal sequence without hazarding, in one's preferred response, an analysis or a reaction to the internal structuring (of whatever kind, including meaning) of the previous speaker's utterance. It is the kind of response that can be attempted even in a totally unknown language, as many discover who are put through foreign-language courses that begin with the audiovisual method.

But, to be consistent with an integrational perspective, it may be preferable to characterize children's utterance imitations as not so much a means of "keeping structures in play" (while, it is implied, further syntactic processing is attempted) as an abbreviated means of "keeping situations — integrated form-context pairings — in play." Utterance imitation keeps the situation "in play" while further processing is undertaken: matching that situation with past situations and calculating (by inferences and analogies themselves guided by assumed present goals and interests — interpretive "fine-tuning") the ways in which the present form-context pairing is similar and different from past ones.

The situation of blind children learning a language is interesting not least since they are evidently constrained in part by their inability to draw on visual cues (gestures, pointing, gaze, facial pose, etc.) in making sense of the language around them. They face, in a rather sharper way, the difficulty of being able to draw on the manifest or ostensively foregrounded, which, as was argued in chapter 5, is always difficult and uncertain. Concerning Seth's imitations, Peters writes:

> In the transcripts of Seth's interactions with his father we find three kinds of imitation. Not only does Seth spontaneously imitate a good deal, but his father also regularly elicits imitations from Seth. Both these kinds of imitations contributed to the teaching and memorization of formulaic chunks of language, including prayers and stories, as well as shorter routines which they eventually performed antiphonally, using the well-established, sentence-completion routine. This kind of contextually triggered reproduction of memorized chunks is really delayed imitation. (Peters 1987: 303)

Triggered representation of the kind Peters describes is at the heart of child language development. Central to the task is "memorization of formulaic chunks of language," the examples mentioned here being prayers and stories. To these can be immediately added songs, rhymes, proverbs, catchphrases and idioms, and standard routines for greeting, saying good-bye, thanking, apologizing, requesting, protesting, and negotiating. Beyond these, in a top-down acquisition of institutionalized chunks of language and in line with earlier arguments, can be added the most versatile chunks, words.

Peters's work helps reintroduce the question of whether direct instruction plays a larger role in first language acquisition than has been assumed in recent years. Ethnographically oriented researchers, such as Watson-Gegeo and Gegeo (1986) on the Kwara'ae of the Solomon Islands, have highlighted the role of instruction via requested imitation, and Miller (1982) shows strategies of imitation at work in learning and teaching the following: (1) names and labels; (2) rhymes and songs; (3) politeness routines; (4) how to talk to third parties; and (5) how to talk to baby dolls. Peters adds an important point: "The observation that delayed imitations may play a crucial role in language development suggests that it is of utmost importance to be able to identify routine situations in order to be able to recognize delayed imitations" (Peters 1987: 307). Among these she lists feeding, dressing, going for walks, playing ball, building block towers, and telling stories and concludes that the evidence raises the possibility that syntactic development may be more tightly tied to situational use than has been generally assumed.

For imitation to function at all, it is vital for the child to have hazarded some kind of rough segmentation and grouping of the myriad stimuli that he or she encounters, in constant succession (as argued in chapter 3). The child must postulate some clustering of processes (of speech, gesture, movements of objects, mood, etc.) constituting what they will later come to know by the abstract label *playing dress up*, or *acting out a nursery rhyme*, or *having a tea party*, and so on. Additionally, the child must be sufficiently attentive and reflective to notice and adopt a basic classification of the ongoing stream of activity-embedded speech, into chunks that situationally are more purely a use and chunks that are additionally a mention. For example, in among the unpredictable sequences and bits of byplay within a performed interaction (such as *answering the door to the mail carrier*), the child must at some stage grasp that certain chunks ("Hello, Ken!" or "Thanks very much, goodbye") are mentions over and above their present use and may be used again in set places in reenactments of this particular routine. For the child learning English, as always in principle, there will be no classification or signaling of language into uses and mentions at the outset. A child may have to witness many occasions of answering the door to the mail carrier and come to participate in those occasions before she will take the inferential step of detaching the chunks transcribed above and adopt the hypothesis that these are some kind of mentions generally usable in the specified situation. As noted, those chunks are transcribed above, in standard English orthography: there is no grounds for assuming that the child does anything remotely similar, in mental analysis of what are essentially sequences of sounds integrated with particular movements. If the child's "repetition" of the first chunk is the sequence of sounds [logen] with fall-rise intonation, that rough matching may suffice for the present. It would be quite mistaken to think that the child at first recognizes that the sequence comprises two words, a greeting and the name of the individual — as becomes clear if the child now starts saying [logen] with fall-rise to any mail carrier to whom he or she opens the door.

At this point, some further speculations concerning the fundamental motivations of contrived or perceived repetition may be made. These relate to claims listed as resources in mother-child interaction in chapter 3: in particular, the claim that the production of repetitions (recyclings or near repeats) is motivated either by interest in some kind of comfort or pleasure (on the positive side) or by a kind of repair of a perceived discomfort (on the negative side). Thus, a mother repeats a swooping intonation and play with the labial articulators, and the baby repeatedly responds with gurgling laughter, with the aim of causing pleasure and amusement and displayed mutual attention. But a baby who cries when feeling hungry or when a toy falls out of reach and who then cries again and again does so because some need or want has not yet been met: each recycled cry constitutes an attempted repair of the previous failed bid for attention or food or action. The "repair"-type uses of repetitions in the pursuit of needs and wants may be seen as instances of what Halliday (1975: 63) calls the instrumental ("I want") and regulatory ("do as I tell you") functions in a child's early language: of the six basic functions, Halliday identifies these two as the more pragmatic ones. The pleasure-seeking type of repetitions, by contrast, would seem to be primarily instances of the interactional ("me and you") function — which "embodies the child's need for human contact" — and secondarily contributory to development of the imaginative ("let's pretend") function.

Repetition and the Neglect of Difference in Linguistic Theory

The role of repetition in linguistic theory, over and above such empirically oriented studies as those discussed above, cannot be overstated. A failing repeatedly (*sic*) commented on in this book has been the tendency in linguistics to deploy the Saussurean binarism of similarity and difference in a sharply imbalanced way (the *Cours* does this as much as any other theoretical text), promoting similarity as central and foundational and setting difference to one side as a distracting complication. (In fact, as far as theory is concerned, similarity is hardly a strong enough assertion: the identity implied by full repetition is what is required.) Such an "orientation to unity," in Saussurean linguistics, is identified and critiqued by Bakhtin, who contrasts it with the sociolingual actuality, which is heteroglossic: "Linguistics, stylistics and the philosophy of language — as forces in the service of the great centralizing tendencies of European verbal-ideological life — have sought first and foremost for *unity* in diversity. This exclusive 'orientation toward unity' in the present and past life of languages has concentrated the attention of philosophical and linguistic thought on the firmest, most stable, least changeable and most mono-semic aspects of discourse" (Bakhtin 1981: 274; see also the counterposing of Saussurean and Bakhtinian linguistics in Crowley [1990]). Accordingly, an emphasis on similarity, identity, and repetition is central in the most influential theoretical formulations in the *Cours*: "The individual's receptive and co-ordinating faculties build up a stock of imprints which turn out to be for all practical purposes the same as the next person's" (Saussure 1983 [1916]: 30). And, in North American linguistics, the emphasis on recurrent samenesses was famously reasserted by Bloomfield: "In certain communities (speech-communities) some speech utterances are alike as to form and meaning" (1935: 144).

In the Saussurean distinction between paradigmatic (or associative) and syntagmatic axes also, we see an interplay of criteria of similarity and difference, with again those of similarity more prominent. In distributionalist fashion, the paradigmatic axis specifies places in the sequencing of utterances and attempts to specify a paradigm (however large or small) of utterances that might acceptably substitute for that utterance actually used, in the given place. Framing the range of structural and semantic differences between items in a paradigm, an overarching sameness is thus asserted: the paradigmatic axis articulates differences within a governing sameness. Furthermore, the paradigmatic axis is as concerned with semantic issues as syntactic ones, as Saussure's own term for the axis, *associative*, suggests: it is represented as the dimension in language activity in which a speaker or hearer might pause, in the incremental production of language, and consider the range of other forms structurally and/or semantically related to that one actually selected.

In relation to the syntagmatic or combinatorial axis, however, the picture is muddier, and the resort to criteria of similarity and difference is even less balanced, for the syntagmatic axis addresses the possibilities and limitations on just what utterances, in what order, can follow a given utterance. The way in which this has usually been interpreted has been rather strictly syntactic: the syntagmatic axis is the syntactic domain of possibilities (and impossibilities) of chaining of utterances. Thus, the syntagmatic exclusion of sequences such as *cow the jumped moon over the* has been attributed to syntactic grounds rather than semantic ones. But the criteria of similarity and difference apply far less neatly here. It is easy enough to see difference (structural, functional, semantic) between succeeding utterances (words, phrases, etc.) in nonrepetitive nonpalindromic sentences. It is less easy to see similarity. Yet linguistic analysis has proceeded with quite restricted attention to those dimensions of difference. What has been privileged instead has been syntactic similarity: no matter what diversity of semantic concerns are articulated within successive chunks of utterance (sentences), the similarity or relatedness of syntactic structure, between sentences and indeed throughout a given language, has been the focus of study. The phrase structure configuration in universal grammar (everything has an X′ structure, comprising a head, modifiers, and specifiers) is just one vivid example among many, speaking to similarity over and above difference.

The point of dwelling on this emphasis on similarity in linguistics is to draw attention also to what it neglects — here, difference along the syntagmatic axis — for, having acknowledged the aspects of recurrent syntagmatic similarity that a developed metalanguage of syntactic description can undoubtedly illuminate, there remain a multiplicity of dimensions of language production, along the associative chain, unaddressed: these include semantic sequencing, intonational sequencing, kinesic sequencing, gaze sequencing, and their interrelations (e.g., constraints on possible combinations of gaze and intonation). It is true that in written language several of these do not apply and that the analytic task therefore seems more manageable. But the most crucial of these aspects does of course apply, in both writing and speech: the semantic aspect, what one might want to call *the rules for sense sequencing*. The questions to be addressed include the following: in terms of meaning, what can follow what, what tends to follow what, what cannot follow what? Only in highly localized parts of language behavior (e.g., openings and closings of conversations, apologies and simple "repairs," invitations, simple narratives, paragraph development in student essays, and travel guides), almost invariably parts of highly institutionalized genres or language games, are there the beginnings of answers to these questions.

The broader reason for this state of affairs seems to be the unspecifiability of "the rules for sense sequencing" — much as we might wish otherwise, and much as our analytic habits might lead us to expect otherwise — for, in the larger context (consider, e.g., the chain of meanings involved in your own experiences in language since you awoke this morning), meanings will succeed meanings in innumerably diverse ways for different situated individuals. As a result, there can be no grammar of meaning sequencing as there can be for sentence syntax; what meaning sequencing we do enact cannot possibly be a matter of following a unified grammar or fixed set of rules. Even conversation analysts discussing the sequencing of turns in a conversational closing are concerned to stress that what is displayed is an awareness of an established pattern for "doing" closings. More generally, and in less monotone activities than exiting conversations, predictability of meaning sequencing is impossible. This unpredictability of future language production, the rich essence of the syntagmatic axis, perforce is speedily glossed over in mainstream linguistic treatments in favor of the manageable associativeness of syntax, whereas the unpredictability of what, in meaningful language activity, will follow what is a natural corollary of the cotemporality, the "here-and-nowness" of language integrated within human behavior, previously noted. It is a principle of linearity that, owing to its unmanageability, Saussure (1983 [1916]: 69–70) acknowledged and then effectively suppressed or diminished (see Harris 1987: 69; and Hutton 1990). More specifically, Saussure reduced linguistic linearity to the notion that signs exhibit and function by means of monolinear sequentiality: signs are produced one at a time and one after another (the paradigmatic and syntagmatic interrelatedness of signs, as a structured system "ou tout se tient," it is asserted, necessitates this view of signification as coming in temporally discrete packets, rather like Morse code). In this way, the *structuredness* of linearity came to be assumed and focused on, while the *temporality* of linearity was largely neglected.

Types, Tokens, and Writing

In this final section of the chapter, an attempt is made further to situate the idea of repetition in relation to integrational linguistics, particularly emphasizing the place that repetition occupies in a literate community's metalinguistic reflections on language activity. I quote extensively from an important essay by Love (1990c), "The Locus of Languages in a Redefined Linguistics." One section of the latter effects a clarification of doubts raised by some (e.g., Pateman 1987a) concerning the integrationists' position on theories of types and tokens. Love comments:

In order to make general statements at all one must indulge in abstraction. Spatio-temporally distinct objects and events must be envisaged as "the same" in some respect relevant to the purposes of the discourse. Something like a type-token analysis is required. If one is to talk about, say, cats, distinct individual organisms have to be seen as tokens of a type "cat." This is true for languages no less than for cats. . . . That utterances can be treated as recurrent instantiations of underlying invariants is an assumption that we take for granted.

261 Repetition

> What is problematic is the further assumption that the analysis into types and tokens — what counts as an underlying invariant, and what counts as an instance of a particular invariant — is uniform for a whole linguistic community, determined for every member of that community by an abstraction called "the language." (Love 1990c: 97)

Without question, types and tokens are real abstractions for speakers. But they are abstractions that begin and end in individuals, individually. No invariant system of types or instances of types underlie these situated interpretive strategies. Neither types, nor tokens, nor that abstraction we call repetition are *realia* of situated language use. They are a part of a now enormously elaborate post hoc and propter hoc activity of detached reflection on that use, at a level of sophistication — which is also to say at a level at which the unwary may be misled — rivaled by no other naturally occurring human activity. It is almost unthinkable to imagine a kind of dance that is a commentary on dancing itself, a dance that analyzes dancing, specifies its necessary parts, specifies the common core of diverse kinds of dancing, a dancing that definitively distinguishes "dancing" from "extradance activity (the dancers, the clothing, the props, the stage, the music)," and further specifies the primary and necessary functions of dancing, and so on. Sometimes, it seems, such metamoves are all too thinkable with language. Language — particularly written language — naturalizes the illusion not merely that some language use may be treated as mentions but further that all language use is in fact a kind of mention, a mentioning (or instantiating) drawing on a fixed and common code. The logical end point of this illusion is the idea that "external" language is but mention by translation of an internal "language of thought" (Fodor 1975).

Beside these metalinguistic illusions we must set the reality of actual communicational exchanges, including actual exchanges about metalinguistic matters:

> When A asks B to repeat *exactly* what he said, he is speaking metalinguistically. If, on the other hand, he merely asks him to repeat what he said, he is not necessarily speaking metalinguistically; and it is significant that now the response may be a different form of words entirely. All that is demanded in this case is another utterance perceived as similar to the first in respect of playing the same role in the communicational exchange. But that, in the end, is all that A gets even when he makes the more specific demand. He may *think* he is being offered a token of the same type (not that he would necessarily use that terminology). That is because he takes for granted the

type/token distinction as a necessary concomitant of discourse about language. But if one asks what its being a token of the same type actually consists in, there is no answer, except that it conforms to the *idea* that it is: an idea validated ultimately by nothing more than the circumstances of the communicational interaction within which, and for purposes of which, it is entertained. (Love 1990c: 98)

In short, it is of the utmost importance that we keep theoretically distinct our account of (*a*) first-order language use and (*b*) second-order ideas and discourse about language use.

This is nowhere more important than when understanding repetition: "Perceiving utterances as manifestations of underlying 'sames' is not a necessary condition of any use of language whatever. It must be at least possible to understand an utterance without relating it to an antecedently given underlying abstraction. Nonetheless, once one has understood an utterance for the first time, one will entertain the possibility of repeating it. This involves *deciding* what would constitute repeating it" (Love 1990c: 100). The first two sentences here summarize an important rebuttal of certain assumptions of iterability. It is the third sentence that invites further commentary. Its emphasis is on "understanding an utterance for the first time," as distinct from merely encountering or using an utterance. So the possibility is allowed — and implied — that an individual may have encountered versions of some utterance, embedded within a social activity, on many distinct occasions before that "breakthrough" occasion on which she understands it for the first time. As stressed before, those recurrent uses of the "same" utterance are strictly no such thing — each is acoustically, auditorily, articulatorily, situationally, etc. different from its brothers, although all may be — from a metalinguistic point of view — repetitions of the same item or, to use overtly metalinguistic terms, "a series of tokens instantiating a single underlying type." But how does the individual's breakthrough to sense, to "understanding an utterance for the first time," conceivably happen? And what degree of detached reflective awareness of one's own behavior is implicit in this level of understanding, such that it enables one, instantly, to "entertain the possibility of repeating [the understood utterance]"?

In line with the sketch of primitive tree felling and mother-child interaction drawn in chapter 3, I propose that understanding language — particularly the child's or the species' development of understanding of its first linguistic signs — including understanding of its detachability (recontextualizability) and recyclability, is not plausibly an abrupt or sudden illumination but a gradual, incremental grasping of things and their uses, or "things in use." According to this view, it simply will not be possible, observing the first humans or any baby coming into language today, to identify any particular occasion as that on which the subject(s) first understood an utterance. Or to so designate a particular instance will be arbitrary. It is not that identification of, for example, an infant understanding a particular utterance is arbitrary, for we have numerous plausible criteria to support such identifications; what is in question is the identification of first occasions, the onset of understanding. The same qualification must apply to characterizations that refer to a distinct point of reflexivity when the possibility of repetition is first grasped. In practice, attempts to pinpoint a discrete occasion at which repetition was "first" perceived as a possibility, resource, etc. neglect the essential prior developing awareness of repeatability, out of which any particular displayed awareness of repeatability must have emerged.

Furthermore, repetition itself is more complex than is sometimes realized since what constitutes a repetition of a given utterance is a situationally variable matter; as Love (1990c) notes, what counts as a repetition varies from occasion to occasion, without detached, abstract, or permanent determination. Sometimes "I don't know" will be a satisfactory repeat of "Je ne sais pas," sometimes not; sometimes the word *grass*, pronounced in a Northern British English dialect, can be satisfactorily repeated with a Southern pronunciation (i.e., with different vowel quality), sometimes not. And, as noted before, even "full repetition" (with no perceptible auditory etc. divergence from a prior token) is never strict iteration drawing on a fixed and permanent underlying system of types, for all so-called repetition is subject to the condition of linearity, of continuous situational development and shift of communicational demands. The very production of a prior token, in its situational priorness, guarantees that any subsequent token counted as a copy is not in fact identical.

Love goes on to ask what "understanding," at the primordial stage, can mean. His conclusions are not dissimilar from my own in chapter 3: the effect of A's noise on B's behavior "suggests" to both that the associations of the noise for B "are similar to" the associations of the noise for A. Inherently, the power of reflection on experience is involved. "The birth of language as an object of contemplation follows hard on the heels of the birth of language itself" (Love 1990c: 107); and, we may add, the birth of language must have followed hard on the heels of the birth of contemplation and self-awareness themselves. As argued in chapter 3, intentionality is a prerequisite of the first language — indeed, it is hard to see how any given individual A, lacking an established practice, could have set about making his given noise intending that it achieve the given effect in individual B. Without benefit of guidelines as to what would or would not count as a replication, A and B would be obliged to take up the faith-driven other-oriented practice of taking on trust: taking on trust that, in seemingly similar circumstances, noises x', x'', and x''', are intended as versions of x, as more tokens of which x is the first clearly remembered token.

This stage, of setting about repeating, is less obvious than Love implies. He writes: "It is no less hard to imagine how even primitive man could have failed to entertain the notion . . . that behavior-eliciting vocal noises might be made on purpose. The obvious way to test this possibility would be to make a second, similar noise and see if it elicited a similar response" (Love 1990c: 108). While making a second similar noise to probe whether a previous noise was intended may seem obvious to us, it is not clear why this should have been so obvious to the protohuman. Here, it seems to me, is an evolutionary crux: how does a semirational, semireflective animal, caught up in the constant flux of living, hit on the very idea of repeatability, of instant or not-so-instant replay? The beginnings of an answer must lie in the abundance of impressions or stimuli already bombarding these hominids, speaking to the repetitiveness of life: the recurrence of animal calls, of eating, sleeping, procreating, of daylight and darkness, and of using the same tools over and over, in the same ways, in hunting and farming.

Love comments further on how a theoretical impossibility (abstract invariance) must have been absorbed into everyday language practice at an early stage: "The basic idea of an invariant abstraction — a class or a type — underlying utterances is a necessary feature of any attempt to make sense of even the most primitive linguistic event. If . . . the essence of the concept of 'a language', as distinct from 'language,' is the idea that there are things which utterances are utterances of, that idea is bound to arise as a result of no more than the human capacity for reflecting on experience, generalising about it, and purposefully attempting to renew it" (1990c: 108). Or, in terms I have used here, the grasping of the idea or possibility of repetition (namely, of recycled relatedness) is what makes language possible; the more systematic and comprehensive that recycling appears, and the more that the actuality of partial replication is displaced in the community's thinking by the operative illusion of full repetition (instantiations from a permanent underlying system), the more entrenched will be the notions of "a language" and "discrete languages." And no technological and intellectual advance has done more to further the illusion of linguistic behavior as the outward repetitive manifestations of an inner system, shared and determinate, than the invention of writing.

There are any number of things that need to be said about writing and the way it has reshaped our perspectives on ourselves, our cultures, our knowledge of things, etc. Here I will simply draw attention to one broad contrast, between what, following Malinowski, may be called the "phatic" tendency in speech and the informativeness of writing. That is to say, as the tree-felling and mother-child scenarios in chapter 3 indicated, it is possible to consider very many of the typical situations in which spoken language is used as ones in which the content of the speech itself is not particularly crucial. There is considerable tolerance of variation in what is said and quite how it is said in, for example, interactions involving speech such as accomplishing tasks, expressing affection, offering sympathy, expressing anger. All such activities are ones in which speech seems most evidently integral rather than necessary supplement or necessary core, such that the activities themselves could conceivably proceed without any speech whatsoever (these activities could certainly be accomplished after a fashion, without using any spoken or signed language). These are examples of speech at its most phatic—although the implication is not that speech here is marginal, accidental, or supererogatory, even if linguistics has, significantly, tended to reinterpret the term *phatic* along just such trivializing lines. This is speech integrated within "proposals" rather than "propositions," to use a distinction in Halliday (1994): Halliday suggests that a basic distinction can be made between language used in the exchanging of information (propositions) and language used in the giving or demanding of goods and services (proposals). Clearly, not all uses of speech are as phatic as this: oral narratives are a clear and common example of speech used more than phatically, to supply information that would not be conveyed anyway, as it were, by other means.

But the phatic embeddings of speech within social actions are in striking contrast with some of the canonical uses of writing, which are united in being the expression of information or representations at one place and time in such a way that they may be received and interpreted at some removed place or time. This is not the only use or situation, but it is surely the canonical one. And one of the ways such a situation can be distinguished from the canonical uses of speech is that, in the case of writing, whatever action is performed is done essentially in and through the writing itself and seemingly alone. Again, the canonical act may be that of informing, although other related acts such as promising, directing, etc. are options too. The chief point is that the written material is essential to the given act of informing: without it, the act of informing cannot conceivably be accomplished. These are cases of writing used within "propositions," in the Hailidayan sense noted above. In direct interaction, on the other hand, between two individuals copresent in some sense (e.g., even if only at opposite ends of an international telephone connection), various social actions for which speech is an ordinary accompaniment can in fact get done even without actual speech. The communicativeness (which is to say, the interpretability) of sighs, silences, and gestures are just some of the potential resources making this possible. Goffman's comments on the enactment of a simple service transaction at a supermarket checkout counter are germane here (Goffman 1976: 282–83). He calls such a clearly sequenced transaction "an occasion of cooperatively executed, face-to-face, non-linguistic action" and adds, "Words can be fitted to this sequence; but the sequencing is not conversational" (p. 283).

The connection of these broad trends to the way we use and think about language is that the burden seemingly inherent in writing, that it self-sufficiently make possible its own informativity, means that people naturally look to it more and more as a means by which clear and full records may be kept, as a mode within which ambiguity and imprecision ought to (and, then, must) be eradicated, and one in which, for example, an informative act may be set down in such a way as to hold, in perpetuity, as that informative act. Writing begins with the promise of defying disjunction of space and time; in their thinking about language, literate communities increasingly attempt to hold writing to that impossible promise, doing so along the only lines that make sense, that is, assuming that writing transcribes the fixed collective system of a language.

By the same token, those literate communities will tend to disvalue speech as a reliable guide to the essentials of language. As noted above, phatic uses of speech seem to be ones where speech is so subordinate a component as to be dispensable. One is even tempted (as in the modern linguistic reinterpretation of phaticness) to suggest that here speech is "meaningless" or that the meaning of the speech itself is somewhat arbitrary relative to the ongoing communicative purposes within which it is embedded. By contrast, the corollary to the instrumental and essential role of writing in written communicative acts is that writing is ordinarily meaningful, that what is meant is "in" the writing (and in the writing alone since all other factors — type and size of print and script, on pigskin vs. onionskin pad vs. billboard, etc. — seem so secondary).

Once the spread of writing has disseminated with it this seemingly inescapable conclusion, that the meaning is in the written text itself (cf. Olson 1983), the long and doomed search for absolute literal meanings, decontextualized semantics, and (de)compositionality discussed in chapter 1 follows. But to think of speech in situated phatic uses as supererogatory and dispensable along the lines suggested above is a major misdirection. It is another case of the tail wagging the dog: because at first glance no simple determinate set of forms or utterances seems detachable from any series of acts of, for example, giving sympathy (i.e., detachable and representable, in writing, as the basic means for expressing sympathy), because even quite unpredictably metaphoric language might be seen to work as well as anything else, spoken language is set aside as too complex (it is then argued that we must start with simpler cases, from written language, before turning to the complexities of speech). Thus, a model of language is brought to bear on an object of inquiry, speech, and speech is found wanting because the model of language does not work on it.

Moving toward a conclusion, Love's elegant formulation of the situation may be offered: "The relation between languages, language-users and linguistic variation is therefore this. A language is a second-order construct arising from an idea about first-order utterances: namely, that they are repeatable. Such a construct may be institutionalized and treated as *the* language of a community. But it remains a construct based on an idea: at no point does it become a first-order reality for individuals" (Love 1990c: 101). Singling out the idea of the possibility of recyclability (metalinguistically speaking, the idea of repetition) in this way should prompt fuller acknowledgment that primitive humans must have been, and infants are, surrounded by experiences signaling the reasonableness and naturalness of repetition. Primitive humans must have been auditorily bombarded by the repetitive calls and cries of other animals, birds, and so on. They could hardly fail to notice the repetitive pattern of day following night, sunrise and sunset, of the necessity to attend to recurrent patterns of food consumption and expulsion, and reproduction of their own kind. The so-called simple life is strikingly repetitive, its cycles and recurrences far more foregrounded than in our more technologized world. Anyone who has cared for a newborn baby knows how, by adult standards, the first weeks of life are extraordinarily monotonous and repetitive. An important part of what newborns get accustomed to in the early months of life must be the recurrent cycle of their own waking and sleeping.

In this chapter, I have argued that repetition must be understood as the perception of relatedness, similarity, and recyclability — not of identity. There is a world of difference (or, as Derrida might say, of *différance*) between similarity and identity, although linguistics tends to treat them as identical. In that similarity is not a matter of identity and does always entail change (and then an abstraction from or situated setting aside of change), both of the linguistic touchstones, similarity and difference, are grounded in first-order difference. The upshot of an integrational perspective is that repetition, identity, and difference are determinations of linguistic value ("I understand this utterance as substantially a recycled use of that utterance") performed by individuals, individually. They are not reflections of individuals' alignment with a preexisting common or collective code of units, identities, values, and criteria for the recognition of repetitions; no such collective code exists. They are rather individual mental representations, revisable *aides memoires*, an abridged and condensed but open-ended set of rules of thumb, culled from the fuller memories of past experience that we each carry with us and that constitute each of us.

Given the integrational assumption of constant potential innovation in language activity and of the logical impossibility of repetition as a first-order language experience, a case can be made for concluding that language is pervasively characterized not by repetition but by quotation. This conclusion, congruent with the "citational heteroglossia" that in chapter 4 was noted as propounded by Bakhtin, may be reached via a consideration of our commitments to past literature. If strict repetition is always impossible and situational conditions ("inside" and "outside" language) are always changing and becoming different, why, for example, do we bother reading noncontemporary literature? Shakespeare's situated language productions of, say, 1604, I have implied, can never be fully repeated at a later date; and the experience of being a contemporary addressee of Shakespeare's cannot be remotely approximated today. Given the relative situational immediacy, by comparison, of literature that has been produced in our own time and to some degree from within our own circumstances, it would seem to be irrational to devote the time and energy to historicolinguistically remote texts, an exercise in frustration. A partial explanation of why, nevertheless, we persist in the reading of remote literature may emerge from even a brief look at a near-contemporary poem such as Robert Lowell's "Home after Three Months Away." This poem interweaves phrases and allusions to *Hamlet*, Cibber's changed version of *Richard III*, the Bible, and other prior texts, as the following extracts reveal:

> Three months, three months!
> Is Richard now himself again?
> ....
> Dearest, I cannot loiter here
> in lather like a polar bear.
>
> Recuperating, I neither spin nor toil.

These are echoes and recyclings, but in their very recycledness they are more than and different from repetitions. They are, rather, quotations and only the most visible instances of a pervasive activity of quotation in this poem and in every poem and in every linguistic act. Quotation in this larger sense, which it must be stressed does not at all need to be intentional or conscious quotation, can be perceived at a variety of levels. The reuse of words, of phrases, of grammatical structure, of rhythms and meters and stanzaic patterns, are all versions of quotation. The phenomenon is so pervasive and foundational that even the wide compass of its characterization in literary studies, as "intertextuality," has too limited a scope. Those elements traditionally thought of as a language's grammar and vocabulary are its institutionalized units of quotation and rules of quotation. It is by means of the echoic, other-aware, community-constructing practices of quotation that the otherwise daunting linguistic conditions of semiotic discontinuity and disjunction, of uncertainty as to whether *these signs now* paraphrase *those signs then*, can be negotiated.

Repetition in this sense — quotation — goes on in language use generally, pervasively, and unnoticed. However, it is better to think of this phenomenon as unconscious quotation, for, in addition to the general process of unconscious quotation, there are those specific occasions of what might in contrast be called blatant quotation (what in everyday speech we call *repetitions* are one instance of the latter, blatant quotations). When two speakers of the same dialect, in ordinary conversation, "recycle" very similar pronunciations of particular words, that is the phenomenon of pervasive uncalculated quotation: for example, when one Northern British English speaker talks about the wet [graes] using something very like the pronunciation of his or her fellow Northern English–speaking interlocutor). But when an outgroup member, who ordinarily uses a dialect — such as standard Southern British English — that has a contrasting pronunciation of that word nevertheless pronounces the word *grass* in the Northern fashion, this constitutes conscious repetition or blatant quotation.

Repetition (in the sense of perceived relatedness and unconscious quotation) is a driving force behind the impressions of homogeneity and continuity that underpin our classifications of language events or samples into distinct dialects, registers, idiolects, and genres. (In addition to these institutionalized kinds of repetition, we could consider here more fluid ones, such as parody and plagiarism.) Every one of the speech events subsumed under any of these abstracting labels (namely, dialects, registers, etc.) can be seen, if examined closely, as unique, distinct, different from its partners. A particular verbal genre comprises texts "all of one kind," a particular dialect comprises speech "all of one kind," only up to a point. Beyond that point, the assumed homogeneity of texts within a genre or dialect, and the explanatory power of the notion of genre or dialect, falls away. What bounds or delimits a genre or dialect, in actuality, is nothing more impenetrable than a collective perception of a group of texts (or a collective way of talking of them as if they were so perceived) as set apart by the degree of repetition present among the grouped texts and the degree of absence of repetition between that group and all other texts.

However, the heterogeneity lying within our genres and dialects has of necessity been given short shrift in the modern linguistic period. The privileging of homogeneity over heterogeneity goes hand in hand with the privileging of similarity over difference, noted above; in both cases, the possibility of "full" replicatory repetition is embraced as axiomatic. Indeed, it becomes not merely a possibility but a necessity. Without such a ranking of tendencies, the argument runs, how could a systems-oriented scientific study of language prevail over what might otherwise look like a chaotic, multilayered patchwork of utterances and contexts? Logically, such a linguistics of repetition, of homogeneous and idiosynchronic genres, dialects, and idiolects, has no intrinsic place for or interest in history or linguocultural change. At best, such things can be examined after the fact of synchronic analysis, for example, by comparing and contrasting two historically disjunct synchronic systems. But, from Saussure onward, such studies have been downgraded as a secondary enterprise, one with little bearing on the perspective of the individual language speaker, whose speech is said to constitute a single synchronic system. In all such ways, the linguistics of repetition has fostered a picture of society as homogeneous and of language as unrelated to history. It is as if Santayana's familiar moral, that those who ignore history are condemned to repeat it, has been ingeniously scrambled. The scrambled version runs, A linguistics that assumes that speakers are condemned to repetition can safely ignore history.

7

Rules

> The ability to communicate by speech consists in the ability to make oneself understood, and to understand. It is only when we look at the structure of this ability that we realize how far we have drifted from standard ideas of language mastery. For we have discovered no learnable common core of consistent behaviour, no shared grammar or rules, no portable interpreting machine set to grind out the meaning of an arbitrary utterance. We may say that linguistic ability just is the ability to converge on a passing theory from time to time — this is what I have suggested, and I have no better proposal. — D. Davidson, *Inquiries into Truth and Interpretation*

This chapter, like the previous ones, concerns a form of overreliance and the distorting consequences that this has had on linguistic studies. Here, the overreliance is on rules and rule following as the basis of linguistic activity — and a particular kind of rules at that: rules that are cognitive instructions. Rules-oriented vocabulary and conversations (in the Rortyan senses of these terms [Rorty 1989]) pervade many areas of linguistics, as will be exemplified below in discussion of an account of a child's acquisition of his or her native-language phonology. As a result, although linguists have characterized language as "rule-governed creativity," it is nearer the mark to describe current linguistics itself, in the ingenuity of its rule-oriented accounts of language behavior, as rule-governed creativity. As for language itself, a much more generous notion of creativity, as productive and interpretive proficiency in new or developing circumstances, is required. While there are indeed prescriptive or normative rules — known, public, and statable — shaping various language activities, at least as important are "mere" regularities, trends, patterns of usage, and situated assessments of salience. Whereas rule following entails agreement and predetermination, language activity is more often reflective of concurrence and convergence.

Language Acquisition without Rules

Linguistic activity in general and language acquisition in particular are widely assumed to be forms of "rule-governed creativity." The rules governing linguistic creativity are said to enable the individual to use finite resources in generating an indefinitely large number of new sentences. The conjunction of rule governedness and creativity in this formulation would seem to be a winning combination — and certainly one that has met widespread acceptance within and beyond academic linguistics. The combination appears to capture the tension, between conformity and innovation, that any participant-observer of language activity can feel. And the implication that willful or solipsistic wrenching of the language by the strong-minded individual is necessarily controlled and constrained by rules external to that individual has also seemed attractive: it seems on a par with the way we qualify notions of human freedom. For just as we see that human freedom is a meaningless principle save when calibrated relative to a background of possibilities and limitations, so linguistic inventiveness and novelty seem coherent only against a background of preexisting rules. It is a small wonder, then, that the thesis of language as rule-governed creativity has become one of the foundational claims of modern linguistics. Matters immediately become controversial, however, when linguists begin to specify the nature of the creativity, and of the rule governedness, that they have in mind. One way to begin a closer examination of what in practice is entailed by the assumption that language is rule governed and of the part that that assumption plays in linguistic explanation is to consider a linguist's summarized account of the process of language acquisition in a particular child. Such an account is given in Smith (1989), a book primarily intended to be read by interested nonlinguists, and this account provides a convenient representative instance.

Smith begins the discussion of his son Amahl's development of spoken English by focusing on some seeming paradoxes at a particular stage in the child's speech production. At age two and a half, Amahl says *puddle* [pʌdəl] for what in standard speech is [pʌzəl], that is, sounds we would normally take to constitute an utterance of the word *puzzle*. Yet, elsewhere, Amahl fails to produce the adult pronunciation for the word *puddle* (instead pronouncing that word [pʌgəl]). Why is it that Amahl fails to pronounce *puddle* correctly, with a medial [d], when on other occasions he consistently produces just the right sounds (although for the wrong word, *puzzle*)?

Smith sets out to formulate a coherent and systematic explanation for these trends, but what is first noticeable is the way he characterizes an apparently preliminary matter: "It was first necessary to establish beyond doubt that his [Amahl's] pronunciation was regular and hence *rule-governed*, rather than random" (1989: 39). By the terms used in this prerequisite, at a stroke, the generative linguistic predilection for rule governedness is declared and invoked. But whether that partiality is appropriate here is open to question. To begin with, the quoted sentence instances a quite widespread tendency among linguists to proceed lightly from showing that something is regular to assuming that it is rule governed: "regular and hence *rule-governed*." A subsidiary opposition is also hinted at here: if it is not rule governed, it must be random. Clearly, neither of these conclusions necessarily follows from the premises of regularity and nonregularity, respectively, although in the former case there is an influential etymological inducement to conflate regularity and rules, in the common Latin root of the words *rule* and *regular*. We can observe pattern or regularity in many things without wanting to take the further step of asserting that the pattern is the output of rules that govern its production.

Before proceeding, it may be worth considering a few practical cases where the presence of regularity or rule governedness seems to be relatively uncontroversial. One example of straightforward rule governedness might be the rule in elementary school classrooms that no child may leave the room without first getting the permission of the teacher. All the children in a given school are likely to know this rule — because teachers will have reminded them of it, many times — and they will tell it to you without much prompting if, for example, you ask them if there are any class rules. They may not use quite the language used above, but the sense will be substantially the same. Nor do children find the rule very remarkable: they are already accustomed to the idea that there are rules at school and that rules are needed. They know also that failure to comply with this particular rule will have consequences; they may be kept in at recess, or worse. And, if you were to observe the class for any extended period of time, you would notice that children almost never leave the room without first getting the teacher's permission; in that respect, the children's behavior reflects rule observance. If you then asked some of the children why they did not simply leave the room whenever they had a mind to, they would say "Because there's a rule ... ," or words to that effect. On the other hand, they know that observance of the rule is not automatic, even if it does become routine: they know that they have to think about the rule, remember it, remember that they are not at home in their living room (where presumably the parents' permission is not required if the child wants to leave the room), and so on. And they can think about not following the rule, too: they can choose to defy the teacher and face the consequences (or try to avoid them). Even with the rule, the child has choices.

Different from the above is mere regularity. If I always and only drink coffee at breakfast and lunchtime, my coffee drinking is regular rather than random; but is it rule governed? What rule am I following, and why hasn't anybody told me about it? Will I be in trouble if I forget to drink my coffee this lunchtime? Grounds are important for my coffee drinking, but there are no grounds here for "coffee-drinking rules."

A third class of cases to consider, in relation to rule governedness, might be ones like the following. If I release an apple from my grasp, several feet above the ground, it will fall to the ground at a steadily increasing speed. Although some might first suggest that the fall of the apple is rule governed, is this really the case? Since apples are inanimate and have no sense of what is happening to them, we usually speak of laws or principles rather than rules in such cases, but is the inanimacy of the apple the only reason for calling gravity a law rather than a rule? The fall is governed by or subject to the laws of gravity. If the movement of an apple on some occasion does not conform to the behavior predicted by the law — for example, if the released apple does not fall as predicted — some important interfering factors can reliably be inferred. In the specified circumstances, we might find, for example, that the apple was located in a gravity-free environment or directly above a powerful jet of air, aimed upward. The kind of interference that we would not for a moment accept as plausible would be that, on this occasion, the apple itself chose not to follow the rule of falling. Nor can it be the case that the law of gravity, a predicted cause-effect relation, is suspended in such cases (in the way that a law about on-street parking might be suspended on certain days).

How, in practice, can one establish "beyond doubt" (a condition that Smith emphasizes) that an activity — for example, a particular pattern of pronunciations — is rule governed? For Smith, it entailed setting aside occasional exceptions and finding "consistency . . . so great that it was possible to predict with almost complete accuracy what [Amahl's] pronunciation would be for a new word" (1989: 40). But then by these criteria my coffee drinking is undoubtedly rule governed. Setting aside the occasional mid-afternoon aberration, the occasional late-night and always regretted, insomnia-inducing cuppa (that'll teach me not to follow the rule), my coffee drinking is consistently at breakfast and around lunchtime. And it can be predicted with almost complete accuracy that at tomorrow's breakfast I will drink coffee. If to treat this pattern as indicative of rule governedness does not seem very convincing, we are led to consider the possibility that consistency and predictability of behavior does not entail rule governedness; but this is deeply disruptive to prevailing linguistic methods, for which the postulation of rule governedness is a first necessity. It is a first necessity since much of the ensuing discourse and attendant conceptualization of Amahl's developing pronunciation is in terms of rules (or a rule set) replacing rules: it is assumed that the simpler and (by the standards of adult rules for the given phenomena) inaccurate rules of infant pronunciation are displaced over time by more complex and accurate ones, much closer to rules modeling adult pronunciation. At this point, it may be objected that analogizing between coffee drinking and pronunciation on the matter of rule governedness is unjustified, on the grounds that nothing interesting emerges in the case of the "rule" for coffee drinking beyond predicting the future occasions on which it will be reapplied. Whether this is so or not, however (someone involved in the coffee market might see things differently), whether or not we find a particular rule explanatory over a wide domain and capturing an important generalization and so on, is beside the point. The point is whether there are rules here, followed by either the coffee drinker or the language user, at all.

The whole orientation of this outline of the development of Amahl's phonology is subtly normative and adult centered, which is to say prescriptive, notwithstanding the evident assumption that strictly unbiased observation and description are being undertaken. The normativity might be defended as a mere *façon de parler*, a convenient shorthand way of expressing things, but the point is that for Smith's readers this way of speaking can become an entrenched way of looking at language. Thus, for example, Smith (1989) writes: "I had established that [Amahl] always left out a nasal (m, n, or ng) before p, t, and k, hence his pronunciation of 'bank' [bak]" (p. 40). There is no justification, however, except from a normative, adult-centered viewpoint, for claiming that Amahl "left out" nasals in certain clusters. His behavior is simply not on a par with, for example, my always leaving sugar out of my coffee (itself a misleading enough characterization: in parallel fashion, what sense does it make to say that "all over America, every day, millions of people leave cream out of their coffee"?). To characterize the absence of nasals in certain positions where they are expected in certain dialects of adult English as a "leaving out" is presumptive interpretation presented as impartial description.

What can the linguist do to confirm that this is indeed a "leaving out"? He cannot profitably ask his two-and-a-half-year-old son, "You're leaving something out when you say what this is [pointing to a piggy bank or something similar] aren't you?" So he cannot get a straight answer to confirm his hypothesis. What he can do is go round in circles, asking Amahl to say *bank* (answer: [bak]), pointing to the piggy bank and saying, "This is a [bak], isn't it?" (answer from Amahl, angrily, "No! it's a [bak]"). These are circles that many parents have traced. As Smith (1989) notes of a child's nonstandard pronunciation of *fish*: "A child who pronounces this '*fis*' will object to adults pronouncing it the same way but will accept the correct 'fish' unhesitatingly; quite often responding along the lines: 'Yes, "fis" not "*fis*"', indicating clearly that he can appreciate the correct form even while unable to replicate it and being, perhaps, unaware that he is not making the contrast appropriately" (p. 41). Prescriptivism surfaces here, too, depending on how you interpret the formulation *unable to replicate* [*the correct form*], depending in turn on what one means by *the correct form*. It would be more neutral to say, not that the child is unable to replicate [fɪš] as [fɪš], but simply that he doesn't, producing instead [fɪs]. And it is in the context of reference to fish that nonproduction of [fɪš] applies: it may still be the case that elsewhere Amahl does say [fɪš] (just as he says [pʌdəl], but not in the desired context of reference to puddles).

The more neutral and preferred formulation is to the effect that, in such and such circumstances, the child does or does not do x, rather than that she *is unable to/cannot do x*. The less presumptive formulation makes it easier to entertain a different account of affairs, which hypothesizes that children can do a lot more, in the way of discriminating articulation mimicking adult speech, even if this repeatedly fails to show up until a later date in the form-centered language games that their parents play with them. Setting aside other considerations, we might hypothesize that Amahl could possibly replicate [fɪš] where his father wanted it. But the diversity of interests and demands bombarding this situated two-year-old, coming to make sense of the vast range of phenomena around him, seems adequate grounds alone for the fact that he simply does not do so. Getting the pronunciation of *fish* right is not one of his highest priorities, and, although he hears an adult's mispronunciation of it well enough, he has not reached that stage of self-aware self-monitoring at which he might attend to his own aberrant (by adult standards) performance.

Similarly, in a child's encounter with puddles, one of the lower priorities, of no pressing interest, is that the name is pronounced [pʌdəl] not [pʌgəl]. At this stage, Amahl simply isn't terribly interested in some of the phonetic distinctions that adults hold dear.

The mainstream linguistic characterization that Smith's account enunciates represents the child, at such and such a stage, as being unable to produce such and such a sound combination. That emphasis meshes with a larger set of standard linguistic assumptions, including the view that a preschool child spends much of his or her time acquiring, aided by limited experiential input and feedback, a discrete system of rules (his or her native language) and that along the way immature and defective rule systems are internalized, only to be supplanted by more sophisticated ones, increasingly approximating the adult language system. Early child language is thus conceptualized as deficient, and the early years of language use are in effect viewed as therapeutic and reparative, as, allegedly largely on their own (again, the evidence from ambient language is said to be a sketchy, incomplete, inadequate guide to the mature underlying language system), children get themselves up to speed in their native language. With the ideology of deficiency so widely banished from other branches of nonclinical linguistics ("difference, not deficiency" summarizes the preferred view), it is striking to find it persisting within child language studies. A term like *deficiency* (or its paraphrases in the literature: "at this stage the child is unable to . . . but later revises this hypothesis and begins to consistently produce . . .") is inherently comparative: relative to a certain norm or standard, such and such behavior is deficient or lacking. The child's language is conceptualized, to an excessive degree, in terms of difficulties to be overcome: difficulties of attention, articulation, processing, interpretation, and so on, increasingly overcome. This is to conceptualize the child as born with a handicap (namely, not being a fluent speaker of the adult form of the ambient language), a handicap rapidly overcome thanks to the incalculable boost of innate linguistic structure-constraining principles. The dimension of difficulty and implied handicap is focused on to the neglect of other considerations. An analogous mistake is to conceptualize the deaf child as, first and foremost, handicapped by his or her lack of access to spoken language and to conclude that the highest priority must therefore be given to the work of training the child in lip reading and producing recognizable speech. In contrast to those assumptions is the emphasis that, in a sympathetic environment, the behavior of all normal children, hearing or deaf, gives copious evidence of triumphs of intelligence and ability overshadowing local difficulties. The deaf child inducted into American Sign Language, harnessing his or her enhanced visual and spatial acuity, becomes linguistically proficient as rapidly as the speaking child, inducted into spoken language. What chiefly characterizes the advance of both deaf and hearing children is not disability gradually overcome but ability increasingly harnessed to a complex and expanding social world.

Smith's account continues as follows: "If perception is not an explanation for the child's divergences from the adult norm, and productive difficulty is only a very partial explanation, we still have to account for Amahl's failure to pronounce 'puddle' correctly given that he could say '*puddle*' for 'puzzle'. I assumed on the basis of the kind of evidence already mentioned that his representations of the words of his language were equivalent to the forms he heard from the adults around him, and that he mapped these representations onto his own pronunciation via a series of rules" (Smith 1989: 42). Thus, Smith is drawn to postulate that Amahl must be following certain rules, which have the effect of deflecting the child's speech away from the recognized adult model. Amahl apparently does not fail to perceive that [blu:] was the adult pronunciation of *blue*; nor does he have any apparent problems interpreting the phonetic detail of the adult pronunciations around him (thus he knew that adults were supposed to pronounce *jump* with a final labial consonant cluster, not just [p], and so on). In short:

1. There's nothing wrong with the input, or with Amahl's grasp of the input.

2. Nonstandardism in Amahl's output ([dʌp] for *jump*, [pʌgəl] for *puddle*, etc.) can be only partially explained along lines of articulatory difficulty (as perhaps for glides and sibilants, particularly in clusters).

3. So Amahl must have some rules — some automatically degenerating device — for converting correct (adult-like) stored items into Amahl-speak.

An example of the kind of rule that Smith assumes Amahl must have formulated is given informally below:

2. A rule eliminating consonant clusters in the child's speech by getting rid of "l, r, y" after another consonant. For example:

blue → *boo* [bu:]
green → *geen* [gi:n]
new → *noo* [nu:] (Smith 1989: 42)

But where did these rules come from; on the basis of hypotheses wrought from what data were they formulated? For, as noted, Smith believes there to be no glaring problems with the data available to Amahl (his caregivers do not go around saying [bu:] for *blue*, etc.). Nor, more to the point, is there anything amiss in Amahl's grasp of that data: he *knows* that *blue* is pronounced [blu:], even if in his own productions it keeps coming out [bu:]. This is a fascinating conundrum, which appeal to stored rules hardly explains adequately, but it should be noted to Smith's credit that his acknowledgment of the adequacy of both the input and Amahl's grasp of adult patterns of consonant + approximant pronunciations highlights the conundrum. By contrast with Smith's account, other generativist analysts of child language are usually — as noted in chapter 5 — keen to emphasize the degeneracy and insufficiency of the linguistic experiences available to the child. For many generativists, the child is akin to a little (untrained, nonliterate) anthropological linguist, genetically primed with the broad pattern for all languages, sorting out the system of the ambient language better and better as she or he goes along; but in sorting out the system, they contend, the child must transcend the inadequacies and gaps in the "database" constituted by the language they actually encounter. This is the "poverty of the stimulus" thesis, which in fact Smith subscribes to elsewhere in his book. Thus, for truly orthodox generativist psycholinguists, the child's early allegedly defective productions are partly explicable as "garbage input, garbage output." Smith cannot avail himself of such a facile solution to his own conundrum since he has made it clear that Amahl has received nondegenerative input and furthermore is perfectly able to detect and reject garbage input when he hears it.

One question to ask about rule 2 above and other rules that Smith lists (e.g., alveolars pronounced as [g] when a velar occurs later in the same word: *doggie* pronounced [gɔgi:]) concerns how typical just these phonetic difficulties or blind spots are. I suggest that phonetic divergences of just these kinds are very common among children learning English as a first language, without interference from other languages, but that there is no strong likelihood that adults learning English will make the same kinds of so-called mistakes. Whatever other errors of production the adult learner of English perpetrates, it is highly improbable that he or she will pronounce *doggie* as [gɔgi:], *bank* as [bak]. The case of *fish* mispronounced as [fɪs] is different, however, and may arise in adult learners' English as well as that of native-language-developing children. Thus, the claim is not that there is no overlap between the specific kinds of phonetic errors in adult learners' English and the kinds of nonadult productions of child native-speaker learners; on the contrary, there should be a considerable degree of overlap — in all those areas involving greater difficulty in articulation. Hence, the intermediate status of [fiš] versus [fɪs]: speakers from some language backgrounds, where [š] is not a standard segment but [s] is, will lack training in the use of [š] and may tend to "slip" back to producing [fɪs]. But the point to consider is the fact that there is not total overlap, that, setting aside articulation hurdles that both groups must clear, there are "mispronunciations" like [gɔgiː] that never show up in foreign learners' English. Why should this be so?

Let us focus on just one of Smith's rules for Amahl's nonstandard English, rule 2 quoted above, which states that initial clusters comprising a cluster and one of the approximants have, as a counterpart in Amahl's speech, the first consonant alone (putting it in this way avoids talk of "eliminating," as in Smith's formulation, deletion, reduction, or other question-begging descriptions). Thus, in addition to the examples cited above ([buː] for *blue* etc.), we can predict, from the rule or pattern, that Amahl says [ten] for *train*, [fuː] for *few*, and [bɪk] for *blink* (here another pattern is also involved, by which Amahl produces, in place of standard coda clusters of a nasal plus /p/, /t/, or /k/, the voiceless stop alone). It may be noted in passing that the fourth approximant /w/, is not mentioned in this rule. Does Amahl say [twɪn] for *twin* or [tɪn]? It may be that, like Timothy Shopen's son Paul, his productions here are a mixture of standard and nonstandard, depending on the preceding consonant. Two-year-old Paul pronounced *quick* and *quack* correctly, that is, with [kw-], but pronounced *twig* as [tɪk] (see Ohio State University Linguistics Department 1987: 236). We should note here, too, the findings of Coppieters (1987), who found that two groups of French speakers, one native speakers, the other nonnatives with native-like proficiency, differed markedly in their interpretations of certain important grammatical contrasts (both the groups also differed internally, to some degree, in their judgments: there was no single native-speaker set of judgments on the tests). One of Coppieters observations is germane here: "In some sense, these contrasts may still reflect the contextually rich environment in which they were initially learned. No matter how close to child language acquisition one conceives adult SLA [Second Language Acquisition] to be, it would seem rather implausible that the initial unanalysed stages of child language acquisition would be duplicated by the adult learner" (p. 569).

The question is, why is just this pattern (of absence of the approximants from syllable onset clusters), this systematic discrepancy with standard adult English, so widespread in the speech of children learning English natively (and rather different dialects of English at that) and yet missing from the interlanguages of adult learners — even when other patterns of discrepancy are in fact common across the speech of native-, second-, and foreign-language learners? The evidence points to there being rather different causes for the kind of production that does without approximants in initial clusters (the children's production) and the kind of production, by foreign learners, that may make other kinds of errors, but not this one. For one thing, we have no hesitation in calling all such divergent productions, by adult learners, *errors*; it is far less reasonable to use the same term of a two-year-old's productions. Relatedly, the adult learner is assumed to have been *taught*, or to have consciously attempted to learn, the standard pronunciation of the words they mispronounce. By and large, the entire process of an adult learning English as a foreign language (i.e., formally: matters may be more confused in the case of learning English as a second language) tends to be profoundly metalinguistic: whether in classrooms, or in language labs, or by imitation or role-play or immersion or direct or communicative or any other method, this is never the same thing as growing up, discovering the world and one's place in it, aided by one's first language (here English), which is integral to the acts of discovery and constitution of world and self. Amahl is learning to be an English-speaking person (but learning in its broadest sense, as, when I take my children for a walk around Green Lake, they are learning to take walks around lakes); the adult foreign student, by contrast, is a person learning to speak English.

Some years after first publishing his analyses of Amahl's developing phonology, Smith revised his views and adopted the view that varying perceptual discrimination was in part the cause of some of Amahl's speech patterns. On the basis of a reanalysis of the data by Macken (1980), Smith concluded that the factors contributing to Amahl's speech forms were more complicated than he had earlier assumed. The evidence that prompted this reanalysis included Amahl's contrasts in production of what, in adult speech, would be nasal clusters: for example, Amahl pronounced *meant* as [met] while pronouncing *mend* as [men]. [e] denotes the vowel in standard pronunciations of, for example, *red* and *neck*. Why, if the [d] is "dropped" after a nasal as predicted by the rules for Amahl's speech, is the [t] not "dropped" also, and why is the [n] here "dropped instead"? Smith accepts Macken's argument that perceptual salience is the cause: the nasal in [ment] is "relatively inaudible," while the following [t] may be articulatorily and auditorily prominent; the [n] in [mend] by contrast is longer and more prominent, hence is perceived and stored while this final [d] is dropped. Additionally, while Amahl's pronunciation of *puddle* as [pʌgəl] could be explained by a generalizing rule (that alveolars like [d] become velars like [g] when followed by "dark" /l/), his pronunciation of *pickle* didn't seem to fit the rules so far formulated, for *pickle* was sometimes pronounced [pɪtəl]: "For words like 'pickle', however, there was no rule converting the velar 'ck' to anything else at all. Crucially, though, he sometimes mispronounced it as 'pittle' [pɪTəl], making it clear that his mental representation was not the same as the adult form, presumably because he had misperceived that form. Accordingly, it was necessary to complicate my analysis by including some kind of 'perceptual filter' between the adult's pronunciation and the form the child set up as his mental representation of the words of his language" (1989: 46).

Before contemplating the perceptual filter, it is worth noting the wrenching of the argument in the second sentence; after citing numerous examples of Amahl's nonstandard utterances and invariably attributing them to the application of some conversion rule operating on an adult-style mental representation, suddenly [pɪTəl] puts the linguist all in a pickle. None of the extant rules copes with [pɪTəl]; accordingly, the following putative explanations may be considered:

1. [pɪTəl] can be dismissed as an aberration, as an exception proving the rule.
2. Some further rule could be devised, suggesting that [k] preceded by a front vowel and followed by dark [l] sometimes gets reproduced as [t].
3. Some other level of interpretation and mediation between the input and the output, between what the child encounters and what he produces, can be postulated.

From outside an orientation bent on "capture" of the mechanisms allegedly operating on what a child hears and knows, so as to determine the form of what he subsequently produces, responses 1 and 2 appear far simpler routes. But, from inside a rule-oriented paradigm, they just won't do: from within that paradigm, one by definition requires rules, and furthermore one wants good rules (i.e., powerfully generalizing, intuitively satisfying, etc.). Responses 1 and 2 are therefore unacceptable: 1 says there's no rule here; 2 offers only a weak and local rule, little more than a description. The rule-addicted analyst is induced to take the extravagant third option, postulating a perceptual filter; the crucial consequence of this, for the theory, is that it is no longer claimed — as it was before — that the child '"stores" representations of adult phonology that become "flawed" at the output stage of pronunciation. Now, the stored representation itself is assumed to be "flawed," having refracted the heard input through immature or otherwise imperfect perceptual filters. The theoretical stages in the revised account may be set out in summary as follows (from Smith 1989: 47):

> Adult Pronunciation

is passed through a perceptual filter to give

> Child's Mental Representation

which is then converted by a slightly smaller set of rules to give

> Child's Pronunciation

Although Smith sees this as an advance on the earlier account, two related observations are worth recording. First, for the rule oriented, a rule by any other name works just as well. Specifically, although perception need not necessarily be so conceived, it seems clear that Smith and Macken understand the perceptual filter as some kind of interpretive processing of input that works in an entirely similar fashion to the rules on output: the filter is in short another layer of rules. In lay parlance, a filter usually connotes a simple +/− device for preventing the transit of either the + or the − property (particles of certain size, metals of a certain composition, light of certain wavelengths). The perceptual filter, however (and this is the second point), will have to be rather more complex and in fact comprise a number of filters. Accordingly, the revision of Smith's model has the effect of supplanting one layer of uninspectable hypothesized mechanics with two layers of uninspectable mechanics. The skeptic may be inclined to say that an analysis that requires two such levels of transformation, so as to account for the transition from *pickle* to [pɪTəl], has resorted to an extraordinarily overbuilt model that flies in the face of criteria of psychological plausibility.

We have seen first the postulation of a set of output rules whose ontological status is controversial, then, on the basis of the failure of those rules to handle certain data, the postulation of a further level of perceptual filtering, also arguably ill motivated. An appeal to perception phenomena is designed to enable the rule oriented account to work for a larger range of data; ironically, it strengthens the doubt whether a model of production as rule driven is needed at all. To reintroduce perception factors into the picture is to reintroduce the language learner, as situated processor of the linguistic evidence in which he or she is immersed; and, if we take seriously the individual's rational, reflective, analogizing, interest-prioritizing, salience-assessing processing of observed language, it may be possible to dispense with the machinery of freestanding rules altogether (in this regard, see MacWhinney et al. [1989], a connectionist account of morphology acquisition, based on numerous learned cues rather than innate rules or algorithms). Nor, thereafter, will it be necessary to elaborate the model further so as to cope with the fact that in Amahl's speech *pickle* sometimes comes out as [pɪTəl] and at other times comes out just fine, as [pɪkəl].

Experiential Salience

Taking perception and salience seriously in a theory of child language involves invoking a more powerfully comprehensive criterion than perceptual salience. A beginning may be made by hypothesizing that a child's speech patterns will reflect his or her developing and revisable assessments of experiential or interactional salience. Significantly, in their careful reanalysis of influential proposed explanations for specific kinds of phonological and morphological development in children's acquisition of language, Wanner and Gleitman (1982: 3–48) place much emphasis on principles of salience. In particular, they argue for the salience, in the acquisition of stress-accent languages, of that material that is carried in stressed syllables. Always in specific contexts of linguistic activity, a child's assessments of interactional salience constitute the situated answer to the following unstated question: What things are there that must — *as priorities* — be displayed in one's spoken contributions to particular interactions so that one may be understood and enable one's larger purposes to be achieved? Along these lines, an alternative to Macken's "perceptual salience" explanation of Amahl's saying [met] for *meant* but [men] for *mend* may be proposed. The contrasting productions may have more to do with the interactionally salient fact that the pronounced final [t] in the utterance of *meant* is salient in a wider lexicogrammatical sense.

To see this it first needs to be noted that a child saying [met] where adults say [ment] is no linguistic beginner; in using the form appropriately in context, Amahl evidently knows that the word carries nonpresent time reference; that is, the child has some notion of tense marking and even knows to say [ment], not [mi:nd], when using this irregular verb. Among other things, then, Amahl's use of the [e] vowel here strongly suggests that he has some grasp of the fact that the verb has an irregular pattern. On this irregular verb, the final segment is a grammatical suffix, part of the past-tense or participle making of the verb. Although [mend] (for *mend*) may also be tensed, the final [d] is not a criterial contrastive marker of that lexicogrammatical information in a parallel way: it is not lexicogrammatically salient in the way that the final [t] of [met] is. It would be useful to know what Amahl said as the past-tense form of *mend*; but whether he said [mendɪd] or [menɪd] (and I am assuming that one of just these two options was his choice) is relatively unimportant: the choice has no major consequences in terms of interactional clarity and effectiveness since either one can be interpreted unproblematically as "Amahl's counterpart for what adults pronounce [mendɪd]." (Incidentally, it may be noted that, for *mended*, in nonformal speech a great many American English speakers say a sequence with nasal release in the medial cluster, thus more closely approximating the transcription [menɪd] than [mendɪd] — seemingly aware, in a parallel way, of the nonsalience of the variation.) By contrast, at this stage in his incremental development of the patterns of English, for Amahl to have settled on [men] or [mi:nt] as an adequately clear and effective utterance of the past form of *mean* would make little sense, for here is a child who has evidently already adopted the community's subtle pattern within which, while most past-time reference verbs simply have an alveolar oral stop added to them, some frequently used verbs do not. (The patterns that are subsidiary to the use of an alveolar stop, such as +/− voice and insertion of a vowel where the final sound in the present-time verb is also an alveolar stop, are similarly explicable in terms of their contribution to articulatory and auditory salience.)

Two further points may be made. First, the argument in terms of interactional salience is not a version of the thesis that utterances of different words will be phonetically distinct to the extent that this is needed to disambiguate matters for some reasonably competent listener. A competent listener may have little difficulty in paraphrasing a particular contextualized remark from Amahl as "He really meant it" irrespective of whether Amahl actually said [hi:wi:lɪmenɪʔ], or [hi:wi:lɪmi:ndɪʔ], or something else besides. Whatever the listener can or cannot rapidly make sense of, it is Amahl's assessments that are the basis for the forms that his own utterances take — informed, no doubt, by the feedback he gets from his interlocutors, whose responses may show him which of his utterances are for them clear, effective, and unproblematic. Relatedly, what count as clear and effective utterances is not an issue that admits of a single logical answer. It is not particularly logical to adopt [ment] as the past-time-reference utterance of *mean*. Adopting the pattern of adding, say, [Id] to present-time verb forms, for all past-reference uses of verbs, might seem clearer and more effective; it would not, however, match the patterns used by the vast majority of one's fellow speakers.

The second point is that to account for the emerging patterns in a child's language development in terms of interactional salience amounts to an account that places proper weight on the question of relevance. As indicated in chapter 5, there is considerable congruence between an integrational outlook and the Gricean view that relevance is a foundational assumption, and thus a basis for implicature, in everyday interaction. Amahl's assessment that, in the circumstances, and relative to the other interactional patterns he has adopted, [met] is adequately salient is in effect his assessment of the articulatory effort that suffices (is most appropriate) to help secure the contextual effects that he intends his interlocutors to derive. Sperber and Wilson's terminology of effort and effects may thus be retained, but it is used here without reference to uninspectable postulates such as implicitly measurable processing effort. The kind of effort that an integrational understanding of relevance will countenance considering must be of an inspectable, specifiable kind, such as the articulatory effort involved in saying [met]; and that effort is to be understood not merely in relation to opting for one form from among such articulatorily similar options as [ment] or [mi:nd] but also in relation to the option of saying nothing at all.

Further conceptual difficulties for standard linguistics are posed by one of the questions that its rule orientedness provokes, namely, how speech-production rules change. How, in practice, can the child amend a rule — a governing instruction quasi-automatically followed — in favor of some preferred formula? Rule revision is clear enough in the case of the second graders and their rule concerning leaving the classroom: this is a learned rule, in the public domain, and the children can lobby for its revision, or the teacher can announce that he or she has changed it, or there can be discussion concluding in a change in the public contractual arrangement, and so on. But, in the case of Amahl's postulated internal rules, how is it possible for Amahl to assess and revise them *as rules*? There are no inherent difficulties with the idea that in his speech productions Amahl unconsciously but rationally constructs and observes working hypotheses (e.g., about how to pronounce what are in adult speech consonant clusters in syllable onsets) and that his speech productions will change over time as he equally unconsciously and rationally alters those working hypotheses, those *modi loquendi*. Even here, however, what actually happens is that Amahl continues to speak over time in ways that accord with the kinds of pattern recognitions that, at a remove, we can call working hypotheses about consonant-cluster production; there is no need to assume that the child, at any level of mental awareness, has a sense of the patterns and systematicities his speaking seems to disclose. If allusions to "working hypotheses" must be thus qualified, how much more so must be descriptions in terms of "rule following." At this early age, there is no possibility of Amahl formulating, testing, and revising a rule about his speech — a rule that, furthermore, is supposed to *govern* the productions that are supposed simultaneously to constitute evidence, when compared to adult speakers' performance, for the rule's inaccuracy and inadequacy. The distinction here, between the activity of following a rule and that of unconsciously developing a hypothesis, is absolutely crucial. As Hacker, whose views are discussed in the next section, puts the matter: "Rules are not explanatory hypotheses about behaviour. One cannot construct theories of rules to explain behaviour that is rule-governed. For the rule-governed behaviour is internally related to the rules that determine it as correct or incorrect, and determination of an internal relation is not a matter of hypothesis construction" (Hacker 1988: 165). To attempt to combine the idea of explanatory hypothesis formulation and the idea of rule following in one's theory of language is to attempt to combine chalk and cheese. One must be rejected.

Hacker on Rules in Language

Hacker (1988) vehemently rejects the mystification, as he sees it, of cognitive linguistic theories of language acquisition: although language acquisition is wonderful — like the ability to draw, with great skill, even things we have never seen — it is not, as most linguists and philosophers imply, a profound mystery. For Hacker, rules are human creations, not found in nature: rules in jobs, fashion, etiquette, driving, the law, are "standards of conduct" that provide "norms of correctness" (p. 162). Rules are distinct from formulations of rules (in a language). A rule formulation is a prescription or stipulation, not a description, of some behavior. And rule-governed behavior is more than merely regular behavior: "For a creature to follow a rule he must act in a way that accords with a rule and intend his action to accord with the rule. . . . For conduct to constitute the following of a rule, the formulation of the rule need not play a part in the antecedents of the action, either physically (by being looked up or consulted) or mentally (by being thought of). But reference to the rule must be involved in any explanation or justification of the act which the agent gives if asked. Otherwise the action is merely an instance of accord with a rule" (p. 163).

Relatedly, rules are used in normative activities that are part of the standard background to rule-governed behavior. Thus, novices are trained or taught what is and is not in accord with the rules; rules may "advise" us, where we specifically consult some formulation of them for guidance; rules often provide a justification for an agent acting in a certain way; and they provide, for the spectator, an explanation of that same action. They also constitute standards by which to evaluate actions; hence they define actions — whether in chess or in law, they define what count as valid procedures (for castling or getting divorced). And, if all the above are typical characteristics of rules, then a host of principles, patterns, and mechanisms discussed in linguistics — from the phrase-structure rule for expanding the VP, to the affix-hopping rule, to nasalization and vowel-lengthening rules, to the complex-NP constraint, C-command, and the empty category principle — are not rules at all. Hacker argues that nothing can then be said to be (the expression of) a rule unless it is *used* as a rule, for example, as a guide to action, part of the rationale for acting in a certain way. Rules must always be at least implicit — often they are explicit — and potentially invocable in relation to some activity if they are to be said to govern that activity; and to know a rule entails knowing what counts as following it.

In summary, rules in language behavior are always possible so long as these are not conceptualized as generative rules, that is, devices that automatically and mechanically produce whatever behavior, in language, is said to be rule bound. We can observe and follow rules in our language practice, but we do not automatically do things linguistically that can be said to be rule bound or rule driven. You cannot automatically follow a rule, no more than apples automatically follow or observe a rule of gravity when they fall from trees. That which is automatic is not rule guided; that which is rule bound cannot be automatic. In the case of the apples, gravity is not a rule to be followed at all but a scientific principle (*principle* is a less misleading a description than *law*) describing what, other things being equal, the motion or behavior of objects must (in the epistemic sense) be. After the fact, we may say that objects behave in a way that conforms to and confirms the equally post hoc formulation of a "law" of gravity.

It is from within the foregoing orientation that strong exception is taken to claims such as the following, in Chomsky (1988: 35): "The language faculty selects relevant data from the events taking place in the environment; making use of these data in a manner determined by its internal structure, the child constructs a language, [here] Spanish.... This language is now incorporated in the mind. When the process is completed, the language constitutes the mature state attained by the language faculty. The person now speaks and understands the language." The particular objection is to the purposive characterization here afforded the language faculty: "A child who does not yet speak a language cannot *select data* for the purpose of theory construction" (Hacker 1988: 138).

One of the more compelling arguments for that part of the generativist account of language that says that the individual is innately endowed with an extensive knowledge of a language in the mind-brain, a mental representation that in turn can be represented in the form of rules (or parameterized principles), emerges from consideration of people afflicted with aphasia. Aphasics are those who briefly or for a long time apparently lose the ability to use their native language but who may subsequently and rapidly recover that ability. Surely, generativists have argued, the nature of this loss and recovery makes it reasonable to infer that such aphasics must have retained an inner competence, a knowledge of language, even though they temporarily lose the ability to apply this knowledge (in performance)? And surely this is strong evidence against the anti-innatist insistence that knowledge of language and linguistic ability are one and the same, multifaceted, learned know-how?

In response to this, Hacker (1990) suggests that, although we employ "pictures" of retention to describe the situations of aphasics and amnesiacs, who temporarily forget or fail to speak coherently, only perhaps to recover those abilities later (without learning anew), still memory and knowledge, respectively, really are lost in the two kinds of disorder. We speak about what is really a regaining as if it were a retaining. More fully, what are really experiences of loss and regaining are misleadingly alluded to as difficulties of "accessing" what is underlyingly retained. Yet, if the fundamentals are indeed retained intact, as the latter "language picture" suggests, doesn't this downgrade aphasia and amnesia, as afflictions, to the level of merely motoric or production disorders, albeit very complex ones? Consider, as just one instance of the general assumption, the following remarks in an influential linguistics textbook: "There is much evidence from aphasia studies to support the distinction that has been made between linguistic competence and linguistic performance.... [In some patients, whose production and comprehension abilities fluctuate from normal to impaired from day to day] the linguistic knowledge must still exist in the mental grammar of these patients, although their ability to access it reveals performance difficulties" (Fromkin and Rodman 1988: 406). The misleading picture, of competence retention, promotes the impression that aphasia is a physiological disorder (failure to "get language out") but not a neurological one, for, it is asserted, the language faculty sits undamaged and waiting to be used, in the cortex. The verb *sits* is used advisedly, for Hacker relatedly suggests that the idea of "regaining" one's linguistic knowledge/ability seems more puzzling to us than it really is since the Chomskyan tendency is to conceptualize that knowledge as a state when the knowledge/ability involved cannot possibly be a state; instead, to know or have a certain ability is to be able, potentially, to perform some particular activities (e.g., speak fluent English, play chess) that count as conclusive proof of having that ability. "Recovering from amnesia or aphasia is not recollecting something one had forgotten, but regaining a faculty one had lost" (Hacker 1990: 134). The dispute can be seen as one between those (e.g., generativist linguists) who characterize fluency in a language as knowledge (in the specialized sense of mastered and internalized rules concerning structures and grammaticality) and those who characterize language fluency as an ability. Interestingly, Cooper (1975: 33ff.) suggests that Chomsky's term *competence* tends to give rise to a confusion of those quite distinct factors. By all established standards, *competence* implies ability or, more precisely "ability under specific or reasonable conditions"; but in fact Chomsky (1965: 4) intends *competence* to denote a speaker's knowledge of their language, via mastery of the underlying system of rules. Thus, the keyword *competence*, drawing on the received usage of the term, suggests that conditional ability is being addressed when something unconditional and much more cognitively represented — knowledge — is intended.

At this point, however, even those sympathetic to Hacker's broad orientation may have misgivings. Even if we concur that recovering from aphasia is "regaining a faculty one had lost," still the question remains whether recovery entails regaining everything necessary for nonaphasic linguistic performance or only those parts temporarily lost, for, if only the lost or damaged components need to be actively regained, then linguists seem entitled to claim that the other contributory linguistic components were indeed retained all along. Clearly, this line of argument involves a theoretical division, into parts, of what enables the whole called *linguistic performance*; and from Hacker's public holist perspective such an analytic strategy, invoking parts of wholes, is anathema: in Hacker's view, only language behavior viewed in its wholeness makes sense. Even if such holism were to be accepted, however, other misgivings would remain. While, in comtemplating recovery from aphasia, it is important to emphasize anew the idea of regaining a faculty as opposed to reactivating or hooking up a dormant module, still Hacker's argument is somewhat strained. At base, this is a rejection of a particular influential conception of linguistic knowledge, namely, as something recorded in the mind/brain in some symbolism or other.

In any event, Hacker's insistence on aphasics' "regaining not retaining" is not needed in order to counter the generativist assumptions about aphasics' retention of "knowledge of language" while failing to display, in any External language, fluent performance ability. To counter that view, it need be shown only that whatever abilities in the language an aphasic has but cannot, for a period, draw on are not innate or genetically predetermined, are not a unitary competence, and, particularly, are not a language faculty of the exorbitant kind. By *a language faculty of the exorbitant kind* I mean one with not only extensive syntax information hardwired but even a conceptual apparatus to which labels—that is, the vocabulary of an External language— simply need to be "attached" (see Chomsky 1988: 27ff.). On some of the relevant issues here, see the arguments presented in Schnitzer (1990).

Part of the attraction of rule systems, for most linguists, must relate to another assumption of standard linguistic thinking, namely, that speech is ordinarily in need of processing or interpreting, by the addressee, in order to be made sense of. That processing or interpreting is conceptualized as a stage, in a circuit, at which incoming sound is "unscrambled" via implementation of a set of decoding rules; this set of interpretive rules is one of the "things" that someone ignorant of the language being spoken lacks. To this Hacker responds: "It is a grievous error to think that in understanding an utterance one always or even usually engages in interpretation.... Obscurities, ambiguities or complexities may call out for an interpretation, but it would be wholly incoherent to think that all understanding is interpreting" (1988: 168). One of the proposals that postulates "rules for decoding" has come from Fodor (1975) and is to the effect that processing heard speech is a matter of translating it into the "language of thought." Yet it seems clear that interpretation (in the sense of a processing) of utterances must be the exception, not the rule, if everyday practice is anything to go by. Any hypothesis, of the Fodorian kind or otherwise, that situated speech is automatically and routinely subjected to a process of hearer-internal decoding is essentially premised on the idea that every utterance we hear (significantly, not just some) is in need of translation of paraphrase in order for it to be understood. But, as Hacker observes, if every utterance stands in need of sense-making paraphrase, then those paraphrases themselves will stand in need of sense-making paraphrase, with infinite regress. This follows from the premise that no utterance is "completely" understood (cf. the related arguments surrounding "complete" and "incomplete" sentences discussed in chapters 4 and 6) unless and until it is subjected to a process of interpretive translation, for that premise will apply as comprehensively to the products of the translation process as to the antecedents. The Fodorian defense at this point would be to claim that "the language of thought" is qualitatively different from external language and the latter's need of interpretation, that "the language of thought" is neither the kind of language that is in need of paraphrase nor perhaps even the kind that allows it as a possibility. But then what kind of language can such a "language of thought" be if it lacks paraphrasability? If the "language of thought" notion can be protected only by such manipulation of its own metaphoric core, its explanatory potential becomes deeply suspect.

There seem to be good grounds, in everyday experience, for rejecting the assumption that utterances are invariably in need of complex rule-governed processing on the part of their hearer. This does not, however, justify the contrasting assumption, that utterances are almost invariably easy to understand. Some instances of seemingly noncomputational or noninterpretative language use may be discounted on the grounds that they are the most banal and routine cases of literal language use, often revolving around understanding and showing understanding of such utterances as the question "Is the door shut?" or the directive "Shut the door, please." But as soon as context is specified more fully and utterances are considered that do not bring with them a powerfully preferred normative understanding, the question of how speech events are understood becomes more interesting. An example of such a more interpretively open case might be that of someone newly arrived in a room asking the group already in occupation "Was the door open when you arrived?" The speaker might, inter alia, be intending the utterance to play a part in a rebuke of the group, or in an offer to close the door, or in quite other kinds of act.

It seems possible to identify a tendency in Hacker's various critiques of linguistic theory (Baker and Hacker 1984; Hacker 1988, 1990), a tendency to emphasize that playing public language games is characteristically unproblematic. This in turn seems symptomatic of what may be called an "accentuating of the normative" in some Wittgensteinian philosophers of language. As noted in chapter 4, this is related to a rather more limited view of the potential semiotic creativity of the individual than is warranted. Hacker banishes mental rules only to reinstate a rather comprehensive set of public language rules, and this leads him to be considerably more resistant to a recent proposal from Donald Davidson than an integrational linguistics need be.

Davidsonian Concurrence: Global or Local?

Quite the opposite of a rule-governed theory of language and interpretation is espoused in Davidson (1986), who reflects on how it is that we are able to interpret successfully such malapropisms as those in Mrs. Malaprop's famous phrase, "a nice derangement of epitaphs." It is implausible to say that the sense-making involves following an antecedently given rule, which has the malapropism as one possible input and "a nice arrangement of epithets" as one possible output. Our ability to interpret the saying of "a nice derangement of epitaphs" as an unintended garbled production of "a nice arrangement of epithets," without benefit of any antecedent theory to effect such an "interpretation" (in the sense of a theory as an automatic and systematic interpreting mechanism), suggests that a priori shared knowledge of a theory of meaning common to speakers of the language is not in itself sufficient. Rather, Davidson says, a speaker or hearer must in addition have a "passing theory" about the interlocutor's theory of interpretation as local grounds for believing that the interlocutor will interpret them as they mean him to do.

Perhaps Davidson rather swiftly proceeds from the example to the idea that no antecedent theory guides our interpretation of the malapropism, for undoubtedly some hypotheses (not "automatic rules") are likely to be adduced in the search for sense and relevance in the circumstances of someone saying "a nice derangement of epitaphs." Two of the circumstances undoubtedly helpful here, even for someone encountering the utterance in Sheridan's work for the first time, are that the phrase occurs in a comic play and comes from a character named *Malaprop*. Additionally, some working hypotheses or rules of thumb may well be applied to the locution. One, for example, is the notion that scatterbrains and verbal climbers are often represented as scrambling their utterances in their efforts to impress their interlocutors. Normally, such scramblings are thus of arcane or sophisticated vocabulary items, which constitute targets "missed" in the linguistic production; typically, phonological substitutions occur to any parts of a word except the most heavily stressed syllable, which usually remains intact. Thus, reflecting the first of these conditions, Mrs. Malaprop scrambles *arrangement* and *epithets* but could scarcely scramble such a routine word as *nice*; and, in line with the second of these conditions, she turns *arrangement* into *derangement* but would be unlikely to convert it to *arraignment*, *amendment*, or *assignment*. These conditions or pointers help "decode" other celebrated paraphasias from Mrs. Malaprop —

An alleg*ory* on the banks of the Nile . . .
If I *re*prehend any thing in this world, it is the use of my *or*acular tongue . . .

— but it is doubtful whether they or any other pointers that might be formulated will invariably apply to all kinds of malapropisms (e.g., *beresk*, discussed below). In that such general schematic prejudgings and context-related clues and rules of thumb are used in recovering an intended saying from an incongruous said, it would seem that the relation between "a nice derangement of epitaphs" and "a nice arrangement of epithets" is not arbitrary even if it is also not determinately rule governed. It should also be noted that many psycholinguists view Mrs. Malaprop's malapropisms as implausible and unrepresentative of natural ones. Certainly, Mrs. Malaprop's errors are a different phenomenon from everyday slips of the tongue: while the distracted adult speaker who says "Did you manage to buy some toothache?" (Aitchison 1987b: 247) would be able to self-correct to *toothpaste* if questioned, we have no reason to believe that Mrs. Malaprop could correct her *derangement* or *oracular* in the same way. But then saying *toothache* for *toothpaste* is not a malapropism at all. Closer to Mrs. Malaprop is the child who talks of taking "an antelope if you swallow poison" (antidote) or of learning to play the "elbow" (oboe) (Aitchison 1987b: 257).

As an account of how an interpreter copes with malapropism, then, Davidson's discussion perhaps moves too fast from the ludicrous malapropism to the meaning that the interpreter assumes to have been intended: in fact, Mrs. Malaprop says (and so appears to mean) something quite vivid and arresting (about deranged epitaphs or the causing of epitaphs to be deranged) that we cannot logically bypass; the vivid description of deranged epitaphs interacts, for the hearer, with the more pedestrian assumed-to-be-intended one. And it is striking that, in the face of malapropisms and the retrievable counterpart target expressions (the status of these utterances as malapropisms is in fact contingent on the retrievability of such missed targets), talk of interactionism and echoism seems absolutely indispensable. That talk of interactionism and echoism seems required here is all the more striking since characterizations of metaphor and irony as essentially of that nature (as interactionist and as echoic, respectively) were expressly rejected in chapters 2 and 5.

The interactionist and echoic nature of malapropism is vividly displayed in an instance of the art reported by Ricks (1990), who recounts how, on a certain occasion of acute marital disharmony, he vented his anger by smashing several windows in the conservatory. Shocked by this violence, his spouse summoned the police. To his surprise, Ricks found that the constable who called was not critical of him, was deferential rather, and confided to him as follows: "You must sympathize with us, sir. . . . We get a 'phone-call, sir, telling us that someone has gone beresk." Ricks confesses that, for him at least, and at a Wordsworthian stroke, spousal strife shrank into the wings: "Beresk! My heart leapt up when I beheld this rainbow in the night sky. . . . Beresk! Bereft, burlesque, grotesque, and berserk as I had become, beresk was exactly what I had gone" (1990: 461). Clearly, without the echoes of *bereft* etc. — and not merely *berserk* — for Ricks to recall and assay in interaction with the malapropism, his heart would surely not have leapt so. Ricks's real-life bobby and Sheridan's comic character perpetrate different kinds of verbal aberration. The likely pronunciation of *beresk* is so unlike that of *berserk* that here one is tempted to put it down to a correctly remembered misreading of the written word, with the remembered misreading giving rise to a mispronunciation.

Despite these qualifications, Davidson's point that neither extant knowledge nor antecedent rules can suffice for the unscrambling of unforeseen deviations in performance, or paraphasia, is hard to deny. His larger argument here is of the greatest importance. Its essence is that prior theories of interpretation (which we might have assumed were shared and convention-governed theories) are always potentially in need of supplementation by ad hoc, for-the-nonce, contingent or passing theories. In view of how the speaker of such nonhabitual language relies so heavily on the suppleness of an addressee's spontaneous passing theory, there is some justification for describing such a speaker as "getting away with it," as Davidson puts it (1986: 440). Such passing theories are always potentially necessary, so that we can successfully interpret — as in fact we do — unforeseen departures from habitual language in malaprops, metaphors, irony, child language, dysphasia, and poetry.

Indeed, Davidson goes on to suggest that passing-theory interpretation is involved even in routine everyday instances ("We do not need bizarre anecdotes or wonderlands to make the point" [1986: 440]), but Dummett's response to this suggestion (Dummett 1986) seems well-founded. Applying the Wittgensteinian distinction between *Auffassung* (way of grasping) and *Deu-*

tung (interpretation), Dummett suggests that Davidson's extension of a rather conscious process of interpretation to all acts of language understanding is a false assimilation. And, indeed, it is hard to see that understanding someone who speaks, appropriately, of "a nice arrangement of epithets" entails an essentially identical interpretative procedure to that involved in a hearer's making sense of Mrs. Malaprop's "a nice derangement of epitaphs." As suggested earlier in this chapter, the fact that there is a routine practice within which the normal use is embedded constitutes grounds for arguing that no reflexive interpretive procedure is involved at all. However, the contrast here between routine practice and interpretation-requiring novelty cannot be pressed too hard, as if they were fundamentally contrasting. In particular, deviances such as malapropism have their own sphere of practice and have their own antecedently learned conventions to be adduced in their decoding. There are simple logics, as noted earlier, that assist us in our interpreting of malapropisms, slips of the tongue, and so on. In Ramberg's view, however, Davidson and Dummet are more in agreement over specific premises than the latter realizes. Thus, both accept that a natural language is an existing pattern, embodying a set of distinctive conventions: "But, [Davidson] argues, while there may well exist the kinds of regularity of language that Dummett claims are the conventions of meaning, it is *not* by virtue of her knowledge of these regularities that an interpreter is able to understand the meaning of what a speaker says. It is *because* he agrees with Dummett on the earlier point [that a language must be an established pattern of meaningful conventions] that Davidson goes on to infer that there is nothing for a language to be" (Ramberg 1989: 106).

Nor is Davidson suggesting that the insufficiency of knowledge of established regularities (the conventions of a language etc.) entails that all understanding involves radical interpretation of the same kind. He is quite clear that different kinds of "passing theorizing" are involved in at least the following three kinds of language activity: coping with new names of individuals; the word conversion that is malapropism ("mere substitution" [1986: 441]); and the "sheer invention" of a James Joyce. In all such common occurrences, the conventions of an established public language and a formulated theory about those conventions are insufficient to the interpretive task. And none of this mentions, beyond the business of acquiring new words for old concepts, the even greater challenge of acquiring new concepts along with new words, which is how Davidson characterizes first language acquisition.

For Davidson, rule-governed repetition is "a usual, though contingent, feature" of speech (Davidson 1984: 280). Taken together with factors mentioned above, this draws Ramberg to argue that Davidson adopts the position that the target of application of a theory of meaning must primarily be neither a language nor even an idiolect but specific occasions of utterance:

> The salient contrast is not that between idiolects and languages, but between *occasions of utterance*, on the one hand, and abstractions, such as languages or idiolects, on the other. Unless we attach a curious kind of semantic significance to the notion of personal identity, the abstraction we arrive at by generalizing over one speaker's utterances is, from the point of view of the radical interpreter, no more nor less significant than the ill-defined abstraction we call English. And to suggest that an idiolect is simply the language spoken by one person at one particular time, and so no abstraction at all, is just to say that what a speaker speaks is not a language, nor even any one idiolect, but a *series* of unique idiolects. And this is to admit that we have not found a way to describe in terms of semantically significant linguistic regularities the knowledge a speaker uses when successfully communicating. And we never will find a way to describe this knowledge in those terms, because it is not the mastery of a shared abstract structure of linguistic regularities, such as a language, that permits communication. What enables us to communicate is the mastery of something like an art, namely the art of theory construction, in the form of interpretation. (Ramberg 1989: 106)

In Davidson's own words,

> A passing theory really is like a theory at least in this, that it is derived by wit, luck, and wisdom from a private vocabulary and grammar, knowledge of the ways people get their point across, and rules of thumb for figuring out what deviations from the dictionary are most likely.... In linguistic communication nothing corresponds to a linguistic competence as often described. There is therefore no such thing [as a language, as usually conceived by linguists and philosophers] to be learned, mastered, or born with. We must give up the idea of a clearly defined shared structure which language-users acquire and then apply to cases. (Davidson 1986: 446)

Hacker's response to this points out, first, that standard linguistic theory's failure to cope with malapropisms and spoonerisms is "a very minor flaw" in an account that, for much more general reasons, he sees as riven with confusion. He complains that Davidsonian "passing" theory seems to conceive of a world in which dictionaries, grammars, and the metalinguistic reflexivity and normativity that is so facilitated and extended by written language simply do not exist. Only without such a supraindividual background, Hacker suggests, would Davidson's radically individualist account, of ad hoc guesswork, begin to be plausible.

The interesting thing about this conflict of theories is that, from an integrational point of view, both arguments are correct. "Passing" theory exists, although over time it may become sufficiently determining, for the individual, that it ceases to be theory of a "passing" kind (directly analogous to this is Hopper's emergent grammar notion, which, similarly, can end up largely "emerged" and complete for particular individuals). Davidson is correct insofar as the world that his theory assumes is precisely the world inhabited by young children, coming into language. That child's world, exceptional in Hacker's view, is indeed one in which dictionaries and grammars and writing-based metalinguistic normativity scarcely exist. (In fact, Davidson refers to first language acquisition as an "infinitely difficult problem" [1986: 441] to which his remarks are not addressed; his concern he says is with the comparatively "simple" problem, of "how people who already have a language [whatever exactly that means] manage to apply their skill or knowledge to actual cases of interpretation," such as malapropism).

At this point, however, it might be argued, against the view that children acquiring their first language inhabit a world where passing theory predominates, that the larger world that such children inhabit, of parents and caregivers and older siblings, is one in which dictionaries and normativity do powerfully prevail. Such a counterargument fails, however, simply because that larger world is not known to the infant, at the stage under discussion. Given Hacker's own unequivocal position on the impossibility of a child having internalized, as a rule, a prescription that he or she cannot in fact express, paraphrase, or refer to, it is beyond dispute that children in the first years of life know and exist in precisely the kind of world that Hacker takes to be the logical setting for a Davidsonian "passing" theory of linguistic convergence, intelligent hypothesizing, and salience or relevance assessment. How much more appropriate it is, incidentally, to conceptualize Amahl's increasingly adult-like speech as a process of convergence rather than of "correction." By *convergence*, here and elsewhere, is meant convergence of inspectable behavior (both the beginning and the end of language study), not convergence of putative mental processing. In a somewhat different domain, Kreckel is able to adapt speech-act theory to the detailed analysis of social interaction by proposing a similar principle of convergence (see Kreckel 1981).

On the other hand, Hacker's forces of reflexivity and normativity increasingly play a shaping role in our use of language, as we are trained, socialized, and inducted into the institutions of our community. Increasingly, a larger world, with established frameworks for conduct (linguistic and otherwise), comes into existence for the inducted trainee. In this world, where culture and its conventions seem to loom larger than nature, established conventions for linguistic behavior—conventions that to some extent may be formulated as rules we act in accordance with—will carry considerable influence; to the extent that they do, a "passing" theory or emergent grammar of extempore interpretive practice is dispensed with, and the individual follows and re-inscribes conventions rather more and adjusts and revises them rather less. But, however normative a practitioner the individual becomes, it needs to be recognized that linguistic conventions are guides, tendencies, and patterns; they set normal (but transgressable) limits concerning the *comme il faut* of the linguistic performance of interpersonal actions (informing, apologizing, warning, arbitrating, persuading, sympathizing, etc.). Speech-act theory attempts to specify all the conditions necessary and sufficient for a particular speech act to count as, for example, an apology. But, in practice, in actual heterogeneous speech communities, the relations between specifiable conditions and specific acts invariably turn out to be many to many: rather different conditions can count as enabling what particular community members would regard as an apology, and rather different acts can count as enabled, for particular members, by any particular set of conditions. Thus, conventions of the speech-act theoretical kind or of any other kind do not and cannot generate or produce the acts specified but rather guide or describe them. Linguistic normativity, conventions, and grammars are all then essentially regulative, rather than definitively constitutive, of actions involving language, notwithstanding speech-act theoretical assumptions to the contrary. What is constitutive of an apology, or a threat, or a warning, is just that complex of situated and cotemporal behavior (linguistic and otherwise) experiencing that an addressee concludes that he or she has been apologized to, or threatened, or warned. Speech-act conditions are abstract standards, without the possibility of being more than regulative—and in fact only weakly regulative at that.

For Hacker, despite the inapplicability of accounts of understanding English as a matter of knowledge or mastery of a shared theory for sentence generation, still "mastery of shared rules manifest in speech and the normative activities that surround it is involved": "Speakers of a given language agree on the explanations of the meanings of the words they use, concur in accepting certain explanations as correct, others as incorrect. They also agree, by and large, in the grammar they employ.... Such agreement is not a mere regularity or convergence in linguistic behaviour, it is a normative regularity" (Hacker

1988: 170–71). Given the specific sense of concurrence that Hacker seems to intend — that is, where concurrence is synonymous with agreement — the claim made for it here is contestable. By contrast with a conceptualization of language behavior as rule driven in the generativist sense, the notion of concurrence or agreement has in its favor that it is at least interactive and social: it takes two or more to agree. Concurrence involves one person concurring with others, whereas within the rule-dominated paradigm (where rules are given as much by genes as by the community) no other individual is *necessarily* required for linguistic production to proceed. This reflects Chomsky's long-maintained view that language, which in his view is not intrinsically interactive, can be kept distinct from the inherently interactive phenomenon of communication.

But, if we look for a standard practice of speakers concurring over word meanings and grammar, we shall look in vain. Where, for example, is concurrence displayed or implicit in a child's developing grasp of the standard sounds and sound patterns, grammatical patterns, and meaning patterns of a language? Any genuine process of concurrence (in the sense akin to "agreement") entails taking up a somewhat detached position in relation to a given problem, which is by the same process somewhat objectified, and arriving by reflection and dialogue with others at a similarly objectified solution. A standard situation might be the judicial arbitration of a legal dispute, wherein one judge delivers a verdict, suitably supported by argument, with which verdict the other sitting judges concur. The analogy with the position of the child being inducted into a language-using community jars, for the child is ordinarily in the position not of the concurring judge but of the plaintiff or defendant.

The child no doubt increasingly has the ability to take up a somewhat detached position in relation to her own or others' linguistic (or other) behavior and formulate relatively objectified or detachable responses to it. Indeed, following the arguments concerning the role of repetition set out in chapter 6, it must be the case that the child can and does objectify and abstract. Such metalinguistic practices are essential to the development of a fully fledged language — for instance, to the formulation of working hypotheses as to what are useful and productive patterns of language in the community surrounding the child. There is thus no denial here that metalinguistic practices of abstraction are involved in language development, from the earliest occasions. But what is not evident is that, ordinarily (rather than in exceptional cases), these abstractions and objectifications are the subject of agreements with or ratifications by others, outside (or inside) the continuous flow of experience. Like the rest of us, ordinarily, children say and do what seems to work best, without the practical possibility of removing themselves from their lives long enough to record agreements or concurrences over the range of emerging patterns that might, in principle, be agreed on. Similarly, when a secretary in the English Department seeks my concurrence with her opinion that *gotten* is slang and uneducated, it is not open to us to go about determining whether we concur over all the patterns of usage we both invoke in the course of discussing the bogey word *gotten*: the condition of being able to play the "concurrence game" is that ordinarily language is not subject to processes of concurrence or agreement. When at the dinner table my five-year-old countered my remark — correctly heard as a complaint — that he was rather talkative by pointing out that his noisy younger sister was worse behaved since she was *shoutative*, what role did concurrence play in the proceedings? The question of concurrence, namely, that *shoutative* is an expression that does not concur with the established usages of the language community, comes a distant pedantic second to other factors, in the context. We (and he) understood perfectly well what *shoutative* meant. We all knew and understood the established pattern for adding -*ative* to a doing word when that "doing" is judged to be going on a great deal: when I then asked him what *fibative* might mean, he suggested at once "lying." What guided production and communication were established and remembered patterns of usage, which rendered the situated production of *shoutative* perspicuous and ingenious rather than problematic. *Shoutative* was in no way underwritten by concurrence, and the only concurrence directly involved was that in the specific situation *shoutative* was accepted and understood. But, if concurrence is typically context tied in this way, then that norm is a "passing theory" of precisely the Davidsonian kind.

Besides that sense of *concurrence* critiqued above, where the term is understood as roughly synonymous with *agreement*, there is an alternative, etymologically encouraged understanding of the term that is worth considering further: *concurrence* in the sense of "going along with an arrangement or state of affairs (where other arrangements are imaginable), but without conscious or formal agreement." Some support for such a distinction comes from the proceedings of the U.S. Supreme Court. There, when an opinion of the court is written by a particular justice, those other justices in full agreement with the bases of that verdict are said to "join the opinion"; on the other hand, a justice who accepts the majority verdict but wishes to argue for it along some other lines is said to "concur separately." This alternative sense of concurrence approximates Lewis's idea of a convention — a rational coordination of behavior that does not involve or presuppose prior agreement or prior rules but is rather a situated solution to a regularly recurring potential problem (Lewis 1969). There are connections here, also, to Garfinkel's ethnomethodological view of conversation, and certainly turn taking in conversation may be viewed as involving Lewisian conventions rather than rules. There is a temptation to interpret Lewis's views as involving the claim that conventions develop because they are of mutual benefit to the parties involved; but maintaining the resistance to assumptions of mutual properties voiced elsewhere in this book — properties "held in common" — I will suggest that what is involved is collective benefit and not strictly mutual or shared benefit. The benefit is collective insofar as each believes that it is in their own best interests to observe and maintain the convention. But no individual can confirm that his or her best interests are identical to those of any other, so mutual benefit cannot be assumed; nor need it be.

In place of conceptualizations in terms of rules, linguistics must explore patterns and habituation, doing what works best or, in Fish's phrase (1989), "what comes naturally." The patterns of our language practices are natural not in the sense of automatic or innate but in the sense that we are naturally rational, reflective, imaginative, sense-making, pattern-seeking, other-oriented individuals. A recasting of linguistics, toward the study of the etiology of patterns of usage, is appropriate in almost every language area to which the mythology of quasi-scientific rules has spread. Thus, even conversational analysis, in its most visible bid for ratification by mainstream linguistics (Sacks, Schegloff, and Jefferson 1974), leans heavily on the supposition that conversation is governed by a simple system for the allocation of turns at talk — a rule-governed solution, it is suggested, to the practical problem of keeping talk orderly. But, as in the other examples mentioned above, it is not clear that the practical regularities of orderly conversation are rules in the sense of "known directives," followed by participants. A characterization of the orderly patterns of turn taking in conversation (at least among white middle-class Americans, ca. 1970) is succinctly expressed in Sacks, Schegloff, and Jefferson (1974); but this characterization constitutes a description rather than a set of rules. Conversational analysis is better understood, quite generally, as descriptive rather than related to rules. Insofar as people take turns, avoid other repair, negotiate closings, do display, design their responses, and so on, they do so on the basis of what, in their experience, they have learned works best, given social constraints of politeness and respect, and given the innumerable purposes and language games within which "turn taking" may take place. Perhaps turn taking is simply an exponent, in conversation, of the Saussurean principle of linearity. At least, it seems that physiological constraints as well as principles of politeness are going to discourage coterminousness — and even extended overlap — of speech. But where politeness is not attended to — rows, enthusiastic encounters, games, and parties — turn taking may be neglected.

Socialization unquestionably involves induction into manifold institutionalized settings within which the individual is guided toward the socially correct or acceptable way of doing things. But this is at best a tacit process of normative compliance or acceptance rather than agreement. More generally, no polls are taken in the course of the establishment of usages; there is no national assembly on the language, with voting delegates from all the recognized (by whom?) dialect communities. A language comprises a host of normative practices, different forms of life, from which specifics we can (if we are so minded — and it is in the nature of literate and regulated societies to be so minded) extrapolate and generalize certain kinds of normative rules of grammar, word meanings, and so on. But how constrained we are by the normative regulation of linguistic behavior is a continually moot point; indeed, it is the essential point.

Before turning from generative rules, the following conclusions from Hacker may be dwelt on:

The concept of a rule there invoked [namely, in the theories of language propounded by linguists and philosophers] is incoherent, at least it is so unless the concept of a rule of language is radically different from the concept of a rule as used in our general discourse about rule-governed behaviour. If that *is* the case, then it must be thoroughly explained, and argument is needed to justify talking of "rules" here at all. But it is not suggested by linguists or philosophers that the expression "rule" is being used in a "special technical sense." (Hacker 1988: 166)

In recent years, however, in the reformulations of linguists of universal grammar (UG), it seems to be implied that whatever parts of the grammar are postulated as psychologically real (or a representation of orientations to particular kinds of structure and structuring that must, in some form, be a distinctive part of our genetic mental endowment) are indeed to be thought of less as rules that govern than as a framework of principles, akin to scientific laws or biological facts, that the normally developing individual cannot avoid using. These deeply embedded principles can no more be set aside or inspected by the child than can one's sexual maturation (one can inspect the physical consequences of sexual maturation, but the phenomenon itself is beyond direct observation). One of the consequences of this theoretical turn, increasingly, is that UG principles have become remarkably abstract. Remote from the "superficial" specifics of any particular external (E) language, they run the risk of being devalued on the grounds of their remoteness from all E languages: it may be argued, in fact, that UG principles are no longer specific to language and are no longer an argument for a mental component specifically reserved as a language faculty or module. In their favor, it might be suggested that their very abstractness means that their theoretical dependency on some of the less plausible outreaches of the earlier Chomskyan paradigm is all the more tenuous. And that would mean in turn that particular topics pursued within generativist linguistics could retain a legitimacy and coherence notwithstanding extensive perceived weaknesses in the framing paradigm. Certainly, it would be impertinent to doubt the intellectual achievements of generativist linguists exploring complexities of scope and quantification in logical form, or abstract principles in phonology, or a host of other topics; what is in doubt is the place of those achievements in a coherent picture of language (its acquisition and use) and of the relations between language and other cognitive activities. In depiction and detail, that picture will have to look very different from the sketch noted earlier and repeated here: "The language faculty selects relevant data from the events taking place in the environment; making use of these data in a manner determined by its internal structure, the child constructs a language, [here] Spanish. . . . This language is now incorporated in the mind. When the process is completed, the language constitutes the mature state attained by the language faculty. The person now speaks and understands the language" (Chomsky 1988: 35).

Pateman's Wittgensteinians

In his important recent defense of a realist theory of linguistics, Pateman includes a densely argued critical review of the objections to Chomskyan linguistic theory that have come from certain "Wittgensteinian" philosophers of language (principally, Baker and Hacker, Itkonen, and Kripke). A particular target of Pateman's critique is the ontological skepticism of the Wittgensteinian concerning the Chomskyan claim that grammar is essentially a mentally represented system of rules (or principles) and largely innate. Pateman, like Chomsky, is a dualist, arguing that two quite distinct conceptions of language must be characterized independently of each other, before attempts to link them are made: a cognitivist account of grammar best captures the nature of language in the mind; but language or languages in society are intentional objects about which people have beliefs, prejudices, and attitudes and must be studied sociologically. Crucial to Pateman's cognitive generativism is a claimed distinction between introspection and intuition:

> I use the term "intuition" to designate that which gives us causally related indexical or symptomatic evidence for the character of underlying psycholinguistic (or, more generally, psychological) processes. Intuitions are not exercises of judgement which claim certainty or any kind of objectivity for the content of judgement and hence which claim the assent of all those implicated by the judgement [as introspections do (MJT)]. Rather, intuitions are reports of appearances, hence subjective expressions. . . . In intuition we tell how something strikes us, how it appears to us and thereby provide causal evidence about our minds. In Wittgenstein's terms, intuitions provide *symptoms* rather than *criteria* of what underlies them. (1987b: 135)

In Pateman's view, the distinction between introspection and intuition can be made clearer

> if the distinction between claims of forms (1) and (2) is clearly drawn, and if it is realized and insisted that intuition is used to establish claims of form (1), not form (2), which involves the exercise of judgement (introspection in my terms).
>
> (1) Sentence *P* seems grammatical to subject *S*.
> (2) Sentence *P* is grammatical in language *L*, according to subject *S*.
>
> Evidence of form (1) in turn provide the basis for the linguist's claim (3); and evidence of form (2) provide the basis for the linguist's claim (4):
>
> (3) Sentence *P* is grammatical in subject *S*'s internally represented language.
> (4) Sentence *P* is grammatical in language *L*.
>
> In Chomsky's terms . . . intuition provides evidence for the character of I-languages (internalized languages), whereas introspective judgement — exercised, for example, when a foreigner asks me whether you can say P in English — provides evidence for the character of E-languages (externalised languages). (Pateman 1987b: 135)

These claimed distinctions are not free of difficulties, however. Pateman wishes to characterize the symptomatic noncriterial nature of intuition sufficiently broadly so that it can cover all kinds of psychological events that may be taken as symptomatically reactive. Thus, he would presumably include, as events or behaviors that are symptomatic of intuitions, such nonintrospective indicators as pupil dilations and infants' head turns in addition to more verbally displayed signs of recognition or rejection. Invaluable though the former indicators are, their use is far from being the norm in linguistic research that probes intuitions. Intuitions, as used in the development of grammars and theories in linguistic science, are rarely spontaneous in that way; rather, they are usually quite openly elicited. This point relates also to an analogy that Pateman uses in pursuing one of his more general criticisms of Wittgensteinians and their declining to explain phenomena such as successful language performance (1987b: 137, n. 13). That declining to explain, he suggests, is an unjustified neglect of important issues, analogous to that which one might condemn in any medical science that was content to explain the disease consumption "anti-scientifically," merely in terms of its symptoms (growing weak, thin, clearheaded, coughing blood, and then dying). But this analogy fails: symptoms of various illnesses are not, at the outset, elicited, in the way that those of linguistic competence are. Medical symptoms are in that sense at least spontaneous: the patient "presents" with various symptoms when he or she goes to the doctor. By contrast, language users do not spontaneously go to the theoretical linguist with their symptoms of UG.

Similarly, one of the significant differences in Pateman's separation of intuitions from introspections is that the former are spontaneous and unbidden while the latter are public judgments where one functions as a spokesperson for the language. Thus, an interactive context is mentioned in Pateman's depiction of introspection elicitation, a foreigner asking about the acceptability in English of a given utterance, while nothing similar is admitted to be involved in intuition disclosure. But, again, the claimed contrast is tenuous: there is nothing particularly natural or unreflective, for the layperson, in being prodded for grammaticality judgments by a linguist. The time is long past when linguists and psycholinguists could be claiming miraculously direct access to naked intuitions, when throughout their elicitation procedures they are construing informants and their responses in line with one framework of linguistic assumptions or another. The idea of intuitions as reflexes or responses free of interpretive contaminations will not hold.

Equally problematic is the distinction then developed from the proposed separation of intuition and introspection. Intuition, Pateman argues, underlies claims such as that made in (1) below:

(1) Sentence P seems grammatical to subject S,

while introspection is said to underlie claims such as that made in (2):

(2) Sentence P is grammatical in language L, according to subject S.

It may be noted in passing that the broader conception of intuition acknowledged above (one that would cover various physiological or psychological tests involving bicameral listening tests, head turns, pupil dilation, etc.) is abruptly narrowed here to the familiar theoretical syntactic domain of judgments of sentence grammaticality. But even to subsume both (1) and (2) under the rubric *judgments of sentence grammaticality* distorts the picture, according to Pateman's account (judgment is involved only in [2], the fruit of introspection). However, it is hard to find any consistent support for Pateman's distinctions in the practices of linguistic grammaticality research. Two contrasts are claimed: "seems grammatical" versus "is grammatical" and "grammatical" versus "grammatical in language L." Yet the latter of these has no status whatsoever from the point of view of the individual whose intuitions or introspections are being tapped (it clearly has a fundamental status in the theory of UG), while the former contrast chiefly relates to speaker perceptions of correctness, attitudes to dialects and nonstandardisms vis-à-vis a postulated standard dialect, and so on — at any rate, centrally to do with different kinds and degrees of orientation toward the so-called external language and not a legitimate basis for sustaining a clear internal language/external language distinction. Any variation between talking of an expression as "seeming" grammatical and "being" grammatical has nothing to do with inward knowledge and everything to do with authority and politeness.

That whether a particular sentence is grammatical, rather than grammatical in language L, is a meaningless distinction for an informant is evident as soon as one attempts to uncover their intuitions on any particular sentence. This is so for the simple reason that, unless an informant is specifically trained to respond to some more obscure standard, the normal basis for judging a sentence grammatical is whether it is judged to be a correct sentence of a particular language. For an ordinary informant, *grammatical* simply means "correct usage in language L." If, on elicitation of whatever means, I show symptoms of judging

Il me l'a donné

as grammatical, it is because I am implicitly evaluating the sentence as a correct sentence of standard French. It is simply impossible to obtain grammaticality judgments that are not tied, by the individual from whom they are extracted, to an explicit or assumed "external" language framework. And when judges are confronted with more marginal cases and asked whether these are grammatical —

Il a donné le à moi,
He gave it me

— it still remains impossible to locate a "no external language's land," shaped by neither French grammaticality intuitions nor English ones but simply pure "grammaticality intuitions."

One of the tensions evident in the foregoing counterposing of cognitivist and late Wittgensteinian views of language behavior centers on two very different conceptions of what is involved in grammaticality. For cognitivists, grammaticality has everything to do with regularity and nothing essentially to do with correctness; for Wittgensteinians, by contrast, correctness cannot be so dismissed, either as inessential or as quite distinct from regularity: a significant part of the regularity displayed in a language is rooted in and nothing but a matter of correctness.

Pateman, along with Chomskyan linguists, will defend the reality of intuitions by citing sentences exhibiting violation of the complex-NP constraint, which is a reflex of the more general subjacency condition (e.g., see Pateman 1987b: 101). The evidence of such sentences is taken as powerful support for claims about the autonomous regularity of grammar. But, significantly, this is some distance from the kind of regularity noticeable by the lay user, of the kind discussed by Taylor (1990: 146–48), regularities of a much more immediate kind, to do with how the community or the postulated elite pronounces words, uses language, and so on. The latter kinds of regularity have everything to do with perceptions of correctness and incorrectness and lay judgments of bad grammar (where the latter phrase extends to nonstandard pronunciations: pronouncing *nurse nois* or saying "I'm singin' in the rain" are said to be "bad grammar"), while generativists are likely to be quite emphatic that the kind of deep grammatical principles in which they are interested have nothing to do with correctness and incorrectness. But in saying this they are more right than they imagine: precisely because the kind of complex-NP constraint–violating sentences that generativists offer to readers, inviting them to concede their absolute ungrammaticality, are in fact the kind of sentences never encountered or considered for possible use by situated language users, their correctness or otherwise can never emerge as an issue. This is an important way in which what concerns UG linguists in fact bears no relation to the issues of grammaticality and correctness that concern ordinary language users. Thus, as far as the average layperson is concerned, it scarcely makes sense to talk about the ungrammaticality of, for example,

> What did Mary repair the car that smashed into?

or

> Who did Mary repair the car that smashed into the garage?

It makes little sense because for the layperson grammaticality and ungrammaticality judgments come into play only over sentences that it might have occurred to them to use, that are fairly readily interpretable, and concerning which they have to make a decision concerning correctness.

In one crucial section (6.5) exploring Wittgensteinians' objections to the Chomskyan "mythology of rules," Pateman notes the Wittgensteinian view of rules as prescriptions that can guide action, that may or may not be followed, and so on. In all those respects, rule prescriptions contrast with scientific laws:

> Wittgensteinians posit an entirely orthodox distinction between the moral and the natural sciences, the latter generally conceived positivistically. And they assign the study of language wholly to the moral sciences, leaving aside the possibility of "scientific investigations into what parts of the brain are causally related to linguistic abilities" [Baker and Hacker 1984: 300, n. 66] — investigations which have no bearing on the study of the normative phenomena of speaking and understanding.

In response to this, Pateman makes the following points:

> Though speaking is an intentional activity, the explanation of which will make necessary reference to the goals, purposes, norms, rules, etc., being followed by the speaker, none the less speaking is not an intentional activity under all its relevant descriptions. Under some descriptions, it is properly explained . . . in causal-mechanical terms . . . [entailing] reference to inaccessible rules or representations. (1987b: 141)

Here, one of the grounds for a causal-mechanical view of certain aspects of speech is reached via rejection of Baker and Hacker's claim that, because speaking is an intentional following of rules, it follows that speakers "can produce at will as many ungrammatical sentences as the theorist wishes" (Baker and Hacker 1984: 299). Pateman criticizes this overly bold assertion from a variety of perspectives. First, he doubts whether speakers can readily speak ungrammatically, for example, readily "mangle" standard intonation patterns. His doubts are justified, but it is not clear that they promote causal-mechanical arguments or undermine those for rule-following normativity. The normativist is entitled to argue that, so ingrained after long training are the normative grammatical patterns, striking out into the realms of ungrammaticality — like breaking out into verse or song for those unaccustomed to doing so — is not done easily. Nevertheless, it can be done (and if speakers were truly causally constrained in this area this could not be so), and, when it is, it is indeed done "at will."

A second objection to Baker and Hacker's claim about free choice over rule following is introduced: even if superficially plausible with regard to speaking, the claim does not extend as it must to hearing and understanding: "It is simply not true that I can freely mishear and misunderstand speech addressed to me in a language I know" (Pateman 1987b: 142). But it begs the question to characterize mistaken understandings as arbitrary mishearings and misunderstandings: Wittgensteinians are no more attracted to the spread of misunderstandings than anyone else, so that Pateman's rejoinder here is somewhat polemical. What this second objection requires consideration of is whether a language user is free to interpret heard utterances in any way other than whichever way is postulated as that yielded by the causal-mechanist apparatus. Put thus, it is clear that the language user is so free, although again it is important to reiterate that "freedom to interpret . . ." is not any form of retreat to mindlessness but on the contrary can be achieved only by that effort of "will" emphasized by the Baker and Hacker formulation, where they write of what a speaker "can produce at will." *Free* (where a speaker "freely misunderstands speech"), it should be noted, is Pateman's term, not Baker's and Hacker's, and it reappears when he contrives a contrast of positions by stating that "the linguist is not interested, *qua* linguist studying linguistic competence, in free speech" (1987b: 142). The term *free* does not apply in the context of the present discussion: the question is not so much whether it is the case that "I can freely . . . misunderstand speech addressed to me in a language I know" but whether it is possible to have variable understandings — some even classifiable as misunderstandings — of a given text.

This in turn highlights the second respect in which question begging is involved in saying

It is simply not true that I can freely mishear and misunderstand speech addressed to me in a language I know.

Here it is presumptive to characterize the language under consideration (such as English) as one "I know," for what is imagined here is the kind of full and seemingly infallible knowledge of, say, English, that appears to be involved when one uses the language in one's accustomed speech communities. By *a language I know* is indicated something quite unqualifiedly and ideally Chomskyan: a language without dialects, representable by a single set of unambiguous and nonoverlapping rules, known by me perfectly and without distractions, memory lapses, etc. The language and the knower are such that when ordinary English sentences are encountered (e.g., *The thief took the haslet*), neither mishearing nor misunderstanding is allegedly possible. Clearly, this is incorrect. As soon as "the language I know" is permitted to subsume dialects, registers, and specialized languages or borrowings from these with which a hearer may be unfamiliar, then the sentence quoted above ceases to be a simple irrefutable truth. Instead, it is quite easy to find cases in which speech in the known language, soberly and after deliberation, may still be misinterpreted. Conversing with a Scottish friend, and trying to remember the surname and particulars of a mutual acquaintance, the friend produces the utterance [smelɪ]. To this, slightly taken aback, I reply "Is he?" whereupon the friend indicates that what he had supplied was the acquaintance's surname, Smyllie. Or, if an Irish friend says, or seems to say, that a certain ultrascholarly retired professor is "a tome," it may take a few minutes before I realize that my creative mishearing must be abandoned for the more mundane knowledge that the said professor is at his place of residence. These are slight examples, but the potential, in a language one knows, for mishearing and misunderstandings that cannot be dismissed as due to inattention or stupidity is quite general. It is particularly evident in school classrooms, where children's talk to their teachers routinely displays the former's relatively limited proficiency in the language. And of course it is readily apparent whenever one grapples with any specialized and unfamiliar register or discourse. Even on the basis of the texts to be found in an English-language newspaper, a commodity clearly aimed to meet the needs of a large readership, discourse misunderstanding is easy to uncover, whether the subject matter is baseball, or cricket, or bridge, or computing, or the stock market.

Indeed, it was in the face of the overwhelming evidence that individuals can and do freely mishear and misunderstand speech even in a language they evidently know that contemporary linguists retreated, in their claims for their grammar modeling, from saying that this modeled the language to saying that it modeled some one speaker's idiolect. As noted in chapter 2, poetry interpretation is perhaps the most institutionalized and publicly displayed language game in which willed diversity of both speaking and interpreting is sanctioned. Even here, however, there are quite firm limits on interpretive diversity, although those limits shift over time; there is a logic to the sanctioned diversities in interpretation. Elsewhere, interpretive independence, being unsanctioned, may incur sizable costs both to the individual and to the fabric of the community. Therefore, we make a normative choice, save in pressing circumstances, not to go out of our way to depart from the standard rules of English.

Pateman's third rejoinder is not so much to question the Baker and Hacker claim but to suggest that it does not address the central Chomskyan or cognitivist position at all. That central position is confronted, Pateman suggests, if we consider the fact that we talk in our sleep and in delirium — "a good argument in favour of a causal-mechanical theory of language production" (1987b: 142).

Why Pateman feels sleep talk is a knockdown argument vis-à-vis Baker and Hacker is that it is assumed that such talk is not intentional or voluntary but "the product of the operation of mechanisms of speech production operating unconsciously and in an ordinary causal fashion": "it is not I, as subject of self-consciousness, who speak when asleep." These assumptions, however, are themselves open to question. As far as my personal observations of sleep talk run, it seems that talking during sleep typically constitutes what one might call "phonated outbursts" triggered by particularly intense imagined enactments of particular dreamed events. Sometimes, where a child wakes from sleep after a particularly intense dream, it is possible quite straightforwardly to relate the substance of the talk to the content of the dream that the child reports having experienced. In view of these factors of mental involvement, it seems possible to pursue a line of argument in which it is not conceded that talking in sleep or in delirium — insofar as it counts as talk at all and is not just random phonation or gibberish — is wholly involuntary or unintentional. Examples like sleep talk (and delirious speech and the language of the insane) press hard on our received conceptualizations of consciousness and intentionality; but it is no easier to accept that sleep talk is on occasion both genuine speech and purely causal mechanical than it is to accept that Searle's cat can produce genuine English sentences.

In the face of the counterarguments that Pateman's claims give rise to, the only satisfactory position to adopt seems to be something not unlike that with which Pateman himself concludes his section 6.5; it is also the essence of the generativist linguistic answer to the claim that language is public intentional practice: it is an answer that invokes strata and modularity. That is to say, while the public normative aspects of actual languages are acknowledged, nevertheless it is claimed that underlying the contingent details of those public practices are strata, of universal grammar, without which none of the developed actual languages would have the structuring that they clearly have. The hypothesis is that there is a unitary mechanism, comprising the necessary framework together with various kinds of options for external-language-specific adjustments of that framework, that is an enabling cognitive basis of all human languages. With the automatic help of this unitary mechanism, the particular (less fundamentally contrasting) design of the native language is replicated by the child in the course of his or her acquisition of the language. The most popular analogy is with vision: there are distinct modules involved in the process of seeing, and those modules are separate even though they operate jointly; they are also physiological, operating causally, rather than at the will of the individual who sees. With these analogies it is hard to have much quarrel. Only a few points need to be reiterated. These all have to do with spelling out some of the implications of the analogizing of the UG mechanism or module to parallel ones in vision.

Just as we can and should study what is basic, an endowment of all ordinary human beings, in the mental equipment that makes seeing (including seeing perspective, depth of field, etc.) possible, so we can and should study what is similarly general and underlying all natural languages. But now apply these distinctions to the case of two individuals each endowed with the relevant neural modules or equipment for seeing who are standing in front of a Rembrandt painting. One of these individuals is a one-year-old child, who has conceivably never seen an oil painting in her life and may never have visited an art gallery before; the other is an adult familiar with some of the subtleties and complexities of Western art, of Rembrandt's life, of seventeenth-century Dutch mercantilism, of brushwork and chiaroscuro and flesh tone and the melancholy that shadows Rembrandt's contented figures, and so on. At some necessary but basic stratum or module, as vision scientists would confirm, we can reasonably postulate that a very similar activation of various cortical sensory visual faculties takes place in child and adult, and the precise nature, interaction, etc. of those activations is what vision scientists are interested in; mutatis mutandis, UG linguists are interested in something as basic, underlying as large a group of natural languages as possible (possibly extending beyond spoken ones to include Sign). All well and good. On the other hand, it would be disingenuous to say, of the child and the informed adult looking at the Rembrandt painting, that they see the same thing. Nor would the vision scientist pretend otherwise; he or she would be quick to explain that what the adult sees, when looking at the painting, is relative to an enormously complex superstructure of culture and history and aesthetics etc. that the adult has learned or acquired over the years. The vision scientist might even be guarded about claiming that the child sees the Rembrandt painting at all (as distinct from seeing a vague mass of colors).

Nevertheless all that superstructure must connect with a substructure (of the kind that even the child has) in order to function properly; if the substructure were lacking in some way (e.g., through blindness), then the adult's kind of seeing could not arise, whereas, for all children with the substructure in place, informed seeing of Rembrandt of the adult's kind is a common potential. All this, too, is well and good; but for anyone concerned to explore contextualized practices (whether this be art or language), one fundamental question remains neglected or ignored in all this. And that is, How can we better understand the factors or steps by which the adult's competence at "seeing Rembrandt paintings" develops from, or in the course of using, the child's genetic visual endowment? This question clearly contains a rather crucial presupposition: that understanding how it is, and what it is, that informed adults see when they see a Rembrandt painting is of some importance. Some but not all vision scientists are likely to respond that such a question is not of importance as far as "the vision module" is concerned; but, in the analogous situation of UG and external languages, virtually all UG linguists would insist that the phenomena involved in linguistic acculturation, like those involved in visual acculturation, are not questions that their work can address, not of foundational importance to linguistics, and not amenable to controlled scientific study. To someone who takes the goal of analyzing and understanding Rembrandt really seriously, the vision scientist's denials of either interest or expertise make it immediately clear that there is no point in going to such a person for enlightenment. And, to someone who takes the goal of analyzing and understanding actual language behavior really seriously, the inappropriateness of seeking enlightenment from universal grammar should be made at least as clear.

In elevating the hypothesized mental mechanism—the genetic grammatical mechanism that might underlie all actual languages—as the major focus of linguistics, the exploration of vast areas of language, as a normative set of practices, is deliberately neglected. The neglect is considered—the judgment being that in modeling UG linguists are modeling factors more fundamental and more deeply embedded in the human mental endowment. A focus on UG is thus grounded on a compelling argument. At the same time, however, no parallel argument seems available for inattention to actual language behavior — any more than a compelling argument justifying attention to human anatomy is equally a good justificatory basis for neglecting human physiology. What is equally unclear is how such a compartmentalization of interests — here, into such compartments as "linguistics as a branch of cognition" and "languages as complex normative practices" — can by that very effort of compartmentalization rank those compartments as of greater or lesser worth, as "core linguistics" versus "social linguistics," as foundational versus "uninteresting." It is only fair to emphasize that generative linguists seem less inclined to claim or assume (via implicit ranked terms) the disciplinary and intellectual high ground that they formerly did. Over the last few years, generative linguists have become quite content to defend their investigative priorities on the basis of some such "horses for courses" or "we do apples, you do oranges" principle. But, in the process, they have rendered themselves vulnerable to the charge that, whatever they are pursuing in their intensely abstract modeling of remotely underlying putative structuring postulated to be represented in some form in the brain, they are not pursuing the systematic study of actually occurring language behavior. Consequently, to call their work *linguistics*, let alone *language studies*, is a misnomer of a nontrivial kind: UG is essentially a brain science. And, once it is acknowledged that the theoretical goal of UG linguists is indeed a richer understanding of "what goes on in the brain" in the acquisition and use of language, that is, once it is recognized that UG studies are brain science, a further nontrivial question relating to terminology arises: namely, why it is that UG generativism characterizes itself as a branch of cognitive science but not of neurological science.

Concluding with Individuals

> In the distinction between "Speech" and "Language", I can see nothing but a sort of transformation of the theory of a "folk-mind" or "collective mind." . . . Mind and consciousness are found only in the individual, and even if all, or nearly all, individuals in a community think the same, and feel the same with regard to this or that, or are accustomed to react in a like manner to this or that situation, we still do not get a "folk-mind" which behaves like this, but many minds which resemble one another. (Jespersen 1946: 14–15)

In this chapter I have argued that it is important to distinguish between, on the one hand, the language-structuring principles, which have the status of scientific laws, whose putative characterization is pursued in UG, and, on the other hand, patterned aspects of actual language behavior, constrained by social rules. Too often these latter human tendencies to develop and observe patternings and to be trained in and conform to normative formats are recast in the linguistics literature as intrinsically cognitive rather than social. For example, the patternings within Amahl's developing proficiency in spoken English are characterized as primarily cognitively powered rather than as arising from the negotiation of the individual's interests and needs (including, let it be noted, a predisposition toward other orientedness) with the normative pressures of that individual's larger communities. Within those larger communities, particular interests and needs have greater power and influence and authority than others, giving rise to equally powerful exclusionary and disciplinary discourses based on partial notions such as standard English, correct English, proper pronunciation, and educated usage. A renewed exploration of these issues and a renewed examination of allegedly "purely linguistic" issues (such as Amahl's "purely phonological" simplification of onset clusters by deletion of approximants — [bl] → [b]) is necessary. In terms of the self-oriented, other-oriented, and normative influences on language behavior, that renewed exploration would draw out the connections, denied in twentieth-century linguistics, between language, law, political philosophy, morality, and ethics. Such connections are of the kind examined by Hobbes and Locke, which descended both to the French *philosophes* and to the framers of the U.S. Constitution (on Locke's views on the weaknesses of linguistic intersubjectivity, particularly if language is to be the medium for inquiries into the foundations of natural science, and on his consequent subscription to the need for normative constraints on the individual's acknowledged freedom "to make words stand for what ideas he pleases," see Taylor [1990]).

What has also emerged in the discussion is the tendency for generative linguistic accounts of, for example, developmental phonology to be themselves a kind of "rule-governed creativity" in two senses summarizable as follows:

1. Wherever a systematicity, patternedness, or "logic" is observable in the data or elicited intuitive judgments, that patterned creativity must be characterized as the working of an internalized rule or set of rules.

2. Within generativist theory, linguists are free to be quite creative in their postulation of multiple abstract levels or strata, constraining input and output in series or even in parallel or with local cyclicity. But there is a governing rule that such creativity of theoretical explanations or "solutions" must ultimately issue in an account that represents the linguistic phenomena as subject to specifiable rules (principles, etc.).

In place of treating language as "rule-governed creativity" I have argued here and throughout for viewing it as something approximating "hypothesis-backed creativity" — a significantly different conception. There is a considerable difference between adopting a form of behavior that follows particular rules (it would be redundant to state that in this context the individual is deliberately following those rules) and behaving adaptively on the basis of a considered adoption of particular hypotheses.

Some may deplore what they see as the unreconstructed and irredeemable conservatism of the integrational position, notwithstanding the hostility to rules, innatism, and homogeneity, in the foregoing arguments. In particular, a cult of individualism may be detected in the arguments here against assuming collective control and group or social determination of language. It may be alleged that the integrational linguistics espoused here recalcitrantly neglects the social. But the intention has been otherwise. It has been emphatically to acknowledge the role of the social, of collective forces, group allegiances, and so on — but not to assume that these are determining or actually control, at every level, the forms and functions of linguistic interaction.

The kind of individualism argued for here is that of individuals necessarily living in and through collectivities but remaining in certain respects individual agents. Not free, not necessarily unitary or unaffected by class, race, and gender contradictions, etc., and not autonomous, but nevertheless in crucial respects individually responsible, accountable, and enabled. Both mentalist-cognitivist and social-collectivist assumptions about the fundamental nature of language tend to minimize the powers of individuals in these respects. To take a single small example, if I, from my particular background of gender, race, nationality, and class characterizations, make some racist or sexist remark, it is incorrect to attribute this in large part to that biological and social-determinative background; I, individually, am primarily responsible and accountable (and not my race, nationality, class, or profession assignments or selections, no matter how they may reinforce matters). Analogously, a racist remark is a racist remark, at some level of assessment that will apply (if not universally) across all the communities that compose a given society: it seems fundamentally inadequate (specifically, morally inadequate) to allow the argument that only from a potentially rather partial viewpoint (e.g., that of allegedly hypersensitive Jews, or Irish, or Native Americans) is a particular remark racist — that is, that racism is, in essence, a socially constructed category. Racism is undoubtedly socially constructed and socially mediated, and individuals and individualism are socially constructed, but those constructions are a shaping of preexisting elements, namely, racism and individuals. Society "constructs" racism; but of what is society constructed? Essentially, of individuals, oriented to other individuals while supportive of self, motivated in their language by faith, hope, and charity as well as greed, fear, and envy. Racism is a constructed category, which will change over time and with other changing circumstances, but it is in the first instance, at the experiential level as distinct from the metaexperiential level, constructed or construed by individuals. Just as a racist remark, in the first instance, comes from the individual to the individual in an integrated situation: in the first place, it causes hurt to individuals.

Gender, class, and so on are all in effect the domain of variables, the argument against individualism runs. We are all subject to these domains, we all have some gender, class, race, or other etc., but just which ones we have, in which combination, are deeply determinative of our so-called individuality. We are, whether we like it or not, shot through with heterogeneous differentiating social categories and histories. But these truths still neglect an aspect of experience that is foundational to criteria of morality and that, although socially experienced in some respects, remains essentially our experience as individuals. It is a determinant that does not apply variably, or in varying degrees, in the way that, within the universal categorization for *race*, there are both contrasting and gradable affiliations to such classifications as *Caucasian*, *Asian American*, *Chinese*, etc. The variable to which I allude is *death*. Death guarantees the end of your participation in the language community, which goes on without you. And, setting aside the atypical situations in which an entire language community is silenced, by emigration, dispersal, or persecution (situations that have come to be called "language death" (Dorian 1981: 198n), the overwhelmingly more common picture is one in which a language-speaking community witnesses a number of minideaths with each passing day, as particular individuals within that community die. Strokes and aphasias give glimpses of the future withdrawal, but with death comes the definitive cessation of the use of language. And that cessation equally irrefutably applies not to the community but to the individual. Too often, linguistics uncritically attributes "possession" of the language to the community, neglecting the fact that the community is in essence an aggregation of individuals of finite life span. It is the individual who creates language, and it is the individual who, in dying, ceases to do so; it is not, ultimately, in the power of the community either to "give" language to the individual or to take it away. But this contingent dependency of the language on what is done by or happens to individuals is reflected in even the commonest language activities such as using names. At least one expression that one might reasonably take to belong to whatever counts as "the language" for the particular community of which the individual is a member is subject to radical change of use when that individual dies: his or her name. How *Peter* and *Peter Smith* will be used, by those familiar with these expressions, when Peter Smith is alive will undergo significant change when their referent dies. Outside of acts of pretense, delusions, and other serious but parasitic uses, such utterances as "Hello, my name is Peter Smith," "I am Peter Smith," and "Good to see you, Peter!" will disappear from the local culture.

Something of the needed reconsideration of individualism in language behavior is captured in a review by Cameron of the contrasting approaches to conversation of social psychologists and conversational analysts (Cameron 1990). Cameron notes that a major contrast lies in the two traditions' views of descriptions of social members in terms of gender, class, tendency to be dominant in interaction, etc. What is the ontological status of such categorizations? For social psychologists, they are given facts, independent variables that preexist any particular interaction or any particular individual. Having "controlled" for these, the social psychologist analyst looks at the emergence or otherwise of some dependent variable — for example, interruption, pitch ranges, or eye contact — within an interaction between individuals already classified as "male, dominant," etc. By contrast, authentic conversational analysis tries to approach the analysis of single interactions without any such predeterminations and without assuming that such categories are a given background; instead, these categorial attributes, as much established through interaction as preexisting it, may be the focus and in the foreground of interactional strategies: "Social behaviour is not to be explained as an epiphenomenon of individual dispositions and characteristics: rather the reverse. Such things as [the social psychologists' category of] 'dominance', and even from a strict ethnomethodological perspective, gender, have to be routinely 'accomplished' in social interaction" (Cameron 1990: 222–23).

In the foregoing chapters, I have attempted to offer an interested but critical scrutiny of how standard linguistic theorizing has addressed a range of issues and phenomena, from literal meaning to irony to correctness, bearing on actual language behavior. To some, the attempt will seem both superficial and impertinent, marred by unsupported generalizations and sweeping claims; and, clearly, none of the major issues addressed here has been treated comprehensively. Nevertheless, the purposes of the discussion, I believe, should mitigate censure of the questionable aspects of such a way of proceeding. The aim has been to uncover a recurring weakness in the recourse, as a means of understanding language behavior, to forms of abstract idealization and freestanding methodology. In some ways, this has made for a negative book, but this should not be overstated; the intended stance is constructively critical rather than radically skeptical. The chief theme of these chapters has been the weakness or limitedness of various extant linguistic categories, models, and methods, not their wholesale incoherence or inadequacy. I have tried to maintain consistency in first showing how, in my view, what is standardly understood by literal meaning, verbal metaphor, or echoism in irony, repetition, or rule governedness suffers from internal contradictions or an inability to account for the diversity of actual language use. But I have repeatedly emphasized that in none of these cases can we then crudely conclude that there is "no such thing" as literal meaning, or echoic irony, or rule following, and so on. Rather, the nature of the thing that literal meaning (or echoic irony etc.) is needs a substantially adjusted conceptualization. Over and over again, this study has attempted not so much a refutation of categories and models as a radical revision of them — a cutting of them down to size — predicated on a skeptical consideration of some of the assumptions underlying those categorizations and models. In short, the criticisms have been aimed at two levels: the level of specific categories (e.g., literal meaning), where the status of and claims for each, I have argued, require substantial revision; and the level of underlying assumptions or theory in the service of which those categories have been invoked (e.g., use of the literal meaning category in theories of determinate linguistic meaning, illocution, and speech acts), where much of that overarching theory, I have claimed, must be redefined.

Attending to "total" or situated speech involves recognizing that an infinitely variable range of contextual factors can, in every particular instance of language use, contribute to the determination of segmentational analyses — analyses that will continue to be the standard materials of linguistics. Because linguistic analysis, at whatever posited level, is never independent of utterance context but rather always proceeds from a tacit interpretation of the encompassing situation, integrationism will always stand above and behind the very possibilities of analytic segregationalism that linguistic studies prefer to foreground. Again, it would be mistaken to present this account as one simply setting up integrationism *against* segregationalism, even if it is sometimes useful to summarize positions by means of such blunt oppositions. Rather, the integrational perspective is the almost invariant condition — that of "total speech" or language taken seriously in context — whether for ordinary language users or for linguists, within which the possibilities of linguistic segregations, categorizations, and modelings emerge. But it is a condition, I have argued, much neglected in those latter enterprises. Just as integrationism is a precondition of, rather than an alternative to, segregationalism, similarly there can be no unitary integrational methodology, to be presented as a rival or an alternative to extant methods and models. The integrational stance is not itself a method or model but such a reconsideration of utterances in their contexts as indicates the limitations or incompleteness of any analytic linguistic methodology one might apply to them.

References

Aitchison, J. 1987a. "Reproductive Furniture and Extinguished Professors." In *Language Topics: Essays in Honour of Michael Halliday*, vol. 2, ed. R. Steele and T. Threadgold. Amsterdam: John Benjamins.
Aitchison, J. 1987b. *Words in the Mind: The Mental Lexicon*. Oxford: Blackwell.
Anderson, A. R., ed. 1964. *Minds and Machines*. Englewood Cliffs: Prentice Hall.
Ariel, M. 1991. "The Function of Accessibility in a Theory of Grammar." *Journal of Pragmatics* 16 no. 5: 443–63.
Auer, P., and A. Di Luzio, eds. 1992. *The Contextualization of Language*. Amsterdam: John Benjamins.
Austin, J. L. 1962. *How to Do Things with Words*. Oxford: Oxford University Press.
Austen, J. 1970 [1813]. *Pride and Prejudice*. Ed. F. Bradbook. London: Oxford University Press.
Austen, J. 1971 [1816]. *Emma*. Ed. D. Lodge. London: Oxford University Press.
Baker, G., and P. M. S. Hacker. 1984. *Language, Sense and Nonsense: A Critical Investigation into Modern Theories of Language*. Oxford: Blackwell.
Bakhtin, M. 1973. *Problems of Dostoyevsky's Poetics*. Translated by R. W. Rotsel. Ann Arbor: Ardis.
Bakhtin, M. 1981. *The Dialogic Imagination*. Austin: University of Texas Press.
Banfield, A. 1981. *Unspeakable Sentences*. London: Routledge.
Barker, N., and M. Parr. 1992. *Signs of the Times: A Portrait of the Nation's Tastes*. London: Cornerhouse.
Bar-Lev, Z., and A. Palacas. 1980. Semantic Command over Pragmatic Priority. *Lingua* 51: 137–51.
Barsalou, L. 1987. "The Instability of Graded Structure: Implications for the Nature of Concepts. In *Concepts and Conceptual Development*, ed. U. Neisser. Cambridge: Cambridge University Press.
Bateson, G. 1979. *Mind and Nature*. New York: Ballantine.
Becker, A. 1984a. "Biography of a Sentence: A Burmese Proverb. In *Text, Play and Story: The Construction and Reconstruction of Self and Society*, ed. E. Bruner. Washington, D.C.: American Ethnological Society.

Becker, A. 1984b. "The Linguistics of Particularity: Interpreting Superordination in a Javanese Text. In *Proceedings of the 10th Annual Meeting of the Berkeley Linguistics Society.* Berkeley: Linguistics Department, University of California, Berkeley.

Becker, A. 1987. "On the Difficulty of Writing: Silence." In *Thinking about Writing and Writing about Thinking*, ed. B. Morris. n.p.

Berwick, R., and A. Weinberg. 1984. *The Grammatical Basis of Linguistic Performance: Language Use and Acquisition.* Cambridge, Mass.: MIT Press.

Bhaya Nair, R., R. Carter, and M. Toolan. 1988. "Clines of Metaphoricity, and Creative Metaphors as Situated Risk-Taking." *Journal of Literary Semantics* 17, no. 1:20–40.

Bierwisch, M. 1967. "Some Semantic Universals of German Adjectivals." *Foundations of Language* 3:1–36.

Bierwisch, M. 1970. "Semantics." In *New Horizons in Linguistics*, ed. J. Lyons. Harmondsworth: Penguin.

Black, M. 1962. *Models and Metaphors: Studies in Language and Philosophy.* Ithaca, N.Y.: Cornell University Press.

Black, M. 1979. "More about Metaphor." In *Metaphor and Thought*, ed. Andrew Ortony. Cambridge: Cambridge University Press.

Blackburn, S. 1984. *Spreading the Word: Groundings in the Philosophy of Language.* Oxford: Clarendon.

Blakemore, D. 1987. Semantic Constraints on Relevance. New York: Blackwell.

Bloomfield, L. 1935. *Language.* New York: Holt, Rinehart & Winston.

Bolinger, D. 1976. "Meaning and Memory." *Forum Linguisticum* 1, no. 1:1–14.

Booth, W. 1974. *A Rhetoric of Irony.* Chicago: University of Chicago Press.

Bredin, H. 1992. "The Literal and the Figurative." *Philosophy* 67:69–80.

Brown, R. 1973. *A First Language: The Early Stages.* Cambridge, Mass.: Harvard University Press.

Cameron, D. 1990. "Integrating Conversation?" *Language and Communication* 10, no. 3:219–27.

Carston, R. 1993. "Conjunction, Explanation and Relevance." *Lingua* 90: 27–48.

Chomsky, N. 1965. *Aspects of the Theory of Syntax.* Cambridge, Mass.: MIT Press.

Chomsky, N. 1988. *Language and Problems of Knowledge.* Cambridge, Mass.: MIT Press.

Chomsky, N., and M. Halle. 1968. *The Sound Pattern of English.* New York: Harper & Row.

Clark, H., and P. Lucy. 1975. "Inferring What Is Meant from What Is Said: A Study in Conversationally Conveyed Requests." *Journal of Verbal Learning and Verbal Behavior* 14:56–72.

Clark, H., and C. Marshall. 1981. "Definite Reference and Mutual Knowledge." In *Elements of Discourse Understanding*, ed. A. Joshi, B. Webber, and I. Sag. Cambridge: Cambridge University Press.

Cohen, L. J. 1979. "The Semantics of Metaphor." In *Metaphor and Thought*, ed. Andrew Ortony. Cambridge: Cambridge University Press.

Cohen, L. J., and A. Margalit. 1970. "The Role of Inductive Reasoning in the Interpretation of Metaphor." *Synthese* 21:469–87.

Cohen, T. 1979. "Metaphor and the Cultivation of Intimacy." In *On Metaphor*, ed. S. Sacks. Chicago: University of Chicago Press.

Condillac, E. B. 1970. *Oeuvres Complètes*. Geneva: Editions Slatkine.

Condillac, E. B. 1971 [1756]. *Essay on the Origin of Human Knowledge*. Translated by Thomas Nugent. New York: AMS Press.

Cooper, D. 1975. *Knowledge of Language*. New York: Humanities.

Cooper, D. 1986. *Metaphor*. New York: Blackwell.

Coppieters, R. 1987. "Competence Differences between Native and Near-Native Speakers." *Language* 63, no. 3:544–73.

Croce, B. 1922. *Aesthetic*. Translated by R. Ainslie. London: Macmillan.

Crowley, T. 1990. "That Obscure Object of Desire: A Science of Language." In *Ideologies of Language*, ed. J. Joseph and T. Taylor. London: Routledge.

Crystal, D., and D. Davy. 1969. *Investigating English Style*. London: Longman.

Culler, J. 1983. *On Deconstruction*. London: Routledge & Kegan Paul.

Davidson, D. 1978. "What Metaphors Mean." In *On Metaphor*, ed. S. Sacks. Chicago: University of Chicago Press. Reprinted in *The Philosophy of Language*, ed. A. Martinich, 2d ed. (Oxford: Oxford University Press, 1990).

Davidson, D. 1984. *Inquiries into Truth and Interpretation*. Oxford: Clarendon.

Davidson, D. 1986. " 'A Nice Derangement of Epitaphs.' " In *Truth and Interpretation: Perspectives on the Philosophy of Donald Davidson*, ed. E. LePore. Oxford and New York: Oxford University Press.

Davis, H. 1989. "What Makes Bad Language Bad?" *Language and Communication* 9, no. 1:1–9.

Davis, H., and T. Taylor, eds. 1990. *Redefining Linguistics*. London: Routledge.

Derrida, J. 1974. "White Mythology: Metaphor in the Text of Philosophy." *New Literary History* 6, no. 1:5–74.

Derrida, J. 1977a. "Signature Event Context." *Glyph* 1:172–97.

Derrida, J. 1977b. "Limited Inc abc. . . ." *Glyph* 2:162–254.

Derrida, J. 1988. *Limited Inc*. Evanston: Northwestern University Press.

Dirven, R., and W. Paprotté, eds. 1985. *The Ubiquity of Metaphor*. Amsterdam: John Benjamins.

Dorian, N. 1981. *Language Death: the Life Cycle of a Scottish Gaelic Dialect*. Philadelphia: University of Pennsylvania Press.

Downes, W. 1984. *Language and Society*. London: Fontana.

Dubois, B. 1989. "Pseudoquotation in Current English Communication." *Language in Society* 18:343–59.

Dummett, M. 1986. "A Nice Derangement of Epitaphs: Comments on Davidson and Hacking." In *Truth and Interpretation: Perspectives on the Philosophy of Donald Davidson*, ed. E. LePore. Oxford and New York: Oxford University Press.

Duranti, A., and C. Goodwin, eds. 1992. *Rethinking Context*. Cambridge: Cambridge University Press.

Durkheim, E. 1915. *The Elementary Forms of the Religious Life*. London: Allen.
Eriel, B. 1984. *Selected Plays*. London: Faber and Faber.
Ervin-Tripp, S., and C. Mitchell-Kernan, eds. 1977. *Child Discourse*. New York: Academic.
Fehr, B. 1938. "Substitutionary Narration and Description: A Chapter in Stylistics." *English Studies* 20:97–107.
Firth, J. R. 1957. *Papers in Linguistics, 1934–1951*. London: Oxford University Press.
Firth, J. R. 1964. *The Tongues of Men*. London: Watt.
Firth, J. R. 1968. *Selected Papers of J. R. Firth, 1952–59*. Ed. F. R. Palmer. London: Longman.
Fish, Stanley. 1989. *Doing What Comes Naturally: Change, Rhetoric and the Practice of Theory in Literary and Legal Studies*. Durham, N.C.: Duke University Press.
Fodor, J. 1975. *The Language of Thought*. New York: Crowell.
Fodor, J., and J. Katz, eds. 1964. *The Structure of Language: Readings in the Philosophy of Language*. Englewood Cliffs, N.J.: Prentice-Hall.
✓ Fowler, H. W. 1965. *A Dictionary of Modern English Usage*. 2d ed., rev. E. Gowers. Oxford: Oxford University Press.
Fromkin, V., and R. Rodman. 1988. *An Introduction to Language*. 4th ed. New York: Harcourt Brace Jovanovich.
Fromkin, V., and R. Rodman. 1993. *An Introduction to Language*. 5th ed. New York: Harcourt Brace Jovanovich.
Furlong, A. 1989. "Towards an Inferential Account of Metonymy." *UCL Working Papers in Linguistics* 1:136–45.
✓ Gadamer, H.-G. 1975. *Truth and Method*. Translated by G. Barden and J. Cumming. London: Sheed and Ward.
Gardiner, A. 1932. *The Theory of Speech and Language*. Oxford: Clarendon.
Garfinkel, H. 1967. *Studies in Ethnomethodology*. Englewood Cliffs, N.J.: Prentice-Hall.
Gerrig, R., and A. Healy. 1983. "Dual Processes in Metaphor Understanding: Comprehension and Appreciation." *Journal of Experimental Psychology: Learning, Memory, and Cognition* 9:662–75.
Gibbs, R. 1983. "Do People Always Process the Literal Meanings of Indirect Requests?" *Journal of Experimental Psychology: Learning, Memory, and Cognition* 9:524–33.
Gibbs, R. 1986. "Skating on Thin Ice: Literal Meaning and Understanding Idioms in Conversation." *Disclosure Processes* 9, no. 2:17–30.
Gibbs, R. 1987. "Mutual Knowledge and the Psychology of Conversational Inference." *Journal of Pragmatics* 11, no. 5:561–88.
Gibbs, R. 1990a. "Comprehending Figurative Referential Descriptions." *Journal of Experimental Psychology: Learning, Memory, and Cognition* 16, no. 1:56–67.
Gibbs, R. 1990b. "The Process of Understanding Literary Metaphor." *Journal of Literary Semantics* 19, no. 1:65–79.
Gibbs, R. 1992. "Categorization and Metaphor Understanding." *Psychological Review* 99, no. 3:572–78.

Gildea, P., and S. Glucksberg. 1983. "On Understanding Metaphors: The Role of Context." *Journal of Verbal Learning and Verbal Behavior* 22, no. 5:77–90.

Glucksberg, S., and B. Keysar. 1990. "Understanding Metaphorical Comparisons: Beyond Similarity." *Psychological Review* 97, no. 1:3–18.

Goffman, E. 1967. *Interactional Ritual.* New York: Anchor.

Goffman, E. 1976. "Replies and Responses." *Language in Society* 5:257–13.

Goffman, E. 1981. *Forms of Talk.* Philadelphia: University of Pennsylvania Press.

Green, K. 1993. "Relevance Theory and the Literary Text: Some Problems and Perspectives." *Journal of Literary Semantics* 22:207–17.

Grice, H. P. 1957. "Meaning." *Philosophical Review* 66:377–88. Reprinted in *Philosophical Logic*, ed. P. Strawson. Oxford: Oxford University Press.

Grice, H. P. 1975. "Logic and Conversation." In *Syntax and Semantics 3: Speech Acts*, ed. Peter Cole and Jerry Morgan. New York: Academic.

Grice, H. P. 1978. "Further Notes on Logic and Conversation." In *Syntax and Semantics 9: Pragmatics*, ed. Peter Cole. New York: Academic.

Gumperz, J. 1989. *Contextualization and Understanding.* Berkeley Cognitive Science Report, no. 59. Berkeley: Institute of Cognitive Science, University of California, Berkeley.

Hacker, P. M. S. 1988. "Language, Rules and Pseudo-Rules." *Language and Communication* 8, no. 2:159–72.

Hacker, P. M. S. 1990. "Chomsky's Problems." *Language and Communication* 10, no. 2:95–125.

Hacking, I. 1986. "The Parody of Conversation." In *Truth and Interpretation: Perspectives on the Philosophy of Donald Davidson*, ed. E. LePore. Oxford and New York: Oxford University Press.

Halliday, M. A. K. 1967. *Grammar, Society and the Noun.* London: University College.

Halliday, M. A. K. 1975. *Learning How to Mean.* London: Edward Arnold.

Halliday, M. A. K. 1994. *Introduction to Functional Grammar.* 2d ed. London: Edward Arnold.

Harris, R. 1981a. *The Language Myth.* London: Duckworth.

Harris, R. 1981b. "Truth-Conditional Semantics and Natural Languages." In *Language, Meaning, and Style: Essays in Memory of Stephen Ullmann*, ed. T. E. Hope, T. Reid, R. Harris, and G. Price. Leeds: Leeds University Press. Reprinted in *The Foundations of Linguistic Theory*, ed. N. Love (London: Routledge, 1990).

Harris, R. 1987. *Reading Saussure.* London: Duckworth.

Harris, R. 1989. "How Does Writing Restructure Thought?" *Language and Communication* 9, nos. 2–3:99–106.

Harris, R. 1990a. "Lars Porsena Revisited." In *The State of the Language*, ed. L. Michaels and C. Ricks. Berkeley and Los Angeles: University of California Press.

Harris, R. 1990b. "Making Sense of Communicative Competence." In *The Foundations of Linguistic Theory*, ed. N. Love. London: Routledge.

Harris, R., and T. Taylor. 1989. *Landmarks of Linguistic Thought.* London and New York: Routledge.

Hasan, R. 1984. "The Nursery Tale as Genre." *Nottingham Linguistic Circular* 13:71–102.

Hewes, G. 1984. The Invention of Phonemically-Based Language. In *Language Development*, ed. A. Lock and E. Fisher. London: Croom Helm.

Hirsch, E. D. 1976. *The Aims of Interpretation*. Chicago: University of Chicago Press.

Holman, C. H. 1972. *A Handbook to Literature*. Third edition. New York: Bobbs Merrill.

Holtgraves, T. 1994. "Communication in Context: Effects of Speaker Status on the Comprehension of Indirect Requests." *Journal of Experimental Psychology: Learning, Memory, and Cognition* 20, no. 5:1205–18.

Hopper, P. 1987a. "A Priori and Emergent Grammars." In *Linguistics in Context*, ed. D. Tannen. Norwood, N.J.: Ablex.

Hopper, P. 1987b. "Emergent Grammar." In *Proceedings of the 13th Annual Meeting of the Berkeley Linguistics Circle*. Berkeley: Linguistics Department, University of California, Berkeley.

Hopper, P. 1988. "Discourse Analysis: Grammar and Critical Theory in the 1980's." In *Profession 88*. New York: Modern Languages Association.

Hopper, P., and E. Trangott. 1993. *Grammaticalization*. Cambridge: Cambridge University Press.

Hutton, C. 1990. "Meaning and the Principle of Linearity." *Language and Communication* 10, no. 3.

Hymes, Dell. 1971. "Competence and Performance in Linguistic Theory." In *Language Acquisition: Models and Methods*, ed. R. Huxley and E. Ingram. London: Academic.

Jackendoff, R. 1983. *Semantics and Cognition*. Cambridge, Mass.: MIT Press.

Jakobson, R. 1960. "Closing Statement: Linguistics and Poetics." In *Style in Language*, ed. T. Sebeok. Cambridge, Mass.: MIT Press.

Jakobson, R., and K. Pomorska. 1983. *Dialogues*. Cambridge, Mass.: MIT Press.

Jespersen, O. 1946. *Mankind, Nation and Individual from a Linguistic Point of View*. London: Allen & Unwin.

Johnstone, B., ed. 1987. "Special Issue on Repetition." *Text*, vol. 7, no. 3.

Jonsen, A., and S. Toulmin. 1988. *The Use and Abuse of Casuistry*. Berkeley and Los Angeles: University of California Press.

Kagan, J. 1981. *The Second Year: The Emergence of Self-Awareness*. Cambridge, Mass.: Harvard University Press.

Katz, J., and J. Fodor. 1963. "The Structure of a Semantic Theory." *Language* 39:170–210.

Keysar, B. 1989. "On the Functional Equivalence of Literal and Metaphorical Interpretations in Discourse." *Journal of Memory and Language* 28:375–85.

Kiparsky, P. 1973. "The Role of Linguistics in a Theory of Poetry." *Daedalus* 102:231–44.

Kittay, E. 1987. *Metaphor: Its Cognitive Force and Linguistic Structure*. Oxford: Oxford University Press.

Kittay, E., and A. Lehrer. 1981. "Semantic Fields and the Structure of Metaphor." *Studies in Language* 5:31–63.
Knapp, S., and W. B. Michaels. 1982. "Against Theory." *Critical Inquiry* 8, no. 4:723–42.
Knapp, S., and W. B. Michaels. 1985. "Pragmatism and Literary Theory, III: A Reply to Richard Rorty, What Is Pragmatism?" *Critical Inquiry* 11, no. 3:466–67.
Knapp, S., and W. B. Michaels. 1987. "Against Theory 2: Hermeneutics and Deconstruction." *Critical Inquiry* 14, no. 1:49–68.
Kreckel, M. 1981. *Communicative Acts and Shared Knowledge in Natural Discourse*. New York: Academic.
Labov, W. 1972. *Sociolinguistic Patterns*. Philadelphia: University of Pennsylvania Press.
Lakoff, G. 1987. *Women, Fire and Dangerous Things*. Chicago: University of Chicago Press.
Lakoff, G., and M. Johnson. 1980. *Metaphors We Live By*. Chicago: University of Chicago Press.
Lakoff, R. 1989. "The Way We Were; or, The Actual Truth about Generative Semantics: A Memoir." *Journal of Pragmatics* 13, no. 6:939–88.
Leech, G. 1983. *Principles of Pragmatics*. London: Longman.
Lehrer, A. 1974. *Semantic Fields and Lexical Structure*. Amsterdam: North-Holland.
Levin, S. 1977. *The Semantics of Metaphor*. Baltimore: Johns Hopkins University Press.
Levinson, S. 1979. "Activity Types and Language." *Linguistics* 17:365–99.
Levinson, S. 1983. *Pragmatics*. Cambridge: Cambridge University Press.
Levinson, S. 1988. "Putting Linguistics on a Proper Footing: Explorations in Goffman's Concepts of Participation." In *Erving Goffman: Exploring the Interaction Order*, ed. P. Drew and A. Wootton. Boston: Northeastern University Press.
Levinson, S. 1989. "A Review of Relevance." *Journal of Linguistics* 25, no. 2:455–72.
Lewis, D. 1969. *Convention*. Cambridge, Mass.: Harvard University Press.
Lightfoot, D. 1982. *The Language Lottery: Toward a Biology of Grammars*. Cambridge, Mass.: MIT Press.
Love, N. 1984. "Psychologistic Structuralism and the Polylect." *Language and Communication* 4, no. 3:225–40.
Love, N. 1988. "Ideal Linguistics." *Language and Communication* 8, no. 1:69–84.
Love, N. 1990a. "Editor's Introduction." In *The Foundations of Linguistic Theory: Selected Writings of Roy Harris*, ed. N. Love. London: Routledge.
Love, N., ed. 1990b. *The Foundations of Linguistic Theory: Selected Writings of Roy Harris*. London: Routledge.
Love, Nigel. 1990c. "The Locus of Languages in a Redefined Linguistics." In *Redefining Linguistics*, ed. H. Davis and T. Taylor. London: Routledge.
Love, N., and G. Wolf, eds. In press. *A Blastschrift for Roy Harris*. Amsterdam: John Benjamins.

Lowell, R. 1965. *Selected Poems*. London: Faber.

Lyons, J. 1968. *An Introduction to Theoretical Linguistics*. Cambridge: Cambridge University Press.

Macken, M. 1980. "The Child's Lexical Representation: The *Puzzle-Puddle-Pickle* Evidence." *Journal of Linguistics* 16:1–17.

MacWhinney, B., J. Leinbach, R. Taraban, and J. McDonald. 1989. "Language Learning: Cues or Rules?" *Journal of Memory and Language* 28:255–77.

Malinowski, B. 1923. "The Problem of Meaning in Primitive Languages." Supplement to *The Meaning of Meaning*, by C. Ogden and I. A. Richards. London: Kegan Paul, Trench, Trubner & Co.

Malinowski, B. 1935. *Coral Gardens and Their Magic*, vol. 2. New York: American Book Co.

Michaels, W. B. 1980. "Against Formalism: Chicken and Rocks." In *The State of the Language*, ed. L. Michaels and C. Ricks. Berkeley: University of California Press.

Miller, G. A. 1979. "Images and Models: Similes and Metaphors." In *Metaphor and Thought*, ed. A. Ortony. Cambridge: Cambridge University Press.

Miller, P. 1982. *Amy, Wendy, and Beth: Language Learning in South Baltimore*. Austin: University of Texas Press.

Milne, A. A. 1961 [1928]. *The House at Pooh Corner*. New York: Dutton.

Mitchell, W. J. T., ed. 1985. *Against Theory: Literary Studies and the New Pragmatism*. Chicago: University of Chicago Press.

Muhlhausler, P. 1985. "Towards an Explanatory Theory of Metaphor." In *The Ubiquity of Metaphor*, ed. R. Dirven and W. Paprotte. Amsterdam: John Benjamins.

Norris, C. 1990. *What's Wrong with Poststructuralism?* London: Harvester Wheatsheaf.

Nöth, W. 1985. "Semiotic Aspects of Metaphor." In *The Ubiquity of Metaphor*, ed. R. Dirven and W. Paprotte. Amsterdam: John Benjamins.

Ohio State University Linguistics Department. 1987. *Language Files*. Fourth edition. Reynoldsburg, OH: Advocate.

Olson, D. 1983. "Writing and Literal Meaning." In *The Psychology of Written Language*, ed. M. Martlew. Chichester: Wiley.

Onishi, K., and G. Murphy. 1993. "Metaphoric Reference: When Metaphors Are Not Understood as Easily as Literal Expressions." *Memory and Cognition* 21, no. 6: 763–72.

Ortony, A., ed. 1979. *Metaphor and Thought*. Cambridge: Cambridge University Press.

Ortony, A., D. Schallert, R. Reynolds, and S. Antos. 1978. "Interpreting Metaphors and Idioms: Some Effects of Context on Comprehension." *Journal of Verbal Learning and Verbal Behavior* 17:465–77.

Pateman, T. 1987a. *Language in Mind and Language in Society: Studies in Linguistic Reproduction*. Oxford: Clarendon.

Pateman, T. 1987b. "Philosophy of Linguistics." In *New Horizons in Linguistics*, ed. J. Lyons, R. Coates, M. Deuchar, and G. Gazdar. London: Penguin.

Pateman, T. 1989. "Pragmatics in Semiotics: Bakhtin/Volosinov." *Journal of Literary Semantics* 18, no. 3:203–16.

Peters, A. 1987. "The Role of Imitation in the Developing Syntax of a Blind Child." *Text* 7, no. 3:289–311.

Pilkington, A. 1991. "Poetic Effects: A Relevance Theory Perspective." In *Literary Pragmatics*, ed. R. Sell. London: Routledge.

Plath, Sylvia. 1981. *Collected Poems*. Ed. T. Hughes. London: Faber and Faber.

Pratt, M. L. 1986. "Ideology and Speech-Act Theory." *Poetics Today* 7, no. 1:59–72.

Pratt, M. L. 1987. "Linguistic Utopias." In *The Linguistics of Writing*, ed. N. Fabb et al. London: Methuen.

Propp, V. 1958. The Morphology of the Folktale. Bloomington: Indiana Research Centre in Anthropology.

Pulman, S. 1982. "Are Metaphors Creative?" *Journal of Literary Semantics* 11:78–89.

Ramberg, B. 1989. *Donald Davidson's Philosophy of Language*. Oxford: Blackwell.

Ricks, C. 1990. "Word Making and Mistaking." In *The State of the Language*, ed. C. Ricks and L. Michaels. Berkeley and Los Angeles: University of California Press.

Rommetvei, R. 1988. "On Literacy and the Myth of Literal Meaning." In *The Written Word*, ed. R. Säljö. Heidelberg: Springer.

Rorty, R. 1985. "Pragmatism and Literary Theory II: Philosophy without Principles." *Critical Inquiry* 11:3, 459–65.

Rorty, R. 1989. *Contingency, Irony and Solidarity*. Cambridge: Cambridge University Press.

Rosaldo, M. 1982. "The Things We Do with Words: Ilongot Speech Acts and Speech Act Theory." *Language in Society* 11:203–37.

Rosch, E. 1978. "Principles of Categorization." In *Cognition and Categorization*, ed. E. Rosch and B. Lloyd. New York: Academic.

Ross, J. R. 1970. "On Declarative Sentences." In *Readings in English Transformational Grammar*, ed. R. Jacobs and P. Rosenbaum. Waltham: Ginn.

Rumelhart, D. 1979. "Some Problems with the Notion of Literal Meanings." In *Metaphor and Thought*, ed. Andrew Ortony. Cambridge: Cambridge University Press.

Sacks, H., E. Schegloff, and G. Jefferson. 1974. "A Simplest Systematics for the Organisation of Turn-Taking in Conversation." *Language* 50:696–735.

Sacks, O. 1989. *Seeing Voices: A Journey into the World of the Deaf*. Berkeley and Los Angeles: University of California Press.

Sadock, J. 1979. "Figurative Speech and Linguistics." In *Metaphor and Thought*, ed. A. Ortony. Cambridge: Cambridge University Press, 46–63.

Saussure, F. de. 1983 [1916]. *Course in General Linguistics*. Translated by R. Harris. London: Duckworth.

Schank, R. C. 1972. "Conceptual Dependency: A Theory of Natural Language Understanding." *Cognitive Psychology* 3:552–631.

Schnitzer, M. 1990. "Critique of Linguistic Knowledge." *Language and Communication* 10, no. 2:95–125.

Searle, J. 1969. *Speech Acts.* Cambridge: Cambridge University Press.
Searle, J. 1977. "Reiterating the Differences." *Glyph* 1:198–208.
Searle, J. 1979. *Meaning and Expression.* Cambridge: Cambridge University Press.
Searle, J. 1980. "The Background of Meaning." In *Speech Act Theory and Pragmatics*, ed. J. Searle, F. Kiefer, and M. Bierwisch. Dordrecht: Reidel.
Searle, J. 1994a. "Literary Theory and Its Discontents." *New Literary History* 25:637–67.
Searle, J. 1994b. "Structure and Intention in Language: A Reply to Knapp and Michaels." *New Literary History* 25:677–81.
Searle, J., F. Kiefer, and M. Bierwisch, eds. 1980. *Speech Act Theory and Pragmatics.* Dordrecht: Reidel.
Shelley, P. B. 1967 [1840]. *A Defence of Poetry.* In *English Romantic Writers*, ed. D. Perkins. New York: Harcourt Brace.
Short, M. 1988. "Speech Presentation: The Novel and the Press." In *The Taming of the Text*, ed. W. Van Peer. London: Routledge.
Slembrouck, S. 1992. "The Parliamentary Hansard 'Verbatim' Report: The Written Construction of Spoken Discourse." *Language and Literature* 1, no. 2:101–19.
Slobin, D. 1982. "Universal and Particular in the Acquisition of Language." In *Language Acquisition: The State of the Art*, ed. E. Wanner and L. Gleitman. Cambridge: Cambridge University Press.
Smith, N. 1989. *The Twitter Machine.* Oxford: Blackwell.
Sperber, D. 1975. *Rethinking Symbolism.* Cambridge: Cambridge University Press.
Sperber, D., and D. Wilson. 1981. "Irony and the Use-Mention Distinction." In *Radical Pragmatics*, ed. P. Cole. New York: Academic Press.
Sperber, D., and D. Wilson. 1986. *Relevance: Communication and Cognition.* Oxford: Blackwell.
Sperber, D., and D. Wilson. 1989. "On Verbal Irony." *UCLA Working Papers in Linguistics* 1:96–118.
Stokoe, W. C. 1960. *Sign Language Structure.* Buffalo, N.Y.: Department of Anthropology and Linguistics, University of Buffalo.
Strawson, P. 1971. "Intention and Convention in Speech Acts." In *Philosophy of Language*, ed. John Searle. Oxford: Oxford University Press.
Supalla, T., and E. Newport. 1978. "How Many Seats in a Chair?" In *Understanding Language through Sign Language Research*, ed. P. Siple. New York: Academic Press.
Swinney, D., and A. Cutler. 1979. "The Access and Processing of Idiomatic Expressions." *Journal of Verbal Learning and Verbal Behavior* 18:523–34.
Szymura, J. 1988. "Bronislaw Malinowski's 'Ethnographic Theory of Language.'" In *Linguistic Thought in England, 1914–1945*, ed. R. Harris. London: Pergamon.
Tannen, D. 1987a. "Repetition in Conversation: Toward a Poetics of Talk." *Language* 63:574–605.
Tannen, D. 1987b. "Repetition in Conversation as Spontaneous Formulaicity." *Text* 7, no. 3:215–43.

Tannen, D. 1988. *Talking Voices: Repetition, Dialogue and Imagery in Conversation.* Cambridge: Cambridge University Press.

Taylor, C. 1985. *Human Agency and Language.* New York: Cambridge University Press.

Taylor, T. 1981. A Wittgensteinian Perspective in Linguistics. *Language and Communication* 1, no. 3:263–74.

Taylor, T. 1984. "Editing Rules and Understanding: The Case against Sentence-Based Syntax." *Language and Communication* 4, no. 2:105–27.

Taylor, T. 1988. "The Theory of Speech and Language of Alan Gardiner." In *Linguistic Thought in England, 1914–1945*, ed. R. Harris. London: Pergamon.

Taylor, T. 1989. "Condillac: Language as an Analytic Method." *Language and Communication* 9, no. 4:289–97.

Taylor, T. 1990. "Normativity and Linguistic Form." In *Redefining Linguistics*, ed. H. Davis and T. Taylor. London: Routledge.

Taylor, T., and D. Cameron. 1987. *Analysing Conversation: Rules and Units in the Structure of Talk.* London: Pergamon.

Thompson, A., and J. Thompson. 1987. *Shakespeare Meaning and Metaphor.* Iowa City: University of Iowa Press.

Titone, D., and C. Connine. 1994. "Comprehension of Idiomatic Expressions: Effects of Predictability and Literality." *Journal of Experimental Psychology: Learning, Memory, and Cognition* 20, no. 5:1126–38.

Toolan, M. 1988. *Narrative: A Critical Linguistic Introduction.* London: Routledge.

Toolan, M. 1989. "Ruling Out Rules in the Analysis of Conversation." *Journal of Pragmatics* 13, no. 2:245–68.

Tourangeau, R., and L. Rips. 1991. "Interpreting and Evaluating Metaphors." *Journal of Memory and Language* 30:452–72.

Traugott, E. 1985. "On Regularity in Semantic Change." *Journal of Literary Semantics* 14:155–73.

Traugott, E. 1989. "On the Rise of Epistemic Meanings in English: An Example of Subjectification in Semantic Change." *Language* 65:31–55.

Traugott, E., and M. L. Pratt. 1980. *Linguistics for Students of Literature.* New York: Harcourt Brace Jovanovich.

Ventola, E. 1987. *The Structure of Social Interaction.* London: Pinter.

Volosinov, V. 1983 [1926]. "Discourse in Life and Discourse in Poetry." Translated by J. Richmond. In *Bakhtin School Papers.* Oxford: RPT.

Volosinov, V. 1973. *Marxism and the Philosophy of Language.* New York: Seminar.

Wanner, E., and L. Gleitman. 1982. "Language Acquisition: The State of the Art." In *Language Acquisition*, ed. E. Wanner and L. Gleitman. Cambridge: Cambridge University Press.

Watson-Gegeo, K., and D. Gegeo. 1986. "Calling Out and Repeating: Two Key Routines in Kwara'ae Children's Language Socialization." In *Language Socialization across Cultures*, ed. B. Schieffelin and E. Ochs. Cambridge: Cambridge University Press, 17–50.

Williams, Patricia J. 1991. *The Alchemy of Race and Rights*. Cambridge, Mass.: Harvard University Press.

Wilson, D., and D. Sperber. 1993. "Linguistic Form and Relevance." *Lingua* 90:1–25.

Wittgenstein, L. 1953. *Philosophical Investigations*. Oxford: Blackwell.

Wolf, G. 1989. "Malinowski's 'Context of Situation.'" *Language and Communication* 9, no. 4:259–67.

Wolf, G., ed. 1992. *New Departures in Linguistics*. New York: Garland.

Wright, E. 1992. "The Entity Fallacy in Epistemology." *Philosophy* 67:33–50.

Wunderlich, D. 1980. "Methodological Remarks on Speech Act Theory." In *Speech Act Theory and Pragmatics*, ed. J. Searle, F. Kiefer, and M. Bierwisch. Dordrecht: Reidel.

Index

abstraction, 238–241, 263–264
activity types, 162–165
Aitchison, J., 38, 47–49, 114, 294
aphasia, 289–291
arbitrariness of the sign, 106
Austin, J., 22, 39, 226–233, 237

background, 30–31, 34–35, 37
Baker, G., 309–310
Bakhtin, M., 18–19, 152–155, 257–258, 268
Banfield, A., 157
Berwick, R., 201–203
Bhaya Nair, R., 57, 66, 73, 75, 85
bicycle, as carriage, 166–169
Black, M., 59, 60–61
Bloomfield, L., 7
Booth, W., 51
Brown, R., 119–120

Cameron, D., 247, 319
Carston, R., 223–224
Carter, R., 57, 66, 73, 75, 85
children: development of language by, 21–22, 98, 119–121, 173–174, 201, 203, 254–257, 271–287, 289, 298, 300–301
Chomsky, N., 141, 288–291, 304, 305
Clark, H., 44–45, 198–199
code theory of language, 192–197, 230
cognitivist-mechanist approach to language, 10–13, 313
Cohen, L., 65–66

coming into language, 14–15, 98–139
componentialism, 37–39
compositionality, 244–252
conceptual metaphors, 85–88
Condillac, E., 100–106, 114–116
Connine, C., 74
Context, contextualism, contextualizedness of language, 3–7, 13, 15–16, 25, 29–30, 166–169, 182
convergence, 298–299
Cooper, D., 65–66, 88–91, 95–96, 217–218, 290
cooperative principle, 204–206
Coppieters, R., 280
cotemporality, 109, 151
Crowley, T., 258
Culler, J., 128–132

Davidson, D., 63, 88–90, 95, 271, 293–298
deaf: language of the, 68, 118–119
Derrida, J., 15, 53, 127–133, 226–233, 237
Dirven, R. and W. Paprotte, 56
displacement, 221
Downes, W., 54
Dubois, B., 235
Dummett, M., 295–296

echoic mention: irony as, 207–212, 214–216
evidence, 197–199, 201–203
experience and experientialism, 32, 85–88

Firth, J., 162, 164
Fish, S., 50–52, 302
Fodor, J., 261, 291–292
free indirect discourse, 155–157
Fromkin, V., 290
Furlong, A., 221

Gadamer, H.-G., 125
Gardiner, A., 145, 148–154
Garfinkel, H., 146–147
genre, 162–165
Gibbs, R., 43–44, 72–73, 74–80, 85, 198–199
Gleitman, L., 284
Glucksberg, S., 69–72
Goffman, E., 64, 253, 266
Grice, P., 14, 19, 41, 153, 181, 197, 203–207, 211, 214

Hacker, P., 287–293, 297–300, 303, 309–310
Halliday, M., 112, 119, 164, 224–225, 257, 265
Harris, R., 3, 9, 20, 103–104, 109, 122, 126, 143–144, 158–161, 166–169, 176, 180, 238–241, 260
hearability, 158–161
Hewes, G., 109
Holtgraves, T., 74
Hopper, P., 115–116, 242–243
Hutton, C., 260

idioms, 43–44, 78, 244–246, 251
individualism, 315–321
integrational linguistics, 3–5, 8–10, 13, 22–23, 44–47, 94–95, 140–180, 245–249, 260–270, 286, 319–321
intentionality, 14–15, 98–139, 237–238
interactionist theory of metaphor, 59–60
intertextuality, 154, 268–270
introspection vs. intuition, 305–310
ironical understatement, 212–214
irony, 19, 124–125, 207–220
iterability, 15, 20, 127–133, 237–241

Jakobson, R., 252

Jespersen, O., 315
Johnson, M., 85–88

Kagan, J., 254
Keysar, B., 69–72
Kittay, E., 56, 69, 93
Knapp, S. and W. Benn Michaels, 15, 40–42, 121–127, 129, 133–135
Kreckel, M., 298

Labov, W., 99
Lakoff, G., 32, 48–49, 85–88
Lakoff, R., 244
language, vs. a language, 1–3, 98–100
language-user: characterization of, 140–142
Leech, G., 39
Levinson, S., 59, 64, 143, 162, 229
Lewis, D., 302
Lightfoot, D., 98
linguistic competence, 98–99, 194
literal meaning, 13, 24–55
Locke, J., 101, 106, 131
Love, N., 20, 54–55, 98, 260–265, 267
Lucy, P., 43–45
Lyons, J., 6–7

Macken, M., 281, 283
MacWhinney, B., 284
malapropism, 293–297
Malinowski, B., 109–110, 113, 265
manifestness, 183–187
Margalit, A., 65–66
Marshall, C., 198–199
meaning, 35, 166–176
memory, 17, 176–179
metalinguistic awareness, 174–179, 260–268
metaphor and intimacy, 90–91, 219
metaphor and metaphorical meaning, 13–14, 42–43, 45, 56–97, 218–219
metaphor as "extra work," 75–79
metonymy, in language development, 106, 115, 117
Murphy, G., 69, 73
mutual knowledge, 16, 117–118, 185–186, 197–200, 302

natural signs vs. artificial signs, 103–105
normativity and authority, 35, 287–295
Norris, C., 227

Olson, D., 267
Onishi, K., 69, 73
orientedness to others, 11–12
ostensive behavior, 186–189
ostensive-inferential communication, 189–191, 193

passing theory, 293–304
Pateman, T., 153, 155–156, 238–241, 260, 304–312
Peters, A., 254–256
phatic communion, 109–110, 265
Plath, S., 81–84
pragmaticism, and literal meaning, 39–42
Pratt, M., 59
principle of relevance, 181–182
proposals vs. propositions, 265–266
prototype theory, 47–49, 160
pseudoquotation, 235
psycholinguistic approaches to metaphor, 69–85

quotation, 269–270

Ramberg, B., 296–297
reformulation, 247–248
relevance theory, 19, 181–226
repetition, 20, 32–33, 226–270
represented discourse, 155–157, 233–238
Ricks, C., 295
risk, 53, 66–67
ritual function of language, 108–111
Rodman, R., 290
Rommetveit, R., 50, 155
Rorty, R., 40–42, 62–63, 271
Rosch, E., 47–49
rule-governed creativity, 21, 271–284, 316–317
rules, 21–22, 271–321
Rumelhart, D., 37–38, 44–45, 64–65
Rushdie, S., 51, 221–222

Sacks, O., 68, 118–119

salience, experiential, 284–287
Saussure, F., 22, 100, 140, 148–150, 152, 257–260, 270
Schnitzer, M., 291
Searle, J., 15, 25–27, 29–37, 122, 132, 135–139, 193, 226–233, 237
Shelley, P., 92–93
Sign language, 118–119, 159, 313
signification, 128–131
similarity and difference, 257–260
situation: influence on meaning determination, 158–169
Slobin, D., 117
Smith, N., 272–284
speech-act theory, 133–135, 142–145, 229–232, 299
Sperber, D., 19, 62, 177, 181–225
Stokoe, W., 159
Szymura, J., 113–114

Tannen, D., 33, 193, 241–245, 251–253
Taylor, C., 102
Taylor, T., 101–104, 148, 151–152, 172, 247, 308, 316
text vs. context, 3–5, 181–182
Titone, D., 74
transcription: influence of, 4–5, 54–55
Traugott, E., 59
Turing, A., 176–177
type and token, 27, 135–139, 165, 260–270

Universal Grammar, 196–197, 303–304, 306–308, 313–315
use vs. mention, 18–19, 233–238

Volosinov, 153–154, 155

Wanner, E., 284
Weinberg, A., 201–203
Wilson, D., 19, 62, 177, 181–225
Wittgenstein, L., 162, 169–173, 191–192, 229, 304–312
Wright, E., 199–200
writing, 20–21, 54–55, 155, 227–230, 260–270
Wunderlich, D., 29

Michael Toolan is *Associate Professor of*
English at the University of *Washington*.

Library of Congress Cataloging-in-Publication Data

Toolan, Michael.
Total speech : an integrational linguistic approach to language /
Michael Toolan.
p.   cm.   — (Post-contemporary interventions)
Includes bibliographical references and index.
ISBN 0-8223-1781-8. — ISBN 0-8223-1790-7 (pbk.)
1. Language and languages — Philosophy.   2. Linguistics.
I. Title.   II. Series.
P106.T666   1996
401–dc20   95-42485   CIP

typo — it's Bottom